MW00443522

LOVE AND DEATH
IN THE GREAT WAR

LOVE AND DEATH IN THE GREAT WAR

Andrew J. Huebner

OXFORD
UNIVERSITY PRESS

OXFORD

UNIVERSITY PRESS

Oxford University Press is a department of the University of Oxford. It furthers the University's objective of excellence in research, scholarship, and education by publishing worldwide. Oxford is a registered trade mark of Oxford University Press in the UK and certain other countries.

Published in the United States of America by Oxford University Press
198 Madison Avenue, New York, NY 10016, United States of America.

Library of Congress Cataloging-in-Publication Data
Names: Huebner, Andrew J., author.
Title: Love and death in the Great War / Andrew J. Huebner.
Description: New York, NY : Oxford University Press, 2018. |
Includes bibliographical references and index. |
Identifiers: LCCN 2017038184 (print) | LCCN 2017040132 (ebook) |
ISBN 9780190853938 (Updf) | ISBN 9780190853945 (Epub) |
ISBN 9780190853921 (hardcover : alk. paper)
Subjects: LCSH: World War, 1914–1918—Social aspects—United States. |
Huston, George Waring, 1896–1918. | Dees, Eliga, 1895–1967. |
Huebner, Arthur, 1891–1918. | Soldiers—United States—Biography. |
World War, 1914–1918—Biography.
Classification: LCC D524.7.U6 (ebook) | LCC D524.7.U6 H84 2018 (print) |
DDC 940.3/1—dc23
LC record available at https://lccn.loc.gov/2017038184

1 3 5 7 9 8 6 4 3 2

Printed by Sheridan Books, Inc., United States of America

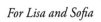

For Lisa and Sofia

Crusades are for generals. War is a more personal thing.

—Edmund G. Love, *War Is a Private Affair* (1951)

CONTENTS

NOTE ON SOURCES

Some of the primary sources I use in this book contain illegible writing, incorrect grammar, spelling errors, or satirical slang. Rather than cluttering the text with "*sic*" or bracketed corrections, I have chosen to let much of this text stand as is. I lightly intervened when I thought clarity required it, but I wanted to keep readers in the period, as it were, and to confront them with unmediated rhetoric of the day. I hope audiences will forgive some occasional confusion.

Love and Death
in the Great War

PROLOGUE

DESPITE THE IMPOSING SCALE of the Great War's origins, horrors, and shadows, many Americans of 1917–18 imbibed a more prosaic tale of their role in that fight: a love story. Civilized white men would demonstrate their personal character, love for family, and masculine mettle by defending women, children, and home from German militarism. This mission of chivalric rescue demanded men and women assume their traditional positions as protector and protected, so a war fought well would showcase, bolster, or redeem the health of the American family. Of course, the nation's grander aims are better known. From the declaration of war in April 1917, newspapers and officials' speeches linked it to free commercial exchange, open diplomacy, antimilitarism, self-determination, democracy, and, most expansively, the preservation of white, Christian civilization. But in those same bursts of persuasive language, and in popular music, film, and the private letters of soldiers and their families, some Americans invested the war with more intimate meaning. Even talk of "civilization," "democracy," or "nation" often translated to the protection of women, family, and the rhythms of daily life. The state and its advocates marketed this story in the constricted culture of wartime America, though private citizens likewise found the family war a powerful way of expressing their obligations.[1]

Yet the romance of American intervention quickly grew cluttered with contradictions. Some people never bought its assurances and opposed the war at their own risk, while others became cynical through personal loss. Many parents worried about releasing their sons to a military environment notoriously inhospitable to virtue. Some women and people of color bristled at the exclusionary assumptions of the chivalric narrative and challenged the white male monopoly on martial honor and its attendant political advantages. Defenders of the wartime love story, in turn, both officials and ordinary citizens, clung to the promise of a war for family, love, and home, whether through the architecture of policy or the rhetoric of hope.

Love and Death in the Great War tracks this battle over the war's meaning through transatlantic correspondence, national propaganda, home front society, and official policy, traversing daily life and public symbolism. Spanning 1917 to the early 1920s, it is anchored in the experiences of three Great Warriors and their families—a quiet German American draftee from Wisconsin; a barely literate career soldier from Missouri; and a patriotic, college-educated, and terribly homesick enlistee from Alabama. Joining them in the story are a young nurse from New Orleans; a teenaged Ozarks schoolteacher; a Marine from Ohio who later wrote a searing novel of the Great War; the African American New Yorkers of the segregated 369th Infantry; a satirist who would go on to postwar fame; the pious Tennessean Alvin York and other winners of combat medals; and a young black military laborer accused of rape. Woven through the book are wartime dissenters, parents, artists, policymakers, songwriters, clergy, teachers, journalists, and local authorities. These Americans left behind a rich record of their behaviors and priorities. Rather than claiming them "typical" or "representative," however one might define such terms, I submit that collectively they offer a vivid picture of wartime society.[2]

To many Americans, the war was personal. Even the loftier justifications associated with the Great War found emotional expression in public and private spaces, sometimes to the chagrin of officials bent on stressing the war's geopolitical objectives. Yet other people and forces defied that narrative or exposed its contradictions. The story of white male chivalry and familial uplift, though repeatedly and forcefully told, absorbed challenges throughout the war's phases. The decision to conscript, propaganda campaigns against the Germans, the suppression of dissent, the moral and religious education of the draftee population, official programs for maintaining the soldier's family, the controversies over black doughboys and women in the war zone, army management of interactions with civilians, the postwar repatriation of the dead—all not only enveloped individual lives but also became venues for public debate over what war meant for family, love, and domestic harmony.[3]

In *Love and Death in the Great War*, then, I am less concerned with the *causes* of intervention than with how Americans (including those in the government) explained, justified, lived, understood, or found *meaning* in it.[4] By putting home and family at the center of that cultural process, the book joins works on other American conflicts that argue for the motivational power of personal appeals.[5] More broadly, it finds common ground between the ways Americans and other populations experienced the Great War, despite their otherwise dramatically different wartime situations. Across the Allies and Central Powers, promoting war as a defense of home proved not only a potent propaganda tool but also a prevalent way of making sense of violence once it came. Many Americans, like other people, did not want war, but confronted mounting evidence their safety and values depended on it. Tales of defending homelands could be told in France, Britain, Germany, Austria-Hungary, Serbia, Russia, and other places, but also in the United States and Canada, though of course the particular character, timing, plausibility, and immediacy of such stories ranged widely from place to place. In America, an ocean away from the fighting, it took until early 1917 for defensive narratives to play a part in triggering intervention and to find purchase among some—though not all—citizens of the republic. We will meet people of different minds on that matter in this book. It thus concurs with much recent scholarship that pictures the populations of 1914–18 neither as witless dupes of the state, unthinking patriots, nor rabid militarists, but rather as people invested in the security of their families and willing to fight for it. Nevertheless, whether because of the asymmetries of sacrifice, the length of the war, or disillusionment with its conduct, patience with that project had limits among both soldiers and citizens. Consent wavered to one degree or another across the belligerent nations.[6] What happens, then, to "heroic narratives of purpose and expectation," as one scholar of Russia has put it, when war's brutalities come home?[7]

To explore such collisions of narrative and experience in the American context, *Love and Death in the Great War* draws on letters, diaries, newspapers, speeches, films, military unit histories, official newsletters, and posters. Those sources link areas often studied separately: combat zone and home front, official propaganda and the private search for understanding, public policy and its implementation, personal emotion and political history, the lives of men and women.[8] The book therefore aims to synthesize and recast much scholarship on America's First World War, which tends to compartmentalize presidential leadership, the mental universe of the doughboy, the stories of women and ethnic or racial minorities, conscription, dissent, propaganda, veterans, and the mobilization and deployment of the army. In merging these subjects, *Love and Death in the Great War* shows Americans wrestling with enduring paradoxes: war has seemed a home-saver and home-wrecker, a clarifier and disruptor of gender roles, a crucible for and destroyer of virtue.

Yet the chapters that follow offer no simple chronicle of disillusionment, a facile and discredited cliché for the Great War experience.[9] Some people reveled in the war's romance even as they lived its terrors, just as soldiers abroad nurtured emotional bonds with family as much as feelings of alienation. Several groups saw liberating possibilities in wartime change. Even if those hopes went unfulfilled in the near term, a longer view suggests that out of the Great War's shattering of families, and the vast public effort to assign value to those tragedies, came a revised story of war and family for the twentieth century.[10]

DURING THE LATE NINETEENTH and early twentieth centuries, Americans witnessed the cresting of two ideas that merged to shape the picture of the Great War developed here. The first held that war could serve as an incubator of personal growth and familial health; the second that those measures of private virtue, so central to national strength, required renewal. These ideas circulated in popular and literary culture, political rhetoric and public policy, reform campaigns, and all manner of debates, spectacles, movements, prophesies, laws, and texts. Heralds of fantasy or apocalypse enjoyed access to political influence or a public voice. They were middle class or elite reformers, journalists, military officers, religious leaders, industrialists, "experts" of various stripes, and officials at all levels of government. More often than not, they were men.

At the heart of their hopes and fears was the white family, an institution of theoretically stable moral qualities and clear gender divisions. War's allure sprung in some measure from its tendency to clarify spheres of activity. It presented men with the opportunity to engage and sharpen their protective impulses, whether by defending their own, other, or symbolic families. The enemies in the ennobling-war story as well as the threats in the familial-decay story often possessed darker skin or "savage" ways or distorted understandings of domestic life. For adherents of such gendered white nationalism, martial victory over racially distinct enemies promised to confirm Anglo-Saxon superiority, save the family, sharpen masculine character, and inhibit white decline.[11]

The Civil War had shown that even a conflict without a vilified racial "Other" could offer redemptive collateral benefit and rest upon personal rather than ideological foundations. Some soldiers fought for home, comrades, or God, even as others dedicated themselves to causes of union, emancipation, slavery, or independence.[12] As the years passed after that war, people North and South continued to revere their veterans, reward them with political influence, and romanticize their exploits. Union veterans benefited from an expensive pension system, while Confederate ones took pride of place in Lost Cause rituals and some collected state-level soldiers' aid. Reconciliation between the sections rested in part on a shared memory of martial honor, a common sense of supremacy over black people (though some Union veterans remained proud of emancipation), and eventually, collaborative military experience against Spain in 1898.[13] War and empire in the Caribbean and Asia, to their promoters, offered opportunities to flex masculine muscle and either save, subjugate, or civilize racial inferiors.[14]

In the meantime, political leaders and public intellectuals expected women both to abet the state's wars and safeguard familial morality. Mothers were to raise dutiful and upstanding sons, nurture future soldiers and citizens, and regard personal loss as patriotic investment. Opponents of woman suffrage thus charged that the movement of women out of the home and into politics would disrupt and weaken both realms. Naval theorist Alfred Thayer Mahan claimed women voting would obliterate the "constant practice of the past ages by which to men are assigned the outdoor rough action of life and to women that indoor sphere which we call the family." Suffrage advocates nevertheless won some state victories in the late nineteenth century, but it was no fluke that the rise of bellicose white nationalism, of strong associations between martial and civic entitlement, coincided with the "doldrums" of that movement. No states adopted woman suffrage from 1896 to 1910.[15]

The cult of regenerative war persisted even as very few Americans joined the army; fewer still fought in significant engagements; and military men were not known for their character. Soldiers spent much of the late nineteenth century serving constabulary functions on the frontier, breaking labor strikes, or appearing during emergencies. Enlistment attracted men seeking high adventure or patriotic fulfillment but just as often served as a last resort. Even as the armed forces professionalized, modernized, and went abroad, the army admitted in a recruiting booklet of 1904, many Americans considered service "degrading." Twelve years later, an exposé reported a good number of "down-and-outers" in the ranks, with lots of them unmarried men escaping manual labor or farming. Recruiters rejected upward of 70 percent of applicants for sexually transmitted diseases and other shortcomings.[16] For those who cleared the bar, military life could corrode virtue. In his Civil War novel *The Red Badge of Courage* (1895), Stephen Crane had the Union volunteer Henry Fleming's mother say,

> There's lots of bad men in the army, Henry. The army makes 'em wild, and they like nothing better than the job of leading off a young feller like you, as ain't never been away from home much and has allus had a mother, an' a-learning 'em to drink and swear. Keep clear of them folks, Henry.[17]

Reformer and muckraker Raymond Fosdick, assigned to investigate soldierly behavior along the Mexican border in 1916, discovered rampant drinking and sex. Fosdick recommended that Secretary of War Newton Baker limit access to alcohol and prostitutes and develop distracting activities to compensate for the absence of wholesome domestic influences.[18]

In audible if quieter channels of public dialogue, critics worked against the war romantics. Many Americans of this period expressed deep ambivalence about large standing armies and what some saw as European-style militarism. Dramatic testimony on the sorrow of war came in the form of seven hundred thousand Civil War dead and one million wounded. Forty-five thousand men circulated back into society with limbs missing. Countless more bore the psychological marks of battle. The federal government ultimately acknowledged the scale of these personal costs in the enormous pension system for Union veterans. Meanwhile, through the late decades of the nineteenth century, popular enthusiasm for spending on the armed forces remained cool. Antimilitarists read books like *The Future of Wars* (1898), which predicted horrific industrial slaughter.[19] That same year, of course, belligerent voices successfully urged war with Spain, although dissenters warned of the private costs. The anti-imperialist Sen. George Hoar (R-Mass.) agreed that countries depended on families but rejected war as a strengthener of them. "A nation is made up of human homes," he explained in opposition to colonizing the Philippines in 1899, "and the glory of a nation and the value of its possessions are in its humble homes. I do not agree with the Senator who thinks that a home is made better by the loss of its boys or the crippling for life of its head."[20]

Pacifist feminists around the turn of the century likewise considered wars irredeemable affairs, recoiling at the notion that they sharpened character and invigorated men for political citizenship. Women should vote and hold office, argued many pacifists and suffragists, precisely to strip American politics of masculinized militarism. Jane Addams, a founder of the Woman's Peace Party in 1915, mocked the dearly held yet "pathetic" certainty of war's "regenerative results." In contrast, as the preamble to the group's constitution lamented, armed violence produced "poverty-stricken widows and orphans."[21]

Still, the mythology or memory of redemptive combat on the frontier, in the American Revolution, and in the Civil War proved durable components of white nationalism. Despite the private suffering of Civil War veterans, popular depictions of that conflict often made personal injury sentimental. Some experts predicted that advancements in prosthetics and the study of veteran wounds might minimize physical suffering in future wars. Military schools, veterans' reunions, hopeful talk of gleaming new weapons and war-bought manliness, valorization of warriors "from pulpit, press, and stump," in the words of Gen. M. M. Trumbull—all persisted into the 1880s and 1890s.[22]

Further fueling the story of romantic war was the expulsion of native peoples from the West. Even temporary setbacks such as Custer's Last Stand in 1876 endured in the national imagination not as embarrassing defeats but as symbols of Indian savagery and American pluck. Tales of troops slaughtering often defenseless or outgunned Native Americans transformed before eastern audiences into affirmations of national greatness and the inevitability of territorial expansion. Coursing through that story was the captivity narrative, whereby white men rescued white women from menacing racial Others. Servicemen of the 1870s and 1880s theoretically saved the continent and thus cultivated a sort of aggregate chivalric virtue. During the Great War, themes of captivity and white chivalry would continue to enthrall and inflame popular audiences. Men of color, meanwhile, did serve from the Civil War through the Indian wars and the excursions to Cuba and the Philippines. But although soldiers in those segregated units drew admiration from the black community and some whites, they otherwise suffered unyielding political marginalization and often outright hostility from officials and civilians.[23]

FROM THE PERSPECTIVE OF reformers, elected officials, and others with a public voice, nearly every development transforming America in the pre-1917 decades threatened the white family. Their crusades may have rested on deeper ambitions—to enforce ethnic assimilation, control racial minorities, preserve working-class productivity, keep themselves safe from crime, stave off social instability or revolution, impose Christian values—but that they so often invoked family suggested its enormous symbolic power.

To those of a xenophobic disposition, new immigrants, depending on their origins, imperiled familial propriety by their moral deficiencies, childrearing styles, and alleged desire for white women. Anti-Chinese exclusionists in the nineteenth century put low character atop their list of imagined flaws. Statutes barred prostitutes and their agents, then the Chinese altogether, and then polygamists, with these measures codified in a major February 1917 immigration law. This legislation contained a literacy test applied only to men, as Congress feared that barring illiterate wives, children, and elderly parents would separate husbands from moderating influences. Family men, in this way of thinking, were the best Americans. "The first essential for a man's being a good citizen," maintained Theodore Roosevelt, was "his possession of the home virtues."[24] By the early twentieth century, nativists found those virtues lacking among southern and eastern Europeans, their exoticisms of religion, dress, and language excluding them from the benefits of whiteness. In 1916, Anglo-Saxon chauvinist Madison Grant warned that even assimilative appearances could mask sexualized threats. "These immigrants adopt the language of the native American," he wrote in *The Passing of the Great Race*, "they wear his clothes; they steal his name; and they are beginning to take his women." From a more sympathetic position, New York photographer Jacob Riis peppered his exposé of tenement life with racially essentialist critiques of immigrant familial practices. He revealed domesticity undermined—the Italian's predilection for gambling, child abuse in Mulberry Bend, the prostitution of girls in Chinese laundries, youth labor in Jewish homes, the Bohemian's derelict housekeeping, an English family sleeping on rags, and armies of homeless children.[25]

Riis and other reformers regarded the American city as a filthy labyrinth of family-killing perils. Saloon-keepers, tenement owners, traffickers in "white slavery," single women exploring financial and sexual independence: all drove urban spaces downward into decadence. Fastidious reformers discovered in movie theaters, dance halls, and amusement parks dangerous gender mixing, while films, "sex novels," and the birth control movement authorized impure thought or action. For temperance advocates, the risk of sexual depravity as well as parental negligence or violence lurked in the liquor bottle. Many states and counties went dry leading up to national prohibition in 1919. Vice crusader Anthony Comstock and the 1873 law that bore his name ultimately judged birth control literature "obscene." The Mann Act of 1910 outlawed the movement of women across state lines for "debauchery" or other "immoral purpose." In cities and beyond, regular panics flared about divorce, low Anglo-Saxon birth rates, and child welfare.[26]

As some of these reforms showed, lawmakers set out with particular zeal to protect families they considered "innocent" or "deserving."

The first two beneficiaries of substantial public assistance in the United States were soldiers and mothers, suggesting not only popular associations of national health with the family but also official admission that war, in addition to the era's other hazards, threatened it. Single mothers, especially widows, had become objects of sympathetic aid programs by the first two decades of the twentieth century. Advocates for mothers' pensions after 1910 aimed to offer succor to the needy, stabilize gender roles, and prevent social upheaval. "Normal family life is the foundation of the State," said a mothers' pension advocate in 1914, "and its conservation [is] an inherent duty of government." Two Supreme Court decisions limited women's work hours—not men's—due to their "physical structure" and primary duties as mothers. Eventually forty states and the federal government had maternalist programs in place to aid women and children.[27] The state and federal veterans' pensions rested on comparable ethics of familial strength mixed with the impulse both to motivate and reward military voluntarism. Abraham Lincoln's government intended the pension as an inducement to enlist in 1862, envisioning its recipients as war widows, dependents, and the disabled. Family life, and the traditional roles of men, women, and children, might thus survive the disruptive impact of war. Later amendments drew in veterans developing postwar health problems, and the 1890 Dependent Pension Act extended aid to all former Union men with ninety days' wartime service. By 1915, expenditures for veterans of the Civil War exceeded the cost of fighting it. Like smaller pensions for soldiers earlier in American history, these laws mainly benefitted whites. Few black veterans applied and they often met rejection when they did.[28]

With men, as with women and children, some Americans saw a crisis. One scholar writes of the late nineteenth century that manhood was "a matter of taking responsibility for one's family and community, embracing citizenship, playing a public role."[29] Civilized white men were expected to protect the home and innocents inside. They should be restrained, resolute, and decent, violent only when stirred by threats. Economic independence formed another key ambition. Yet some observers sensed diminishing opportunities for white men to command these roles in the age of industrialized labor, disorienting economic cycles, and state woman suffrage victories. Critics of the bloated Civil War pension system claimed it emasculated veterans by making them dependent on government rather than restoring their workingmen's status as true heads of household. Others found this sort of breadwinner masculinity not manly enough. Newer standards, borne of the insecurities of the late nineteenth century, added urban, muscular, working-class, and physical notes, but still maintained their white racial exclusivity. For heralds of such masculine virtue, war could be a good thing. Concerns over withering male vigor, once again, helped provoke war against Spain in 1898 and the seizure of the Philippines thereafter.[30]

These fears of decline and emasculation fired much of the violent, sexualized, and apocalyptic urgency of white supremacy. Among other conjured threats to white familial health, cried the terrorists of Jim Crow, was the black rapist, supposedly incapable of manly restraint. Untold numbers of black men, accused of crossing the sexual color line, died at the hands of local law enforcement and white mobs. Race riots in Wilmington, North Carolina, in 1898, Atlanta in 1906, and Springfield, Illinois, in 1908, to one historian of race and sexual violence, were "sparked by rumored incidents of rape or manufactured 'rape epidemics' involving black men and white women."[31] Indignation at alleged African American arrogance undergirded a riot in New Orleans in 1900. Throughout these and other cases of retributive aggression, white southerners often justified their violence in chivalric terms, but they aimed to eliminate black political and social as well as sexual competition. More squarely revealing of those prejudices were black codes, disfranchisement, segregation, limited access to military service, the sharecropping system, and other forms of economic discrimination, which both exerted white control and withheld from black men the markers of masculine standing. One of the oldest and most horrific weapons in this arsenal, of course, was the sexual assault of black women by white men. The Ku Klux Klan rose to new heights of membership in the 1910s, meanwhile, warning of a racialized moral emergency. Targeting immigrants as well as African Americans as polluters of white purity, the Klan attracted a larger, more urban, and less southern following.[32]

The diverse social critics of the progressive movement, finally, across its humanitarian, illiberal, religious, and political wings, derived coherence in part over their relentless emphasis on the integrity, health, and even survival of the white family. Preserving the future of the middle-class home drove much of what progressives did, including at times attempting to spread their values to other groups, at others to segregate those groups, but usually with the goal of social stability. With compassion as well as arrogance, according to a perceptive scholar of the movement, progressives fought for their particular way of life even as they sought to humanize industrial work, reduce political corruption, and discipline corporations.[33]

THE PEOPLE IN THIS book thus grew up learning a powerful story about war and family, about white men's monopoly on martial service and the political benefits it brought, and about war's chivalric or regenerative possibilities. They may have perceived challenges to that vision. Some, perhaps, sensed or shared fears about the shape of the family. Other people in the book were the ones reformers found threatening to that institution.

When the United States entered the European war in April 1917, after years of watching the carnage from afar and lurching toward partnership with the Allies, these Americans began hearing or reading a lot about war, the family, and the home, about heart and virtue and love and death and emotion. What was familiar to millions of Europeans by that point was about to become familiar to Americans.

1

Johnny Get Your Gun

STANDING BEFORE THE UNITED STATES CONGRESS on Monday, April 2, 1917, in his speech asking for a declaration of war against Germany, President Woodrow Wilson vowed, "But the right is more precious than peace, and we shall fight for the things which we have always carried nearest our hearts."[1]

The day Wilson spoke was the first day back at school for a young woman in rural Wayne County, Missouri, named Mae Dupree Bilbrey, who rejoined the junior class at Williamsville High School.[2] In those early days of April, both Mae and the president had the army on their minds. Wilson concerned himself with how to make the force bigger. Mae thought about Eliga Dees, a private in the Sixth Infantry stationed on the Mexican border.

They came from big families in Black River Township, nested in the Ozark highlands of southeastern Missouri. Mae was the oldest of seven children of John and Ida Bilbrey, who had welcomed her on the last day of 1896. When the census takers came by in 1900, the Bilbreys were calling her "Minnie M." and renting a farmhouse.[3] Lige arrived to William and Sarah Dees on June 20, 1895. They gave him the name of his grandfather and an uncle, Elijah, which over the years became Eliga and eventually Lige. He had at least nine siblings and was one of the youngest.[4]

Sometime in their teens, Mae and Lige had developed a mutual fondness. But Lige's relatives and Mae's father had forbidden the youthful romance. "He thought I was only a little girl and you was a kid and that we would change our minds and not be satisfied," she once remembered of her father in a letter to Lige. While Mae boarded with a Mr. Lewis, he kept Lige from visiting.[5] Then, in late 1916, Lige left town. Rumors trickled back that he had married someone. In fact, on January 2, 1917, he had joined the army at Jefferson Barracks outside of St. Louis.[6] Lige signed up alongside many unmarried men otherwise headed for manual labor or farming. After testing clear for venereal disease, he signed up for three years of active service then four in reserve. Lige trained at Jefferson Barracks for about a month before coming home on leave in February or March 1917. Mae saw him at a gathering but ignored him out of spite. She thought Lige had married and also heard he was saying nasty things about her.[7] Soon after that snub, Lige left town again to fulfill his new assignment to the Sixth Infantry in El Paso. The unit recently had returned to Texas from Mexico, where it spent several months chasing Pancho Villa under Gen. John J. Pershing. With tensions between the United States and Mexico subsiding, Lige traveled against the tide of a hundred thousand National Guardsmen withdrawing from the border just as he arrived to join the Sixth.[8]

The young man reached out to Mae by post. Around the time of Wilson's speech, he sent her his picture and then a scrawled letter. Lige possessed a seventh-grade education and modest literacy.[9] His command of the written word stopped somewhere short of punctuation, capitalization, penmanship, and spelling, but he could make his meaning clear. In this letter Lige conveyed surprising news. He'd enlisted in the army. Rumors of his cruel words were just that. He had not married, and in fact thought *she* had. Learning otherwise, he hoped to revive their courtship.

Twenty years old and clear of the obstructionists, Mae replied to Lige on April 12, 1917, to reciprocate his feelings and retire the misunderstandings. She planned to teach school. Like an increasing number of people, she determined to pick her own mate.[10] Wary of gossipers, Mae asked Lige to keep the relationship secret. Meantime she promised Lige she had been a "good girl" since they last spoke. To Mae, their situation heralded tragic as well as romantic possibilities. "When I see the flags and see the cars of soldiers pass and when we sing 'America,' 'Stars [*sic*] Spangled Banner' and all the patriotic songs, I almost cry," she sighed. "Why? Because I can't help but think of the soldier boy I once loved to dream dreams about."[11]

IN WASHINGTON OFFICIALS WERE busy assigning purpose to the intervention. Much of the country along with the president originally had opposed joining the catastrophe in Europe. "He Kept Us Out of War," went a slogan of Wilson's 1916 reelection campaign, even as the administration and vocal interventionists were accumulating grievances against Germany and sensing American security at stake. Now, in April, although escalating German attacks against maritime traffic in the Atlantic may have provoked American belligerence, Wilson sought to imbue it with higher meaning. "German submarine warfare against commerce," the president thus declared on the rainy evening of April 2, "is a warfare against mankind." The United States would fight "to vindicate the principles of peace and justice" and for a world "made safe for democracy."[12] In place of autocracy, intrigue, deception, and militarism would come self-determination, collective security, and the rule of law. These were the ideals Wilson found "nearest our hearts." The president later disavowed any crusade to force a form of government on anyone, and even his quotable line about democracy implied cultivation more than imposition. But audiences may have heard in his words something like global salvation at stake in this war.[13]

Then the war resolution went to Congress for debate. Over several days, the senators and representatives delivered long-winded oratory, bitter denunciations, heartfelt proclamations, patriotic one-upmanship, and bookish dissertations on history, morality, and the law. Most members favored war, but they parted company on aims, attaching a variety of sometimes imprecise ideals to the intervention. The United States fought for *honor, independence, human freedom, democracy, modern civilization, the sovereign rights of the American Republic, dignity in the councils of the nations of the earth*, and *humanity and the preservation of its ideals*. And it fought against *organized barbarism, German Prussianism, Austrian absolutism, Prussian militarism*, and *the unspeakable Turk*. While some voted for war to defend or nurture "democracy," others renounced any such motivation altogether, preferring commercial or legal arguments. Almost every lawmaker wrapped his remarks in patriotic outrage.[14]

For many supporters, however, the war implicated a personal goal: protecting the family. In the House debate, Rep. Henry D. Flood (D-Va.), chairman of the Foreign Affairs Committee, made the opening statement, speaking of love, honor, and respect. The Germans had dared to

> insult our flag, to destroy American property, and to murder American citizens, and a nation that will not fight for its honor and for such wrongs to its people is not worthy of the love of those people or the respect of the world and will not long retain either.

Flood cited Germany's violation of an ancient principle: "In the calamities of war children are exempted and spared on the score of their age and women from respect to their sex."[15] Speakers pledged to protect or avenge the innocent, introducing into the record constituent petitions vowing to defend American lives. To Sen. Henry Myers (D-Mont.), submitting to Germany would render vain the efforts of both sides in the Civil War—one that fought for, and one that surrendered in good faith to, a government obliged to protect its "sons and daughters."[16]

These appeals depended for their power on years' worth of stories about German contempt for masculine behavior—stories that animated few Americans to cry out for intervention but lent it purpose once it came. Adherents of either restrained or muscular manliness took offense at German sexual depravity and disregard for chivalry. Press coverage of the "rape of Belgium" publicized images of maimed children and defiled women, inspiring donations to Herbert Hoover's Commission for Relief in Belgium.[17] In 1915, when the Germans executed Edith Cavell, a British nurse found guilty of spiriting their enemies to safety, a writer in the *New York Times* said, "Man's love of life, the chivalric sentiment of man for woman, tender consideration for the helplessness of age and of youth, all these she [Germany] has maimed and bruised and effaced with her mailed fist, all these she has trampled under foot."[18] In his speech at Cooper Union before the 1916 election, Theodore Roosevelt played to protective impulses when he mourned "babies gasping pitifully as they sank under the waves."[19] The German declaration of unrestricted submarine warfare and the Zimmermann telegram of February and March 1917 then confirmed, for the president and those urging intervention, that the German threat against America was neither distant nor abstract. More and more organizations, newspapers, and individuals, whether with relish or resignation, publicly declared war necessary or inevitable, despite the improbability of a German-Mexican alliance and its rather brief life as a trigger of media alarm.[20] The business of the U-boats, though, Wilson termed "unmanly" in his war message of April 1917, a speech whose "virile simplicity" the French minister of justice appreciated.[21] The so-called Hun wasn't so much *un*-masculine as *hyper*-masculine—muscled, bestial, loathe to subdue his sexual impulses. By abandoning restraint, Germans became eligible for simian portrayals of racially suspect groups, the Irish, the Spanish, and African Americans before them (figure 1.1).[22]

Germany's descent into primitivism surprised admirers of that nation. Since 1890, Kaiser Wilhelm's young empire had embodied modern technological progress and a future-oriented *Kultur*, albeit amid more sinister notes of expansionism and militarism. German immigrants, meanwhile, had compared favorably to the Irish in the 1840s and more recently had weathered the storms of scientific racism and xenophobic "hyphenism." Although a bit clannish and too fond of beer, griped the nativists, they were Christian, family-loving, and hard-working, especially compared to southern and eastern Europeans. The congressional Immigration (or Dillingham) Commission's report of 1911 placed the Germans high in the ethnic rankings.[23]

This esteem melted away in 1914 and thereafter, when Germany revealed not only sinister geopolitical ambitions but also an uninhibited style of war. Those who had once venerated the Teutons, even believed Anglo-Saxons their descendants, found this style unbecoming of an advanced white people. Sometimes this thinking percolated upward from the body politic. Late in 1917, a school principal in Louisiana sent the War Department a poem he'd written for dissemination:

We admire her commercial progress
And her scientific stride
But alas for German Kultur
When She took an Army bride

FIGURE 1.1 "Destroy this mad brute . . . Enlist!" 1917. World War I Poster Collection, Library of Congress.

From this unnatural union
Has sprung the German State,
A nation of Military pirates
Who live, to plunder, fight and hate[24]

This armchair observer of world affairs visualized state behavior in familial or matrimonial terms, although he imagined the (raping and pillag-
ing) German army as a woman. Better-known figures such as English
poet Rudyard Kipling published articles expelling Germany from the
ranks of the civilized.[25] Madison Grant, the noted evangelist of eugenic
theory, issued a revised version of *The Passing of the Great Race* in 1918
that removed Teutonic settlers from the American origins story. For
these critics, what did *Kultur* really mean? Inscribed on a club in popular imagery, it bludgeoned rather than edified. After the war, famed psy-
chologist G. Stanley Hall recalled, "There was something fundamentally
wrong with the Teutonic soul."[26]

Before that, in early April 1917, assumptions about German moral
decline freighted the war with righteous urgency. In words spoken
or introduced into the record, senators and citizens from Montana,
Nevada, New Jersey, Ohio, Texas, Washington, and Wyoming testified
to failed virtue and derelict masculinity—*outrages, ravished, tortured,
massacre, dismember, barbarous, atrocities, cold blood, cruel, despotic,
inhuman, ruthless, brutality, terrorism, murder, piracy,* and *tyrannical.*[27]
For Americans to tolerate affronts against civilized restraint would be
cowardly and *craven*, as one speaker put it.[28] But the war's supporters
had faith in national resolve. Sen. Thomas Hardwick (D-Ga.) granted
Americans were praying for peace. "But, Mr. President, I deeply mistake the temper of American manhood, the mettle of American citizenship," he declared, "if the prayers from those homes are for peace at any
price."[29] War had a price too, but Hardwick assumed Americans were
ready to pay it.

NATALIE VIVIAN SCOTT, TWENTY-SIX years old at the time of Wilson's war
message, was appalled at German behavior in Belgium. She had been
born to parents who called themselves "Boss" and "Muddie" in Bristol,
Tennessee, on July 18, 1890. Boss, or Nathaniel, owned a small railroad
construction business based in New Orleans, but the family followed

him to jobs in Alabama, Tennessee, Georgia, Kentucky, and Indiana, before settling in Bay St. Louis, Mississippi, in late 1896. Natalie had two older brothers, Nauman and Wyeth. The family lived through a yellow fever epidemic in Bay St. Louis, watching neighbors die and then seeing them burned within four hours per the instructions of the state board of health. The fever almost claimed the life of Muddie, or Martha, who survived the dehydration, black vomit, headaches, and chills, but remained a partial invalid the rest of her life. Natalie never forgot what she saw as a seven-year-old.[30]

In 1903, the Scotts moved to Carondelet Street in New Orleans. Natalie excelled at the Garden District's Newcomb High School and entered Newcomb College, affiliated with Tulane, at the age of fifteen (figure 1.2). Natalie cultivated her interests in sports and art and eventually her political consciousness and activism. The young women of Newcomb received the full education typically reserved for men

FIGURE 1.2 Natalie Vivian Scott in 1907 or 1908, while a student at Newcomb College. Natalie Scott Papers, Louisiana Research Collection, Tulane University.

but experienced both the culture of Victorian-era decorum and the civic engagement of the progressive age. Wearing a long skirt, Natalie played center on the basketball team. She acted in plays, helped edit the yearbook, and served as class poet and historian. Natalie endeavored to draw out timid young women, forming an organization called the Student Club to assemble members on what she called an "equal footing." In the summer of 1908, with her friend Hilda Phelps, Natalie worked successfully to match the extracurricular sports, clubs, and other activities offered at Newcomb to those serving the men at Tulane. Soon the university's board of administration had its first female member, and three of the six students running the yearbook were Newcomb women. A line in a student poem of June 1909—*Natalie's voice was hoarse from talking*—suggested the young woman's role in the reforms.[31]

After graduating in 1909, Natalie went to Washington, D. C., where she studied ancient Greek drama. By 1911, she was back home, acting in plays and teaching at Newcomb High School. For six years she held that job while earning a master's degree in Greek literature from Tulane. In 1914, while on a trip to Guatemala with Muddie, Natalie learned of the outbreak of the Great War.

Upon her return to New Orleans, Natalie worked to aid Belgian refugees. She read Edith Cavell's appeals to donate funds for her overrun hospital and Belgian civilians fleeing to France. Natalie and Hilda organized a production of the play *Christmas Boxes* late in 1914 as a benefit for women and children in Belgium. She joined in the outrage over Cavell's execution. By 1916, Natalie had taken a Red Cross nursing course and put in a request to go to France should the Americans intervene. Her ambition concerned Natalie's family, although physical danger wasn't the issue. Natalie's brother asked her, "please promise not to join the red cross? Really I would hate to have to think of you thrown among so many soldiers, and the work you would have to do."[32] Wyeth, like other Americans, found the war zone no place for a lady. Natalie disregarded these worries and learned French and wireless telegraphy. Weeks after the war declaration, Natalie's application for overseas service reached the desk of Dr. Alexander Lambert, former personal physician and friend of Theodore Roosevelt, who was heading the American Red Cross Medical Operations on the Western Front.

AS CONGRESS CONSIDERED THE war measure, George Waring Huston was studying law at the University of Alabama. He was born in Selma on June 1, 1896. Short and slender, with brown eyes and dark hair, he went by Waring. In the days after President Wilson's speech, Waring applied for admission to an officers' training camp. He counted two Confederate veterans and the Revolutionary War hero Brig. Gen. Andrew Pickens among his ancestors.[33]

Waring's father put particular pressure on him to seek a commission. R. Walter Huston worked in Selma as an assistant cashier at the City National Bank and in the insurance business. He had two children from a previous marriage—Harry, born in 1885, and Helen, in 1887. After Walter's first wife died in 1891, he married Nellye Augusta Smith, who came from a wealthy family down in Mobile. A year after the wedding, Nellye gave birth to Waring.[34]

The Hustons and Smiths were big families. Relatives often visited Walter and Nellye's large house on Church Street in Selma. A report card for December 1902 revealed that young Waring possessed a fine deportment. He was learning to read, write, and do math, but needed to work on spelling. As for drawing, the lad was "trying his best."[35] In 1914, Waring graduated from Selma High School with sixteen others (figure 1.3). The yearbook noted he ran longer on brains than diligence, just like his best chum Pressley Cleveland. It predicted Waring would be president of the country, though his own cryptic ambition was "To Have 'Good Win.'"[36] That fall, Waring and Press and another friend, William Harper, enrolled at UA in Tuscaloosa.[37] Waring hated the food, suffered beatings from upperclassmen, and missed his family. Eighty miles was a long way from home at a time when traveling out of town merited mention in local newspapers. Waring schemed to leave Tuscaloosa whenever he could. His homesickness grew so severe it became a topic of correspondence among his relatives.[38]

During the summer of 1916, Waring received a letter from UA President George H. Denny imploring him to sign up for the Reserve Officers Training Corps (ROTC), established just days earlier by the National Defense Act.[39] It is likely that he numbered among the four hundred students who enrolled, although none of his letters survive to confirm it. The next year, a few days after Wilson's war message, Waring and his well-connected family began working to place him in the armed

FIGURE 1.3 Waring Huston high school photograph, 1914. Edwin Condie Godbold Local History Collection, Selma-Dallas County Public Library.

forces. He sought admission to one of the new officer training schools, where the army ultimately would commission almost half of the 182,000 new junior officers needed to fight the war.[40] For the Hustons, Waring's efforts had military, familial, and social implications. Earning a commission would make the boy an officer *and* a gentleman—and uphold a cherished tradition of martial service.

THE ANTI-INTERVENTIONISTS IN CONGRESS deployed the symbol of the family with the same fervor as the war's advocates. These dissenters declared *themselves* the true protectors of women and children. Whether they made isolationist, anti-corporate, or pacifist arguments, the war's opponents consistently laced their opposition with tragic predictions for the wartime family.[41]

President Wilson himself had called entrance "solemn and even tragical" in his April war address.[42] During the Senate debate, skeptics foresaw weeping widows and pitiful orphans in Europe and America. Sens. James Vardaman (D-Miss.), George Norris (R-Neb.), and Asle Gronna (R-N. D.) claimed to dread the looming anguish of *devoted wives, orphaned children, broken-hearted women, babes, beloved ones,* and *loving mothers,* all for ill-defined or nefarious purposes.[43] One mother, Mrs. H. A. Woods, had her letter on this subject read into the record. The North Dakota farmwoman saw heartbreak where others saw the maintenance of honor:

> Did the mother of the poorer, thrifty classes, who spent many wakeful nights during the infancy of her boy, who went faint and weak, who got along without necessities in the way of clothing, who patched and stinted, in order to feed and clothe her boy, go through those sacrifices to send her boy to a slaughterhouse to be butchered? And what has that boy done to be sacrificed, to be made to suffer until he goes insane, to lose his eyesight, to lose an arm or a leg or both? Where does the humanity and the justice come in?

She likewise regarded gender propriety under threat, but not from the Germans. What were women doing sailing on ships into a war zone? "Let the women stay at home, where they belong," she said. To sympathize with the drowned women seemed "maudlin" and "ridiculous."[44] For different reasons, the antiwar progressive Robert La Follette (R-Wisc.) found chivalry misapplied. It hardly seemed honorable to join a blockade currently "starving to death the old men and women, the children, the sick and the maimed," all in the name, he charged, of base commercial interests.[45]

Antiwar Rep. Henry Cooper (R-Wisc.) embraced the standards of masculine gallantry but didn't find them at stake in the European war. In a testy exchange, Cooper argued, "a brave man might well defend his own home, his wife and children from marauders and yet not be willing to go 100 miles away to engage in a brawl."[46] His Democratic colleague from Missouri, Perl Decker, likewise perceived no sacrifice of honor in voting for peace. In an early morning speech on April 6, antiwar Democratic majority leader Claude Kitchin (N. C.) echoed these points but altered the familial metaphor. He likened himself to a son trying to keep his father out of a fight, but pledged if a fight must come, he would be "taking off his coat and struggling with all of his soul and might in defense of that father."[47] But no true affront had yet been suffered.

Cooper, Decker, and Kitchin were not pacifists, but Jeannette Rankin was, leading her to a deeper critique of the chivalry argument. The first woman elected to Congress, Rankin (R-Mont.) found nothing ennobling in war, and she objected to this war's commercial justifications and dubious Allied propaganda. When Rankin's name was called around 3:00 a.m. on April 6, she paused. "I want to stand by my country," she finally said, "but I cannot vote for war."[48]

These dissenters collectively imagined war as familial tragedy, a notion circulating in antiwar plays, films, music, and books of the 1910s. War's imperilment of families infused two popular songs of 1915: "Don't Take My Darling Boy Away" and "I Didn't Raise My Boy to Be a Soldier" (figure 1.4). But now, such motherly protectiveness offended the interventionists, as patriotic rather than antiwar motherhood carried the day. When Mrs. Woods's letter was read in the Senate, John Sharp Williams (D-Miss.) ridiculed its "cowardly nonsense." "If you raised your boy right, you raised him to do whatever he had to do for his own honor or for his country's honor," he sneered.[49] Sen. Key Pittman (D-Nev.) offered a more temperate version of the point. "I have the deepest sympathy and consideration," he claimed, "for those loving women who have written letters to various Members of this body. . . . They feel more deeply than I can ever feel the loss of a dear one." No one wanted to leave "widows out in the little homes to take care of the orphans." But better to lose a few hundred thousand now than a few million in an inevitable showdown with Germany.[50] What was more, soon doctors and journalists began peddling a "safe war" argument in the press, claiming that medical advances and the more "rational" war of 1917 meant a less lethal battlefield for doughboys.[51]

Six senators and fifty representatives voted against the resolution. Peace activists believed it contradicted the popular will, something a coalition including William Jennings Bryan, the Woman's Peace Party, the Socialist Party, and several congressmen from the South and Midwest had vainly struggled to prove by calling for a national referendum on the war. But many in the antiwar minority in Congress pledged to get on the team, implicitly disowning their earlier predictions of war's

FIGURE 1.4 Sheet music for "I Didn't Raise My Boy to Be a Soldier," 1915. Wade Hall Collection of Southern History and Culture (Sheet Music), University of Alabama Libraries Special Collections.

catastrophic dimensions. Said one former skeptic, "The people of this Nation should stand as one man."[52]

A FEW DAYS LATER, on April 9, Waring Huston wrote to a top military official in New York seeking information on becoming a Second Lieutenant in the Reserve Corps, just as his father appealed to their congressman. Meanwhile, E. W. Pettus, a law associate of Waring's brother-in-law, implored Secretary of War Newton Baker himself to consider the young man. Ten days later, Sen. Oscar Underwood of Alabama forwarded Waring's credentials to the Commanding General of the Eastern Department, the man in charge of officer training schools. His parents fretted. "Nothing new has developed in Waring's case," his father Walter reported to Nellye while she visited New Orleans.[53]

Waring heard in early May he had been admitted to the training camp at Fort McPherson outside of Atlanta. Applicants had been selected through "no partiality," said officials. The *Atlanta Constitution* printed the names of the lucky ones on May 12, the day Waring arrived.[54] Leaving home never got easier. On May 26, 1917, Waring complained to his mother of loneliness, arms sore from typhoid shots, and feet tender from long, rainy treks. He worried the folks back home at 702 Church Street were going on with their lives. "Write real soon and don't forget me," he pleaded. "I love you and Papa more than you realize and my! how I miss you all."[55]

JUST AFTER WARING LEFT Selma, Thomas Alexander Boyd and Martin Gus Gulberg enlisted in the Marine Corps in Chicago.[56] Thomas was just short of nineteen, brought up by a widowed nurse in Defiance, Ohio. He was a good student at Elgin Academy in Illinois at the time of Wilson's call to arms. "Very lukewarm" was how he described his enthusiasm for the war in a letter to his aunt, but he wanted to contribute his service as an ambulance driver. When that effort failed for unclear reasons, he joined the Marines, enlisting so he could be one of the "atoms in the great struggle."[57] The redheaded Gulberg, a shipping clerk, wanted a part in what he called "the big fuss." On May 23, the boys left a train station full of tearful relatives for Parris Island, South Carolina. From the road, Boyd joked to his mother, "I expect to embrace my trials and tribulations with great fortitude and much reticence thereby favorably impressing my superiors."[58]

Heat and hazing met the recruits at Parris Island. For dropping his rifle during drill, one young man had to search the grounds for exactly one thousand burnt matches. Nothing Thomas Boyd did in boot camp, nor the impassioned rhetoric of public culture, raised the temperature of his enthusiasm. In fact he resented the state and its claims of collective interest and civic duty. "Personally," he declared to his aunt from Parris Island, "I have nothing to fight for. The individual is much better off than the citizen." But he nonetheless worked hard to qualify for the Corps. When his mother asked if he regretted enlisting, Boyd replied no.[59]

In mid-August, Thomas and Martin traveled to the new Marine training grounds at Quantico. The Corps put them in a rifle company, the Seventy-Fifth, part of the First Battalion, Sixth Regiment. It was a new regiment led by hardened veterans. They spent four weeks at the camp, hiking the surrounding hills and learning to drill and use grenades and bayonets. Boyd had to reassure his mother that Quantico was not on the Western Front, but in Virginia.[60]

THERE WERE NOT ENOUGH volunteers like Waring Huston, Thomas Boyd, and Martin Gulberg to field the million-man force Wilson wanted. America's military was small—the day before his April war speech, the regular army consisted of 121,000 enlisted men—and the Allies' needs were big. "We want men, men, men," French Marshal Joseph Joffre famously requested of the president during a visit in April, dashing the hopes of those in Congress who thought no American bodies would be necessary. The National Defense Act of 1916 had called for the expansion and professionalization of the army and state militias, but strategists understood that modern conflicts required conscription. Every major warring state in 1914 had a draft besides Britain, and it came there in 1916. Congress quickly considered a conscription bill to which Wilson had referred approvingly in his speech of April 2.[61]

The debate roughly followed divisions of class and geography, with many southern and midwestern Democrats opposed, and many elites and northeastern Republicans in favor. Speaker of the House Champ Clark famously said, "there is precious little difference between a conscript and a convict."[62] Clark's Missouri colleague in the Senate, James Reed, had called his antiwar colleagues traitors but opposed the draft, warning the secretary of war, "You will have the streets of American cities running red with blood."[63] Rep. George Huddleston of Alabama raised the specter of a "rich man's war, poor man's fight" like the one some southerners resented in the 1860s. From the blood of unwilling draftees, who would profit? "The old guard of munitions makers," he answered, "war contractors, captains of industry, Wall Street speculators, metropolitan financiers."[64] Other opponents perceived no chivalry at stake. "If this war was to protect the free institutions of America, our homes, our women and children," speculated a farmer in North Carolina, "selective conscription might be justified; but in that case there would be no need of conscription."[65]

None of these arguments worked. Appeals to nationalism and duty, and the shortage of volunteers, carried the draft to passage. Many former antis, including Reed of Missouri, switched sides under pressure from Wilson. His bill won 397–24 in the House, and 81–8 in the Senate. On May 18, the president signed the Selective Service Act, requiring males between the ages of twenty-one and thirty to register. The administration had favored lowering the age by two years, but for people in states where teenagers weren't legal adults, or who thought the military posed moral risks, nineteen was too young. In an attempt to soothe anti-statist anxieties, Wilson empowered the 4,647 local draft boards, not federal officials, to conduct registration and conscription.[66]

The president argued that wartime service was a citizen's obligation, an old idea now enforced by law. By this maneuver of logic, only traitors would evade their obligations. The masses of young men who were expected to register, whatever motivated them, thus appeared to be "willing." Without irony Wilson introduced the Selective Service Act to the country:

It is in no sense a conscription of the unwilling; it is, rather, selection from a nation which has volunteered in mass.

Was "volunteered" the right term? Section 3 of the Selective Service Act warned,

[A]ny person who shall willfully fail or refuse to present himself for registration . . . shall be guilty of a misdemeanor and shall . . . be punished by imprisonment for not more than one year, and shall thereupon be duly registered.

In this climate of "coercive voluntarism," the apt phrase capturing the letter and spirit of the policy, newspapers urged consensual patriotism alongside warnings about the consequences of dissent. "Jail for Slackers," cautioned the *Washington Post*. Whatever its incongruity, Wilson's position marked the meeting point—or break—between the voluntarist past and the American state of the present.[67]

Once the registration ended, local boards would draft some 12 percent of those registered, though draftees wound up constituting 72 percent of all soldiers in the wartime army.[68] The government articulated guidelines for exemptions, mainly for men with dependents or jobs crucial to home front productivity, but the local boards would manage their allocation. This arrangement bent local dynamics of reputation, shame, and obligation to the needs of the state. It funneled loyalty to the federal government through loyalty to one's friends and neighbors.[69]

Registration day was set for June 5. At Parris Island, Thomas Boyd heard of the law and wrote to his mother. Although he harbored reluctance about war and the power of the state, he shared popular associations of military service and masculine virtue. "I suppose the conscription will get a lot of the cold footed boys," he jeered, "who have attempted to evade their share of the big fight."[70]

AMONG THE 10 MILLION MEN expected to register was a quiet twenty-five-year-old laborer in the town of Ixonia, Wisconsin, named Arthur Wilhelm Ludwig Huebner (figure 1.5). The unassuming Arthur, blue-eyed and blond-haired, worked as a farm hand for a Welshman named Evan Evans.[71] His parents and six younger brothers and sisters lived in nearby Watertown.

Arthur's father, Christian Huebner, had come to Wisconsin in 1887 from a German-speaking part of the Russian province of Poland. Christian ultimately opened a shoemaking shop but first worked for a Prussian farmer named Carl Braunschweig. He married Braunschweig's daughter Louise in early 1891, and in November they had a son named Arthur. Two years later came Otto, then Martha in 1895, Johanna in 1896, and Alvina in 1901, when Arthur was enrolled in a public school

FIGURE 1.5 Arthur Huebner, 1917. Author's collection.

and spoke better English than his siblings, who attended Lutheran schools in German. In 1903 came another boy, Walter, then a move to nearby Ixonia. The family grew again in 1908 when Louise gave birth to Carl. Then, on July 8, 1910, Louise and Christian had their eighth child, a girl they called Irene Louise. Arthur was eighteen years old. He hadn't gone to high school and was working on the farm of a German American named Theodor Jaeger.[72] The little girl inherited her mother's poor constitution and lived only two and a half years.

In 1917, the Huebners moved to Watertown, Wisconsin, a settlement of 8,829 residents near Lebanon and Ixonia. Christian found work with the railroad. Passage of the Selective Service Act converted Arthur and his younger brother Otto into prime candidates for conscription. Neither had dependents. The community would be watching German behavior in particular, and the Huebners were undeniably German. In Christian and Louise's house in Watertown hung a plaque: *In diesem Haus ist Deutsch gesprochen*—"In this house German is spoken."[73]

WISCONSIN'S POLITICAL TRADITIONS and ethnic character made it a hotbed of antiwar feeling. Pacifism, socialism, and progressivism circulated through the state's bloodstream, adherents of each suspicious of war in general, while the Germans hoped to stay out of this war in particular. On a Sunday evening in November 1915, an appreciative and heavily German audience filled the Turner Opera House in Watertown to hear speeches advocating neutrality, part of a broader pattern that included thousands of Irish and Germans packing Madison Square Garden to demand American noninvolvement.[74] Inside the Watertown hall, Northwestern College musicians led the audience in song—"America," "The Star-Spangled Banner," and the German anthem "Die Wacht am Rhein" ("The Watch on the Rhein"). The citizens adopted a series of resolutions condemning the lopsided traffic in arms to Britain, "the bully of the oceans," and demanding true neutrality.[75]

Even as Congress debated the war resolution seventeen months later, people in Wisconsin continued to oppose entrance. In the city of Sheboygan, a referendum showed 4,082 against fighting, seventeen in favor—and out in the county, it was 2,051 to zero. A vote in Monroe went 954 to ninety-five in favor of staying out. Citizens in Grand Rapids, Milwaukee, Arpin, and Campbellsport sent antiwar petitions to senators.[76] Sen. Robert La Follette cited this sentiment in his broad, long-winded attack against intervention and was one of six senators to vote no. Wisconsin provided nine of the fifty members of the House of Representatives who stood with La Follette. As late as May 1917, the *Watertown Weltbürger*, a German-language paper in press since 1857 but losing readers to assimilation, still talked about British and French "lies" concerning Germany.[77] Such activities earned Wisconsin a steady Justice Department presence during the war.[78]

As in other parts of the country, Wisconsin officials and newspaper editors vocalized a more interventionist strain. During the April debates, Sen. Paul Husting (D-Wisc.) introduced into the record proclamations of "loyalty" from citizens in Madison, Janesville, Fond du Lac, Racine, and Reedsburg. Four hundred fifty women in Milwaukee signed a petition supporting war "no matter what the sacrifice."[79] At the University of Wisconsin, every one of the 420 faculty members save two repudiated La Follette's antiwar heresy. The state legislature registered its condemnation.[80]

Watertown followed the trend. In May 1917, civic leaders welcomed federal officials to implore citizens to meet the town's $300,000 Liberty Bond goal. One of the government men made clear what dollars would buy—domestic, even personal, stability:

> Those families which stand together and boost each other, and who look to the interest of each family, is [sic] the most successful. . . . [Buy a Liberty Bond because] we in this country are receiving opportunities that no other country can offer its citizens and [live in] an ideal place to raise and make a happy family.[81]

The same month, Watertown businessmen underwrote the creation of a National Guard unit, Company E, drawing exclusively from area volunteers. Local papers reported that citizens in the local *Turn Verein*, a German club, later wined and dined Company E before its departure.[82] Amid passage of the Selective Service Act and La Follette's allegations of class warfare, the patriotic *Watertown Daily Times* ran a cartoon denying this would be a bourgeois war fought by the proletariat, listing a "roll call" of draftees that included "rich man," "poor man," and "banker" alike.[83] This message was so important to the Wilson administration that the Committee on Public Information (CPI) eventually stitched it into its "Bulletin for Cartoonists," which instructed artists to discredit the class warfare claim as a German lie.[84] Even before such mandates, leaders in Watertown demanded that anyone with familial ties and a patriotic pulse should support the war. A poem published on Memorial Day beseeched Watertowners to "renew allegiance to home and flag."[85] In 1917 America, it was rapidly becoming clear that to defend one was to defend the other.

WITH THE JUNE 5 REGISTRATION approaching, two months into the American commitment, the war's meaning still proved elusive. A huge rally in Chicago on May 27 pivoted around the question, "Why war and what for?"[86] Even true believers expressed confusion. In New York, Rabbi Samuel Schulman pledged absolute loyalty to the war, though he politely submitted, "We have the right as soon as possible to know in definite terms what we are actually fighting for."[87]

The confusion arose less from a shortage of justifications than an abundance. Some people envisioned a religious crusade, others glimpsed a chance to Americanize immigrant-soldiers. Many progressives, once skeptical of the war, bent it to their purposes, pinning their dreams of a more activist state on wartime needs. Philosopher John Dewey regarded war as an opportunity to audition progressive pleas to elevate the community over the individual, harness state and commercial enterprises to the common good, and deploy science and reason on behalf of social endeavors. Above all, a just war fought efficiently would blend the progressive goals of bureaucratic organization and human decency. Other than Randolph Bourne, Jane Addams, Robert La Follette, and a handful of like-minded dissenters, most progressives joined the team.[88]

Often those authorities seeking to clarify the war's aims added new ones. Newspapers published Secretary of the Interior Franklin Knight Lane's capacious defense of the intervention's objectives. It was a war for self-preservation; it pitted followers of Christ against those of "Mahomet"; it would punish Germany for "outraged" Belgium, "desecrated" France, and attacks on the *Lusitania* and *Sussex*. It would defend Britain, the source of Anglo-Saxon civilization, and nurture infant democracy in Russia. And combat militarism. And maintain American "self-respect."[89]

When popular newspapers tried their hand at explaining the war, the results could be quite different. A piece in the *Boston Globe*—"Why I Will Be Ready on June 5th"—included a few geopolitical justifications but otherwise invested national goals with personal meaning:

BECAUSE I am an American citizen and want to do my duty.
BECAUSE My country needs me.
BECAUSE I don't want to be called a slacker.
BECAUSE I am not afraid.
BECAUSE I want to keep my name untarnished.
BECAUSE I want my folks to be proud of me.
BECAUSE I don't want the world to say I'm a coward.
BECAUSE I realize that it is deeds and not words that count.
BECAUSE I want to show the Kaiser that we are not bluffers.
BECAUSE I am patriotic.
BECAUSE I am going to fight for the flag that waves over all the
    world and has never known defeat.
BECAUSE I am not a quitter.
BECAUSE I want to maintain my self-respect.

BECAUSE I believe in freedom and personal liberty.
BECAUSE I am a Man.[90]

The *Globe* suggested that literally protecting the family was not war's only potential contribution to domestic tranquility. Personal motives might share space with, trump, or coincide with diplomatic objectives. Here war offered an opportunity to burnish one's standing in the community, relationship with family, and individual character. The *Globe* conflated patriotic and personal virtue, asking young men to renew their masculine credibility, make families proud, and serve national military goals. In spring 1917, such ideas reverberated across the landscape of popular and quasi-official culture. A verse from George Cohan's tune "Over There," written days after Wilson's address, aligned personal and national motivations:

Make your mother proud of you,
And the Old Red, White and Blue.[91]

Whatever the president had meant in that speech, for Cohan these were the things people carried nearest their hearts.

MANY PEOPLE FROM MISSOURI, Mae Bilbrey's state, harbored cynical views of the intervention. Missouri was home to German-speaking immigrants, but dissent drew from other reservoirs. Traditions of localism and anti-corporatism flowed from the 1870s through the Grange movement and the Populist insurgency into April 1917. Papers like the *Missouri Ruralist* and *Missouri Farmer* reported widespread resentment of northeastern war profiteers, even as the state's big Democratic sheets supported Wilson.[92] One of the six votes against war in the Senate had belonged to William Stone of Missouri, governor when Mae and Lige were born in the mid-1890s. The Democrat thought intervention would constitute "the greatest national blunder of history," although he avoided abuse by pledging loyalty should war come.[93] Four of Missouri's sixteen representatives in the House voted against war.[94]

Dissent quieted down in Missouri, as in Wisconsin, after the declaration of war, although some observers noted the sobriety of patriotic rallies. On Saturday, April 15, 1917, Wayne County citizens in Greenville watched flag-waving children march from the school to the courthouse plaza. The crowd listened to oratory from local attorneys and teachers, including a Wayne County member of the League to Enforce Peace, headed by former President William Howard Taft. An ex-sailor raised the American flag while a band played "The Stars and Stripes Forever."[95] Local papers peddled the war's chivalric underpinnings. A headline screamed that the government in Vienna let "BABIES STARVE IN THE STREETS."[96] A man named York Lovelace, sheriff of Wayne County, publicly pledged to protect the personal rights of enemy aliens, although he reminded his constituents, "every citizen owes undivided allegiance to the American flag."[97]

Poignant as the tale of starving babies may have been, many Missourians associated war with corporate voracity rather than humanitarian compassion. For them, a different story about the pathos of small children would have been more persuasive, one predicting domestic bliss shattered by the appetites of business. On April 1, 1917, the *Missouri Farmer* imagined familial tragedy:

Laughing, crowing baby boy, what knows he of tears,
Partings bitterer than death, anguished hopes and fears,
Cooing, babbling joyously, little does he guess,
Soon the darkling war clouds may make him fatherless.[98]

TO THE SOUTHEAST, ROBERT and Nellye Huston's boy, himself familiar with anguished hopes and fears, endured lonely spells at Fort McPherson.

After checking in on May 12 and receiving his identification card, Waring went to the barracks of Company 7, a narrow building with four rows of cots. He met the company commander and collected a blanket, pillowcases, and sheets. Within a day, Waring filed through the camp hospital for vaccinations as other men fainted. On Sunday he received his uniform. "You sure would laugh to see me in my outfit," Waring wrote his mother in Selma. "I have the biggest shoes I most ever saw." Posted notices revealed the schedule: Up at 5:30, march to assembly at 5:40, breakfast at 5:50, drill and assembly from 6:50 to noon, then dinner, more drill and assembly from 1:20 until supper at 6:00, study hours from 7:30 to 9:30, then back to quarters for lights out at 10:00.[99] A trainee in Illinois grumbled, "It is like hoeing the garden on a rainy day and lying down every few minutes. Then, when you get tired, come in the house and sit on the edge of a bed and read a few columns of Webster's Dictionary (that's the nearest layman's book to a 'Drill Regulations'). Then go to bed and get up at five o'clock in the morning by bugle, and do it all over again."[100]

Eventually Waring accumulated a haversack, meat box, canteen, rifle, bayonet, cartridge belt, first-aid kit, knife, fork, spoon, and pick. He asked his mother to ship his bathrobe and slippers and socks. He sent home his suit, hat, shirts, and collars. He marched and drilled and studied books in the evening. He ate mediocre food, though once enjoyed a feast of beef, potatoes, celery, tomatoes, corn, lemonade, and strawberries. He was exhausted and missed his family, although the papers found the men in "the best of spirits."[101] "I miss you all so and your letters help a whole lot," Waring wrote. "Don't feel like you have to write, but when you can, do so, even if it is a short one." He asked for a wristwatch for his birthday, coming up on the first of June.[102] Waring inquired after his sweetheart, Carrie Goodwin, the "Good Win" of his yearbook entry. He sent her photos of the camp and himself. She sent him a picture in late May, making him "right homesick."[103]

On May 20, 1917, the candidates were called to Atlanta to fight a fire that Thomas Boyd and Martin Gulberg had seen from the train to Parris Island. "Just think of blocks and blocks of beautiful homes going up in smoke," Waring lamented to his mother. It was their second trip to Atlanta in a week. They had just passed in review before Gen. Leonard Wood and had their parade photographed for the *Atlanta Constitution*. Then they had two more inoculations.[104] Of his feeling on Fort McPherson, Waring said, "I can't say that I am delighted to be here but it is as good as they could make it."[105] The *Constitution* reported the same thing in upbeat tones. "There is nothing which could contribute to the comfort of the men," the paper assured, "that Uncle Sam has overlooked."[106]

TWO WEEKS LATER, THE sounds of laughing children heralded the coming of registration day. On June 5, families gathered in a Washington park to hear Secretary of War Newton Baker announce the arrival of conscription. Baker recounted the chivalric story, then argued that the war, rather than disrupting the family, would prove compatible with, showcase, or even stimulate domestic virtue.

To make his point, Baker contrasted familial tranquility and gendered order in America with the heartbreaking personal dislocations of Europe. Here "fathers and mothers are escorting their sons to the places of registration," and brave sweethearts are "mak[ing] woman an inspiration to man in an hour of trial." In Polish territory it was said not a single child under five survived. Here a woman dressed in white sang "The Star-Spangled Banner" to a line of young men waiting to register. In Serbia little boys of nine or ten carried arms. Here "you can hear the laughter of children at play." Around the war zone children died as they entered candy shops. Here Americans channeled familial devotion to patriotic ends, there the Germans mocked it with their "surrender to the bestial." But wouldn't war itself disrupt American family life, make orphans of children, or at the very least, confuse everyday patterns? Yes, but "it is a happy confusion."[107]

Baker's hopeful message appeared in the CPI's *Official Bulletin*, a government publication circulated to every post office, university, magazine, chamber of commerce, governor, and mayor in the country.[108] It reverberated in newspapers, just beginning to operate under the advisory gaze of the CPI.[109] "American Manhood Responds to Country's Call," announced the *Racine* (Wisc.) *Journal-News*. Papers gushed at the commitment of young men. Millions stood in line for hours, endured confusion over the location of polling places, and refrained from drink in towns closing saloons for the day. All this they did "voluntarily," though prison sentences awaited slackers. No masculine righteousness accompanied registering for the draft at the tip of a bayonet, so the press reported men who were willing. The words people used to describe the act of registration, like Racine's "responds," suggested volition: *ready to serve, they answer, youth of state enrolls for Uncle Sam, whole nation answers call.*[110]

Women and girls, in turn, poured themselves into the war effort in ways becoming of women and girls. They pinned ribbons on registrants in New England, all across Tennessee, and in Arthur Huebner's Watertown. They mobilized automobiles to ferry boys to the registration. New York's Committee on Aliens dispatched emissaries to immigrant wards demanding women encourage their men to register. Mothers, whom Baker had urged to give their sons "gladly," escorted sons to enroll.[111] In Wisconsin, the *Eau Claire Leader* used a drawing called "The Democracy of Motherhood" to visualize maternal chaperones.[112] Women handed out Wilson's war message at registration places in Chicago, Atlanta, and Nashville, an effort driven by the leader of a national women's group who thought the men needed reminding of it. They did the same in Montgomery, fifty miles down the Jefferson Davis Highway from Waring Huston's hometown, as a preacher insisted before a crowd, "our richest gift [is] the gift of our sons on the altar of our country."[113] Across America, women prodded slackers to the centers.[114]

Even those who stepped forward voluntarily, said the war's backers, only reluctantly took up arms. A New York minister called Americans "home-loving fighters" and not "mechanical professionals."[115] Such men would imagine family as the inspiration for their martial exertions. The Woman's Liberty Loan Committee circulated that chivalric narrative for nationwide consumption:

Bonds or Bondage!
Which Do You Choose?
Will You Let Your Country Be Conquered?
Or Will You Do Your Part to Help Her Now?
The Men of America Are Fighting *Your* Fight.
Stand Back of Them![116]

An Iowa ad for a Liberty Loan drive put the future doughboy's motivation more bluntly: "He fights for you and your family as well as his."[117] Children found the Hun in lessons furnished by the CPI, meant to appeal to "the imagination and to the emotions," teaching that soldiers were going to Europe to keep Germans from "coming to our country" and ravishing Americans.[118]

Newspapers often distilled the war's bigger promises down to everyday terms. A war ostensibly about democracy and rights and humanity in fact guaranteed things more concrete—lifestyles, values and traditions, comforts and happiness. The *Baltimore Sun* honored the political and religious dimensions of American patriotism but also keyed its vision for the postwar world to the prosaic:

But still for God and land our song—
    A safe world for democracy!
*A world in which we still can live
    In our own place and our own way.*[119]

If protecting ordinary life stood at the heart of the conflict, men faced a stark choice—demonstrate devotion to family by going to war or reveal its absence by staying home. An editorial in Atlanta laid bare what registering for the draft revealed about a man:

> Patriotic citizens, men and women, will gather at the registration booths to cheer and encourage the men who will respond to the country's call. And these thousands of young and virile Georgians will respond as readily and as willingly as did their fathers and grandfathers when there was need for them in other wars.[120]

One young woman in Worcester, Massachusetts, even refused to marry her boyfriend unless the local draft board lifted his exemption as a skilled worker. "Down my way," she lectured the board, "all single fellers between twenty-one and thirty-one are divided into just two classes, those who go, and those who don't go. That's my classification. Now if [he] don't go, I'm through with him."[121]

BLACK PEOPLE WEREN'T SO much marginalized as invisible in registration day culture. Other than the occasional statistic or story about African American registrants, the normative model of the doughboy-to-be was a white man. Although it wasn't necessarily aimed at them, the wartime promise that enlistment would burnish masculine virtue, familial strength, and patriotic mettle held potent appeal for many black people in 1917. They had endured decades of humiliation, terror, marginalization, discrimination, segregation, exclusion, and sexual assault. For these reasons, some wanted nothing to do with fighting. A "prisoner of war" was how one black draftee from Brooklyn later saw himself, not a "patriotic soldier eager to defend a flag that defends me and mine."[122] A. Philip Randolph and a few other black leaders held to their antiwar positions and suffered persecution for it. A good number of African Americans protested induction or avoided the state's grasp, like some whites, because of their transience, illiteracy, or isolation. But Adam Clayton Powell Sr., W. E. B. Du Bois, the editors of the *Chicago Defender*, and other leaders saw an opportunity to secure rights. Many southern racial demagogues opposed their service, which itself had the effect of changing some black minds. Sen. James Vardaman declared in

August the "negro" would clamor more loudly for equality should the government "inflate his untutored soul with military airs."[123]

For many black citizens, serving in the armed forces offered theoretical access to elusive masculine honor, especially if they measured it by the newer standard of defiance rather than the older one of uplift. Whatever their position, a large number of African Americans regarded military service as a chance to accrue martial experience and the trappings of manhood and citizenship that went with it.[124] Black leaders loudly declared the patriotism and masculinity of the race. The National Association for the Advancement of Colored People (NAACP), the Tuskegee leadership, the author James Weldon Johnson, the National Equal Rights League, and others differed on tactics and tone but agreed on the dangers of disloyalty. Black papers reported dutiful registration. The *Kansas City Advocate* found no slackers among black men in the city, although a number of whites "were known not to register."[125] The *Chicago Defender* printed this letter in October:

> When the President sounded the tocsin of the war, summoning the chivalry of the country in the defense of the nation, then it was the duty of every loyal and able-bodied Race man to place himself unreservedly at the service of his Race and country.

White supremacists believed—correctly, the author said—that "military training and placing of arms in the hands of the Negro makes him a new man, and every class will feel the uplift."[126]

Few black advocates entertained predictions of overnight war-won equality. The *Afro-American* threw its support to President Wilson but remained skeptical of his democratic promises. The key question for Du Bois, his NAACP colleague Joel Spingarn, and others was how blacks would be used. Civil rights leaders wanted black men in combat and in the officer ranks, not service roles, all the better to prove their masculinity. The *Cleveland Gazette* printed an appeal to its African American readers from a correspondent in France calling forth the doughboys for this mission of rescue. "Widows people this land," he reported. "Mourning is the national costume."[127] Many black people, vocal leaders and draftees alike, wanted in on the fight.

ACROSS REGISTRATION DAY CULTURE, the nation affirmed itself as a collective and almost wholly white family. Sons were to fight, parents and wives to sacrifice willingly. But the national family had a rift running down the middle of it, east to west. Sectional healing accelerated in preparation for war. On June 4 and 5, the Sons of Confederate Veterans (SCV) and the United Confederate Veterans (UCV) met in Washington to honor the Dixie past. Speakers at both events turned public memory of the Civil War to new purposes, declaring it a model for the Great War's chivalric character and regenerative promise.[128]

Three thousand SCV attendees were reminded that heroes Washington, Lee, Wilson, and even Lincoln had been born in the South. Speakers called for a burial of regional hatreds,

> an acclamation of a reunited people, a death knell to the last burning embers of sectional differences and a spirit of confidence in the President to carry the nation through the present crisis, just as other heroes of the South have in days gone by.

Whatever the new war was about, it now required "all our patriotism, heroism, and manhood." Men must protect what they treasured. If the audience needed reminding, on the stage appeared a Confederate girls' choir singing old favorites. Later, "maids of honor" from southern states, including Miss Mary Custis Lee, daughter of Robert E. Lee, ascended to the platform. "There is nothing for this country to do," cried an overheated Sen. Duncan Fletcher (D-Fla.), "but raise her flag, unsheathe her sword and strike with all her might."[129]

The next day, the UCV celebrated its reunion by staging a commemorative and patriotic exhibition. President Wilson took time out of his registration day schedule to deliver a classic speech on redemptive war. The Virginian reminisced about men on both sides, part of one "race," devoting themselves to "chivalric gallantry." God had reunited the nation to meet the challenge in Europe. American men, in millions of gestures of obligation, volunteered their services as the Civil War generation had. Wilson saw no irony in equating the Great War's conscription with the Civil War's voluntarism. "No really thoughtful and patriotic man" could object to the draft law of 1917:

These solemn lines of young men going today all over the union to the places of registration ought to be a signal to the world, to those who dare flout the dignity and honor and rights of the United States, that all her manhood will flock to that standard under which we all delight to serve.

Grave threats from abroad awakened the country's sense of civic and moral obligation, cleansing it of selfish instincts. "There comes a time," Wilson explained, "when it is good for a nation to know that it must sacrifice if need be everything that it has to vindicate the principles which it professes." The Confederate veterans stood and cheered, grateful Wilson associated the war with tradition and pleased he admired their honor. The president called for restoration—of duty, unity, courage, clarity of purpose. The challenges of 1917 demanded a "renewal of the spirit which has made America great among the peoples of the world."[130]

Once again women figured prominently in this call for renewal, appearing on the dais as objects of protection and admiration. This UCV ritual dated to the 1880s, organizers deploying female "sponsors" to reinforce southern chivalric traditions and confirm the manhood of the aging Confederates.[131] With America's visual culture awash in German ape-men and dead children and unconscious white women, the presence of comely maidens carried urgent meaning. A speaker from Texas proudly presented "a bevy of pretty sponsors and maids of honor, whom he calls 'prides of the prairie.'" The conference-goers fêted an older woman for spending years tending a Confederate cemetery in Ohio.[132]

One matron of honor, a Mrs. Kimberly of Mississippi, disclosed to a reporter how hard it was for southern women to join their Yankee counterparts. As the custodians of commemoration and principal mourners of the dead, women stubbornly "held their prejudices." But now the national family must shed old animosities. That spirit of reunited sisterhood had marked the dedication of the new Red Cross building a couple weeks earlier. Loyalty and unity so established, southern elites in particular channeled their energies to a new war for personal and national honor.[133]

OTHERS IN WARING'S ALABAMA saw things differently. Some didn't perceive a threat to honor in this war, some rejected Wilson's linkages between the bellicose spirit of the 1860s and that of 1917, and some suspected northeastern capital of driving America into Europe's destructive internal affairs.

The national preparedness movement of 1915–16, ultimately backed by Wilson and culminating with the National Defense Act (1916), had attracted the support of northeasterners, urbanites, and the comfortable classes, people like Waring Huston's family and UA president George Denny, who had campaigned to bring the ROTC to Tuscaloosa.[134] It met opposition in the Deep South, where agrarian constituents of the Democratic Party harbored profound suspicion of elites and standing armies. When Congress debated war and conscription, antimilitarist resentments intensified—only 470 men from Alabama had enlisted voluntarily by April 27, 1917—but so did calls by pro-war and patrician southerners to defend American honor.[135]

In Congress in April, Reps. Huddleston, Burnett, and Almon claimed to speak for rural antiwar Alabamians like G. H. Simpson, a Confederate veteran. He wrote Burnett that he believed in honor but didn't think it imperiled. His words entered the record:

Now have we got to have our sons conscripted and forced to leave the home land and go across the ocean just to let rich people get richer, and our dear boys never see home again? . . . [If Germany comes here] we will whip them before breakfast.[136]

On the floor of Congress, war advocates hounded Burnett with charges of dishonor. Rep. Heflin of Alabama spoke for a southern gentry enamored of Confederate heritage, declaring ready for service people like Waring Huston—"the descendants of the men who followed Stonewall Jackson and Robert E. Lee."[137] John Burnett shot back that all he remembered were shattered veterans sent to war by leaders happy to sacrifice other people's loved ones: "They were willing to have their sister's sons go; they were willing to have their neighbors' boys go; but they never got where the death grapple raged between brave men." Barely five feet tall, Burnett stormed up and down the aisles, claiming *he* was the one keeping chivalric vigilance over the "women and children of my country." Voters had opted for Wilson and peace in 1916, he cried, to avoid seeing "their loved ones torn from their homes and butchered in a war for which we were not responsible."[138] In the end, two of Alabama's ten House representatives voted no on the war. Burnett and Huddleston cast two of the six southern votes in the House against conscription.[139]

As in Missouri and Wisconsin, skeptics in Alabama kept their voices down after those votes passed. Newspapers filled with support for war and conscription, even as some southern draft boards quietly reported upwards of 80 percent of young men requesting exemptions.[140] A "great wave of patriotism" surged over the citizens of Montgomery on registration day, said a paper there. The *Selma Mirror* asked, "Is Your Boy in the War?" and implored people to buy Liberty Bonds.[141]

"IS YOUR BOY IN the war?" Robert and Nellye Huston hoped he would be. They belonged to the class tending to favor intervention—urban, well-to-do, proud of Confederate ancestors. Waring shared his parents' dreams, although he was terribly conflicted, desperate to go to France in one breath and afflicted with paralyzing homesickness in the next.

It wasn't clear whether the Hustons would get their wish. Waring worried constantly about failure. Would he make it through the camp and join the army? In what role and at what rank? Waring tended to write his parents separate letters, and these matters he took up with his father. "I really wanted the field artillery," he lamented the evening of May 25, "but the Captain said a lot of math. was required." "[S]o I put the Cavalry—after all that drilling today I know I was not fitted for the infantry." He so badly wanted to avoid serving as a foot soldier that he talked about quitting and risking conscription. Waring allowed he'd be satisfied with a noncommission but that wasn't the prize he was after.[142]

Failing the course would render such questions moot. Men were kicked out because they lagged in their studies or physical fitness or couldn't adjust to discipline, with which Waring struggled. He caught hell for incorrectly sheathing his bayonet in its scabbard.[143] In another case, the blanket slipped on his horse, and an officer threw him out of the exercise. "There was no use to argue with him," he complained, "for it does not [do] a bit of good up here." Waring feared the incident would hurt his chances for the cavalry.[144] In late May, the candidates learned they would undergo a new physical exam soon. Rumor had it being underweight would get you tossed out, which worried Waring. He reminded his parents in almost every letter that the test loomed.

NINE DAYS AFTER THE draft registration, President Wilson warned in a Flag Day speech, "The military masters of Germany [have] filled our unsuspecting communities with vicious spies and conspirators." The CPI spread the president's message in seven million reprints. In the weeks and months that followed, officials and citizens changed German place names, banned Beethoven, renamed German foods on menus, prohibited teaching the German language and German literature, and generally harassed German Americans around the country.[145]

Yet many of the slacker stories of 1917 had nothing to do with German-ness. Attacks on loyalty constituted attacks on the interlocking attributes of manliness or womanliness, whiteness, and even sanity. Rational, civilized white people had their gender roles straight. In a time of war, this meant committing sons to battle and families to patience. Against the drumbeat of mandatory patriotism and familial virtue, slackers seemed barely human. Theodore Roosevelt called them "miserable creatures."[146] Waring Huston's hometown paper preferred the term "mongrel agitators" for a biracial gang of anti-conscriptionists.[147] A governor on the Great Plains explained to a reporter, "Like Russia, Kansas has its wild men, socialists, agitators, some of who are sincere in their belief, but none the less insane."[148] The *Milwaukee Journal*, a paper leaning Democratic in a heavily Republican state, questioned the manhood of Robert La Follette and his antiwar cronies: "All their talk about free speech is pretty, but disloyally so. When a man is trying to burn one's house or murder one's children, men cannot talk about free speech."[149]

A farmers' union member in Texas vowed to resist conscription, arming himself and hiding in the woods. A posse of officers found the man, E. H. Fulcher, and riddled him with twenty-three bullets. Fulcher was a serial abuser of chivalric standards, sought for beating his wife as well.[150]

In this climate, any suggestion that the draft threatened rather than strengthened the stability and health of the family, any mobilization of grief, met shrill rebukes. To Teddy Roosevelt—who had been pushing for war all along to stave off "national emasculation" and would send four sons to fight when Wilson rejected his own offer of service—the song "I Didn't Raise My Boy to Be a Soldier" was as ridiculous as a tune he invented called "I Didn't Raise My Girl to Be a Mother."[151] Good women had children, good sons joined the army. Here military service was less a disruptor of domestic virtue than its logical culmination. Thus the Soldier and the Mother—two figures so dear to conceptions of national strength that they were the first to collect public welfare spending—became an inseparable pair in wartime iconography (figure 1.6).[152] Registration authorities demanded people follow models of militarized familyhood. "[L]et no parent, sister, or sweetheart try to stop the natural operation of the draft law," warned one.[153] Attorney General Thomas Gregory lumped those worried about their loved ones into a rogue's gallery of slackers including "weaklings," the "disloyal," and people "lacking in patriotism."[154] Families behaving properly made the news. A man in Kansas City so shamed his relatives by refusing to register that he changed his mind, from his jail cell, at the pleading of his weeping sister.[155] A Columbia University student only did the "manly thing"—register for the draft—at the urging of his disgraced parents and sister. In the popular film *The Slacker*, in theaters that fall, it was the wife's exhortation rather than the example of his enlistee brother and best friend that stirred the husband's patriotic mettle.[156] People were to usher men to the polling places and symbolically transfer their obligations from family to state, or to align their familial virtue, their appreciation of proper place, with martial obligations.

To expect women to abet the disruption of the family in these ways overturned some traditional middle-class attitudes about feminine propriety. Women normally bore a social responsibility not only to give life but also to keep the family intact.[157] But in the resurrection of another tradition—of patriotic, sacrificial maternalism—it was "natural" for mothers to give sons to war. In this environment, women who agitated against the draft appeared misguided, unpatriotic, and above all unwomanly. The press often depicted them committing violence, looking haggard, and carrying on like savages. In Montana, said the newspapers, anti-draft women attacked the police.[158] A "hatless young woman in a frowsy dress" rushed a group of passing soldiers in New York in a spectacle of unfeminine rage. "Take off their uniforms, boys!" she allegedly cried as she tore at the jacket of a sergeant in the army. For their flaunting of gender conventions, these non-women surrendered

FIGURE 1.6 Sheet music for "America Here's My Boy," 1917. Wade Hall Collection of Southern History and Culture (Sheet Music), University of Alabama Libraries Special Collections.

the protections of chivalry. The New York police gave no quarter to the frowsy woman and her associates, leaving men and women alike with "bruised faces and torn clothing."[159] In a scorching patriotic speech in the same city, the Rev. Billy Sunday asked God to "strike dead" men and women who interfered with registration day.[160] From here forward, purveyors of official and imaginative culture would insist on the incompatibility of female radicalism and motherly virtue. Feature films excoriated pacifist women who stood in the way of conscription.[161]

A prime offender was the anarchist Emma Goldman. She and the other founders of the No Conscription League had issued a manifesto against militarism, coercion, and the suppression of liberties. At a registration day protest in the Bronx, Goldman invoked the personal tragedy she saw in war. She called the registration a "funeral march" of young men. Her associates issued a leaflet assuming a parent's point of view: "Don't Register, Son." The meeting attracted infiltration by government agents, and once again the authorities made no distinctions of gender when they rounded up and pummeled the dissidents.[162] Goldman and her colleague Alexander Berkman were arrested ten days later and charged under terms of the Selective Service Act with leading a "conspiracy to induce persons not to register." The same day, President Wilson signed the Espionage Act, which outlawed interference with the armed forces and assistance to enemy governments. The act criminalized antiwar rhetoric if judged to disrupt conscription, incite insubordination, or otherwise impair America's military effort through "false statements." It prohibited distributing such rhetoric through the mail. The law wasn't as powerful as Wilson wanted. Legislators voted down a press censorship provision and tried to separate criticism of the war from interference with it. But zealous judges interpreted the Espionage Act broadly, quelling dissent in Wisconsin, Alabama, Missouri, and elsewhere. Congress amended it with the Sedition Act of May 1918, which stretched restrictions on speech to include language abusive of the United States.[163]

Under these laws, the courts prosecuted two thousand people. Ten years in prison awaited Rose Pastor Stokes for her antiwar remarks before the Women's Dining Club of Kansas City in 1918. Her words, the court ruled, would "chill enthusiasm, extinguish confidence, and retard cooperation" among the nation's women in particular.[164] For supposedly saying American mothers had become "brood sows" for the army, socialist Kate Richards O'Hare received a five-year sentence. (She denied using that term, but freely admitted opposing the state's expectation that mothers produce soldiers.)[165] In the summer of 1917, *The Masses*, a radical journal of satire and the arts, ran afoul of the Espionage Act's "nonmailability" provision in part for a drawing called "Conscription" that showed dead women and children draped over a cannon. Judge Learned Hand bucked wartime hysteria and decided for *The Masses*, but he swam against the current. Soon the journal's legal battles ended its run. Few other publications dared to test the administration.[166]

SINCE APRIL, IT HAD become clear that questioning whether the war's promise warranted its price in sorrow would induce charges of treachery or prosecution in the courts. People in Missouri, Alabama, Wisconsin, and other places surely harbored doubts about giving over their boys for this war, but they either subdued those doubts or made sincere efforts, in the absence of clearer national objectives, to endow the conflict with personal meaning. Government officials, as well as their advocates in communities around the country, peddled this hope—that intervention would protect or even strengthen the family—in the context of a much broader effort to mobilize opinion behind the war effort. Keying the fight to private affairs, they claimed it afforded men the chance to be proper sons and husbands, women to be proper mothers and wives. In other words, the war's architects and promoters did not ask Americans to subordinate their needs to the state's but rather to regard those needs as overlapping. Framed that way, giving sons was a duty and privilege less than a sacrifice.

This assignment of meaning would bear considerable power for anyone concerned with domestic virtue, but especially for those who believed the conventions of gender propriety and bonds of family were crumbling. For them, war demanded a welcome return to custom. "[F]oolish violations of those laws of God and nature which have been falling into contemptuous neglect in the United States," lectured a traditionalist in the *Atlanta Constitution* in July, "must be brought to a sharp end at this time of crisis in the world's affairs."[167]

IN THE NATION'S FIRST Great War registration, 9.6 million young men, often with families by their sides, had signed up for the draft. Lige Dees may have registered but was already in uniform and therefore exempted from conscription. Waring Huston registered from Fort McPherson and would be eligible if he failed his officer training course.[168]

Right around this time, the Huebners visited a Watertown photography studio. Though of modest means, the family put on its finest dress, Christian and Louise's children arrayed around them, and Carl, their youngest since little Irene's death, seated in between them (figure 1.7).

FIGURE 1.7 The Huebners in 1917. *Back row*: Alvina, Otto, Johanna, Arthur, Martha, Walter. *Front row*: Christian, Carl, Louise. Author's collection.

Up to that point, Christian had lived the classic immigrant's fantasy—escape poverty, have a family, earn a living, commit to life in America while preserving something of Old World culture. A state subjecting sons to military service was not part of the dream. Many immigrants from the Russian and German Empires, including Christian's half-sister, had left Europe specifically to avoid the imperilment of their families by conscription.

Now Arthur and Otto were vulnerable to the first large-scale draft in American history for a war against the Germans. What did Christian and Louise think of this? They had likely hoped war with Germany would not come but remained faithful to America once it did. Indeed, most German-language newspapers in April 1917 held this position. For all the Huebners' devotion to German culture, they dedicated their political loyalties to the United States. Christian's wife and children were American citizens, and he would later put in his papers. Many German Americans likewise felt no allegiance to the Kaiser even as they read German newspapers, spoke the mother tongue, and worshipped in German churches. As a popular saying put it, "Germania our mother, Columbia our bride." Why should affection for the mother prevent fidelity to the wife?[169]

Arthur W. L. Huebner demonstrated his fidelity to the United States by registering in Watertown on June 5. He described his height and build as "medium." And in the era of Kaiser Wilhelm II, he elected to put his middle name down as "William."[170]

2

Make Your Daddy Glad

MAE BILBREY SPENT A boring summer in 1917 living with her uncle in Williamsville, Missouri, the monotony broken only by soldier trains and drifters passing through town. Sometimes Mae skipped Sunday school to laze about reading romances, which she worried made her seem a "very bad girl" to other people. Meantime, the constant crowing of roosters drove the young woman crazy. She distracted herself with her stories and crocheting projects and by writing to Pvt. Eliga Dees.[1] Three months had passed since their exchange in April. In that time, the War Department had transferred a few infantry and cavalry regiments from the Mexican border to mountainous Fort Oglethorpe in Chickamauga Park, Georgia, where it reorganized them for training and deployment to France.[2] As part of this process, the army moved Lige from the Sixth Infantry to the newly incorporated Fifty-Third Infantry around the time of his twenty-second birthday.[3]

The military past endured at Chickamauga Park, scene of critical Civil War battles. By January 1918, in fact, officials had renamed Lige's part of Fort Oglethorpe "Camp N. B. Forrest" for the Confederate general and founder of the Ku Klux Klan. Fading was any sense of irony surrounding United States troops training at a cantonment named for the "great confederate cavalry leader," as the Fort Oglethorpe newsletter put it.[4] Winners and losers, North and South, had dissolved into a singular memory of shared honor. Mae had imbibed that history. She knew about the battles of the Chattanooga campaign, in which one of Arthur Huebner's immigrant ancestors had fought, and wished she could see the sites as Lige could.[5]

Like many Americans of their era, Mae and Lige eased the burden of separation by writing letters. The transportation and mobility revolutions were pulling people away from their loved ones, bringing the words "nostalgia" and "homesickness" into the popular vocabulary. Nostalgia was even known to kill people.[6] War generated separations of great duration and distance, potentially made permanent. As the spaces widened, and across the populations of the belligerent states, notes, pictures, gifts, food, postcards, parcels, and letters assumed tremendous meaning. Of course censorship limited what people could say. Every warring army deployed censors to protect information on troop movements, keep abreast of the soldier's mood and commitment, and sniff out subversion in the ranks or on the home front. Broadly speaking, in Germany, Austria-Hungary, and France, censorship was randomly enforced, difficult to maintain, or implemented later in the war. The Russians, British, and Americans screened the mail more consistently, although morale and social unrest remained matters of concern in every government at some point or another. Yet none of this surveillance diminished the value of correspondence. Soldiers and families may have avoided certain subjects but kept up a brisk traffic in emotion.[7] They literally counted the days since the last letter or package and anxiously awaited the next one.[8] Mae deployed a common epistolary strategy, numbering her letters so Lige would know if ones were missing.

The wartime post brought reminders of separation along with mementoes of intimacy. As such, they only went so far. "I will write you and try to cheer you up if I can," Mae once wrote to Lige, "for I know you must be lonely." Mae, though surrounded by people, was lonely too.[9]

AT FORT MCPHERSON, WITH the physical exam approaching, Waring Huston's fellow officer candidates dropped out in clusters. In early June 1917, Selmian Mickey Brislin injured his foot, saw the camp doctor, and got thrown out, just like four others in Waring's company the same day. Mickey welcomed his dismissal, Waring divulged to his mother, though he asked her to keep that quiet in a world watchful for slackers.[10] Apparently many others in the camp felt similarly disillusioned, including Waring, although his displeasure had limits. "A bunch of boys have resigned but I could not think of such a thing although I don't like military life much," he wrote to Mama.[11] Candidates picked for aviation, coast artillery, and field artillery left for other camps. Waring regretted not selecting one of those branches.

As he waited for the physical, Waring's homesickness worsened. Turning twenty-one on June 1, 1917, dragged his mood lower:

> Well today is my birthday and here I am away from all those I love so dearly. I have sure had the blues all day and still have them for that matter. You just don't know how bad it is to be so far away. I miss you and Papa more than you imagine and wish constantly that I was at home with you all. I don't mind the work so bad it is just the being away from home.

Waring's parents sent him the watch he wanted, a Radiolite, but they didn't write, which hurt his feelings. Nothing reassured a lonely enlistee, or a melancholy sweetheart, like a letter. Waring graciously wondered if they were sick.[12]

It was not that Waring feared death or missed the comforts of home. He realized, rather, that service tore him from the very familial bonds that partly had inspired him to sign up. Public culture in 1917 acknowledged little irony here, the roles of faithful son and good soldier utterly compatible. Waring and his family appear to have accepted this idea. On May 29, Waring's brother Harry wrote to Nellye,

> I am certainly proud of that boy, and I told him so, and you and the whole family should be proud of him, here he was a boy who had no military training at all, and I rec[k]on had no thought of ever going into this sort of thing, then at the first call to jump right in and grab hold and not sit back and wait to be made to go. Waring has always been mighty dear to me, ever since, he was a little bit of a kid, I have loved him more than any one ever knew, and I have watched him grow up and become a man, and a good one too.[13]

Harry moved so smoothly from Waring's patriotic to brotherly qualities that they almost seemed of a piece. But the situation had its incongruities. Waring was terrified that in the process of honoring family and nation he would lose his "real" life and forfeit his place in Selma. Not being forgotten would become Waring's constant project.

ONLY A SMALL NUMBER of American soldiers had left for Europe by the summer of 1917. Among them was a teacher from Mae's Williamsville High School named Roy Thornburgh, an April enlistee who went overseas in June with the First "Big Red One" Division.[14] But as the cantonments filled up and bigger departures loomed, the ways women should handle the imperilment of their sons or sweethearts occupied a great deal of space in public culture.

Back in April, the debate between patriotic and pacifist maternalism had been uneven—"America Here's My Boy" had drowned out "I Didn't Raise My Boy To Be a Soldier."[15] Those mothers who saw no conflict between a son's obligations to family and nation—whose pride in their boys as sons drew from their pride in them as servicemen—continued to have their say. The songs "I Have Raised My Boy to Be a Soldier" and "If I Had a Son for Each Star in Old Glory, I'd Give Them All to You" served as the new anthems of nationalistic motherhood.[16] Newspapermen created a subgenre of wartime journalism when they wrote pieces on mothers of astonishing generosity with their offspring. Mrs. Mary J. Lamb of Chicago had given three sons to the military and wished her fourth were old enough. She found mothers who whined about their fears maudlin and selfish. "No mother loves her family more than I do," she boasted to the *Daily Tribune*, "but I look at this war as God's laundry."[17] So be it if her sons gave their lives to cleanse the world of Germany's moral delinquency. Another Chicago woman had six children in active war service and savored the contribution.[18] Mrs. A. W. Cook of Savannah, Georgia, felt "proud, not sad" about her four boys training at Fort McPherson, while the paper in Arthur's Wisconsin hometown found a woman in Madison with the same number of doughboy sons.[19]

At the same time, newspaper reporters found conflicted mothers. At a recruiting station in the Windy City, a young man tried to enlist against his mother's wishes. A passer-by, herself the mother of seven boys in France, talked the woman out of her objections and the son signed up.[20] Some women struggled to reconcile their devotion to sons and country. Mae Bilbrey's local paper, the *Greenville Sun*, wrote in July 1917, "The mothers of all nations are asking, with streaming eyes and breaking hearts, as they send their sons into the welter of world-war; 'To what end, O God?'" The paper answered its own question: "[M]others of today know that back of their supreme sacrifice shines the glory and joy of world-freedom."[21] Would that be enough to overcome loss and grief? Even some who considered themselves patriotic, who would have hated to be called slackers, could not stomach the thought of losing their sons. A writer for the *St. Louis Post-Dispatch* quoted a suffragist in the Ozarks named Tillie on just this point:

> I read in the paper about a mother who had give her two sons to the war and had wrote the President that she had a third to give. I cain't understand it, somehow. I know that I ain't that kind of mother. I jist know that the war is here and that the fault ain't ourn. I know we've got to stand by the President, and I shore aim to stand by him—but I jist cain't give my boys willin'.

Tillie asked the woman interviewing her if this made her unpatriotic. The writer didn't think so and Tillie hoped not. If her sons had to go, she pledged, she would accept it without complaint. But her boy, though "manly and growed up," still seemed like a child, barely removed from the time "his little head was layin' on your breast."[22]

Some antiwar women—and Tillie never would have sanctioned this behavior—confronted their more unabashedly bellicose counterparts. A woman wrote the *Chicago Daily Tribune* to address the "many" women she knew, including some at a recent dinner party, who regarded her as a "murderer" and a "cold and unnatural mother" for her willingness to give sons to the war. The editor responded publicly that the "weak and selfish" women who would level such charges didn't understand civilization depended upon sacrifice for its comforts and rights.[23]

Although limited for now, the war's tragic dimensions and their impact on families were coming into view. In September 1917, a German air raid on a hospital in France killed Oscar C. Tugo of Washington, D. C. His mother fainted when she heard the knock at her door.[24] The same month, the *Nashville Tennessean* ran a long piece on a devastating feature of battle: "Soldiers have told and have written of the cries for 'mother' that have come from the ghastly No Man's Land where the wounded lie; of the same cry on the hospital beds." War and injury so shocked the boy's sensibilities, the piece explained, that he longed to be cradled by the arms that had held him as a baby.[25] From a broader perspective, the progressive Jane Addams continued her assault on warmongers and their pretty promises. She and the Woman's Peace Party suffered no claims of war's regenerative value: "What are American women going to win [in] the great war? Child labor, long hours, scant food, high prices, lowered standards of living, loss of constitutional guarantees of freedom, martial law, venereal disease, infant mortality, bereavement, and desolation." For women nearer the fields of battle, in this view, war upended chivalric fantasies, delivering only violence and deprivation.[26] Where other progressives saw opportunity for their causes, Addams saw an irredeemable nightmare.

The serialized story of a fictional soldier's bride named Patty, printed in June 1917 in Wisconsin's *Eau Claire Leader*, charted the range of emotional responses to war circulating throughout the national press. Patty and her husband Bertram are recently married. Bertram, educated in a military academy, volunteered for the service after the war declaration and is awaiting orders. Patty dreads the prospect of her husband going away. "I thought I could bear it, but I can't, I can't. Don't go, dear. I have no one else. I shall die without you."[27]

Who should go in Bertram's place? In an inversion of wartime culture, Patty suggests *bad* family men. Those who love deeply, cherish their wives, and are "brave noble men" should get to stay home. "There are so many drunkards and worthless men whom the world would be better for losing . . . why not let them do the fighting?" Patty would have an army of abusers and derelicts battle the Hun. Bertram smiles condescendingly and tries to reassure her—but by reciting the war's personal rather than political or humanitarian implications. "You could not help losing respect for a husband that was a slacker," he says.[28]

Her husband is not a slacker, although it's only later, when she visits Bertram at camp, that Patty realizes her luck. The sight of her husband drilling overcomes her: "All men must be six feet tall, and I tell you they are upstanding young gods in their fine uniforms with their martial bearing. The tears ran down my cheeks as I saw Bertram pass."[29] The soldiers are so willing to sacrifice themselves—Patty calls them "martyrs"—that she is inspired to sacrifice as well. She embraces war because it reveals her husband's manly character. "Your devotion to him will take you as far as his devotion to liberty," her sister-in-law Eleanor says.[30] Wayne County's *Greenville Sun* made this point when it eulogized a favorite son departed for the army. "Few of us had realized the meaning of this war," the Missouri paper confessed, "until one so popular among the younger set and so universally liked by all, harkens to the call of his country."[31] For the imagined Patty and the real people of Wayne County, political causes played much smaller motivational roles than love, honor, and admiration.

Would this thinking hold up under the strain of separation? Even the chastened Patty admits of watching her husband, "the lofty view of the war passed as he faded from view."[32]

FOR POLICYMAKERS, THE POSSIBILITY of familial disruption posed a contradiction. They could hardly let a conflict keyed in part to domestic tranquility destroy the family. More important, the government dreaded the social upheavals of such destruction. As conscription began, officials endeavored to keep the American family literally intact, financially solvent, and morally pure.

The state used the draft to stabilize families, marriage, and gender roles—but to a point. Married men with dependents garnered the largest number of exemptions from service. Forty-three percent of all registrants won such reprieve.[33] But those exemptions mostly went to families with a single male breadwinner, the preferred domestic model of the white middle class. Selective Service directed boards to grant dependent exemptions to men with high, hard-to-replace incomes, leaving poorer men with families vulnerable. Throughout the war, in fact, 25 percent of married men called for examination were conscripted.[34] African Americans were overrepresented in those ranks. National policymakers and local draft boards struggled to imagine black men as providers, and they cited chronically low black wages to prove it. This circular logic protected white, property-owning patriarchs, and without threatening their masculinity, as it acknowledged and rewarded their breadwinner status.[35] This release from military obligation of most middle-class husbands with children left a population of draftees that was 90 percent single. Some men thus hoped to avoid service by getting hitched, eventually leading Selective Service to ban local boards from exempting registrants married since the war declaration. It commanded boards to sniff out dependent claims exaggerated or invented to dodge service.[36] But the official message of the war's early months, despite caveats for poor, black, or hastily married men, held that families should not be disturbed. A registrar in New York spoke for many others when he said, "great effort should be made not to dissolve the home ties."[37] These developments confirmed the symbolic character of the war for family in a nation distant from the fighting. In contrast with some of the continental belligerents, it would be waged largely by men without families of their own.[38]

Just as pressing for familial stability was the moral health of the doughboy, something undermined by vice in past martial adventures. One mother wrote President Wilson that she and others like her would sooner see their boys die than have them return "ruined in body and ideals."[39] Alcohol and prostitution posed the gravest threats in the popular mind. Just two weeks after Wilson's address of April 2, 1917, the War Department created the Commission on Training Camp Activities (CTCA) to discipline behavior. Noted reformer Raymond Fosdick assumed its leadership, stoking progressive hopes that war might lend urgency to moral uplift. Sexually transmitted diseases threatened not only to undermine a man's virtue but also his fighting ability. The popular narrative of the war's purpose likewise stood to suffer by debauchery. If soldiers were defending womanhood from sexual predators, they could hardly prey on girls around the camps or in France. Worse, to consort with European women of low morals, cautioned reformers, would jeopardize the honor and health of sweethearts and wives at home.

In the spring and summer of 1917, the CTCA prepared a moral curriculum for the conscripted masses. In line with the government's ambition to rescue civilization, and to showcase or redeem American domestic qualities in the process, the CTCA set out to create a morally pure army. Optimists expected returning doughboys to be ambassadors of good conduct in their communities, particularly urban ones. Secretary of War Baker entrusted the CTCA with helping to solve the "troublesome city question" that "for so many years [has] hung heavy on the conscience of our country."[40] The war for family had many different enemies—not just the Germans but America's inner demons as well.

THE ARMY REHEARSED ITS moral program at Fort McPherson, where officials busily converted Waring and other candidates into soldiers. Even as the recruits underwent transformations in dress, posture, and habit and learned the arts of violence and survival, they had to stay civilized.

One expects journalists covering Fort McPherson had the trainees' families in mind as they filed stories. Food was healthy and appetizing, intended to "build flesh and muscle where fat once predominated."[41] Accommodations were more comfortable than in traditional military camps. A candidate's visiting mother, the surest judge of domestic order, found everything satisfactory:

> Mother inquires if he washes his teeth regularly, and son replies that he has to. She asks if he is comfortable on a bed without springs, and son says "Betcha life," even though he might not be—at first. Mother surveys the interior of the dormitory from wall to wall, overlooking not a detail, and appears well pleased with everything in general.

The reporter and mother next stopped outside of Waring's barracks, where two regular army men marveled at the bedclothes: "Sheets for soldiers!"[42] No danger of the boys becoming degraded here. They might even mingle with the ordinary citizens of Atlanta without embarrassing themselves, their families, or the military. On a holiday in May, the candidates were free to travel into the city. (Waring just went in to shop and have a haircut, hurrying back to the base to study, he assured his mother.) For the *Atlanta Constitution*, the Fort McPherson student-officers seemed "[n]eat and courteous and quiet, every inch gentlemen and every inch soldiers and men."[43]

Yet camp officials feared temptation might overtake character. A small piece in the newspaper announced on May 19 that alcohol and gambling would be barred from the camp.[44] Henceforth soldiers could not see guests in their barracks, but had to meet them publicly in the Young Men's Christian Association (YMCA) building for no longer than thirty minutes. That facility had writing desks, pen and ink, and stationery, the better to direct the men's attention home. If they wished to congregate with women and had no visitors, camp leaders organized wholesome gatherings.[45] Soon these efforts were repeated on bases in the YMCA's "hostess houses," places reflecting Fosdick's personal commitment to replicating domestic values in the military environment.[46] These gathering points turned the doughboy's gaze toward his female relatives and away from the seamier possibilities lurking around the camps. "Yes, it is a wonderful place, the Hostess House," gushed the *Christian Science Monitor*, "and this is the dominant thought of all the wives, the mothers, the sisters, the sweethearts, who have found it."[47]

ON SATURDAY, JUNE 16, WARING took his physical examination. He had hoped to come home that weekend, see his family and Carrie Goodwin, but the exam took too long. The next day, he wrote a melancholy letter to his mother.

Waring didn't think he had passed the exam. He had a foot injury and was underweight, though he felt hard as nails. He asked his mother to keep his civilian clothes ready for delivery in case he got turned out. If so, Waring hoped, maybe he could go to the second officer training camp planned for August. He enclosed photographs, ever concerned with preserving the record of his existence and experiences. Waring asked Nellye to give his love to his father and kiss his sister Helen Lapsley's children for him, who lived just across Church Street from Waring's parents. "Sure would like to see those brats," he said, then closed, "With lots of love, Waring."[48]

THE LETTER WENT TO Dallas County, Alabama, a thousand-square-mile patch of gently undulating land. Alabama owed its possession of the territory to Gen. Andrew Jackson's 1814 victory over the Upper Creeks at the Battle of Horseshoe Bend. Out of those spoils the Alabama territorial legislature created Dallas in 1818. A year after Alabama became a state in 1819, settlers incorporated Selma, the future Dallas County seat of justice.[49] Among the white inhabitants of the area were William Henry Huston (b. 1833) and Mary Elizabeth Prestridge (b. 1842). They married on December 10, 1857, and had a son, R. Walter Huston (Waring's father), on January 5, 1859. George Waring Smith, meanwhile, was born in Dallas County about 1837. Five years later, a wealthy Mobile lawyer and his wife welcomed the infant Charlotte Elizabeth

Hamilton. These two children later met and married, most likely in the late 1860s, and had Waring's future mother Nellye in 1875.[50]

When the secession crisis came, both of Waring's grandfathers—William Henry Huston and George Waring Smith—enlisted in the Confederate army. George suffered four wounds and brief imprisonment with the Federals. William's experience is less clear, but he managed to travel home regularly to Dallas County. His wife Mary gave birth in 1861, 1863, and late 1865, providing young Walter three new siblings. In either of William's two possible units, he would have been present for the dramatic events in Selma at the close of the Civil War.[51]

Manufacturing and transportation infrastructure made Selma a key arsenal, protected by a fortified defensive line of earthen works, ditches, and stockades. In March 1865, a northern cavalry corps launched an extended raid toward the city, slowed only by Lt. Gen. Nathan Bedford Forrest's much smaller cavalry force. The Union men paused to send a detachment to Tuscaloosa to torch the University of Alabama, a military training site, before continuing south. On April 2, the Yankees faced Forrest's rebels at the doorstep of Selma. He ordered every male to defend the city, but the northerners overran the works. Civilians, Union soldiers, Confederate regulars, rebel stragglers, and local militia all mingled in a wild scene. Outraged locals reported the worst depredations. On Forrest's way out of town, he executed four Federals allegedly taking liberties with local women. Such insults would long endure in the city's collective memory.[52]

After the war, the Huston family moved to Mobile, where William worked as a cotton broker, but by the 1870s he was back in Selma serving as sheriff of Dallas County. His son Walter, twenty-one in 1880, worked as a clerk for the railroad. Walter married his first wife soon thereafter. In 1895, four years after she died, he married Nellye Augusta Smith. They had Waring the next year.[53]

Amid the cyclical depressions and deteriorating cotton prices that would plague Dallas County through the onset of the Great War, Selmians were proud that two local men, former Confederate generals, represented Alabama in the United States Senate—John Tyler Morgan and Edmund Winston Pettus—where they fought aggressively for states' rights and white supremacy. Edmund Pettus's son Francis, speaker of the state House of Representatives, spearheaded the campaign to disfranchise black voters in Alabama's revised constitution of 1901.[54] It was Francis's son Edmund Pettus, law partner of a man named John Lapsley, who wrote the letter on behalf of Waring Huston in April 1917 to Secretary of War Newton Baker. Waring's half-sister Helen was married to Lapsley, and Waring listed the law firm as his employer when he registered for the draft.[55] Apparently Lapsley's associate Pettus had taken an interest in the boy and had the ear of the secretary of war.

AMONG THE SOLDIERS RUNNING with Nathan Bedford Forrest during the Civil War was a thirteen-year-old boy named Nathaniel Graves Scott. He was from northern Alabama and signed up in 1861 with the First Kentucky Regiment. Nathaniel made himself useful to Forrest as a spy, scouting out enemy camps and towns and masking his purposes with his youth. Later in life, he went by "Boss" and ran a railroad construction company in New Orleans.[56]

Boss Scott's daughter Natalie, while she awaited word on her application to go to France with the Red Cross, had been named state secretary for the Louisiana Woman's Committee of the Council of National Defense. Her job was to coordinate women's war efforts in New Orleans. The number of volunteers underwhelmed Natalie and her friend and fellow Woman's Committee member Hilda Phelps. In that city and Louisiana more broadly, citizens divided over the matters of war and conscription. Many draft-eligible Louisiana registrants, in fact, were hiring attorneys to prepare exemption claims. Natalie and Hilda became involved in the debate when they directed a successful campaign to compel every woman in the state above the age of sixteen to register with the Woman's Committee. Then, in August, Natalie received a letter from Dr. Alexander Lambert, chief medical officer for the Red Cross in France and Belgium, inviting her to come to Paris immediately to join his staff.[57]

MAE AND LIGE HAD weathered the rumors of each other's marriages and Lige's enlistment in the army only to have the European war threaten permanent separation. The growing literature aimed at soldiers' wives offered reminders of the tension. "Your wedding, although by God-law and by man-law it will symbolize eternal union," went a piece in the *Atlanta Constitution*, "may be made, instead, a preface to long, and, tragically, even final separation."[58] The prolific composers of Tin Pan Alley quickly put those ideas to music:

> So, send me away with a smile little girl
> Brush the tears from eyes of brown.
> It's all for the best
> And I'm off with the rest
> With the boys from my hometown.
> It may be forever we part little girl
> But it may be for only a while.[59]

The hope of reunion and the fear of tragedy likewise mingled in the letters Mae and Lige wrote each other. But in the meantime, other problems occupied their attention.

Sometime in June or early July 1917, another suitor approached Mae. She rebuffed him but wrote of the incident in a long letter to Lige. A soldier's mail carried enormous emotional power, liable to either calm or inflame jealous impulses, and this letter set Lige off. His angry response doesn't survive but Mae's does. "You scolded me too much," she wrote on July 6, "and I know you haven't any room to get so cranky." But to a man prone to insecurities, her next words could have seemed alternately reassuring or foreboding. In either case they highlighted his excruciating absence:

> I did not want to go with the other fellow and that's the reason I came home by myself. And I do not go with any one and don't expect to until Lige comes home. When are you coming anyway? Soon I hope. . . . You know I would be yours any time if I only could but how can I honey, when you are where you are?[60]

Mae had no shortage of admirers. About a week later she wrote that she had "quit all the fellows here. They do not interest me anymore." Lige nonetheless asked her what she did nights. She answered that she spent them at prayer meetings and the ice cream parlor and who knew "where all." One evening she stayed up talking to a well-educated wanderer who came begging for food. The boy had gotten sick and was making his way home to Van Buren, Missouri. He so appreciated the scraps he almost wept. Mae made a point of telling Lige the traveler was "dandy good looking."[61]

More difficult for Lige was the matter of swimming. Like lots of rural folks, Mae and her friends spent a good part of the hot months in the water. Lige didn't like this. If she was going to swim, he should be there to chaperone her. Sometime early that summer, he forbade her from swimming with other people, but she didn't get the letter in time. In her note of July 6, she reported going to the creek with some friends, but only because she hadn't received his directive. He wrote back angrily. She tried to soothe him, but recounted going swimming again, contrary to his wishes. Her words showed both her devotion to Lige and her rejection of his control, however playful:

> I never said I went swimming with Mr. Lord. I said he went with us.
> If you was here I would be afraid to go in. You might hang me. But
> I listen to you anyway if you are not here. And I'll not go in much
> more, not over a dozen more times; that wouldn't be many would it?
> I want to learn good so when you come home, I can go swimming
> with you, ha! Would you care? Or would you let me drown?

In Lige's stead, other men were assuming responsibility for Mae's safety and maybe taking liberties from that position of access and intimacy. He worried the situation left her looking vulnerable or even available. Fighting to protect women in general, as so much of public culture had it, pulled Lige from his duty to protect "his" woman in particular. Mae's insecurities ran in the same direction. "I bet you have a girl out there though?" she wrote in July. "What did you ever do with those pictures I used to have? I bet you gave them to some other girl."[62] During one of their separations she had returned his pictures, safeguards against forgetting. Now she wanted them back, and presumably Lige sent them. But she would continue to worry about him straying into the arms of another.

Even as she pointed out and perhaps needled Lige about his inability to protect her literally, Mae reveled in his mission to protect her figuratively. She basked in Lige's status as a "noble, good boy," and submitted to the allure of the uniform currently circulating in American culture (figure 2.1). "I have always been proud of you ever since you

FIGURE 2.1 "Ain't It Nice to Be a Soldier?" Postcard from Camp Meade, Maryland, 1917. Author's collection, courtesy of George Rable.

became a soldier more than ever," she cooed to Lige. Mae even tried to get her friend Ella similarly fixed, telling Lige, "She said for you to get her a pretty soldier boy. . . . But she said be sure that he is as nice a fellow as you are. You never will find one for her will you honey-boy?"[63] War might enhance love or destroy it, and Mae felt both possibilities at once. She expressed her affection for Lige at every turn, but the painful prospect of tragedy colored their exchanges. Echoing the fictional Patty, mingling thoughts of love and death, Mae fretted in July, "If you have to go to France, I know I will simply die while you are gone. I am afraid I will never get to see Lige any more."[64]

MAE'S MELANCHOLY MORE OR less matched the mood of Williamsville, Missouri, part of a cluster of small towns in southern Wayne County making up her social terrain. Citizens in that area were uneasy about the war, and their region was stagnating. Both problems had deep roots.

White settlers in Missouri Territory organized the county in 1818 and drove native peoples out. Soon came migrants from Virginia, Tennessee, and other parts of the South, including David and Gracy Dees of South Carolina in the 1820s. They had at least six sons, all of whom lived and farmed in St. Francois Township. As these boys married, the county filled with Dees children. David was kin (probably brother) to an Eliga Dees, a Missouri preacher who in 1819 built a Methodist log cabin church, Dees Chapel, about seven miles from Williamsville. Sometime thereafter, David Dees's son Elijah (nephew of Eliga) erected a frame church to replace the cabin. It still stands today. Eventually at least seven generations of Eliga Deeses, including the doughboy Lige, would worship there.[65]

When secession came, many citizens hoped either to join the Confederacy or follow Kentucky's path and remain neutral. Missouri's governor and commander of its militia both declared their allegiance to the South. Only after federal troops drove local forces to the state's southwest corner did Missouri stay with the Union. But partisans of both sides—Union "jayhawkers" and Confederate "bushwhackers" William Clarke Quantrill, "Bloody Bill" Anderson, and the James and Younger brothers—kept up a campaign of terror and guerilla warfare. In the fall of 1864, a Confederate force invaded the state, but its failure by October more or less ended rebel activity. Wayne County seat Greenville, held at different times by blue and gray, lay in charred ruins.[66]

At war's end, parishioners of Dees Chapel trickled back to the little church from both armies. At least two Dees men had thrown their lot in with the Union, including Elijah, grandfather of Lige and builder of Dees Chapel. Wayne County lore later had it that former enemies quickly reconciled. Mae Bilbrey herself reported as much in the history of her beloved county she wrote much later (*A Little Bit of God's Country*). But Wayne's residents had seen war and detested it.[67]

The area proceeded to grow in infrastructure and population, but retained its rural character and much hostility toward banks, railroads, and "special interests." Some people called Missouri the "mother of outlaws" for these attitudes.[68] Into this region came John Bilbrey from Tennessee in the 1880s or 1890s. He married a woman named Ida and they had Mae at the very end of 1896. Nearby were Sarah and William Dees, the son of the Civil-War-era Elijah. They had a new baby of their own, one-year-old Lige. As Mae and Lige grew up, the expansion of Williamsville and Wayne County slowed down.[69]

AMERICA'S FIRST DRAFT SINCE the Civil War commenced in Washington on July 20, 1917. After the registration in June, local draft boards had assigned serial numbers to every draft card, from 1 to 10,500 (the largest number of registrants in any jurisdiction). Secretary of War Newton Baker pulled serial numbers randomly, establishing the order in which the men attached to those numbers would be called for physical examinations. Once officials communicated the sequence to the country's 4,600 draft boards, those panels set to examining men and granting exemptions until they reached quotas assigned to them by Selective Service. Especially in small communities, men probably knew the person who ushered them into the army.[70]

Hundreds of thousands of draftees would soon make their way to new training cantonments, forming a huge army with men already in the armed forces as well as those serving in the National Guard. Eventually the military organized its ranks into three sorts of divisions. Draftees made up the populations of new "National Army" divisions. Regular army divisions were created from existing units like Lige Dees's Fifty-Third Infantry. Militia from the various states anchored National Guard divisions. At least initially, the three varieties of soldier (regular, draftee, and guardsman) would train in different settings. The government built thirty-two training camps over the summer of 1917: sixteen for the National Army and sixteen for the National Guard. Draftees in camp got to sleep in wooden barracks, while National Guardsmen resided less comfortably in canvas tents. Ultimately both the regular and National Guard divisions pulled conscripts from the National Army to achieve battle strength. By 1918, those transfers had rendered the divisional designations meaningless.[71]

THIRTEEN PERCENT OF DRAFTEES were black, numbering around 370,000 and exceeding their proportion (10 percent) of the population. About ten thousand African American soldiers served in existing units, including the Ninth and Tenth Cavalries and the Twenty-Fourth and Twenty-Fifth Infantry Regiments. Although the General Staff deliberately mingled foreign-born with native-born troops for assimilative purposes, it never integrated white and black men, other than to have white officers command black enlisted men. For a time, the leadership did consider using the majority of black draftees as combat soldiers and training them in cantonments around the country. White officers reported good black combat service in past conflicts to the army brass.[72]

By August 1917, that plan was dead. Southern political leaders and the communities surrounding Dixie cantonments objected to hosting large numbers of "armed Negroes," as they phrased it again and again. Many such critics pointed to what happened that month in Houston, Texas, soon after the race riot in East St. Louis. One of the black regular army units that predated the war, the seasoned Twenty-Fourth Infantry, was stationed in Houston to guard the construction site at Camp Logan. The black men in the unit came from all over the United States and refused to abide by Jim Crow. One day, Pvt. Alonzo Edwards witnessed the abusive arrest of a black mother of five by two white police officers. Edwards asked that the woman be handed over to him. Furious at this breach of racial etiquette, one of the policemen whipped Edwards with his pistol and later beat and arrested another black soldier who turned up to investigate. When word reached Camp Logan, roughly one hundred members of the Twenty-Fourth marched into Houston to attack the police and others who stood in their way, killing at least fifteen whites, including law enforcement officials. The first generals of the Thirty-Third Division arrived at Camp Logan on August 25 to find it under martial law due to the "lamentable shooting affray" of two days earlier.[73]

The affair in Houston reinforced southerners' opposition to arming and training black men in their midst. In this climate, despite the outcry from W. E. B. Du Bois and other black leaders, military officials submitted to political pressure. The majority of black draftees would funnel to the Quartermaster and Engineer Corps, essentially labor units. Leaders in the black community, meanwhile, ranging from Du Bois and Joel Spingarn of the NAACP to student activists at Howard University, lobbied for black officers to serve on the Western Front. The War Department refused to admit black candidates to the officer schools like the one Waring attended, so Du Bois and others reluctantly accepted the creation of the separate Fort Des Moines Colored Officers' Training Camp, which opened in June 1917.[74] "The leaders in the movement wish it understood," clarified the black-owned *Cleveland Gazette*, "that they do not accept the camp as segregation—they are wholly opposed to such discrimination—but they do accept it as a means to an end."[75]

Despite Houston's impact on broader policy, black women there and around the country saw an inspiring defense of black womanhood at

Camp Logan. Many African Americans in this period imagined military service as an assertion of their profoundly interrelated (and chronically undermined) senses of manhood and citizenship. "You dared protect a Negro woman," a schoolteacher in Texas wrote. This was the "most sacred thing on earth," she said, echoing national standards of masculinity that in part underpinned intervention in the European war. But here whites were the enemy, what one woman of color called "Southern huns." That fall, when sheriff's deputies arrested several black women on false prostitution charges in Waxahachie, Texas, a crowd of black draftees gathered to plot their rescue. "You are going to fight for Democrasy," exhorted a man named Ely Green. "This is where you should start, at your own doorstep, to defend your women." Though Green's association of chivalry with democracy actualized so much persuasive public rhetoric, jittery white officials found the militancy it provoked unacceptable—threatening, in fact, to white social space and comfort. In this way of thinking, the black soldier's masculine prerogative to gain was the white man's to lose. Secretary of the Navy Josephus Daniels thus reasoned that the men rioted in Houston because "the Negro in uniform wants the whole sidewalk."[76]

Few whites could tolerate that prospect. For their offenses in Houston, thirteen black soldiers were sentenced to die by hanging in San Antonio. Six other executions followed subsequent courts-martial. Citizens in Waring Huston's Selma could read a detailed account of the first hangings in their newspaper, right next to a piece asserting, "South Best Place for the Negro."[77]

In the meantime, to appease leaders disappointed by the relegation of black servicemen to menial work, the War Department created two black combat divisions. The Ninety-Second, headquartered at Camp Funston in Kansas, contained four regiments of drafted infantrymen and Fort Des Moines officers but the white Maj. Gen. Charles Ballou as its commander. Large aggregations of black trainees continued to frighten white officials, however, so the men of the Ninety-Second, in a blow to divisional cohesion, trained at seven different cantonments in the North. Three black National Guard regiments plus a drafted one made up the Ninety-Third Division. The black units in the regular army, in the meantime, spent the war guarding the Mexican border and American island territories. Secretary of War Baker, however, rebuked southern authorities when he allowed several black National Guard units to drill in places like Virginia, Texas, and Alabama. One of them, the New York Fifteenth Regiment, traveled to Camp Wadsworth in Spartanburg, South Carolina, in October 1917 for a brief and tumultuous stay.[78] The mayor of the town warned the men would be treated as pariahs, whatever they had come to expect in the North. Sure enough, "dirty nigger" was what a Harvard-educated African American officer heard as he was being kicked off a streetcar. There was similar trouble in a hotel lobby involving nationally famous musicians and members of the unit's regimental band, Drum Maj. Noble Sissle and Lt. James Reese Europe. The War Department, thinking of Houston, sent the Fifteenth immediately to France. An officer in the regiment remembered soldiers of the white New York National Guard division sympathetically serenading their exit from the camp to the tune of "Over There." When the Fifteenth arrived at Camp Mills on Long Island, they got in another fight, this time with the Alabama-based 167th Infantry of the Forty-Second "Rainbow" Division, the brainchild of Douglas MacArthur. The 167th regiment included Waring Huston's boyhood friend Pressley Cleveland. In this case, though, the Dixie unit's commander admitted his men's blame and punished them. Then it was on to camp in New Jersey and to France in December 1917, where the Fifteenth became part of the Ninety-Third Division.[79]

The cumulative effect of the August decisions was to preserve the hierarchy of masculine honor cherished and reinforced in much of the broader society. Most white men would fight, and most black men would dig ditches, clean camps, fix machines, unload ships, and carry heavy objects.

IN EARLY AUGUST, ARTHUR HUEBNER and his family learned that he and 179 other young men from Jefferson County, Wisconsin, had been summoned to the county board for their physical exams. The vast majority had German-sounding names: Schrieber, Dietz, Mueller, Luedke, Frohmader, Becker, Schultz. Another was Bernhard "Ben" Fluegel, a sheet metal worker from Lake Mills, Wisconsin. Daniel J. McCarthy of Watertown, who had one set of grandparents born in Ireland, the other in Germany, also got the call.[80]

The Watertown boys reported for their physicals in mid-August 1917. A local man and Philippine-American War veteran named Nig

Preusse described the process for the *Watertown News*. The examiners tested Arthur's eyes and inspected his feet and hands. They put their fingers in his mouth and checked his teeth. They related his height to his weight to gauge overall health. They measured his chest.[81] Arthur had to withstand "great mechanical stress," with his senses, nervous system, and "organs of emotional control" all in tiptop shape, according to a study of drafted men.[82] Ben, Daniel, and Arthur all passed. If they were needed to help fill Wisconsin's quota, they would be inducted. Arthur presumably continued working for the Welsh farmer in Ixonia. His family waited in Watertown.

THE HUEBNERS' HOMETOWN LAY at a bend in what white settlers called the Rock River. The enormous immigration wave of the antebellum decades had fed European newcomers into the region, joining "Yorkers" from the east coast who had expelled the indigenous populations. Between 1830 and 1860, almost five million transplants arrived in America, a third of them German, a third Irish. Both groups gravitated to Wisconsin, but by the 1840s Germans predominated, attracted by the state's familiar climate and geography, opportunities for free worship, and existing German communities. About half of Watertown's four thousand residents in 1853 came from German-speaking regions. Signs reading "English spoken here" popped up in store windows to reassure other shoppers.[83]

In 1845, this pattern of movement brought Louise Braunschweig's future parents to Lebanon, a German enclave about nine miles from Watertown and part of neighboring Dodge County, Wisconsin. Toddlers Carl Braunschweig and Henrietta Maas traveled with their respective parents in a contingent of almost three hundred "Old Lutherans" facing religious persecution in Prussia. The German revolution of 1848 spurred another exodus to Wisconsin, granted statehood that year, of highly educated "Forty-Eighters." Among them was Carl Schurz, who arrived in Watertown in 1853. After entering local politics, Schurz served as Abraham Lincoln's minister to Spain and a major general in the Union army, then as senator from Missouri, and finally as secretary of the interior in the Rutherford B. Hayes administration.[84] His wife Margarethe Schurz, in 1856, established in Watertown the first kindergarten in America.

The two young Prussian immigrants of 1845, Carl Braunschweig and Henrietta Maas, married in 1860 in Lebanon. While two of his cousins fought, one of them dying at Gettysburg, Carl and Henrietta began a family of six girls and one boy who survived infancy. Among them was Louise, born March 16, 1869. This was Arthur's mother, always the sickliest of the sisters. Across the Atlantic, Arthur's father, Christian, was born in 1867 to ethnic Germans in the village of Rybitwy, part of the Russian province of Poland. Christian's parents died soon after his birth and relatives separated the four children. Christian went to live with an aunt and uncle. At fourteen, his adoptive parents uprooted the orphan once again, sending him to Thorn, Prussia—part of the newly unified German Empire—to train as a cobbler. Christian soon decided to search for opportunities in the United States. Germany in the 1880s was undergoing a dramatic economic transformation, increasing agricultural imports and developing an industrial base. Farmers found domestic markets drying up. These conditions, along with Otto von Bismarck's conscription program, drove 1.7 million Germans to America between 1881 and 1892.[85]

Around the age of twenty, Christian borrowed money from his half-brother Gustav to fund passage to America. On June 1, 1887, he boarded a vessel of the North German Lloyd shipping line, the *Fulda*. Christian probably bunked below decks with a thousand other poorer travelers. After more than two weeks, he disembarked at Castle Garden in New York, reported himself a citizen of the Russian Empire, and passed the physical. With uncertain English, he traveled overland to join relatives of his father's first wife in Lebanon, Wisconsin. He soon found work as a farmhand, opened a shoe business, met and married the farmer's daughter Louise Braunschweig, and welcomed Arthur on November 23, 1891.[86]

Several years and children later, in 1906, Christian and Louise's family gathered with her aging father, Carl Braunschweig, and his many descendants from two marriages (figure 2.2). The next year the old man died. Some of the people surrounding him that day comprised part of a massive demographic trend recorded in 1910. Twenty-seven percent of Wisconsin's residents had been born in Germany or had both parents born there. Meanwhile 8 percent of the entire United States was first- or second-generation German, although the latter category required

FIGURE 2.2 The Braunschweig family, 1906. Christian is fifth from the left, back row, with Louise directly in front of him and teen-aged Arthur two spots to his left. Carl Braunschweig is bearded figure in the center, middle row. Author's collection.

only that one parent be born in Germany.[87] Even these measures, which rendered Germans the largest immigrant group in Wisconsin and the nation, understated the situation. Louise would have been considered German, but not Christian, a Russian immigrant, or their children. It probably annoyed Christian to be counted a Russian. But in 1917 it spared him an even more disagreeable prospect—registering as an enemy alien.

WARING'S NOTE OF JUNE 17, 1917, was his last of the summer. He failed the physical and went home, undoubtedly devastating Waring and his family. Though he finally got to see Carrie Goodwin and his folks and escape camp discipline, he surely wondered what would become of his ambitions. Nearby, in another room in the big house on Church Street, Waring's Confederate grandfather and namesake lay ill. On July 11, 1917, George Waring Smith died at about eighty.[88] Waring decided to give camp another shot, putting in for the second officer training course.

While the family awaited news of Waring's application, a piece of art-work called "Their Boy" appeared in the August 3 edition of the *Selma Mirror*. It showed proud parents gazing at a sign they were about to put up: "A Man from This House Is Fighting in France with United

States Army." The father declares it the proudest moment of his life.[89] No record survives of whether Walter and Nellye took the paper that day or how they may have reacted to it. But the drawing, and many others that showed doughboys making their daddies glad, unquestionably captured the man's hopes for his son. Walter belonged to a generation of southerners awkwardly positioned for military glory. It is likely his first memories involved wartime Selma and his father's service in the Confederate army. As an adult, he witnessed respect for his Civil War–era elders everywhere. Just three weeks earlier, Walter and Nellye had buried her father at Live Oak Cemetery, not far from where the Confederate celebrities and United States senators Morgan and Pettus lay. Men Walter's age lived in places steeped in Civil War memory, but they had not fought a major war of their own. Sons offered the best hope for recharging the family's honor. If Walter saw the drawing, it would likely have chafed at this moment of uncertainty.

The waiting ended a week later when Waring received word about his application to the officers' camp at Fort McPherson: "You are hereby notified that your application at the Second Training Camp was duly received and carefully considered, but due to the limited number of candidates who could attend, you were not selected."[90]

THE DAY WARING'S REJECTION letter was written, Congress began considering the matter of soldier's insurance, a key piece of the effort to stabilize American families. The bill proposed in August had four parts. First, it provided for the wartime financial support of a man's dependents through "allotments," compulsory payments of at least $15 a month drawn from his army salary, and "allowances," supplemental payments from the government. Second, it delivered "compensation" in case of death or disability, in accordance with the severity of the harm done and the size of the man's family. Third, it mandated government-funded rehabilitation services for the wounded. Fourth, it offered voluntary life insurance to servicemen at reduced rates.[91] In an open letter to President Wilson, Secretary of the Treasury William McAdoo made the bill's passage a moral issue. Should we hesitate to protect "the widows and orphans, the dependent and the injured, who, after all, make the greatest sacrifices of any part of our people, for the safety, security, and honor of our country?"[92]

Just as compelling to the bill's champions were opportunities to preserve social stability and domestic roles. Women and children cared for in a doughboy's absence, whether temporary or permanent, would be less likely to seek work or fall into ruin. Compulsory savings and affordable life insurance would channel soldiers' money homeward rather than to bar and brothel. A man wounded in combat, if properly rehabilitated, might still provide for his dependents. McAdoo argued that fewer candidates would seek draft exemptions if they knew the government would step in as surrogate breadwinner. Morale among the soldiers and their home folks would improve.[93] Women, above all, should welcome the steadying influence of insurance. "This is a great opportunity for women," explained Ida Tarbell, oil industry muckraker and member of the Woman's Committee of the Council of National Defense, "to urge the maintenance of families from the outset, to prevent untold suffering, to bring us through this war with families stronger than they otherwise could be."[94] The government also hoped to save money, particularly by requiring wounded men to undergo rehabilitation and get back to work. They would thus maintain masculine credibility while staying off the dole currently pouring outward to Civil War veterans.

The bill passed as the War Risk Insurance Act (WRIA) on October 6, 1917. The only substantial change to the proposal came when lawmakers opted to distribute the death and disability compensation without respect to military rank or salary. Much of the WRIA was meant to replace the existing veterans' pension system, which critics found rife with corruption, nepotism, inconsistency, and great expense—and which, they claimed, had discouraged familial health by underwriting a generation of dependent men. The new law thus aligned with the state's wartime and progressive-era goal of keeping the family intact and gender roles clear.[95]

NATALIE SCOTT IMMEDIATELY ACCEPTED Dr. Lambert's invitation to join the Red Cross in Paris. Advocates for the war, disappointed by the lukewarm support for it in Louisiana, relished the news. Natalie became a model of civic virtue and selflessness in the New Orleans press, which claimed her story had turned the "opposition and defiance" of Louisiana women in a more patriotic direction.[96]

Late at night on September 4, Natalie arrived with her luggage at the New Orleans train station. She cried as she kissed her brother goodbye. Her mother traced a small cross over Natalie's heart. Over nine days, she made her way to New York. Natalie sent several telegrams and sixteen letters to her mother in that short time. She boarded the ship *Touraine* in New York on September 13, 1917, bunking with the wife of one of sixteen accredited correspondents assigned to Gen. John Pershing's staff. Natalie passed the time playing bridge and shuffleboard. There was a concert, minstrel show, and auction to aid French orphans. Natalie was taken with the romance of soldiers and ambulance corpsmen on board, writing to her mother of the ship's "wonderful looking men." Unaccompanied by a convoy, the vessel zigzagged and kept its lights off at night. When France came into view, Natalie wrote her mother, she realized the scale of her commitment. "You know I am not emotional," she said, "but the tears come to my eyes when I think of it. All the significance of it,—hands across-the-sea, danger, service, wonder at nautical science, everything swells indistinguishably in one big emotional heave."[97] The *Touraine* landed at Bordeaux on Sunday, September 23. Among the first things Natalie noticed were French women in mourning dress.

She gave her address in Paris to new friends met on the voyage, then boarded a train bound for the capital. After she arrived on Monday night, she checked in to the Hotel St. James on Rue Saint-Honoré, and the next morning reported for work at the offices of the Red Cross.[98]

ON SEPTEMBER 16, 1917, Thomas Boyd, the conflicted young Marine, left Quantico, Virginia, for the 180-mile rail journey to Philadelphia. Recently, Thomas had written to his mother about his future. "[I]f I go to France," he said, "I stand a chance to return and I stand a chance to remain there—Leave the rest to Fate, Providence, or anything else." He joked to his aunt that the only way he would be home by Christmas was in a wooden kimono. News of his unit's imminent departure for France put the jinx, Thomas wrote, on any thoughts of "home and mother." He also mocked a young woman who had written of longing to see his "big blue eyes" and kiss him one more time. "Isn't she the sentimental little devil?"[99]

In Philadelphia, Boyd and the Chicago shipping clerk Martin Gulberg of the Sixth Regiment were serenaded by music from a Navy band as the unit boarded the transport ship *Henderson*. Women of the Red Cross, also bound for France, cheered from the top deck. The vessel sailed for New York and then Europe on September 23. Rough seas afflicted many of the Marines. One night, while walking his post, Gulberg noticed Cupid at work on the ship. "There in the moonlight," he later wrote, "the officers and nurses were playing the old, old game." Nothing else noteworthy happened during the crossing, except that Thomas Boyd was promoted to corporal. It was a sunny October 5 when they arrived in Saint-Nazaire, France. After almost three weeks on the ship, Gulberg exulted in the town's green trees and red-roofed houses.[100] Thomas Boyd's experiences from that point forward, observations he accumulated in combat and in conversations with other Marines, would generate material for a searing literary account of love and death in the Great War.

WHILE BOYD AND GULBERG were at sea, Louise and Christian Huebner's suspense finally ended. On September 28, a notice appeared in the *Watertown News* calling Arthur, Ben Fluegel, and Daniel McCarthy to report for duty at Camp Grant in Rockford, Illinois, about seventy-five miles south of Watertown. Arthur gathered his things and boarded the train for Rockford on October 3, 1917. Army regulations permitted him to bring soap, shaving accessories, toothbrush and tooth powder, towels, socks, underwear, and extra shirts and collars. All this had to be bundled into hand baggage, not trunks. No bedding would be necessary, authorities promised. Official instructions recommended draftees appear in dispensable shoes and clothing, unless they wished to mail their civilian attire back home.[101]

A few days later, Arthur wrote his brother Otto, in German, to tell him he'd arrived. The postcard showed a scene of the conscript's life at Camp Grant, men shaving under a tree in a rustic version of a nevertheless familiar domestic ritual. On the reverse Arthur wrote, "Dear brother: We arrived at the camp yesterday evening at 7:30 and everything is going well. From Arthur."[102] In his second month at Rockford, at the urging of camp promoters of the WRIA, Arthur purchased a life insurance policy.[103] The *Watertown News*, meanwhile, printed an ode to Arthur and other draftees, which read, in part: "You felt the call and left your all, / Your loved ones and your babies, too; / But then, the Hun snarled at our gates; / The fight was up to you."[104]

Arthur's mother, four years after her daughter's death, was feeling the sting of separation. That she would give her sons gladly or wait with optimism was unlikely. Christian later wrote to a cousin, "All this my wife took very very hard."[105]

WARING HUSTON SAT IN the Atlanta railway station for four hours, a long wait on a hot day after the 200-mile trip from Selma. Finally he boarded a train to his next destination, a recently erected cantonment in Chamblee, Georgia, called Camp Gordon. The railcars took about an hour to cover the fourteen miles, making it 2:30 a.m. before Waring put his head down. He slept a couple hours until reveille at five. It was early September, and the young Alabamian was back in the army, preparing for service in what some officials were calling the War of 1917.[106]

Drawing on his experience at the first officer training camp, Waring had enlisted in the Eighty-Second Division at the rank of acting sergeant. Headquarters assigned him to the new 325th Infantry Regiment, commanded by Col. Walter M. Whitman. The military needed noncommissioned officers to help process and drill Arthur Huebner and the hundreds of thousands of other draftees pouring into cantonments around the country. The all-draftee Eighty-Second, formed at Camp Gordon on August 25, was putting together its own training cadre of noncoms. Setting aside his broader ambitions, Waring filled one of those posts. He was lucky that Camp Gordon had wooden barracks, though they weren't finished as thousands of "rookies" arrived in September.[107]

Recruits in Waring's 325th Infantry came from Alabama, Georgia, Florida, and Tennessee, part of a massive movement of half a million conscripts into the National Army.[108] Their mobilization demanded unprecedented exertions of the state. Secretary of War Baker called it a "stupendous" task to turn an "unmilitary country" into a world warrior.[109] Officials monitored, disciplined, and sometimes accommodated the doughboy's behavior, even as they provided him food, clothing, shelter, and medical care. Waring began on a very hot Saturday, September 8, to train recruits in the military way. He applied for the third officers' program, to be held in early 1918 in a remote corner of Camp Gordon.[110]

The young man's happiness and aspirations continued to run at cross-purposes. Waring didn't hide his misery from his mother. "Well here I am again in one of these d_____ camps," he griped in his first letter from Camp Gordon. "Believe me Mama army life is not what it is cracked up to be—not by a long shot." The struggle to belong, to feel comfort in the hard world of camp, to ensure his family and hometown remembered him—all weighed heavily on Waring as he rejoined the service. An invitation to a community dinner in honor of local draftees, a ritual held a couple days before Waring left and repeated across the country, may have helped if he attended.[111] He tried to find relief in the presence of a few guys from home and a favorite captain from Fort McPherson, but they failed to deliver the emotional security Waring craved. "Please write me just as soon as you can Mama and just as often as you can 'cause' I am blue and lonesome—I miss you all more than you can ever imagine," he wrote. "You know I always did hate to leave home and believe me it is hard on me now. I feel like if I could have a good cry it would do me worlds of good—it would not take much to make me do it either."[112]

Homesickness affected enough trainees to be addressed in *Trench and Camp*, a newsletter distributed in all the cantonments. The cover image showed a sympathetic Uncle Sam consoling a sad-looking rookie. "Alone Boy?" he says. "The Whole Darned Country Is with You."[113] Notwithstanding its comforting message, the picture departed from the spirit of the national registration in June 1917, when the prospects of sorrow and homesickness had been quiet in discussions of the wartime family. For Waring, the support of the whole darned country did not change the fact that he was lonely, a feeling familiar from his Tuscaloosa days. "[I]t is awful to be here with so many boys," he had written his father from college, "and to think that they don't care a darn about you."[114]

Yet Waring, ever conflicted, vowed to acquit himself commendably overseas. He had a "duty to perform" and hoped he could do it well. The boy's versatile disposition could accommodate self-pity and hopefulness. "I am getting along all right," he wrote his mother in September, "and hope to make good up here even if it kills me."[115] He acknowledged the paradox creeping into popular culture—that he might make his family proud but endure personal suffering in the process.

Service in France looked imminent. The *Atlanta Constitution* reported in early September 1917 that the Eighty-Second would be one of the next divisions to cross the ocean. Military authorities thought

Waring and the other instructors needed about three months to prepare the draftees.[116] Atlantans were proud of their own men in those ranks, sending them off in a caravan of patriotically decorated cars just days before Waring left Selma. A reporter recognized the same incongruities Waring expressed in his letters. The farewell pulsed with "the real pathos of grave partings despite the pomp and glory of flying colors and braying bands."[117]

If those elements did battle in the mind of Waring Huston, pathos was winning. "Look after my Girl for me please Mama 'cause' you, Papa, and she are all I have," he closed that first letter. "Mama I love you all three and it nearly kills me to stay so far away."[118]

3

Tell Your Sweetheart Not to Pine

IN MAE BILBREY'S NOTE to Eliga Dees of July 15, 1917, she talked hopefully of him coming home to Missouri for a visit in September. If he made that trip, Lige would have returned to a Wayne County stirring with war preparations. In August, the county draft board began calling and examining men in the order determined by the national serial number lottery. Wayne County sheriff and board officer York Lovelace put a notice in the *Greenville Sun* warning those summoned not to dodge the authorities or claim phony dependents. This was Missouri, where such evasions would surprise no one. Over the next few weeks, the board filled Wayne County's quota of ninety-six men, declaring them ready for departure to the National Army's Camp Funston in neighboring Kansas.[1]

While these gears turned, the *Greenville Sun* joined the national chorus on war's redemptive potential. In August, the paper ran a piece on the single man without marriage prospects, a sorry sufferer of hole-filled socks, loose buttons, and unmet needs. In normal times, he wandered about aimlessly, adrift of meaningful loyalties, a nonparticipant in the propagation of the species and therefore a man without a stake in the future. Heading a family, in that world, showed real masculine virtue and civic character. But war offered the bachelor another route to manly citizenship. Even better for the bachelor, the military might serve as surrogate family. "He marries war," wrote the author, "and the government sews his buttons on and darns the holes in his socks."[2] Domestication, not degradation, was what the *Sun* saw coming for the army man.

The mostly young, single draftees left Wayne County in two groups to elaborate farewell rituals. The first send-off began with a banquet on a Thursday night for the soldiers-to-be and their families, sweethearts, and friends. The women of Greenville fed four hundred guests before everyone retired to the courthouse lawn for a gathering of two thousand. Voltaire V. Ing, the local lawyer and conscript's uncle who had called for the demonstration, delivered appreciative remarks. The selectmen slept in Greenville homes that night. On an overcast Friday morning they departed by train, stopping in Williamsville, where Mae Bilbrey and the other high school pupils lent their voices to the farewell. The students, school band, and rookies marched in a rainy procession. Though most people kept their composure, reported the paper, such an occasion "necessarily brings grief to the hearts of many families."[3]

For the men and their loved ones, the passage of time had converted the heady promises of April 1917 into tangible experience: the sound of a high school band, the recruit's last glimpses back at his loved ones, the clatter of a train chugging away, the first night at home with an empty chair or bedroom. *Trench and Camp* pictured the scene for readers at Lige's Fort Oglethorpe with a drawing of the draftee departing a sad group of onlookers. Most heartbroken is a small figure in the corner, labeled "HER," a weeping girlfriend or wife.[4] Mae hadn't attended a farewell for Lige—he had enlisted before the spectacles of the war era—but just the passing of soldier trains made her sad.[5]

Once the young men had gone, Wayne County people worked hard to stay connected to them. Newspapers printed trainees' letters to their families, mothers mailed packages to sons. Voltaire Ing organized a mass meeting to publicize the recently launched, $35-million fundraising drive of the YMCA, which, like many American parents, wasn't as sure as the *Greenville Sun* about the military's salutary impact on young men. It pledged to use the money to provide wholesome entertainment and facilitate communication with families to reassert the civilizing influence of home and community. In November, the citizens of Wayne County gave six thousand dollars for the campaign to "make the life of the soldiers and sailors as much home like as possible," as one advocate put it when he spoke to Mae and her classmates. A public letter of thanks from "Wayne County's Sammies," another nickname for doughboys, praised the Y for always making us "feel at home."[6]

WARING HUSTON COULDN'T BELIEVE how fast the boys came into Camp Gordon—five thousand one day, two thousand the next, seven thousand soon to follow. Processing men into the 325th Infantry, which reached war strength in early October, kept Waring in a frenzy.[7] Then, just as quickly, many of them left. The War Department transferred thousands of Camp Gordon draftees to National Guard units around the South, only to replace them with more recruits for Waring and the other instructors to drill. Col. Whitman and divisional leadership seethed at these threats to unit cohesion and readiness. The new arrivals came from the North—New York, Maryland, Pennsylvania—transforming the once-southern Eighty-Second into the "All-American" division. In line with the prevailing analogies of wartime culture, the division's officers viewed the new regiments as their children and used the word "infanticide" to condemn the October transfers.[8] They upset earlier hopes that the Eighty-Second would be ready for Europe within three months.

All across the camps, efforts to implement a standard training program ran up against the staggered arrival of trainees, construction delays, equipment shortages, and divisional transfers. The draftees reported in various conditions of fitness. Many had never handled a weapon before. Even many of the noncoms and officers—Waring among them—possessed the barest of military experience.[9]

There were other challenges. Waring struggled to communicate with less educated recruits. Some 21 percent of white soldiers and 50 percent of black ones couldn't read, according to army intelligence examiners, a real problem in a modern military with forms, written signs and orders, and camp newsletters.[10] The illiterate drove Waring to frustration. "I was out drilling all morning and believe me it is a job to teach these recruits anything," Waring wrote home in September. "I had three that could not read or write so you see what a job it is going to be." An unfortunate boy named Israel I. Thomas Skinner couldn't name the state he came from.[11]

Camp Gordon's smallest man, five-foot-one-inch Louis Goldberg, who only spoke broken English, was part of a large camp population of immigrant soldiers.[12] Roughly 18 percent of men in the entire army were foreign-born, and about one hundred thousand could not speak English.[13] The draft alone produced half a million immigrants from forty-six countries. With the October additions to the All-American Eighty-Second, the division's proportion of immigrant doughboys stood at 20 percent of the twenty-eight thousand incoming conscripts to date.[14] At Camp Gordon and around the country, such diversity elicited a complex reaction—fulsome praise for the assimilative benefits of conscription mixed with condescension toward, prejudice against, or, occasionally, admiration for the foreign-born. It irritated the *Atlanta Constitution* that men who couldn't speak English made it to the camps, but the editors liked the idea of an All-American division training near their forward-looking city. How exciting to host such exotic arrivals from New York! There was "Chinaman" Harry Low who could discuss American literature with intelligence; Cuban Amelio Garcia, a "fine fellow"; and an Italian veteran assigned to Waring's regiment named Carmen Leconte.[15] The paper hailed the well-known *New York Evening Journal* cartoonist and Camp Gordon draftee Milton Gross, an American-born Russian.[16] Ultimately, the wartime state asserted assimilationist pressures on such draftees but also endeavored to boost their morale, respect their traditions, and cater to their needs.[17]

For its part, the Eighty-Second's divisional history still sounded annoyed in 1920 about the camp's "confusion of races and speech."[18] The burdens of necessity may have dictated widening the pool of draft-eligible men beyond the native-born and thus generated assimilative hopes, but xenophobia ran through the cantonments. An Italian-born rookie at Camp Gordon named Anthony Pierro remembered losing his appetite on the chow line after being called an ethnic epithet. "I hated that name: Wop, Dago, Guinea," he recalled. "I hated all those names."[19] Col. Whitman of Waring's 325th Infantry recalled such enmity but recoiled from it, citing the shared bond of combat. "Our men of foreign birth who were rather contemptuously classed as 'Wops,' 'Bohunks,' 'Dagos,' and 'Guinies,'" he wrote, "will hereafter be classed as our comrades in arms."[20]

The most famous newcomer to Camp Gordon was neither an immigrant nor famous, yet. Alvin Cullum York arrived at Camp Gordon from Tennessee on November 15, 1917.[21] The devout Christian from Pall Mall initially had claimed exemption for his religious beliefs but adjusted his view of God's wishes to incorporate military service. Three days after York got to camp, the illustrious preacher Billy Sunday gave a speech in Atlanta called "When the Chickens Come Home to Roost." Waring admired Sunday's celebrity and intended to go, but we don't know if he or Alvin made the trip.[22] In his remarks that afternoon, Sunday started with the prospect of tragedy, saying rather more bluntly what the architects of the War Risk Insurance Act had pledged the month before. "I am so glad to see you fellows here," Sunday greeted the assembled soldiers, "and when you have to go, if you never come back we will take care of your mothers and wives and children." Then Sunday railed against the moral dangers of unsupervised male behavior. Camp officials shared that concern and labored energetically to make the cantonments congenial to virtue.[23]

Waring read his bible and appears to have stayed out of trouble, not that he would have admitted otherwise to his parents. But his chief mission as 1917 ended was to impress his superiors. Throughout this period, Waring framed his motivations in personal terms. He never mentioned America's war aims or its enemies but could not abide letting "some one else do my fighting."[24] The respect that came with wearing the uniform was the prize, and sometimes Waring even hoped to avoid combat, though he did feel a bit guilty about that:

Capt. Askew came down to see me this morning. He has been talking to the Adjutant and says I have a good chance to get Sergeant Major—that is not a Commission, but it is a pretty safe job if we have to fight "cause" then I would stay back with the Adjutant and the Adjutant stays with the Colonel so you see we would be behind the line. I don't know whether I care to stay so far behind when the others are fighting tho.[25]

At other times, he mentioned the appeal of a safe position without the qualifying remarks. His search for the credibility of service if not the experience of violence lined up with some of the motivations the *Boston Globe* had listed a few months earlier:

BECAUSE I don't want to be called a slacker.
BECAUSE I am not afraid.
BECAUSE I want to keep my name untarnished.
BECAUSE I want my folks to be proud of me.
BECAUSE I don't want the world to say I'm a coward.[26]

Walter Huston likewise thought of his son's service as a personal quest. Success would come with a commission. Walter prayed Waring would be admitted to the officer training camp, he wrote in December. "You must not fail."[27]

WARING'S HURRIED TRAINING OF the draftees formed part of a tremendous scramble to get the American Expeditionary Forces (AEF) to a rapidly changing war. The first, very limited contingents had come in mid-1917, greeted by French people who so associated the Americans with Rooseveltian bellicosity they called the doughboys "Teddies." They arrived just as a general mutiny crippled the French army. Authorities responded with guilty verdicts for more than twenty thousand, executions for fifty, and reforms in leave and provisioning policies for millions. In November, Waring Huston's old classmate and friend Pressley Cleveland's Forty-Second "Rainbow" Division drew from National Guard units in twenty-six states and steamed to Europe. The Allies had just gained some ground after several months of fighting at Passchendaele, or the Third Battle of Ypres, in Flanders. It cost almost 250,000 casualties, including many Australians, at first only injured, drowning in mud in the battle's last days. The Germans lost nearly double that figure, but soon were cheered by Russia's November revolution. The Bolsheviks withdrew from the war in December, ending fighting on the Eastern Front and freeing almost a million German soldiers to surge west.[28] At the end of the year came the black New York Fifteenth National Guard regiment, men who had scuffled with whites in South Carolina and Long Island. In January 1918, this first-arriving regiment of the "Colored" Ninety-Third Division became the 369th Infantry Regiment or "Harlem Hell Fighters." For now, there was no hell fighting or any other kind. The 369th spent its time at the French port of Saint-Nazaire working with Service of Supply troops building railroad tracks and not training for combat at all.[29]

Among the early arrivals in France were Thomas Boyd and Martin Gulberg, the young men who'd enlisted in the Marines in Chicago and now served with the Second Division.[30] Upon landing in Saint-Nazaire, France, in October 1917, Thomas and Martin's First Battalion moved into a leaky bunkhouse. Boyd sent letters back home to Illinois to ask why his sweetheart De Ette hadn't written and to report his home-sickness. "Well, I have two things to look forward to," Thomas wrote, "the trenches and home, one way or another."[31] He and Gulberg spent much of the autumn and early winter working as stevedores and military police. In the months spanning 1917 and 1918, the expeditionary divisions underwent further training and occupied quiet parts of the front.[32]

Thomas Boyd's experiences in Saint-Nazaire later inspired the opening of his novel *Through the Wheat* (1923). Thomas began the book with William Hicks, his alter ego, feeling humiliated by low duties. In the first of many jabs at sentimentalized wartime culture, Boyd ridicules doughboys (maybe including himself) who believed it their white privilege to win masculine glory. For nine months, Hicks thinks, he has been "shunted from one place to another, acting out the odious office of the military police, working as a stevedore beside evil-odored blacks, helping to build cantonments and reservoirs for new soldiers ever arriving from the United States." How could Hicks have come to France for this? "A hell of a way to treat a white man," he thinks, reflecting and perhaps mocking the racialized hierarchy of martial virtue not to mention the letter of military policy decided in August 1917.[33]

With greater venom, Thomas Boyd lampoons the chivalric promises of wartime. He has a hateful drill sergeant, the fictionalized Sgt. Harriman, bark at his men during a bayonet exercise, "Now you forget that these are sacks of straw. They are not at all. They are dirty Huns— Huns that raped the Belgians, Huns that would have come over to the good old U.S.A. and raped our women if we hadn't got into the war. Now, men, I want to see some action, I want to see some hate when you stick these dirty Huns." The man closes this bit of motivational speech with burlesque sexual innuendo: "I want to see how hard you can *grunt.*" A few moments later, Boyd (via Harriman) hollows out another of the war's cherished justifications. "Did you ever hear that you were supposed to be saving the world for democracy?," the sergeant screams. "Now, try it again, and put some punch in it this time. Let's hear your *grunt.*"[34]

Boyd's parody of the sexually charged soldier reflected a very real crisis for American officials in Saint-Nazaire. Arriving doughboys entered a brisk trade in pleasures of the flesh, disrupting the army's plans for a morally pure expeditionary force. From his arrival in France in the summer of 1917, Gen. John J. Pershing, commander of the AEF, had led a personal war against venereal disease. He called first for educational lectures and semi-monthly inspections. Next, there were chemical prophylaxis stations. If the amorous lad didn't reach them in time to stave off infection, about three hours after contact, Pershing threatened him with court-martial. Propaganda materials, meanwhile, tapped into the age-old demonization of prostitutes and French women. Posters blared, "A German Bullet Is Cleaner Than a Whore." The arrival of Boyd and thousands of other soldiers and Marines in Saint-Nazaire quickly strained Pershing's moral program. Late in 1917, he dispatched Dr. Hugh Young, a respected physician from Johns Hopkins University and the director of the AEF's Division of Urology, to investigate.

Young found Americans behaving nothing like paragons of restraint. Alcohol and women were the key corruptors. "The first Frenchman I met," Marine Martin Gulberg later wrote, "wanted to sell me some pictures of nude women. These fellows were wharf rats and preyed upon newly landed troops. They also sold liquor." As a member of the military police, a large part of Gulberg's job was to round up "half soaked gobs" from the French cafés.[35] Dr. Young reported that rum from the West Indies and other "rotgut stuff" robbed the doughboy of his inhibitions and good sense. Lines of American soldiers snaked out from the town's six legal *maisons de prostitution.* Many of the prostitutes weren't actually infected, it turned out. They transmitted the diseases from soldier to soldier in quick succession and remained free of infection through regular washing and inspection, leading Young to call the women's bodies "septic tanks." An outraged Pershing read the report and took the next train to Saint-Nazaire. He issued strict orders holding commanding officers responsible for detaining infected men, ringing brothels with military police, and enforcing prophylactic treatment on any man admitting to a liaison or even arriving in camp drunk. The disciplinary crackdown reduced the rate of venereal disease in Saint-Nazaire dramatically.[36]

Thomas Boyd, Martin Gulberg, and the Marines stayed at Saint-Nazaire until January 1918, when they made the train journey across France to the Vosges Mountains. They rode in the infamous "forty and eight" railcars, meant to hold forty men or eight horses, to Gulberg's sardonic mind one of the "horrors of war." Everybody mashed together and made it intact except one cook, who lost an arm when he fell off the train.[37] The droll Boyd wrote to his family from "somewhere else in France" of war's effect on a man's constitution. "This is unquestionably a gay life," he said, "if one does not weaken but unfortunately there is a very slight chance of one not weakening."[38] His mother apparently was considering joining the Red Cross, but he urged her to stay home and abandon fantasies of the "Florence Nightingale stuff."[39]

Once in the mountains, Cpl. Boyd's company stayed in a village called Champignuelles. There they trained for service at the front, received gas masks, and donned metal helmets. One day, early in the battalion's time in the Vosges region, Boyd was posted as corporal of the guard. He took off his rifle belt and sat down, violations of Marine protocol. The acting commander of the battalion busted Thomas down to private. In *Through the Wheat*, Boyd subjects his character William Hicks to a similar fate. The fictional Hicks fears the worst—home front embarrassment. "What the hell was he to do? It was the first time he had thought of his family. What would Maisie say when she discovered that he, William Hicks, was in Fort Leavenworth? What would the gang at the office say? And his mother? Maybe they might order him to be shot. This was a mess."[40] It was the judgment of sweetheart, pals, and mother, almost more than the threat of execution, that concerned Hicks.

THE DOUGHBOYS ARRIVING IN 1917 found women devoted to the "Florence Nightingale stuff" in the American Red Cross (ARC). Long before American intervention, the ARC had established itself as the primary agency for the medical and material relief of imperiled civilians and had tried with mixed success to spread that relief across the various belligerents. But with the April 1917 declaration of war, the ARC turned its humanitarian energies toward Allied and American soldiers, civilians in the Allied countries, and prisoners of war. Its once international and neutral character became more patriotic, ideological, American. And as the ARC brought men into leadership roles and into the rank-and-file, the organization's publicity materials began investing its mission with what conventional wisdom held to be masculine virtues. The Red Cross still brimmed with the "female" impulse to care and help, still called its archetypal nurse "our greatest mother," but in wartime stressed courage and competence as well.[41]

Natalie Scott of New Orleans embodied the mixture of elements that animated the ARC's humanitarian ethos. In a vaguely parallel way, she captured by word and deed the greater wartime tensions between sentimentality and realism, between tradition and change, between the idea of war as a romantic event and a venue for carnage and terror. After arriving in Paris in late September 1917, she wrote dozens of letters back to her mother that showed her to be at once clinical and sympathetic, rational and compassionate, strong and nurturing. She behaved selflessly but also cultivated her own professional skills and efficiency. War both invigorated and nauseated her. Natalie found soldiers glamorous and went on lots of dates, but ultimately devoted herself to her work. "Things seem too intense just now," she once wrote, "for the lighter fancies; and I'm not material for a grand passion."[42]

Early in the morning on Tuesday, September 25, 1917, Natalie reported for work at the Red Cross headquarters. A fog enshrouded the Place de La Concorde. The whole "majestic" scene, the towering statues of "heroic size," left Natalie feeling inconsequential. She met Dr. Alexander Lambert, chief medical officer for the ARC and former personal doctor to President Theodore Roosevelt. Natalie gushed about the "great" and "lovable" Lambert, a man burdened by responsibilities but cheerful and kind, a combination of traits she would emulate. After settling in, Natalie began working on a report with Dr. Tom Williams on combat's psychological impact on French soldiers.[43]

The casualties of wartime, who had fired Natalie's sympathetic activism, now came to life. She chatted in French with the clerk who issued her identity card. He was about fifty, serving in the army in 1914 but now discharged on account of age. She asked if his sons were in the war. "One sick, one prisoner, one dead," he answered. All had fought for France, together, in the First Battle of the Marne.[44] During a hospital visit, Natalie watched young amputees singing and laughing and racing around in their "rolling-chairs."[45] When she surveyed the rehabilitation program at a vocational school for wounded French veterans, Natalie mourned the "hopeless" and "listless" stage that residents seemed fated to endure, but also cheerfully reported to her mother the restored masculine productive abilities of the men. She purchased jewelry from French *mutilés* and sent them home as gifts. In December, Natalie helped organize Christmas functions for hundreds of French orphans and refugees. At one event two quiet children sat off to the side, their mother unwilling to let them grab toys with the other kids, "so starved for pretty things" and "wild with fear" of being left out. Natalie went over to the youngsters, took their hands, and helped them acquire a gun and a wagon. "And when I left," she wrote home, "I had a glimpse of a caisson driver and a soldier, happily oblivious of everything around them—my two little friends." Here Natalie, no less than the children, seemed unaware of the tragic irony of the episode. She also sent her mother perceptive accounts of war in all its colors. She saw in the wounded men, "even when they are smiling and happy, a reminiscence of pains, or perhaps surprise at finding themselves still on the old familiar earth. . . . They suggest, each one, vistas of the most stirring, varied kinds,—families distressed, battle-fields, suffering, heroic acts."[46]

In between these experiences, Natalie had fun in Paris with American military men, which occasionally made her feel guilty, but she justified it with the progressive logic of wartime. A wholesome young woman like herself could brighten the life of an American and do it in a way that surely risked no harm, "which is more than can be said for some of the pleasures of Paris," she told her mother after a single Sunday that saw her go on eight separate dates.[47] By the end of the year, the neuropsychiatric report complete, Natalie had moved into the direct employ of Dr. Lambert, and she was tasked with creating a filing system for the Red Cross office's medical reports, supply and equipment inventories, and correspondence. She continued to work with refugees and veterans but became known as an impeccable source of knowledge on the ARC's activities. One colleague called her "Miss Information."[48]

FOLLOWING ELIGA DEES'S SEPTEMBER visit to Missouri, assuming he made it, his correspondence with Mae disappears for seven months. Later missives would reveal that old patterns—fears of infidelity, bruised feelings, and above all, the strain of distance—had interrupted their courtship.

That fall and winter, Lige trained with the regulars at Fort Oglethorpe, Georgia. In November 1917, the brass incorporated his Fifty-Third Infantry with other units into the Sixth Division, for now a pure regular army division. The next month the regiment received a big class of officers from the training camps of Waring Huston's ambitions.[49] Meanwhile, Lige and the others conducted exercises in the recently finished trench system on Snodgrass Hill. "Will we dig, dig, dig for Kaiser Bill?" asked a soldier's ditty. "You can bet your bottom dollar / On Der Tag his nibs will holler / Every bullet sings a song for Kaiser Bill!"[50]

All the attention lavished on the new conscription and camps aggravated the regulars at Fort Oglethorpe. In *Trench and Camp*, they trumpeted the impressive scale of their cantonment—"no back number," of which they were "justly proud."[51] Though possessed of their own ragged public reputation, the regulars harbored contempt for National Guardsmen and conscripts.[52] In the poem "Only a Volunteer," they resented the appreciation draftees enjoyed when in fact they had been first to step forward:

Why didn't I wait for the banquet
Why didn't I wait to be cheered
For the drafted men get all the credit
While I only volunteered."[53]

Mae shared such views. In the spring of 1918, when her letters reappear, she mocked the drafted man. "Think of the boys that haven't the nerve to go to their country's call," she wrote, "and even when they are drafted they do all they can to keep out. I would rather be dead than be a 'slacker' or a coward. Wouldn't you dear?"[54] Mae preferred the love of someone like Lige, exposing how thoroughly insinuated into courtship war had become. You could take the measure of a man, Mae suggested, by the volition behind his payment to society. By that rubric, conscripts were only marginally better than outright dodgers. The volunteer truly impressed her, the one enlisting without fanfare. Of course the regulars had to agree. A member of Lige's unit later wrote home that the regulars regarded the draftee as "about three shades lower than a yellow dog."[55] "The Regular Army Man," went another bit of doggerel circulating at Fort Oglethorpe, was the man "fighting for his country—and his home."[56]

THE CONSCRIPT ARTHUR HUEBNER arrived at Camp Grant in early October 1917. His impressions of basic training survive only in the four-word phrase he sent his brother Otto: "Everything is going well." One presumes it meant he did what thousands of others did: situate himself in frame barracks and accumulate possessions when available. Draftees picked up sleeves of fabric filled with straw to serve as mattresses ("bed tickings"), and blankets if they were lucky, though these gave little comfort in a chilly October without steam heat at Camp Grant.[57] *Trench and Camp* printed this soldier's verse:

I'm here with my two army blankets,
As thin as a slice of ham,
A German spy, I think was the guy,
Who made them for Uncle Sam.[58]

Soon Arthur and the other recruits received much-dreaded inoculations for tetanus, typhoid, and smallpox, a new experience for many men from the country.[59]

Uniforms were hard to come by at first. For whatever reason, the draft army contained men both bigger and smaller than the peacetime army, complicating the usual procurement calculus. And there were simply far more bodies to clothe than ever before. Eventually Arthur did get his uniform, helping effect the transformation of boy into soldier (figure 3.1).

Although the Quartermaster Corps ultimately secured more than 26 million shoes, how quickly any of them made their way onto Arthur's feet is another question.[60] A fellow drafted man at Camp Grant named Clayton K. Slack, of Madison, Wisconsin, went more than a month before receiving footwear.[61] Another German American Watertown draftee in this period wrote home, "I got everything but shoes, so I'm quite a soldier now."[62]

Arthur acquired two other items that reinforced both his Christian values as well as the broader program to safeguard his moral character: pocket editions of the Book of Psalms and the New Testament. By

FIGURE 3.1 Arthur Huebner, 1918. Author's collection.

taking possession of the latter, Arthur pledged to read at least one chapter a day and carry it with him at all times. It suggested members proselytize and pray for the "unsaved." He listed his address as "331st M. G. Bn. Co B." Arthur and Ben Fluegel had been assigned to the 331st Machine Gun Battalion in the National Army's Eighty-Sixth Division.[63]

Camp Grant's capacity of forty thousand draftees was four times greater than Watertown's population. From the perspective of a rookie like Arthur, those masses contained a blend of the familiar and the new. The great majority of men who passed through Camp Grant came from

Illinois and Wisconsin, but this included recruits from city and country, from the immigrant wards of Chicago and remote parts of northern Wisconsin.[64] "I was a naïve farm boy when I entered," remembered a Wisconsin draftee named William Helberg. "I found myself in with a really rough tough bunch from Chicago. It was rough all the way."[65] The Camp Grant newsletter made much of the cantonment's diverse roster of occupations—chemist, doctor, attorney, motion picture camera operator, sewer digger—yet a large number were farm workers like Helberg and Arthur.[66] Draftees tended to congregate with men of like background, and for Arthur there were probably a few familiar faces and German-speakers.[67] Yet the shock of change could be great. A camp doctor in New York reported almost everyone he examined suffered from what he called "anxiety neurosis."[68]

As a farm laborer Arthur would have been accustomed to hard work, but training camp subjected him to a new degree of control. A poem published in *Trench and Camp* a couple of days after his twenty-sixth birthday in November addressed the change:

We never heard it back on the farm,
Fall in!
It makes us leave our fire so warm,
Fall in!
We hear it before the morning light,
We hear it the last thing every night,
The Top Serg crying with all his might,
Fall in![69]

Camp discipline could be harsh. According to firsthand reports, conscripts held back tears at Camp Meade in Maryland, bristled at "hard boiled language" at Camp Dodge in Iowa, and were "humiliated" by noncoms at Camp Grant.[70] Arthur got a taste of that hard treatment. Arthur's younger brother Walter remembered decades later that Arthur told him at the time that his instructor mercilessly upbraided the trainees but only to save their lives, he said, once they got to France.

Arthur's day began with the blow of the bugle at 5:30. Recruits tidied their quarters, ate breakfast, and went outside for individual and group instruction ("school of the soldier" and "school of the squad"). Arthur learned to march, drill, salute, and handle his rifle and bayonet. After official inspection of the barracks, the draftees might head outside again for hikes, drill, or calisthenics. Camp officials sanctioned little rest between these labors, obliging recruits to keep the grounds cleaned and maintained ("policed") and to assist the camp cooks. The men needed every one of the 4,761 daily calories allotted to them.[71] The Camp Grant newspaper reported the food wholesome and filling. Clayton Slack later recalled "lots of meat, lots of vegetables."[72]

Equipment shortages plagued the camps. In Waring Huston's Eighty-Second Division, members of Stokes mortar platoons only laid eyes on that weapon once they got to France.[73] At Camp Grant, the men trained with wooden pistols, horses, and artillery pieces.[74] It was big news in the cantonment newsletter when machine gun companies finally got their hands on the real thing two months after arriving at basic training.[75] City boys, Clayton Slack said, couldn't handle the weapons and often left the branch.[76] People in Watertown read that machine gunners at Camp Grant were learning to use a weapon "appalling in its vicious-ness," which the Rockford trainees couldn't wait to train on the advanc-ing Boche, as they called the Germans.[77]

Citizens of Watertown, like those in Selma and Wayne County, faced pleas to contribute to the YMCA's program of uplift. An advertisement for a public talk in November pictured the YMCA as both surrogate family and facilitator of contact with home folks. Arthur and other doughboys must have "the things that will take the place of the restraints of home." The specter of "temptation" threatened the servicemen and thus threatened the very objects of protection in this war—"our chil-dren and our children's children."[78] With some effort the Y would keep the men clear of liquor and worse sorts of trouble.

THE LEISURE ACTIVITIES OF working-class men had long drawn progres-sive scrutiny. Saloons and prostitutes in particular, reformers taught, degraded the husband and father and threatened the wife and child. The muckraker Raymond Fosdick, who had studied soldierly vice along the Mexican border in 1916, counseled Secretary of War Newton Baker to curb alcohol and prostitution among those troops and promote more wholesome alternative pastimes. Edifying middle-class pursuits, prom-ised Fosdick and other progressives, not only helped combat idleness but also encouraged proper male behavior. By the time Lige Dees arrived in El Paso in early 1917, the restrictions were in place but not the diversionary program.[79]

That changed with America's entrance into the Great War. The day of Wilson's war speech to Congress, Baker reported to the president that homesickness and boredom had led men astray during the Mexican affair.[80] The scale of the looming mobilization augured even greater moral collapse—or greater opportunity. As conscription funneled hundreds of thousands into the camps, progressives sensed a chance to restore character they saw threatened by industrialization and urbanization, to educate the masses in middle-class sensibilities and moral conduct, and to overturn historical precedent by training citizen-soldiers of whom families could truly be proud.

The result was the Commission on Training Camp Activities (CTCA), headed by Raymond Fosdick. Through the YMCA and six other civilian partner agencies, the CTCA would oversee the doughboy's character and fighting fitness.[81] Reformers organized activities meant not only to act as "counterweights to temptation," as Secretary Baker put it, but also to build muscles, voices, camaraderie, and stamina. Troupes performed magic, comedy, and music.[82] Athletic directors coordinated physical activity, good for cultivating fitness, military skills, and teamwork. Basketball and volleyball were popular at Camp Grant. Brawlers from Chicago helped make boxing a favorite pastime of officers and rookies alike.[83] The trainees spent an inordinate amount of time singing, which CTCA reformers believed promoted group coordination, patriotic élan, good morale, timing, memory, and even physical strength—a "strong back, chest, and lungs." On Halloween, Arthur and Ben's 331st Machine Gun Battalion belted out wartime tunes. A recruit named Arthur Lanze sang the paean to militarized motherhood, "America Here's My Boy." Groups of three to four thousand selectmen gathered regularly to rehearse "Over There," "Keep the Home Fires Burning," and "Good-by Broadway, Hello France."[84]

Whatever broader goals of moral enhancement animated the CTCA and its allied agencies, military officials wished to keep the boys out of trouble and free of disease. To that end, alongside the recreational programs the CTCA developed a program to promote "social hygiene." It resembled the package of policies Gen. Pershing was implementing in France. The CTCA issued to every enlisted man a pamphlet entitled *Keeping Fit to Fight*, which offered frank sex education in "man-to-man" language. One of the first feature-length government films, *Fit to Fight*, made a readiness plea obvious from its title. But these materials made deeper arguments as well. Soldiers in a war for women and family must not do anything to threaten them. "It would never do for the avengers of women's wrongs," went a cantonment handout on venereal disease, "to profit by the degradation and debasement of womanhood."[85] Equally unfortunate would be to bring disgrace to relatives. Beneath a picture of a home front mother serving food to her family, one social hygiene poster read, "Remember—the folks at home. Go back to them physically fit and morally clean. Don't allow a whore to smirch your record."[86] No doubt these reformers had their pragmatic motivations, but they channeled the power of familial devotion and the war's chivalric meaning to serve those ends. "Your Mother has been Unselfish and Devoted to you," a YMCA poster advised. "WILL YOU be Worthy of Her? Protect the honor of all women and girls."[87]

The next line of defense sent a more complicated message. The CTCA sponsored camp prophylaxis stations for the lapsed doughboy, who faced court-martial, like his comrades in France, if he didn't reach one in time. Some reformers thought this chemical bailout condoned, or at least diminished the undesirable side effects of, the very behavior the CTCA was trying to prevent. They didn't win the argument. Preventing disease and keeping the soldier in the field were always first priorities. But moral considerations still had power to trump military ones. Distributing condoms would have reduced disease, but the army stopped doing so when traditionalist critics objected.[88]

Finally, the Selective Service Act had prohibited the sale of alcohol to those in uniform and facilitated the banning of prostitution around camps. The CTCA would close seventy vice districts by May 1918, even if men continued to pursue sex with prostitutes and other young women. Yet the reformers had successes to boast. In February 1918, venereal disease rates in the camps reached a low of roughly sixty-two per thousand. A later study estimated ninety percent of these cases resulted from pre-enlistment dalliances. A mixture of diversion, coercion, treatment, and persuasion dropped disease rates three hundred percent over the course of the war.[89]

In the moral vocabulary of these programs, the doughboy was an innocent to be protected from prostitutes and venereal disease. Anyone who heard tales of moral breakdown in Saint-Nazaire, including the military officials tasked with fixing it, would have blamed what they considered to be notorious French sexual permissiveness. "Is it inevitable," an American woman once wrote Raymond Fosdick, "that our troops . . . be exposed in Europe to the French policy of 'laissez-faire' in all things sexual?"[90] Stateside prostitutes likewise seemed more dangerous than ever, and authorities policed and criminalized their activities with greater intensity. Once again, war offered the chance to attack long-standing hazards to the health of the family. If the army could gather and educate men on the threat of prostitution, it could build an American manhood, wrote one reformer, "such as this country would never have had if the degeneracy of Germany had not forced us into the war."[91] The enemy's morality squandered was Americans' gained.

IN LATE OCTOBER, WARING began planning a trip to Selma. Though awfully busy—he'd been made Battalion Sergeant Major, a job with lots of paperwork—he felt he "simply *must*" come home. Waring's homesickness and his mother's recurring health problems generated the urgency. He arranged to travel on Friday, November 2. A few days earlier, he wrote a petulant and self-pitying note to his mother about her lack of communication. "I am beginning to believe that you all don't want me to come home," he complained. If she wasn't happy to see her "little boy," he threatened, "he will come right on back to this man's army."[92]

It was a misunderstanding—Waring wrote her again to say a letter had arrived—yet it revealed the fragile state of his sense of belonging. In this note, Waring made a delicate request. Could Carrie Goodwin stay in the family house on Church Street on Friday night? He planned to go visit her on Saturday anyway but wanted to maximize his time with everyone. Lest this look unseemly, he offered to stay in his parents' room. They agreed and Waring spent pleasant days at home. Rather predictably, he saw more of Carrie than his family. Waring returned to discouraging news at Camp Gordon. A friend from Selma named Claiborne Blanton had been given Regimental Sergeant Major, "a great disappointment to me." Yet he remained "right proud" of the warrants certifying his rank, and would send them home for preservation.[93]

Soon after Nellye received that letter, she fell ill again, slowing down her correspondence. Carrie Goodwin visited Nellye and brought some flowers. Waring wrote home on Thanksgiving to say he hoped his mother would come see him once she recuperated.[94]

PART OF THE YMCA's mission to connect doughboy and home was the newsletter *Trench and Camp*, the product of a partnership with newspapers near all National Army, National Guard, and regular army cantonments. These sheets disseminated announcements and news and features of local interest. Military officials, realizing the paper's potential for maintaining ties between camp and home, changed the masthead between the first and second issues from "Army News for Army Men" to "Army News for Army Men and Their Home Folks." Every issue implored trainees to send it home if they didn't have time to write, or even if they did. After all, "Mother Will Like It!"[95] The inaugural issue in October 1917 featured a message from President Wilson demanding there be "no loss of touch between the nation and its soldiers."[96] Commensurate with that purpose, the paper had much to say about the relationship between war and the American family.

Like other voices in American official and quasi-official culture, *Trench and Camp* imagined familial surrogates in the military and affiliated agencies. American families had "loaned their sons" to the government; the YMCA was the soldier's "army mother"; the boys were under the "fostering parental care" of federal authorities.[97] Warriors in the past had suffered through "cheerless yuletides," went a piece on Christmas Eve, but now the efforts of the Quartermaster's Department, as well as wonders of rail and mail, kept the recruit well provisioned with material and emotional succor.[98] The YMCA "makes it possible to hold to the home ideals," providing a place in the camps to write letters, take in films, and practice religion.[99] The army even assumed parents' traditional control over marriage. The post commander at Fort Oglethorpe decreed in December that Lige Dees and other enlisted men must get his permission to marry, lest they fall victim to "wiley women" hungry for a piece of the war insurance pie.[100] By the winter of 1917, *Trench and Camp* essentially had become a weekly salve against home front anxieties. For thousands of families, the Huebners among them, their sons were traveling outside the orbit of community and familial surveillance for the first time.

Doughboys fought, *Trench and Camp* reported, for the benefit and appreciation of the home front family. The minister Dr. Frank Crane wrote that Americans aimed to prevent the "lewd ravisher" from having his way with "our most tenderly reared daughters."[101] More expansively, *Trench and Camp* urged soldiers to visualize an audience for their actions in parents, communities, and future offspring to both make families proud and reflect well on them. "When the war is over, we shall have no apologies to make," went a piece in the Fort Oglethorpe edition at Thanksgiving. "Children can never ask us, doubtfully, what we did in the great war for democracy."[102] Geopolitical goals were relevant, like usual, but the admiration of future generations was the real prize. For morality advocates, as well, ensuring not just the pride but health of those generations superseded the war's other purposes. A poem published in *Trench and Camp* suggested coming back "clean" for one's family trumped battlefield valor:

I may not leave for my children
Brave medals that I have worn,
But the blood in my veins shall leave no stains
On bride or on babes unborn.[103]

In December, a Maj. Wieser encouraged rookies at Fort Oglethorpe to do right by their family members and later "throw out your chest and look them all in the face."[104]

Nothing revealed the purchase of such ideas more vividly than the outcome of a doughboy's cartoon contest in *Trench and Camp*. In late November, the paper awarded the prize wristwatch to a trainee at Camp Logan named Frank Hines. His drawing imagined the Sammy's triumphant return—not before cheering throngs but before his immediate family. Once again, the defeat of German militarism figured conspicuously, but just as vital was "the enthusiasm, joy and admiration of the American people, as typified by one family, over the victory."[105] Home folks gave war purpose.

These features acknowledged no conflict between a soldier's martial and domestic obligations. But when a choice must be made, there was little question which should come first. In October, the Camp Grant edition of *Trench and Camp* printed a photograph of a happy family reunion at the Rockford cantonment immediately above a piece on draftees attempting to sneak home. The image acknowledged the man's durable obligation to family, while the story reminded him of his more important one to the state. Apparently recruits had been lodging an inordinate number of requests for leave to pay last respects, settle financial affairs, or see a loved one. Though many of these invitations were dubious, camp officials accommodated some of them. But what would happen if a rookie insisted on visiting his girlfriend against army regulations? "The price is the most dear a soldier can pay—his life."[106]

"HAVING NOTHING BETTER TO do," the recruit wrote his sweetheart, "I take up my pen to write you."[107] So began the fictional epistolary relationship between the guileless trainee Bill Smith and his girl Mable Gimp of Philopilis, New York. Their creator was Edward Streeter, a Harvard graduate and former reporter for the *Buffalo Express*. In the fall of 1917, Streeter was training at Camp Wadsworth, outside of Spartanburg, South Carolina, with the Twenty-Seventh Division. He introduced Bill and Mable in the divisional newsletter, *Gas Attack*, and in the summer of 1918, gathered the columns into a bestselling book called *Dere Mable: Love Letters of a Rookie*. Others ended up in a second volume published in early 1919, *"That's Me All Over, Mable,"* and a third called *"Same Old Bill, Eh Mable!"* the summer after the war ended. Meanwhile, an author named Florence Elizabeth Summers published Mable's replies as *Dere Bill: Mable's Love Letters to Her Rookie* (1919). Apparently she sent the drafts to Streeter in France for his approval.[108]

Streeter shared his contemporaries' inclination to render the Great War in personal terms, though with more satirical edge than almost anyone else in American popular culture. That his *Dere Mable* sold so many copies suggested a public appetite for this rather less sanguine and considerably funnier look at what war did to love. Streeter covered the tensions of separation—jealousy, heartache, financial stress, and the widening gap in experience between soldiers and their families.

Bill's letters of December 1917 charted his drift from civilian life. He soaked up a bit of French, learned military tactics and jargon, and earned the affection of girls near the camp. Mable shouldn't bother feeling jealous or angry. "Couldn't help meeting them," he wrote of women at a dance in Spartanburg. "They just crowded around me."[109] He got mail from girls he didn't know, just as real soldiers in the encampments corresponded with surrogates. "I would have wrote sooner," the fictional Bill explained, "but I had to answer a couple of letters from some strange women who keep writing to me wanting to adopt me. I ain't accepted their offers yet, on account of you, but I wrote for their photographs."[110] Mable was neither passive victim nor patient waiter, as audiences later learned from *Dere Bill*. "I better close," she wrote, "as a bunch of fellos said they was comin about eight an its most seven-thirty, an I got to dress."[111]

In *Gas Attack*'s last issue of the year, with a wounded French child and doting American on the cover, Bill reported his reduction from corporal to private, just like the Marine Thomas Boyd, though Bill's crime was a messy tent. He closed with New Year's greetings and nudged Mable again about a flashlight he wished she'd given him for Christmas.[112]

"WITH CHRISTMAS TREES ABLAZE with light and color; with a plentiful supply of . . . confections, and with friendliness and good cheer truly typical of the season, soldiers at Camp Gordon spent the last night of their 38-hour holiday at the camp making merry in the various civilian organizations on the reservation." So went the festivities of December 25, 1917, reported the *Atlanta Constitution*, on a day that saw domestic rituals recreated in camp and city. Four thousand men in the Eighty-Second Division traveled out to private dwellings in a program arranged by the newspaper. For those remaining on the base, the YMCA's dinner was best, the *Constitution* reported—turkey, cranberries, celery, olives, potatoes, macaroni, layer cake, and candies.

The day after Christmas, rifles were back on shoulders in preparation for the "grim task" awaiting the men in France.[113] Waring's mind was elsewhere, however. On December 27, he asked for a pass home. "The reason for this request," he wrote, "is that my Mother is ill in Selma, Ala."[114]

THE RECRUITS AT CAMP Grant shivered in their barracks that winter, though Clayton Slack recalled, "two hundred men make quite a bit of heat."[115] The men of his 331st Machine Gun Battalion also warmed themselves with outdoor activity. After the New Year, they built a snow slide at the camp (figure 3.2).

FIGURE 3.2 The 331st Machine Gun Battalion builds a ski and toboggan slide at Camp Grant, January 25, 1918. Arthur Huebner may be somewhere in the photograph. Charles R. Reuber Collection, Wisconsin Veterans Museum.

North Georgia was cold, too. Over the winter at Fort Oglethorpe, Lige's Fifty-Third Infantry Regiment trained for overseas service and heard lectures on beating the Germans from French and British authorities.[116] At Christmastime, *Trench and Camp* looked forward to a future holiday season of peace. What would be the true reward for victory? "Home will be a thing achieved!"[117] The paper didn't explain exactly what it meant by this, but perhaps it didn't have to. Back in Wayne County, Missouri, the Greenville newspaper kept vigil over everyday things as well as the world situation. In a single edition in early December, the *Sun* reported that Mae Bilbrey's sister had measles and called for volunteers to defend the Mississippi should the Germans "come knocking."[118]

Something drove a wedge between Mae and Lige at year's end. Her first note after the long gap in correspondence gives some hints. "If I said anything in my last letter to worry you or hurt you," she wrote in March, "I am truly sorry." She admitted that she had treated Lige badly, that she'd gone with other boys (one of whom Lige knew and was now in France), and that she'd failed to write letters.[119] Here Mae had violated prescriptive rhetoric on war and love—*write your soldier boy, or he will think the worst.* A piece in Arthur's hometown *Watertown Daily Times* declared it a woman's duty to keep the doughboy stocked with letters. To do otherwise would sow doubt about "the sincerity and faith of continued friendship he placed in you."[120]

Mae's actions had led Lige to think her "ashamed" of him, which she promised was nonsense. "I have always been proud of you ever since you became a soldier more than ever," Mae wrote. Lige's martial character gratified her because it put him "above a few people who have treated you so bad and acted so smart." As for the other fellows, she reassured Lige he was the "first boy that I ever counted as my lover." She said *first*, not *only*, and in fact implied she'd gone with other men recently "because I thought you wasn't true to me."[121]

Edward Streeter's fictional Bill and Mable were mired in comparable difficulties. Amid concerns about Mable's drifting attention, Bill gave her a gift:

> I'm sending you my picture in a uniform pointing to an American flag. It's kind of symbolical the man said, if you know what that is. I thought you'd like to put it on the mantle in a conspikuus place so as to have something to be proud of when your girl friends come in to talk.[122]

Would this stabilize Mable's affections, soothe her sadness over Bill's absence, or impress her peers? However comforting the picture may have been, it didn't stop Mable from talking in her letters about a fellow named Broggins. Bill assumed any men left at home were alien enemies or slackers. He pledged if he ever caught someone "winding your victrola" or "shinin his elbos on the top of your baby grand" he'd kick him out of the house. There are plenty of girls waiting for me, he reminded Mable.[123] In February, Bill warned her off Broggins again, the author Streeter exposing the ironies of the war's chivalric foundations. "It aint askin much with me down here defendin you," Bill reasoned. "Although I dont see why I had to come down here to do it."[124]

Finally, Bill heard that Mable took Broggins everywhere she went. One informant arrived at Mable's house to witness Broggins sitting on her lap, sticking his tongue out at Bill's picture on the mantle. Even worse, this man surely was a member of the "Home Defense" and therefore no man at all. "Are you going to have a military weddin," Bill sneered. He instructed her to burn the photo of him with the flag and stop her letters. "Its no use writin any more," he vowed, "cause Im firm as the rock of Gibber Alter. Concrete. That's me all over, Mable."[125]

In Missouri, Mae Bilbrey was ready to put such troubles behind her. Whatever liaisons had occurred during the separation, "there was never any body that could take your place." These were new obstacles in a long history of people trying to separate them, Mae remembered, incorporating the war into a broader narrative of embattlement and love. "When this horrid war is over," Mae wrote, she'd be waiting for him. George Cohan's "Over There" evoked the two impulses of her letter:

Tell your sweetheart not to pine,
To be proud her boy's in line.[126]

In her inability to meet the first directive but acceptance of the second, Mae captured the tension at the heart of wartime love. Though she perceived personal virtue in Lige's military service, that didn't begin to mitigate the strain on her emotional resources. "I would be a happy little girl," Mae wrote, "if I could only have you back again and see you look at me with those blue eyes."[127]

ON THE FIRST DAY of 1918, Waring Huston left Alabama after a furlough at home, the local paper reporting that day on a German air raid in Italy that killed scores of women and children.[128] In Selma, Nellye was fine. Whatever had been ailing her had subsided enough for him to enjoy his visit. His train left Montgomery late and it was almost four o'clock when he arrived at the camp. He pulled off his leggings and shoes and collapsed in bed for an hour's sleep. The next day brought snow to Atlanta. By the afternoon, when Waring sat down to write his mother, everything was covered. He found it pretty but was a "sad-bird," uncertain and lonely. He still hadn't heard about the officer training camp. His Selma buddy Blanton felt sure they'd get in, but what did he know. Waring signed the note and put it down to send in the morning.[129]

Sometime that night, Waring pulled out the letter and in a bigger hand added a postscript: "I AM GOING TO THE TRAINING CAMP." Two days later, he packed up to move over to the corner of Camp Gordon where the new officers would be trained. "I <u>must</u> have a commission," he wrote the night of January 4, "and am going to get one if possible."[130] Waring's new quarters had sheets and a mattress but no blankets. Between January and April, he shot at the range, fought mock trench battles, trained with gas masks, and bummed around Atlanta. He accumulated debts to his father to buy stamps. His mother Nellye sent him cakes and candies.[131]

On March 7, Pressley Cleveland wrote Nellye from France. Press's Rainbow Division was training with the French near the front, but the Selmian had prosaic things on his mind. He had read about Nellye's illness in the newspaper and hoped she'd improved. Pressley's letters to Waring were going unanswered, but he had heard a rumor his friend was "contemplating leaving me pretty soon," which presumably meant marriage. Pressley sure wished he could be "present at the event." What really bothered him, though, was his own romantic problem. For two months he had gone without letters from his sweetheart. Maybe they were lost. But he chided Nellye for somehow failing to put in a word for him back home. "You people should look out for my interests a little," he scolded, "and not let me lose every thing while I am away." Press backtracked a bit with some kind words, and assured Nellye that others in the "Selma bunch" over there were getting on fine.[132]

In late March, Nellye received a letter from Camp Gordon, but it wasn't from Waring. The mother of a young recruit in his regiment had been incessantly writing her son to come home. When he made the illegal trip, the chaplain of the 325th Infantry sent a stern letter to the families of all his charges. The young man might be shot as a deserter for misunderstanding his obligations. Mothers must keep the doughboy's spirits high: "We shall be fighting for you, and we must fight with a will if our lives are to be saved and our cause to be won. So put the sunshine in your letters."[133]

About a week later, Waring gloomily reported he'd be returning to his 325th Infantry without a commission, though candidates would be eligible for them in France. On April 9, Waring wrote that his division would be leaving shortly for Camp Upton, New York. France would be next. He was terribly blue. He had been trying for weeks to finagle a trip home but it never worked out. Waring went to Atlanta to mail home two packages of letters he'd received that he wanted kept. Around lunchtime the next day, April 10, he wired his mother to tell her the 325th would be departing the South at four o'clock.[134]

IN THE EARLY DAYS of March 1918, Arthur Huebner's younger brother Carl went with his mother Louise to run an errand on Main Street in Watertown. During the journey, Louise suffered a stroke and collapsed. She died on March 7. What nine-year-old Carl thought is impossible to know, as he revealed little about it the rest of his life. Arthur received word at Camp Grant of his mother's death and made arrangements to travel home to Wisconsin for the funeral.[135]

The occasion of Arthur's visit allowed the Huebners to gather for photographs at the family house on Eighth Street in Watertown, something businesses urged families to do if they could. "Have a Family Group Picture Taken," read an ad in the *Watertown News*, "Before the Boy Leaves for the Front."[136] In one shot, Arthur stands with his three brothers, Otto, Carl, and fourteen-year-old Walter (figure 3.3).

FIGURE 3.3 Arthur, Otto, Walter, and Carl (in front) at their mother's funeral, March 1918. Author's collection.

The image of Arthur brings to mind what a historian of the Great War wrote many years later: "In thousands of family albums there is a photograph of a young man standing somewhat uncomfortably in uniform—broad-brimmed, peaked campaign hat, high-collar olive drab blouse and trousers with the unsightly and bothersome wrap leggings. He is saluting or awkwardly holding a rifle. Obviously he is a recruit."[137] Arthur's brothers here, especially the younger ones, appear uncomfortable and stiff in the uniforms required of the day. However melancholy that event may have been, family memories convey that Walter and Carl cherished the presence of their soldier-brother.[138] A Camp Grant edition of *Trench and Camp* ran a cartoon on just this sort of brotherly pride, picturing a youngster walking with his doughboy sibling and basking in "The Thrill That Comes Once in a Lifetime."[139]

IT MAY HAVE BEEN Mae's plea to look into his blue eyes again. Lige left Camp Forrest for home around the moment Arthur buried his mother in Wisconsin. Whether Mae's letter of March 8 could have reached Lige in time to spur his visit is uncertain. On Wednesday, March 13, 1918, before a justice of the peace in Greenville, Missouri, the couple eloped.[140]

By all indications this was a spur-of-the-moment decision. In that letter of March 8, Mae said nothing of an impending marriage. Lige likely failed to ask his commanding officer for permission to marry. "I will try and find out what they are going to do with me I don't know if they can do much or not But I had to tell a lie about it," he wrote with his usual allergy to punctuation. According to Mae's sister Clara, the news shocked her family. Her mother cried all day and swore she never wanted to see Mae again. Her father was stunned into silence. Rather quickly, both thought better of it and invited Mae to call on them. Her father's initial objection, after all, had been Mae's youth. She accepted the invitation, but her tolerance for interference had run out: "I think I'll go home Sat. and if they get mad and quarrel at me I never will go anymore."[141] It seems Mae boarded in Williamsville while she attended high school there. Her parents lived close enough for visits.

Edward Streeter's imaginary Bill and Mable reconciled around the time Mae and Lige married. On March 2, 1918, readers of *Gas Attack* learned the Broggins business had been a misunderstanding. Mable could send back all his stuff, Bill said, and put his photo back on the mantle if she hadn't burned it. But what of her lap-sitting, tongue-wagging beau? "How was I to know Broggins was a dog?" Bill began his letter that day.[142] Mable regretted Bill had spent so many sleepless nights thinking a home front slacker was "stickin his tongue out at your picture."[143]

Lige left Missouri on Friday, March 15. The next night, Mae's sadness and distraction nearly killed her. At some point in the evening, in the room of her friend and fellow boarder Etta, Mae sipped from a bucket of lye, used for washing, mistaking it for water. Mae drank grease to soothe her stomach but still vomited all night, drifting in and out of consciousness. She recovered enough to notice and resent Lige's failure to write quickly. People in Williamsville, who by Mae's accounting loved to torment her, put doubts in her head. A girl named Nellie, erstwhile enemy of Mae's, spread rumors Lige had married a Red Cross girl in France. Even Etta taunted her about the unreliability of regular army men: " 'I told you that you didn't know anything about a soldier and that you couldn't trust one.' " Mae could barely take the harassment. "[Y]ou don't know how I feel and how anxious I am to hear from you," Mae wrote Lige, "or you would have written to me as soon as you got back."[144]

Apparently their letters passed each other in the mail. His began, "Dear wife, I will drop you a few lines as I have nothing else to do." Lige asked for their marriage certificate so he could send the allotment payments mandated by the War Risk Insurance Act of 1917. "Be sure and ans[wer] soon for I want to hear from you and be sure and send that [certificate]."[145] Lige's mood darkened a couple weeks later. First, he had a terrible headache and cold at a time when 10 percent of the soldiers at Camp Forrest were sick with a nasty influenza virus that was likely to have migrated south from Camp Funston in Kansas.[146] Second, Mae disclosed she was thinking of earning money by "keeping house" for a man named Ed. Lige prohibited this as long as she intended to stay with him. "[H]ell no you must be crazy," he wrote the evening of April 2, "to think of such for when you keep house it will be for me unless I die then you can talk about keeping house for someone else ask him where his wife is that he don't get her to keep house for him." Perhaps to clinch his martyrdom, Lige reminded Mae of her allotment payments and the thousand dollars' worth of life insurance coming her way so she could "live happily if I get kilt."[147]

Fears of that prospect terrorized Mae's sleep. "I dreamed that you had to sail and that a submarine sunk your ship," she wrote on April 11. "I can see you drown so plain and your face so cold and white." Her waking hours proved just as upsetting. That morning, Mae's history teacher, Mr. Davidson, had taught a lesson on "America in the Trenches." *Can you define pillboxes and camouflage?* he asked Mae. She was so depressed she didn't respond, and her classmates laughed at her. Meantime another teacher led the class in a rendition of "A Soldier's Farewell":

Goodbye, sweetheart darling, I'm off to a foreign land,
Columbia calls her sons to go and fight a tyrant band.[148]

Mae barely kept her composure. The teacher noticed and apologized.[149] For a serviceman's wife, anthems of wartime culture bore considerable power. Even more difficult for Mae was a lecture she attended by a former prisoner of war. She was terrified Lige would end up in German hands.[150]

Over the next couple of weeks, Mae and Lige both confessed to frequent crying. But their sadness coexisted with firm belief in the fight. In one of the couple's few statements of this sort, Mae wrote on April 18 of their agreement that "God will guide us and victory will be ours." Following broader patterns in contemporary public culture, it was *victory* rather than *cause* that inspired the young woman. And bleaker thoughts were never far away. "But how long must we wait?" Mae continued. "It makes me heartsick to think of it all, I want you so much." Though she left the details mysterious, apparently another woman had tried to "take my dada away from me"—Mae often called Lige "dada"—but at least in this case she trusted him and wasn't worried.[151]

In the beginning of May, Lige casually mentioned to his wife that his unit was moving to Camp Wadsworth, South Carolina, the current training ground of Edward Streeter and the Twenty-Seventh Division.[152] From there he would continue to keep up his end of the couple's long-distance romance.

"THE SWEETEST LOVE STORY ever told."[153] So did the entertainment trade magazine *Variety* announce the debut of D. W. Griffith's new war picture, *Hearts of the World*, on March 29, 1918. The film had opened two weeks earlier to enormous throngs, eventually becoming the most popular film of the war.[154] Its promotional material showed a pitiless German soldier whipping a prone woman.

Hearts of the World presented the tale of Girl and Boy, two Americans living in a French village. When war comes, he fights with the French. Griffith works hard to establish her purity. "With white thread and whiter dreams," reads one intertitle, "she works on her wedding dress." After battlefield dramas, the couple is reunited, but not before repugnant Germans terrorize women and children and nearly rape Girl. Americans come to save the day, a pleasing message in a film intended to rally public opinion in the United States. The film closes with a thorough visual conflation of family and nation: Boy and Girl, clutching American flags, surrounded by a halo of light. The scene invited viewers to venerate an almost holy montage of associated virtues—love, patriotism, piety. Other pictures of the day echoed the threats Germany posed to all this: *The Unbeliever, To Hell with the Kaiser, Stake Uncle Sam to Play Your Hand, The Heart of Humanity*, and *The Kaiser, Beast of Berlin*. The Four-Minute Men, dispatched by the Committee on Public Information (CPI) to movie houses and other public gatherings to explain the war, likewise leaned on atrocity stories to make their case, and the agency had just begun circulating a pamphlet on "German War Practices" that boiled the enemy's military policy down to its emotional core: "frightfulness."[155]

More introspective voices continued to acknowledge how difficult, though not impossible, it was for families to find redemptive meaning in war. As *Hearts of the World* opened, the *New York Times* reviewed two books: W. J. Dawson's *The Father of a Soldier* and Richardson Wright's *Letters to the Mother of a Soldier*. Both volumes dealt with the "universal and harrowing experience" of having a son in the military. Fear so consumed Dawson when his sons enlisted that he could barely function. "I was afraid because I loved," he wrote. The mother in Wright's account worried her boy would come back "changed and hard." Even the authors of emotionally honest works, though, eventually found their way to the Great War's regenerative potential. "I saw War revealed as a constructive force," wrote Dawson, a "clean flame" burning away decadence and selfishness. To give his sons was an honor. Wright describes the mother in his story after losing her boy: "Courage picks up her burden after Death has passed, and she carries it on, tireless, unreluctant, her eyes fixed upon the horizon."[156] The identical transition from pain to understanding marked *Over Here* and *Silver Lining*, two accounts of soldiers' brides published in 1918.[157] For the women in both stories, optimism defeats worry. In *Over Here*, released soon after *Hearts of the World*, even the death of Elizabeth's new husband and the father of her unborn child doesn't diminish her patriotic mettle, her willingness to sacrifice family for nation and to honor both without conflict. *Silver Lining*, as its title suggests, delivered a comparable moral. Americans looking to public culture for models of emotional comportment, when they confronted heartbreak at all, found it moderated by resolve.

TO REACH BATTLE STRENGTH, the Thirty-Third "Prairie" Division needed men. It was a federalized National Guard division anchored by Illinois units, training at Camp Logan in Houston, Texas, the cantonment whose construction site the black Twenty-Fourth Infantry had been guarding before the terrible violence of August 1917. In November of that year, the Adjutant General of the Army had ordered the Thirty-Third to sail for France, and transferred almost six thousand recruits from Arthur's Eighty-Sixth Division to make it happen. But too many of these men had been "discards"—alien enemies, illiterates, the physically unfit. Shortages of equipment had hindered training. In April 1918, the Thirty-Third finally received replacements it had been promised. Among them were Arthur Huebner, Ben Fluegel, Clayton Slack, and Daniel McCarthy.[158] Back home in Wisconsin, a Liberty Loan advertisement in the *Watertown News* asked readers to imagine their sons in the trenches. "Lend Him a Hand! Here is your Boy— going over the top." It was rather vague on what the war was about, but very specific on who this boy was: "*your son—your husband—your brother—your friend*." Similar appeals drove Selmians to buy bonds beyond their quota.[159]

The Wisconsin boys stepped off the train in Houston to what Clayton Slack remembered as unbearable heat. A screw-up along the line had the transplants outfitted in heavy uniforms and underwear, and a few fainted on the march to their barracks. In Slack's recollection, National Guardsmen in the Thirty-Third were condescending toward recruits from Camp Grant, even though in his unsurprising estimation the draftee transfers were the better soldiers.[160] To determine their place in the division, Huebner, Slack, McCarthy, and Fluegel underwent physical examinations and intensive daily training.[161] By the end of April, all four had been assigned to the six-month-old 124th Machine Gun Battalion. At full strength, the unit had 750 enlisted men and thirty officers.[162]

Even as the Thirty-Third Division frantically incorporated these late arrivals, it was ordered to proceed to Camp Upton, in Yaphank, New York, halfway out on Long Island.[163]

WARING HUSTON WAS ALREADY there. He had left the South by rail on April 10, sharing a stateroom with Blanton on the Pullman and enjoying the scenery and hot meals cooked in the baggage car.[164] In Philadelphia the men marched around to stretch their legs. After a ferry ride from Jersey City to Brooklyn, another train delivered the men to Yaphank near midnight on the twelfth. Snowy, cold weather greeted the men. Waring's comrade in the 325th Infantry, Fred Takes, wrote in his diary that no one had proper covers and no one slept.[165]

Camp Upton invited low opinions. *Barren* and *ugly* came to mind when a Connecticut trainee thought about it later. It could be dusty or muddy and had a warm-weather mosquito problem. The 325th's commander, Col. Walter Whitman, recalled "ten disagreeable days" spent there. Waring suffered a cold and wisdom tooth pain.[166] He had to calm his mother's jealousy over the number of letters he wrote Carrie Goodwin compared to the number he wrote her.[167]

Simmering racial friction added to Camp Upton's tense atmosphere. The trouble had started weeks earlier and fourteen hundred miles away, at Camp Funston in Kansas, headquarters of the black Ninety-Second Division. L. E. Mathis, an African American sergeant stationed there, had traveled to Manhattan, Kansas, to see a show. The theater owner refused Mathis service. In a fury he reported the incident to Charles Ballou, the white divisional commander. Ballou sided with the theater proprietor. It was the black soldier's responsibility, he claimed, not to provoke "a conflict of races" and jeopardize divisional effectiveness and racial progress. In a blow to the masculine dignity of all men in the

Ninety-Second, Ballou translated his views into an order called Bulletin No. 35:

> Avoid every situation that can give rise to racial ill-will. Attend quietly and faithfully to your duties, and don't go where your presence is not desired. . . . White men made the Division, and they can break it just as easily if it becomes a trouble maker.

The directive went out to the far-flung training grounds of the Ninety-Second Division. Black soldiers erupted in reaction, ripping down the order at Camp Upton. The black press assailed Ballou's action, bristling at the suggestion that uniformed people of color should forfeit their "manhood rights." A large protest meeting in New York issued a resolution demanding black doughboys be granted "proper dignity appertaining to their manhood."[168]

Waring arrived in the thick of this controversy. He confided to his mother that some boys in the Eighty-Second clashed with the "'nigger' officers up here," using the epithet that came so easily to southern lips and which the army actually had tried unsuccessfully to ban.[169] A couple of Waring's acquaintances refused to salute African American officers, who reacted with rage. One white soldier "left the officer standing in the road hollering for him to come back," Waring wrote with approval. In a different regiment, he reported, a white man knocked a black officer cold.[170] It was clear how these Dixie boys ordered their obligations to race and nation, how their racial views trumped military protocol, how they policed access to masculine, martial authority. Similar things happened almost everywhere black officers demanded respect from whites.[171]

On April 23, 1918, Waring wrote his last letter before the crossing. His face was swollen from having his tooth lanced. He had lots to tell but little time, so it would have to wait until he returned. He counseled his mother not to worry. If she didn't hear from him it would probably be the mail. He hoped to please his parents. "Oh! Well I hope Mama darling that you and Papa will have a son that you can sure 'nuff be proud of," he wrote. "I am going to do my best."[172] Two days later, the 325th traveled to New York City, and after some technical problems with the first vessel, boarded the British *Khyber*. They set sail on April 25.[173]

On May 3, Lige departed Georgia. In his last message to Mae from Camp Forrest, a Western Union telegram, Lige tried to govern his wife's expectations:

> I have written you today I am leaving here today but I will write you again Sunday and don't be so blue as I will write as often as I can, so look for a letter most anytime.

The destination of the Fifty-Third Infantry and Sixth Division was Camp Wadsworth, former home of Edward Streeter and celebrity musicians Noble Sissle and James Reese Europe.[174] After a terribly cold winter, Wadsworth was now hot and dusty.[175]

Lige's first day at camp was the newsletter *Gas Attack*'s last. May 4, 1918, saw the publication of the final "Dere Mable" column. Edward Streeter's Twenty-Seventh Division would soon be on its way to France.[176] If Lige read *Gas Attack* that day, he would have found Bill planning a furlough home to Philopilis and expecting Mable would want him to marry her. Streeter refused to sugarcoat the tragic possibilities. Lige would have appreciated Bill's bluntness though he had come to a different decision about marriage. "I guess you know I would [marry you] if I had time," Bill assured Mable. "Besides I dont believe in gettin married before the war cause like as not Ill be killed. I don't want you to worry though or nothing like that."[177]

Beginning on May 6, Arthur Huebner's 124th Machine Gun Battalion traveled by rail from Texas to New York. Over two days, the train took Arthur through the Deep South and mid-Atlantic, past New York City and out to Camp Upton, where he missed Waring Huston by two weeks. Clayton Slack enjoyed seeing the country. He remembered the 124th bunking in crowded sleeper cars and eating hardtack for the first time. The men stayed at Camp Upton about a week. Marching and hiking kept them in good shape. They did no additional military training. The Vickers machine guns they would be using in France finally arrived, though the men were too busy preparing for departure to fire them. The 124th stayed in Yaphank until the evening of May 15, when Arthur packed up his New Testament and Book of Psalms and other possessions. That day, in his hometown in Wisconsin, papers asked readers to recognize Mother's Day by contributing to the Red Cross's campaign of parental surrogacy: "Give Watertown Soldier Boys a Mother's Care."[178]

Arthur Huebner spent his last night in America on the move, traveling sixty-five miles by rail and ferry from Camp Upton to Hoboken, New Jersey. As the sun rose on the cool, fair morning of May 16, five thousand groggy soldiers of the Thirty-Third Division assembled on the piers at Hoboken.[179] With lumbering movements, Arthur and the men from Wisconsin and Illinois and other places boarded a troop transport bound for France.

4

The Yanks Are Coming

THE JOURNEY THAT BROUGHT Waring Huston before the King and Queen of the British Empire began on the morning of April 25, 1918, when the ship *Khyber* sailed from New York. It steamed past Sandy Hook, New Jersey, and joined a convoy led by the seized German vessel *Vaterland*, one of the largest passenger ships in the world. Out in the Atlantic, the soldiers' days settled into a routine of emergency drills and watch duty. Some squeezed into narrow bunks and others slept in hammocks. For three stormy days, waves battered the small fleet and churned stomachs in Waring's 325th Infantry Regiment. The more seaworthy doughboy Knud Olsen, a Danish immigrant, remembered cleaning up vomit as punishment for allegedly falling asleep on watch. As the convoy neared Europe, British officers prohibited lights on board. (To speed up the Americans' arrival, British ships transported almost half of them to Europe.) Early on the morning of May 6, destroyers from the United Kingdom guided the boats through the most dangerous waters of the journey, the *Khyber* enveloped in a smoke screen thrown across its bow. At Liverpool, one dead man and eight sick ones came ashore.[1]

On May 8, Col. Walter Whitman heard the 325th Infantry had been selected to parade before King George V, a ritual of gratitude marking the opening stages of a 1,600,000-doughboy surge between April and

October.[2] The men disembarked, walked a mile to a train station, traveled by rail to Winchester, and hiked three miles to camp. Over two days they drilled, washed, and prepared for the review.[3] In Selma, Waring's family received a telegram reading, "I have arrived safely overseas." In an unintentionally meaningful error, the typed signature described his imminent condition: "Warring."[4]

The men awoke early on May 11 and were in London by eight. They hiked to Wellington Barracks under a bright sun and blue sky flecked with clouds. After tea and sandwiches, Waring and his comrades filed out for a three-mile tour of London. From a window at the War Office, Prime Minister Lloyd George peered down at the procession. It passed the American embassy, thousands of Londoners lining the route. At Buckingham Palace, King George gestured to Whitman to join him. The doughboys turned eyes left to see the royal family. They returned to the barracks at 1:15 for ginger ale, chocolate, buns, and cakes stuffed with meat and eggs. Back in Winchester, the farm boy Fred Takes wrote in his diary of blistered feet and exhausted men.[5]

The British press heralded these specimens of chivalric white manliness, the three interlocking virtues of character, race, and gender critical to the American wartime self-image. The march of the 325th signaled collaboration between the world's two great "English-speaking races," reported the *London Times*. Britons welcomed them as blood brothers and cousins. The American soldiers, paragons of *manhood*, were *tall, clean-shaven, sturdy, gallant, workmanlike*. Newspaper readers in Selma, Alabama, and Watertown, Wisconsin, consumed praise of the men's physical bearing. They were *husky*, in the *pink of condition, eyes straight ahead*, possessed impressive *physiques*, and made up a *fine looking body*. A London bystander told a reporter, "When Kaiser Bill sees that little lot coming over, he won't be half sorry he sank the Lusitania, eh, wot?"[6]

As these testimonials suggest, the most profound gesture of appreciation the British could muster was to regard the Americans as family men. They were just boys stationed far from family and camp. As the *Star* of London put it, in language reprinted in the *New York Times*,

London is a shy old lady, but today she is throwing her bonnet in the air. She is not staring at the American boys, like a stepmother; she is taking them into her arms, like a mother. Their own mothers will be comforted when they hear how London has hugged these gallant American boys.[7]

Imbuing London with motherly compassion implied a new surrogate parent for the doughboy. The United States shared with Britain, France, and other nations this patriotic maternal symbolism, with "dame Columbia" and "Lady Liberty" joining "Britannia" and "Marianne" as female embodiments of nation.[8] Men at arms in those countries imbibed appeals to put the symbolic and literal protection of women at the heart of their understanding of war. But feminizing the nation carried disciplinary as well as motivational power. The London newspaper invited Americans to consider "every British mother his mother, every British girl his sister."[9] The first part offered warmth, the second warning. Of course this message aligned with official American hopes for soldierly restraint, although the Yankee reformers' version of the morality tale usually cast the doughboy as innocent and the British (and more so, French) woman as threat.[10]

After parading in London, men in the 325th Infantry awoke at 4:45 a.m., ate sandwiches, and went by train to the coast at Southampton. Overnight, they steamed across the channel for Le Havre, France. Cold, wet conditions shrouded the seashore as day broke.[11] From France, Waring Huston had a moment to write his mother. He gave the news about passing in review before the royal family, which they could see in theater newsreels. Waring and the other sergeant majors would be visible right behind the mounted staff. "Wish you could see this country, it is beautiful," he wrote of France. "[S]till I would rather be in good 'old' Selma."[12]

THE CONFISCATED SHIP *VATERLAND* owed its construction to the ocean liner battle between Germany and Britain. That struggle for technological and commercial mastery had escalated in 1907 when the Germans unveiled the extravagant *Kronprinzessin Cecilie*, one of four "Kaiser class" vessels commissioned by North German Lloyd, the company whose ship the *Fulda* had brought Christian Huebner to America in the 1880s. The British Cunard Line answered with the *Lusitania*. Britain's craft was bigger and faster, reported the American press, but the German one offered the poshest comforts. Together they comprised the grandest means of transportation in human history. "For Size, Speed, and Equipment," the *New York Times* marveled in August 1907, "the Lusitania and Kronprinzessin Cecilie Never Before Equalled."[13] Four years later, the Germans launched the massive *Vaterland*.

The *Kronprinzessin Cecilie* was on its way from America to Europe in August 1914 when it received wireless news of hostilities. Fearing seizure by the French, the German vessel made a ponderous u-turn. The move put the moon on the wrong side of the ship and passengers in a state of worry. After steaming back to the States, the *Cecilie* docked in Maine to wait things out.[14] In May 1915, a German U-boat sunk the *Lusitania* off the coast of Ireland, killing twelve hundred people. With the war declaration of April 1917, the navy seized the *Kronprinzessin Cecilie* and renamed it the *Mount Vernon*. The same thing happened to the *Vaterland*, moored in the United States for three years until recommissioned in 1917 as the *Leviathan*. Vessels that had carried Germans to America began ferrying Americans to fight Germany.

On May 16, 1918, Arthur Huebner boarded the *Mount Vernon* in Hoboken. Five thousand soldiers in the Thirty-Third Division crowded onto the ship. Clayton Slack recalled they exceeded the boat's capacity by fifteen hundred. Several hours later, the *Mount Vernon* passed the Statue of Liberty.[15] There was so little room that Clayton and Arthur had to sleep on open decks without blankets. Dusk meant lights out, though the chaplain of the 124th, C. M. Finnell, showed movies down below. On May 23, destroyers came out from Brest, France, to usher in the convoy. The harbor was clogged with seventy thousand men waiting to disembark. Somewhere in the jumble were units of Edward Streeter's Twenty-Seventh Division.[16] "Were on a German boat," Streeter had the imaginary Bill write. "I bet it makes them sore Mable to see one of there own boats bringin over fellos like me."[17] Before departing, Streeter had deposited half his columns with the publishing house of Frederick A. Stokes, which released them in 1918 as the bestseller *Dere Mable*.[18]

Arthur waited two days before coming ashore in seedy Brest. Patrolmen beat up so many Americans seeking sex and drink that surgeons at the naval hospital demanded they wrap their clubs with soft cord.[19] These skirmishes were part of Gen. John Pershing's campaign to educate, coerce, or cure the curious doughboy. After Saint-Nazaire in late 1917, he had placed brothels off limits or shut them down, held commanders responsible for unit behavior, and required the reporting of disease rates to General Headquarters. In Brest, commanders forbade Americans from being seen with local women, reflecting suspicions about soldiers' intentions as well as Frenchwomen's. The YMCA erected huts to provide recreational alternatives. When these measures failed to stop sexual traffic, the army lodged prophylactic centers in every regiment. Pershing was determined to field an uncompromised force and reassure American mothers of their sons' virtue. He vowed never to let a man return home with symptoms of moral failure.[20]

The men of Arthur Huebner's 124th Machine Gun Battalion, in the meantime, developed their own sexualized way of seeing war. They spun a revenge fantasy suited to the Hun's allegedly lustful character, vowing to deliver a retributive blow to his manhood. A chanted ditty promised to hit Wilhelm where it hurt: "We'll circumcise the Kaiser with a piece of broken glass; And stick a rusty bayonet right up the bastard's ass!"[21]

THE RAIN SET A dreary backdrop for Waring Huston's landing at Le Havre. Throngs of hungry, ill-clothed children dotted the route through the city and up a hill to a British camp. The hosts took away the 325th's clothing and rifles and replaced them with their own Enfields. After making the Americans march five miles for gas masks, the British commander pronounced Col. Whitman's unit lacking "click." After two days the men marched back to Le Havre, sustained only by a thick cracker, cheese, and raisins. On May 15, the Americans embarked on a train journey to a place called Eu. From there, they broke up by battalion for a month of training with the British, part of a scattering of the Eighty-Second Division in towns west of Abbeville. The countryside echoed with shouts of "In—Out—On Guard!" as the doughboys drilled with bayonets.[22] Sgt. Alvin York of Tennessee recalled being inspected by British Field Marshal Douglas Haig and Gen. Pershing. His comrades in the Eighty-Second knew more about hunting women, he said, than he knew about hunting coon and fox.[23]

Waring often wrote his folks and Carrie Goodwin. Their letters reached him about a month after leaving the States. He assured them he was comfortable and fine and sleeping in horse stalls. He asked after Papa's allotment payment, reported he was broke, and harbored no hope of retrieving his clothing. There was no telling when he and Claiborne

Blanton would get commissions. As for the war, "I don't know how the battles are coming out," he wrote on June 5 by lantern light in his tent, on a table made of boxes, "and couldn't tell you if I did." The same day, Waring took his first real bath since leaving Camp Upton. It had been about forty days.[24]

The unit was close enough to Abbeville to perceive its bombardment. Waring, although committed to promoting vicarious familiarity with his suffering, didn't want his parents to worry and knew censors watched for revealing content. So he avoided graphic revelation, restricting his account of the violence to, "[we] are about used to bombardments now as we have witnessed some few."[25] Fred Takes, writing more freely in his diary, described the same events:

> May 20, Monday—There was another big bombardment at Abbeyville last night. The explosions woke me up at 11 P.M. It kept up for a half hour. Then quit and at 1 A.M. it started again and lasted a half hour. Around 2 A.M. it started again for a half hour. It sounded like war. Some of the shots shook our billet. I got up and looked out of the door and saw the flash of light from the bombs exploding and the flash of the shells breaking up in the sky at the Jerry planes and the streak of light thrown in the sky to find the plane. It reminded me of lightning far off on a warm night. The dogs of the village were all barking and all the people were up and outside, some crying. There was a great roar while the firing was going on. It sounded just like a big storm was coming. That made a person think of war and its effects.[26]

Waring preferred to devote his attention to predictions: "The Americans are giving them ____ and when a few more of us get there we will finish the job."[27] Yet his self-censored bravado did nothing to mitigate his isolation from family and desperate desire to be remembered.

He felt most forgotten at night. After his birthday on June 1, Waring asked Mama, "Did you think about me?" He instructed his mother to have a baby picture of himself sent to Carrie. "Don't let C. G. love anybody else," he wrote on June 13, "for I worship her Mama dear," deputizing Nellye as Pressley Cleveland had to lock down his girlfriend's loyalty. Although he comprehended the delays in mail, he bemoaned the stretches between letters and warned his parents never to think the worst. Waring treasured the cigarettes, tobacco, and newspapers from America, delivered by his mother and stateside charities, signals of home front gratitude. "We are all mighty glad to see America 'wake up' like she has," he said. "[I]t puts new life in us to know the folks back home are backing us up and appreciating the sacrifice we are making."[28]

THE ARMY GAVE ARTHUR HUEBNER no time to get in trouble in Brest. After disembarking, the men marched in the rain three miles to teeming Camp Pontanezen, once home to Napoleon's troops. Machine gun battalions were attached to units within the brigade or in allied commands. Arthur's unit left Camp Pontanezen quickly to join the British Expeditionary Forces near Amiens. He spent June training and moving. To get to Oisemont, the soldiers rattled about for two days in the austere forty-and-eight railcars, then on June 9 walked twenty-six miles to Grandcourt, where they handed over their baggage. For twelve days, Arthur's unit worked with British Vickers machine guns. The men received half the British rations, small bits of bacon, cheese, and hardtack. After Grandcourt, a trek of twenty miles brought the 124th to Pont Remy, on the Somme River, then Vignacourt, then to a tent camp in dense woods at Molliens-au-Bois. The German lines were very close now. It was July 2.[29]

THE RUSH OF AMERICANS came under intense time pressure. Eager to win before the United States got organized, the Germans launched a major offensive in March 1918. Gen. Pershing agreed to hurry mobilization and give temporary command of infantry units to the French and British, compromises that informed the experiences of Arthur and Waring as well as the lodging of Edward Streeter's division with the British. The heavily draftee army of doughboys desperately needed training, transport, and equipment, and the Allies desperately needed reinforcements. These movements swept up as well the recently demoted Pvt. Thomas Boyd and his comrade Martin Gulberg, whose Marines of the Second Division moved from the Vosges to the Verdun front. Elements of the division joined the French along the edge of the Saint-Mihiel salient, a bulge occupied by the Germans since 1914.[30]

The spring saw American divisions training or holding quiet parts of the front under French or British tutelage, while a few moved into the path of the assault. In early April, the Kaiser's army threatened Amiens. A small number of doughboys helped hold the line. In May, German troops came within fifty miles of Paris and the French government planned a move to Bordeaux. French commanders ordered the Second Division to Château-Thierry. On May 31, 1918, Thomas and Martin boarded French trucks bound for the front.[31] The German onslaught had displaced a stream of refugees. "It was a most pitiful sight," Martin Gulberg later wrote. "There were women, old men and babies, all wandering like lost souls in a chaos of confusion."[32]

At the end of May, in the first big American action, Wayne County teacher Roy Thornburgh fought in the First Division's seizure of Cantigny. Soon more than twenty-seven thousand doughboys were helping slow the German advance. The Second and Third Divisions arrived at the Marne River near Château-Thierry in time to hold the enemy there in early June. Thomas Boyd and the Marines counterattacked and took Belleau Wood, at great cost, in the middle of that month.[33] The front was stabilizing. But Gen. Pershing coveted a nimble and independent American army, undiluted by disposition to the French and British and exempt from exhausting trench battles. At a conference in Abbeville in May 1918, he wrested a commitment from the Allies to endorse a separate United States force. Although events required concession in the short term, Pershing never abandoned his dream of an autonomous American army with its own sector of the front. He'd soon have the men to make it happen.

NATALIE SCOTT FELT THE German campaign long before American soldiers did. Since the beginning of the year, she had worked in Dr. Lambert's Red Cross office in Paris under threat of zeppelin and airplane raids and long-range guns. Natalie wrote her mother during the raids: "Good night. Pleasant dreams. And don't mind the Zeps any more than I do." However unfazed the bombings left Natalie, she ripped into the gutless, unmanly warfare that had inflamed her outrage in 1915. "The noble Germans have not lost the glory which is theirs uniquely in history," she wrote, "of warring on women and children, and a peaceful population."[34] The raids continued through March and April, killing scores of

Parisians and some doctors and nurses and generating talk of a looming offensive. Stateside papers reported evidence of German "barbarity,"
according to a piece in Selma about dead and injured orphans in Paris.[35]

Natalie spent one air-raid evening with the army's overseas over-
seer of virtue. She had gotten to know Dr. Hugh Young, serving in
the American Expeditionary Forces (AEF), during her time in Paris.
He was the urologist Gen. Pershing had sent to Saint-Nazaire in late
1917 to investigate doughboy sexual behavior. Now Young directed the
American Medical Service for Civil Population, tasked with curbing
the spread of disease in the AEF and among the French.[36] When she
"introduced" Maj. Young to her mother in a letter, Natalie remarked he
was "not handsome at all" and that "there are no romances imminent"
with him or other doctors.[37] (She otherwise described military men
with terms like *soldierly figure, dashing, handsomer, smart, well-groomed,
good-looking, divine,* and *boyish smile.*) The two became friends. On this
night in early March, the doctor invited Natalie to dinner to meet an
American officer eager for her company. The group went to Fagot's. No
sooner had they ordered drinks than the air raid sirens wailed, clearing
the restaurant of customers, including the officer. This left Natalie and
Maj. Young to enjoy the full attention of the wait staff, which shut the
doors and windows against the bombs and cannon fire. The pair ate
hors d'oeuvres and broiled lobster and drank champagne. When it came
time to leave, they found no taxis and the Metro closed and began to
walk. From the shadows a boy beckoned them to a shelter. After a deep
descent, Natalie realized they were in the catacombs, a series of former
mines filled with six million skeletons transplanted from old cemeteries around Paris. A big crowd and damp air sent Natalie and the major
hurrying back to the surface, where they caught a taxi home. "The last
thing I heard as I tucked myself sleepily in," Natalie wrote her mother,
"was the pounding of the cannons."[38]

Natalie's talents earned her reassignment as head of a new medical library at Place Vendôme. There she met and flirted with Quentin
Roosevelt, son of the former president and an AEF aviator. "Very slim
and <u>very</u> boyish" was Quentin. They shared a joke about the perils
of war when she confused him with his wounded brother Archibald.
"I get up high," the young man said, "so I can keep out of all those
dangerous things." Natalie replied that elevation was the "charm" of

aviation—"that, and the officers." An embarrassed Quentin giggled and ran behind some curtains. He emerged to mention some "corking good-looking French girls" he'd met at the Red Cross.[39]

Then, on March 21, 1918, the Germans launched their offensive, throwing Paris into chaos and Natalie into refugee relief. With evacuees leaving the French countryside, she counted herself as "happy as any one can be in the midst of misery."[40] Natalie worked in Paris train depots, doing translation and distributing mattresses and sometimes sleeping in stations. Old people, women, children, and wounded veterans rushed to the capital with meager belongings. One night, Natalie butted heads with a "lady doctor" named Dr. Mosher, whom she found unkempt and incompetent and thus deserving of neither designation. One patient was a psychologically wounded Belgian laborer. The man's story gave the lie to narratives of wartime masculine uplift:

He talked to his children, his voice soft and gentle, coaxing . . . "Come, little girl. It's Papa." And on and on. You know I am not emotional or easily affected, but it simply tore through me more horribly than a physical pain to hear him. I can never, ever forget it. It was last Wednesday night. I have dreamed of him, thought of him in the midst of all the stress and turmoil since. It simply seems too hard. A poor, good man, happy in his work, unoffending,—torn, hurled, crammed into this horrible maw of war, and spit out again a wreck, a half-man, with no one in the world to turn to, unable to work, not sick enough for the hospital, not well enough for the world, and <u>no one to care.</u>

Some people around Natalie thought her worn down by long hours. Dr. Mosher tried to get her to return home, but Natalie refused, writing her mother that she felt "bound up heart and soul in that work, almost more than I have ever been in anything in my life."[41]

In early April, Natalie left Paris for a post as nurse's aide and translator in Gisors. Very quickly, her unit moved with Roy Thornburgh's First Division to a French hospital in Beauvais, where she spent six months as nurse, translator, and record-keeper. Beauvais was fifty miles north of Paris and close to the British front, serving English, American, French, and German wounded. Between shifts, Natalie entertained soldiers, doctors, and journalists as a dinner companion. One was the famous *Saturday Evening Post* writer Irvin Cobb, a southerner known for folksy prose, preposterous black characters, and, in 1915, warnings of German atrocities coming to American shores.[42] On a day in May, Cobb suggested he and Natalie pretend to get married. The chaplain gave a blessing, photographs were taken, and everybody laughed.[43]

AMONG THE ARRIVING YANKS were the segregated divisions. The Ninety-Third came in pieces and stayed in pieces. New York's black National Guard unit, the Fifteenth Regiment, after its short, turbulent training period, had gotten to Saint-Nazaire, France, in December 1917 and become the 369th Infantry. In the new year, the men were laying railroad track with the army's Service of Supply (SOS) units. Soon thereafter came the other three regiments: the Eighth Illinois National Guard (370th); assorted draftees (371st); and miscellaneous National Guardsmen (372nd).[44]

At first, Gen. Pershing planned to use the Ninety-Third for labor, a direct betrayal of the division's mission. Soon Pershing, who had promised the French four infantry regiments, decided to "loan" them these units. While the general later claimed the arrangement temporary, the regiments never came back to the AEF, contradicting Pershing's broader reluctance to carve up his forces. "It is safe to assume," went a later history, "that Pershing's image of his American army was white in color." The French already deployed black colonial troops and welcomed the assistance. For the duration of the war, men in the Ninety-Third ate French rations, fired French weapons, wore French helmets, and, most dangerously in American eyes, interacted with French women.[45]

The unit eventually known as the Harlem Hell Fighters, the 369th Infantry, saw combat under French command. In March 1918, the men traveled from Saint-Nazaire to Givry-en-Argonne, and a month later took charge of a sector of the French line. Budding artist Horace Pippin later recalled terrible weather and constant bombardment. This part of the front featured strongpoints linked by wire but not trenches, inviting frequent enemy infiltration. A white officer ordered small groups to hold positions ahead of the line to intercept German raiding parties. One night in the middle of May, about twenty Germans slipped past these points and approached an isolated post held by five men. Black doughboys Sgt. Henry Johnson and Pvt. Needham Roberts kept vigil while three comrades slept in a bunker below. Johnson and Roberts heard someone cutting the wire. To warn the Americans, they fired a flare, which drew a barrage of grenades. Explosions wounded both men, but armed with knives, rifles, and grenades, they killed, injured, or drove off the attackers. Johnson used his nine-inch bolo knife to stab one man in the skull and disembowel another. Both earned the French Croix de Guerre.[46]

The black press brimmed with pride. German cowards had been "put to flight" and had "slunk away" during the skirmish. Roberts and Johnson, in these accounts, had revealed the masculine character typically assigned to the broader doughboy population. That summer and for months thereafter, readers saw attached to the pair words like *courage, bravery, fearless, good, heroic,* and *glory*.[47] Advertisements in the *Chicago Defender* peddled pictures of the "two Race men" for black homes.[48] Newspapers run by white people granted the two men *gallantry, stanchness, daring, bravery, valor,* and *heroism*.[49] Such language implied not just soldierly but also moral virtue, perhaps meant as a corrective against ingrained stereotypes. The white commander, Col. William Hayward, wrote in a letter to Johnson's mother that her son was "a good boy, of fine morals and upright character."[50] People eagerly claimed the men as kin. A black reverend in Savannah shared with the local paper the "delightful information" that Needham Roberts was his first cousin. In late June, their families were guests of honor at a party hosted by the woman's auxiliary organization of the former Fifteenth Infantry. Seven hundred celebrants packed the Harlem Casino to welcome the relatives and accept a silk flag sent by Theodore Roosevelt.[51]

Civil rights leaders had long understood that continuing mistreatment of African Americans on the home front undermined rhetoric about saving the world for democracy. The news of Johnson and Roberts, however, coincided with a revolting racial crime in Valdosta, Georgia, exposing hypocrisies that ran deeper than the withholding of political rights. As the black press and white allies linked the skirmish with violence in Georgia, they challenged the wartime story of an honorable America fighting a barbaric enemy for the future of civilized life.

The trouble in Valdosta began when someone shot and killed Hampton Smith. The white farmer's wife, whom the *Atlanta Constitution* later wrote was "attacked" the night of the shooting, pointed the finger at a black man. When the gathering mob couldn't find him, they killed several other black people in retaliation. One victim was Hayes Turner. His pregnant wife Mary protested to police, who took her into protective custody, only to release her to angry white Georgians. They hung her upside down and set her on fire. Then they cut open her abdomen and yanked out the baby one month short of term. The infant cried out before dying under the boots of the mob.[52]

Journalists erupted at the crime and its connection to the war. In a piece called "Courage and Cowardice," the *Chicago Defender* praised the exploits of black doughboys before condemning the white mob, borrowing terms from stories about the rape of Belgium. "This was a woman," fumed the paper. "She was not permitted even the attention of another woman in this trying and ending crisis of her existence."[53] A few weeks later, the *Defender* approvingly reprinted an editorial from the white-run *Lexington Herald* entitled "Lynchers Are the Allies of the Huns." In the eyes of the *Herald* editor, Valdosta proved hollow the war's deeper purpose, a purpose that promoted decency, a way of life, and values—in a word, civilization. "[S]uch lynchings as have recently occurred in the South," he wrote, "tend to give the lie to the claim that we wage a war for civilization. They weaken our denunciation of the brutality of the Germans."[54] Here again were the "Southern huns" an African American woman had called out in the wake of racial violence in Houston in 1917.[55] To the *Herald*'s editor, the lynch mob showed contempt for black innocents and undercut claims of chivalry. In other words, he wrote, the killers both aided and mimicked the enemy.

Yet even laudatory coverage of Needham and Roberts, in the meantime, resorted to stereotype. Papers attributed their deeds to savagery or ignorance rather than bravery. One quoted Gen. Pershing:

Only regret expressed by colored troops is that they are not given more dangerous work to do. They are especially amused at the most dangerous positions and all are desirous of having more active service than has been permitted them thus far. I can not commend too highly the spirit shown among the colored combat troops, who exhibit fine capacity for quick training and eagerness for the most dangerous work.

Here was the key to the military usefulness of black warriors—"their characteristic penchant for amusement!"[56] Pershing and the *Atlanta Constitution* interpreted black readiness not as a political quest for equal treatment but as evidence of inexorable racial characteristics. This meant Johnson and Roberts weren't exactly heroes. The *New York Times* lent them a hint of barbarism:

> Bill, as his wife calls him, also brought a bolo knife into play, handier than a razor; and shot, clubbed, cut, and grenaded, the Germans soon had enough of Bill and Needham, leaving some dead men and fragments of others on the ground.

"Rash" and "demoniac" were other words the paper used or quoted.[57] When Johnson used his knife, he revealed a savage character, thirst for close combat, and comfort with blood. Soon, Natalie Scott's friend Irvin Cobb wrote a series of articles called "Young Black Joe, the Fighting Negro in France" for the *Saturday Evening Post*. Cobb aimed to valorize the black doughboy, declaring that from now on the word "n-i-g-g-e-r" would only spell "American," but ultimately reduced him to stereotype.[58] The pieces were filled with dialect and echoed the preoccupation with the black soldier's disregard for danger.[59]

After its actions of May, the 369th aided the French near Château-Thierry and at Belleau Wood. For valor under fire in those engagements, Sgt. Bob Collins earned the unit another Croix de Guerre. The four regiments of the "Colored" Ninety-Second Division, after training separately in stateside cantonments, gathered in Hoboken in June and sailed to Brest. Gen. Pershing had wished the men to train with the British, but someone in the U.K. war cabinet claimed a bureaucratic misunderstanding. So the Ninety-Second traveled to the French Vosges section. Once again the regiments split up. They confronted the same problems with equipment shortages and inexperienced officers as other American divisions.[60] As the summer would show, that was where the experiences of black and white doughboys diverged.

THE SAME MONTH NEEDHAM ROBERTS and Henry Johnson performed their acts of martial heroics, Eliga Dees and the Sixth Division moved into the place those men had trained, Camp Wadsworth. Although Lige warned

Mae to expect a gap in correspondence, he arrived at camp to a scathing letter. Her vitriolic note doesn't survive but his intense response read, "You know that you are the only one in the world that could sleep in my arms and if I did not want to marry you why you know that I did not have to and I held up my right hand and said that I love you and you are the only one in this world that I could love and I want you to keep this on your mind." The matter so handled, Lige told Mae the camp housed mainly National Guardsmen and his job a corporal was to train them. He raised the possibility she could come for a month and closed with another rebuke. "Now listen honey please do not send me another letter like the one that you wrote the other day," Lige warned, "for I felt like killing myself all day and I don't want to get another like it either."[61]

Mae and her senior classmates at Williamsville High School were busy with graduation events. In the class play she had the role of Clara, a girl trying to dodge the amorous pursuits of a male acquaintance. Her big scene came when she ran off the stage to avoid his kisses. Mae's friends ribbed her for fearing this might hit too close to home for Lige. Another day the students skipped school to play around and take pictures with their Kodaks. She went to a banquet but sadly took a female friend rather than Lige. Her teacher—the kids called him "Prof"—spoke often about the absence of "Mae's soldier boy." She reminded Lige that through all these experiences she "wouldn't do a thing . . . that I thought you would not want me to do."[62]

Mae waited until the end of May to work in other news. "I do hope you can get a furlough and come home," she wrote, "and let me go back with you and stay until my school begins. But I don't guess you knew that I had a school. You don't care if I teach do you?" She had taught before but given it up to finish high school. Mae had been invited to fill a slot in tiny Otter Creek but didn't have time to run it past Lige before accepting:

> I think I can teach a good school. I would rather do that as anything else except keep house for my darling dada and since I can't do that I must do something to pass away the time and then Lige I can save all the money you send me and part of mine and then when you come home we will have some money to get the things we will need. Do you care honey?

Mae's reasoning confirmed her commitment to a traditional domestic future but conceded the overruling exigencies of wartime. Only the price of goods and strain of separation, she suggested, pushed her into the workforce.[63] The thought of Mae earning wages had upset Lige's masculine confidence before, but she caught him in an accommodating mood. On May 11, he granted her permission for what she'd already done. Yet he worried about how this arrangement might erode his breadwinner's credibility. "[Y]ou must know," Lige wrote, "that Dada can keep you up without you having to work and maybe the people will think that you have [to do] it."[64]

The couple's exchange mirrored broader patterns. War promised to reinforce gender traditions, yet in its execution and mobilization threatened to weaken them. Federal officials encouraged female employment, but hoped to minimize its dislocations, just as progressives were laboring to limit doughboy immorality. The framers of the War Risk Insurance Act had mandated soldiers send pay home to keep women from working. Doctors wrote about physical labor's damage to female reproductive organs. Working women stimulated fears of economic independence and sexual dishonor. One federal agency said women should avoid employment in saloons or poolrooms. In factories, some men sabotaged or ostracized female counterparts, whether they felt their jobs or gender sensibilities under threat. Many women earned unequal wages. All this limited the entrance of new women workers into the paid labor force, though existing female workers moved in dramatic numbers into the industrial sector and other new areas.[65]

For Americans protective of gender roles, the safe arena for women was home front voluntarism. To coordinate it, President Woodrow Wilson called upon an established network of women's clubs in forming the new Woman's Committee of the Council of National Defense (Natalie Scott had served as state secretary for Louisiana).[66] Clubwomen helped with draft registration, identified deserters, and sold war bonds. Appeals for women's assistance steered them toward contributions domestic in character, subordinate to male war work, and congruent with middle-class attitudes. Female Red Cross volunteers knitted millions of garments and hospital items. Housewives signed pledges to ration meat and wheat. The state urged women on with the same coercive energy driving other wartime demands. Those who shirked new burdens might earn the epithet "women slackers," violators of both patriotic and gendered standards.[67]

Mae framed her work as a teacher along those lines: temporary, war-driven, feminine, and useful. "I will feel like I am not a 'slacker,'" she wrote on May 15, "and that I am doing a little bit of good." Her employment need not undermine his breadwinner status. "Darling, I know and everybody else knows that you can and will support me," she said. "I don't intend to teach always anyway. When my good old dada comes home I don't want to do anything only keep house for you."[68] Mae acknowledged war's disruptive impact but implored him to trust it would expire. A good home with genders in place would reward Lige's service. On May 4, the Camp Wadsworth newsletter featuring Edward Streeter's work ran a poem called "When We Come Back":

When we come back, remember . . . the things we planned to do:
The little house upon the hill with room enough for two,
The casement with the ivy, the grass so soft and deep,
The singing roof where drops of rain would lull the night to sleep.[69]

Mae shared these dreams. Her flirtations with individuality and assertiveness, she suggested, would evaporate when Lige came marching home. "We will be so happy when we are in our own little home," Mae wrote, "and can tell each other all of our troubles and share our joys and love each other. Won't we dear?"[70] Streeter satirized the prevalence of such visions of postwar domestic utopias through his popular characters Bill and Mable. "We may have to go at the house kind of gradual," the doughboy cautioned Mable. "Buy the blinds first say."[71]

Even as Mae soothed her husband's anxieties, she likely inflamed them with her independence. On May 7, 1918, she mentioned swimming again. "You ought to be here," Mae wrote. "You would let me go in swimming if you was here wouldn't you? You could keep me from getting drowned. I can swim and I'm not afraid but I will not go in because you might be afraid."[72] She granted Lige a monopoly on her protection but reminded him she didn't need it. Soon Mae told him she didn't fret about him leaving her. Lige should feel the same way and not worry. After all, she wrote, with a blend of reassurance and its opposite, "I try to have a good time and not worry so much or get so old just because we are married."[73]

Mae's good mood proved temporary. Two weeks later, she said Lige's latest letter had found her "almost dead with the blues." "I get to think-ing of you some-times," she wrote, "and I can't keep from crying to think of it all. The way we have to be apart and so far from each other all the time and we don't know how long it must be that way."[74] The doughboy poem from Camp Wadsworth's *Gas Attack* acknowledged this side of wartime separation as well:

I'll know you will have suffered far more than even I,
I'll know the sleepless nights when you could only walk and cry.
Remember, proud of heart, dear, if I should chance to fall,
You'd rather I had not come back, than never go at all.[75]

Mae would have identified with the sleep and sorrow parts. Whether she agreed with the last line she never said.

THE BATTLE IN MAE'S letters between war's unsettling and redemp-tive possibilities for domestic life continued to concern surveyors of the public mood. Americans were reaching the battlefield and taking casualties, and any wavering of support could slow the mobilization. Military and government leaders agreed that doughboys and families were having trouble understanding the war. On April 12, 1918, offi-cials from the War Department, the Committee on Public Information (CPI), and other agencies gathered for a conference on civilian and soldier morale. Unless Washington could clarify the war's purpose, said Col. E. L. Munson of the Medical Corps, casualty lists would have a "depressive" influence and maybe even provoke "active opposition especially from mothers." The Wilson administration had long wor-ried about alienating mothers. A judge convicted Rose Pastor Stokes, arrested in March for an antiwar speech to a women's club, because of the threat she allegedly posed to motherly enthusiasm.[76] Now, said history professor and CPI education officer Guy Stanton Ford, parents were demanding to know what the intervention was for. Despite the chorus of war advocacy in popular culture, Americans remained skep-tical, even if or especially if they had sons in the army. An observer of soldiers in France found "too large a proportion ignorant of war aims." Raymond Fosdick found the same contagion of ignorance among rookies in stateside cantonments.[77]

Emotional appeals to hatred, revenge, and gallantry, some officials felt, had outlived their inspirational value. They preferred something enduring, as CPI head George Creel later wrote:

> Could we be sure that a hundred million—the fathers, the mothers, the children of America, alien born and native alike—understood well enough so that they would support one loan after another, would bear new burdens of taxation and send wave after wave of America's young manhood to die in Flanders fields? . . . We wanted to reach the people through their minds, rather than through their emotions, for hate has its undesirable reactions.[78]

In early 1918, those who shared Creel's outlook feared propaganda had played to hearts rather than minds, generating hysteria not comprehension. Sentimental and chivalric pleas, some propagandists thought, distracted people from the war's global stakes. One official said,

> On this side every billboard capitalizes war emotion. Uncle Sam and the Goddess of Liberty protecting our children thrill the community spirit and the paternal instinct, although they do not contribute much to understanding the conditions of real liberty or sensitizing our obligations to a world community. Too few of our posters have visualized our deepest purpose to make a <u>world</u> safe for democracy.[79]

Leaders confirmed a comparable narrowness of vision among the boys in France. Col. Munson wrote in a memo for the surgeon general that "many of our men do not have a clear idea of what they are fighting for."[80] In place of clearer objectives, Americans battled to chase adventure, rescue France, cultivate personal honor, kill Germans, or prove their patriotism. Letters home from soldiers, said censors, focused less on context and more on private matters.[81]

The CPI's *own output*, in fact, contributed to the privileging of feeling over principle. The agency circulated a pamphlet to the camps in March called "Why America Fights Germany." A doughboy had to wait until number four on the list to see mention of "democracy." Ahead of it were grievances against German cruelty, insults, and treachery. All threatened "peace and happiness."[82] The Liberty Loan poster "For Home and Country" mentioned the nation but made family the star (figure 4.1).

FIGURE 4.1 "For Home and Country," 1918. World War I Poster Collection, Library of Congress.

To refocus attention on country, officials sought not to abandon personal justifications but invest them with expansive significance. The state and its surrogates pledged to "direct the nation's emotional energy," as the CPI's historians put it, "into channels of constructive patriotism."[83]

This strategy of persuasive clarification, for one high-level official, called for "psychological control" of both the "military forces" and "the civilian body" in the United States.[84] The ensuing campaign fueled the creation of the newspaper *Stars and Stripes* in February 1918; the establishment of an army "Morale Division"; a program of interviews with combat veterans; and the distribution of pamphlets to the camps in February and March with titles including, "How the War Came to America," "Battle Line of Democracy," and "War of Self-Defense."[85] This mandate to inform and convince had driven the organization of the CPI, in April 1917, and its education programs, film advisors, cartoonist guidebooks, Four-Minute Men, and *Official Bulletin*. The education division of the CPI, headed by

FIGURE 4.2 Drawing from *Stars and Stripes*, March 15, 1918. Serial and Government Publications Division, Library of Congress.

Guy Stanton Ford, produced millions of pamphlets and syllabi and had its words repeated in countless public speeches and media stories. Creel later boasted that citizens confronted the official view at "every turn of the road."[86]

These leaders now keyed the war's private impulses to collective ambitions. Nowhere was the shift more dramatic than in *Stars and Stripes* in the spring of 1918. Two drawings, two months apart, redirected the soldier's chivalric impulses from the personal to the national (figures 4.2 and 4.3). The second image charged the protective instinct with political meaning, casting the nation as the damsel in distress. It promoted the CPI's goal of converting emotional verve to constructive patriotism. It also reflected official desires, though unevenly realized in

FIGURE 4.3 Drawing from *Stars and Stripes*, May 10, 1918. Serial and Government Publications Division, Library of Congress.

public culture, to elevate the war's purpose beyond defense of loved ones. Grand political aims now seemed to propagandists more potent than tangible personal ones. President Wilson, however, at this very moment, was telling foreign journalists that he'd never intended the intervention as a crusade to spread democracy. But he said it off the record.[87]

THE AMBITION TO CHANNEL private emotion to broader understanding guided the celebration of Mother's Day on May 12, 1918. In his proclamation declaring the first such holiday in 1914, President Wilson had honored the home as "the fountain head of the state" and called for Americans to fly the flag to convey their "love and reverence" for mother. Following a tradition dating back generations, he located the nation's strength in the moral and religious environment of the home.[88] During the Great War, amid mass conscription and concern about mothers' support, war advocates credited the doughboy's character and fighting prowess to domestic tutelage. Mother's Day 1918 stimulated a burst of testimonials like that of Secretary of the Navy Josephus Daniels: "It is always true that the morale of a nation's soldiers and the ideals for which they fight are born in the spiritual heroism of a nation's mothers."[89]

Stars and Stripes called every man to desk, YMCA hut, or Red Cross canteen to write his mother. Beleaguered postal officials pledged to meet the surge with dispatch. Soldiers should write "Mother's Letter" on envelopes for expedited delivery and stick to personal matters to simplify the censor's task. "[T]he boat that carries the Mothers' Letters to America," *Stars and Stripes* said, "will be a boat laden with as rich a freight as ever craft bore from shore to shore."[90] There was almost no limit to the regenerative potential of this shipment of mass sentiment. An Atlanta editorialist said a doughboy's letter to mother "will do her a world of good, and it will make him a better man, a more contented man and a better soldier—stronger in purpose and will to fight valiantly for country, home and Mother!"[91] In Beauvais, Natalie Scott passed out flowers for patients to wear in recognition of the holiday.[92]

The House of Representatives passed a resolution supporting the campaign. A group called the National Association for Mothers of Defenders of Democracy called on Americans to pray for moms.[93] To commanders in France, Gen. Pershing issued an order that also appeared in the stateside *Official Bulletin* of the CPI:

To write home frequently and regularly, to keep in constant touch with family and friends, is one of the soldier's most important duties. . . . When no letters are received from over-seas, the greatest distress is caused to those at home. They either feel that letters have been written but lost en route, or else they imagine all sorts of evils, such as sickness, wounds, even death. Both are bad for the active militant spirit which every true American man and woman must possess if our Army is to obtain the real victory that all so earnestly desire.[94]

Officials encouraged doughboys to send messages of love, words of appreciation, and reassurances of good health. At the same time, they reminded the public that motherly sacrifices undergirded a war with implications for the future of human life, reinforcing other campaigns of 1918 to expand the public's perspective. In his Mother's Day statement, President Wilson said,

I take advantage of the occasion to suggest that during this day our attention be directed particularly to the patriotic sacrifices which are being so freely and generously made by the mothers of our land in unselfishly offering their sons to bear arms, and, if need be, *to die in defense of liberty and justice . . .*[95]

Stars and Stripes compared the Great War to the Civil War, quoting Abraham Lincoln's letter to the mother of five dead Union soldiers tendering her "the thanks of the Republic they died to save."[96]

The postal service handled tens of thousands of homeward letters and 1,400,000 pieces of mail from mothers.[97] The press filled with conflations of family and country. From the *Nashville Tennessean*: "An organized tribute to the mother's love resolves itself into higher love for country, for comrades and for God."[98] A representative of the Red Cross "tied up the idea of Mother's Day and patriotism" by talking about love. The *Baltimore Sun*'s coverage of an event included a Red Cross poster depicting "the two noblest emotions," according to the author, "mother love and patriotic devotion, in a composite picture gripping in its appeal" (figure 4.4).[99] A similar image ran in the *Selma Journal* depicting a Red Cross woman of obvious compassion, competence, and love.[100] Talk of love was everywhere—love for country, love for family, love for national

FIGURE 4.4 Red Cross poster, 1917. World War I Poster Collection, Library of Congress.

symbols, and love for an amalgam of all those things. "Look at the flag as it goes by," said Mae and Lige's hometown *Greenville Sun* right after Mother's Day, "and look with love, pride and veneration."[101] Ditties in the book *War Facts and Patriotic Songs*, found in doughboy packs, rang with emotional patriotism:

> Off with your hat as the Flag goes by!
> And let the heart have its say;
> You're man enough for a tear in your eye
> That you will not wipe away.[102]

Mae Dees wrote of how intertwined personal feeling and nationalist resolve had become. "I can't see anything patriotic any more without crying," she divulged to Lige. "It makes me think of you so much. This afternoon at school 8 little girls had a flag drill and marched to 'Columbia' and then sang it and somehow it all seemed so sad and yet so sweet that it made me feel miserable."[103] Perhaps to the frustration of some officials, the merging of personal with national appeals could rather easily drift to "war emotion."

Implicit in Mae's misery, as she said again and again, was the fear that war could destroy her life, that death could rob her of love. But voices in popular culture increasingly promoted the compatibility of familial and national obligations, of grand cause and private virtue, and, in a way, of love and death. A Tennessee newspaper told the story of John Webber, killed in the war and buried just before Mother's Day by his widowed mom. A nurturing family had fashioned a "chivalrous soldier abroad, as well as at home." However terrible his death, John's surviving loved ones are "ours to remember, to comfort and to envy, for they have given a hero to the cause that means so much to all of us."[104] Here was a "good" mother, entrusting her son to the state whatever the dangers.[105] Wives met similar counsel in the two 1918 narratives of wartime brides, *Silver Lining* and *Over Here*. In the former, a memoir, the author Ruth Wolfe Fuller recorded this vow, readymade for readers:

> I, _____, give thee, _____, my Husband, to be our Country's Soldier—to have and to hold, for little time or long—until Peace do us unite![106]

The fictional *Over Here*, released right around Mother's Day 1918 and serialized in the *Chicago Daily Tribune*, ended with a stunning pledge of maternal sacrifice. Elizabeth marries Tommy and they conceive a child before his departure. Tommy dies in France. Nevertheless, says Elizabeth, in a book otherwise three-dimensional in its depiction of grief, "I *am* going to raise Obadiah to be a soldier."[107]

NO RECORD SURVIVES OF Lige Dees writing his mother. Waring Huston was traveling from England to France. Louise Huebner had died two months earlier. To doughboys like Arthur, who had suffered "the greatest loss that can come to a man," *Stars and Stripes* suggested writing to a friend or relative who filled the void.[108] Back in Watertown, a business called the Stuebe Floral Company encouraged locals to wear white flowers to honor mothers who had passed.[109]

A few weeks later, during the official campaigns to clarify the war's purposes, observers of American life still sensed confusion. "There are doubtless some who do not understand," wrote Elihu Root in a piece published in the *Watertown News* in June, "what this struggle really is." Root, a former senator, secretary of war, and preparedness advocate, served as honorary president of the National Security League. His explanation revealed the durability of emotionally charged rather than geopolitically oriented justifications for the war, despite the mission of the past few months to invest it with broad meaning. "This is a war of defense," he said, to preserve cherished "blessings of liberty." Fighting in France meant defending the American way of life.[110] Arthur's hometown paper enumerated what German rule had brought: "[the] sinking of hundreds of neutral ships, the burning of cities, the deliberate devastating of the fair lands of France, the ravishing of women, the enslavement of workmen and the murder of little children."[111] Readers in Selma learned of a "new phase of Hun brutality," the one Natalie Scott witnessed, as Germans drove villagers from homes.[112]

"WE HAVE ALWAYS HEARD talk of the goat," Mae wrote to Lige on May 9, "but believe me, we saw it last night." So began Mae's account of her initiation into the ranks of the Williamsville High School alumni. In the spring of 1918, military metaphors lent the hazing rituals their organizational logic. Mae endured a "physical examination," "vaccination," a "nerve test," and filled out a "questionnaire," all administered by graduates and teachers bent on separating the young people from their dignity. Should Mae be "killed," Lige would be sent a telegram, an inversion of the dreaded wartime prospect. For the nerve test, blindfolded seniors sat in a collapsing chair while somebody fired a revolver to coincide with the plunge. Crying out—which Mae did—earned you a trip "over the top." Older students dumped the senior into a wheelbarrow, rolled her up to the edge of a plank, and sent the barrow and its human cargo crashing back to earth. Fortunately Mae managed to avoid the goat, dragged to the school by the alumni for vague purposes. All Mae said was, "I didn't get shut in with the Billy goat and didn't have to ride it. My heavens! I would have been dead now."[113]

"Over the top" proved a versatile motif in the Missouri imagination. The *Greenville Sun* deployed it to describe rivers running high and money spilling forth for war charities. In April and May, locals bought bonds and donated goods for sale at a generous clip for the "42 splendid young men with the colors from this community." Mae sent Lige the newspaper story, scribbling in the margin, "I suppose you are counted as one of those 42 young men." Personal behavior and public good were growing ever more entangled. Buying eggs, candy, pies, cakes, and ham provided succor for the troops overseas.[114] The newspaper's front page on a single day in April, in fact, showed how the press kept up with private and public registers of experience and the sinews linking them. The April 25 edition belatedly announced the marriage of Mae and Lige; lauded county Liberty Loan contributions; and warned parents to watch out for requests for furlough money from con men posing as trainee sons in camp.[115] Private choices and sympathies, like in most times of war, were becoming ever more subject to public scrutiny, mobilization, and manipulation.

Yet private behavior still attracted private scrutiny. Lige couldn't grab hold of the fact that mail delivery was unreliable, raging or whining when Mae's latest letter hadn't reached him. "I treat you so good and rite to you," he said on May 17, "then you don't give a dam if I hear from you or not I think I will just quit riting to anyone and then all of you will know how I was treated." In a punctuation-less soliloquy of woe, Lige took aim at the popular narrative of soldiers' allotments. To Lige's mind, the money wasn't buying him anything and, worse, made him a sucker. "[D]id you get the lotement?" he wrote. "[L]ooks like you would not be having so much fun with them slackers that you could tell me if you got that stuff."[116] Here was a man struggling to maintain masculine prerogative at great distance. Despite the reassurances of policy and culture, allotments offered a poor substitution for breadwinner's pride. Cowards, Lige felt, had closer access to his wife than he did.

Mae forcefully rebuked this impression of things. She was staying on her parents' farm near Chaonia, Missouri. Mae liked the place better than Otter Creek, enjoying the chickens and ducks and an old turkey gobbler. Her family grew plums, apples, and peas, although much arable land lay flooded. Rising waters blocked the mail cars, which explained the delay in letters and the allotment check. But Mae didn't hinge her case on logistics. She rejected Lige's mapping of her allegiances, denying having "had any fun with these slackers here as you say and I don't see how you could say that." In fact, slackers enraged her. Mae recently had berated a "coward" who lived nearby. He had kids but still expected to serve. President Wilson was no better than the Kaiser, he said, and only a fool would enlist. Mae shot back by associating patriotic duty, as so much of public culture did, with familial devotion:

> I told him I was glad that some of them were true to their *country and homes* enough to go and protect us all. And that I would rather go because I was brave enough and loved my country than to have to be drafted and then curse my country and government.

Mae didn't say how the slacker reacted, but her father laughed at her for being so bold.[117]

Lige nonetheless felt his romance with Mae undermined by separation and home front provocateurs. Apparently Mae suspected her acquaintance Nellie Frazier of writing to Lige with lies of Mae's infidelity. Nellie harassed Mae about an old beau of hers, a fellow called "Bigum," who had married Nellie's sister Ethel. Nellie crowed to people that Mae had missed an opportunity with Bigum, a better provider than Lige. Defenders of Mae shot back that she loved Lige and he sent her money. The only thing Bigum could do that Lige couldn't, they said, was father a child, a stinging reminder of absence. "It made me despise Nell," Mae wrote, "for she is a fool if she thinks I ever loved any body but you." The next time she saw Nellie, Mae would say she preferred a man like Lige over a "slacker and a coward" like Bigum.[118]

Readers would soon encounter an astonishingly similar scenario in the Bill and Mable saga. Florence Elizabeth Summers's *Dere Bill*, which provided the voice of Mable to Edward Streeter's Bill, reinforced popular conceptions of manly mettle:

> Now I aint got nothing against Nellie, Bill, but she sure is hateful an jealous hearted when it comes to you. Shes been flyin round with that Guffy fello just for your and my benefit. She tries to act like shes crazy about him. When she come in she says "I reckon youre lonesome with your fine soldier gone to war." Then she says "Guffy dont have to go to war. Hes workin his brains here for the government, an doin more good than fightin." And I just up and says a little hateful—but composed, "Buddin young citizen, eh?" An she flew off red an mad as whizz an says "I'd ruther have a buddin young citizen at home than a bloomin idiot in the Army." . . . I like Nellie but she sure does say mean things.

Later in the story, Mable delighted in telling Bill that Guffy had been imprisoned as a slacker once his job ended.[119] Mae and Mable found doughboys the archetypes of masculine virtue, service evaders the archetypes of unmanly timidity. Soldiers in France of course held the home front man in low regard. Marine Thomas Boyd accumulated or observed enough resentment during his time in France to include this exchange in his novel *Through the Wheat*:

> "If you could git them home guards away from home you'd sure have to hump. They're home guards—they guard our women while we're over here." The speaker seemed afraid that his listeners would not understand that he was stressing the word *home*.
>
> "Yeh, they's one of 'em guardin' my gal too close. I got a lettah . . ."
>
> "You're lucky to get any kind of letter. Here I been for three months and not a word. I don't know whether they all died or what," Hicks ended gloomily.

"Aw cheer up, Hicksy, old boy. Maybe your mail was on that transport that got sunk."[120]

Doughboys tended to articulate unambiguous hierarchies of male character, with themselves at the top, but the Nellies of reality and fiction never let them get comfortable. News of home guard appreciation rituals couldn't have helped. Servicemen from Watertown, if they were sent copies of Arthur's hometown paper in this period, would have seen banner advertisements inviting women to a dance with the home guards at the local armory.[121]

Lige soon dialed back his wariness and claimed he had been "kidding," but kept up his long-range campaign to assert authority. He asked again if she received the allotment and promised more money if she needed it. He demanded she stay out of swimming holes. He talked about a future visit he might spring on her. He directed she write him two times a week: "I'll spank you if you don't rite to Dada that often." Was this a joke, an admonition, a sexual flirtation? If the latter, it aligned well with a daydream Lige shared with Mae. Perhaps on a visit home, he asked, would she go swimming with him? "We will go all a lone," Lige wrote, "and take off all of our cloths."[122] Nighttime dreams, both of them started telling each other, were edging in this direction. Lige wrote that he had some dreams he could tell Mae about and some he couldn't. After one vision, Lige woke up spooning the man in his tent, and reported the dialogue:

Doughboy: "Dees, what in the h. is the matter?"
Lige: "I was dreaming of my wife."
Doughboy: "Well I wish she was with you instead of me."
Lige: "You are not the only one that wishes that."[123]

Mae wrote Lige of her own dream she couldn't talk about, though it was because she thought he would laugh at her. Mae hoped it would come true, "but not as long as you are in the army."[124]

NATALIE SCOTT HAD A tumultuous May.[125] Her work in the Beauvais hospital tested her "untearful" character, though she vowed to her mother not to let the horrors "get possession of me." She sat with men suffering from survivor's guilt and insanity, gas wounds and illnesses. Natalie heard another nurse ask a dying boy if he wanted anything. "I want to go home," he said. Natalie attended funerals of two Americans, "and I thought of their mothers through it all."[126]

At the end of the month, hospital staff rejoiced at the nearby victory at Cantigny. Then the Germans launched a month-long wave of air attacks against Beauvais. The first night, Natalie awoke to bombs crashing into the hospital. Nursing a bad foot, she limped out of bed, grabbed a helmet, and helped patients evacuate. The action killed children in the town, Natalie heard, and mortally wounded a French nurse. When a sobbing general presented the nurse with a Croix de Guerre, the dying woman directed it be given to her little girl. The next night, Natalie slept on the ground floor of the four-story hospital with her clothes on. Bombs struck right after she fell asleep. She put on her helmet and rushed for the top floors "to get my boys down," as she told her mother. Natalie dodged flying glass and fleeing men on her way upstairs. She found a gas patient lying in rubble, unharmed, and shouted for two Americans to bring him down. Four more boys she rescued herself, arms draped across her shoulders. News of injured children and deaths filtered in. The top two floors of the hospital were gone. "Hell had broken loose," Natalie wrote. She reassured her mother things would calm down but urged her not to worry if no letters arrived. Besides, should the worst happen, Natalie had lived "happily" and "fully" and been "useful."[127]

Audiences in America quickly heard about the courageous professionalism of the nurses. "It was an exciting time," Natalie said in a *Washington Post* article, "but there was no panic." The piece noted the German killing of small babies and wounded soldiers, of doctors and nurses and women and old men.[128]

GEN. PERSHING INSPECTED THE 325th and other units of the Eighty-Second Division around June 5. A few days later, a 326th Infantry captain named Jewett Williams became the first casualty in the division when he was killed on a tour of frontline trenches. Then, rather to the surprise of the British and Americans, the Eighty-Second received orders to reclaim its rifles, cease training, and return to the town called Eu. Ferdinand Foch, supreme commander of the Allied armies, wanted the All-Americans and three other divisions to shore up the French sector.[129] On June 16, the men undertook a train journey of 270 miles to the Toul area. Fred Takes recorded miserable details in his diary: open flat cars, airy and warm by day but cold and rainy by night, some men separated from their coats, much shivering and hunger. Waring managed a spot in a boxcar with two horses and eight men, and found the trip slow but beautiful. Chugging around Paris, they saw Versailles and the Eiffel Tower. The regiment arrived in Maron, on the Moselle River, on June 17.[130]

In a letter home, Waring said only he had "traveled all over France." He quickly figured out a way to reveal his location: "In one of my future letters I am going to put the name of a town in there—it will be the town that we are right near." He soon slipped the word "Toul" randomly into the middle of a sentence. (One wonders why the censor didn't see through the ruse.) Waring's family thus learned he was a few miles from the front and Germany proper.[131]

IN MAY AND JUNE 1918, Lige Dees trained in brutal South Carolina heat. He was planning a visit home, perhaps his last for several months, and expected skinny-dipping and a "big dance."[132] Mae agreed but pointed out Lige usually disapproved of her dancing, though as with swimming, his presence made the difference. She promised not to worry about anything "as long as you don't have to go to France." Meanwhile, Lige had sent Mae a picture of himself. She replied,

> Darling you don't know how sad and lonely you look in that picture. It makes me want to be with you and kiss away that troubled look. Do you really feel that lonely Lige? If you do I certainly am sorry for you. You looked as if you was worrying yourself to death. I hope you are not.[133]

Despite his melancholy, the tenor of Lige's letters to Mae improved, and she noticed. "They are like I love to get," she wrote on June 8, "and they make me love you more every time and I can't hardly wait to get them. But when you used to scold me in your letters it would almost break my heart and I would cry for almost a week." Mae did find hilarious the story about Lige cuddling his tent mate.[134]

Restlessness gripped Mae in the weeks before her teaching job started in July. She picked berries and worried about getting lost in the woods. She asked Lige if there were many girls in the vicinity of camp. She kept up with the romantic career of her former friend Nellie, now stringing along a boy named Trout who served alongside Lige. With sympathy for the cuckolded one, Mae asked, "Does Trout still write to her? Poor kid! I think she has more sweet hearts than she can manage."[135] To her question about cantonment girls, Lige wrote of official efforts to segregate soldiers from temptation. "Mae you know that there is not any girls at any army camp," he said, "for they are not aloud around unless married but a woman would go crazy here in this place."[136]

The Sixth Division received orders to prepare for immediate overseas transfer, shattering Lige's hopes of going home. He confessed to Mae on June 15, "this leaves me all heart broken I can't come home any more until after this war is over unless you are sick." Mae might never see him again, Lige reminded her. In his latest dream, Mae had given birth to a baby boy. Lige also cautioned her against hanging out with the wrong crowd in Williamsville. He granted that "you should know by this time what you want to do and how to take care of your self," but nonetheless accused her of acting like she wasn't married and lectured her on the perils of ruined character.[137]

Doing me dirty: these were Lige's words the next day, a Sunday, in an angrier letter he wrote lying on his bunk. It had been several days since he had heard from Mae, and a recent attempt to ring her on the phone found her absent. He took the snubs as violations of a bargain. Mae was supposed to be a "noble little girl" while Lige was busy making "Old Glory fly high," but instead, while he served his country, she was running with other people. If Mae neglected her obligation to write, "I will not let you teach that school," he warned.[138] Lige bounced from pride to self-pity to outrage to sarcasm to desire to hope to sadness, his letters ensnarled with contradictory impulses. In American public culture, wartime romance looked orderly, if potentially tragic, but in Lige's experience it was befuddling. He wanted to respect his wife's autonomy but considered it at odds with his interests. He urged Mae to live fully but seemed to hate it when she did. He was convinced the manly credibility he earned in the military undercut his position at home. He wanted her material needs met and feared other men meeting them but resented it when she provided for herself.

Then, in his last days at Camp Wadsworth, Eliga Dees did something that brought jealousy roaring back in his direction. Looking ahead to his departure, he sent Mae a package of letters and photographs he had received from *other* women. Lige anticipated trouble but couldn't bear to burn them. He softened the news by nesting it within an epistolary charm offensive. Lige clarified he in fact did trust Mae and thanked the lord "I have got a sweet little woman like that and always tells me the truth." He reinstated his consent for Mae to teach school. He updated her on his cantonment dreamscape with news of a recent snuggle session with blankets, not a doughboy.[139] As for the confession of extramarital correspondence, he pleaded with Mae, "if you read them please don't get mad about it for you are the only one that I rite to now." With that emotional time bomb traveling to Missouri, Lige thought it prudent to remind Mae of hazards he would face and coach her on how she should think about love and death. "[P]lease don't worry about me until you know that I am dead," Lige asked, "and than don't worry for I don't want you to worry honey for it mite make you sick."[140]

IN LATE JUNE, COL. WALTER WHITMAN's 325th relieved French positions in the Toul sector. Waring's Third Battalion took over billets at Saint-Jacques. Other men occupied trenches outfitted with deep, safe dugouts. They could see across No Man's Land to a line of timber shielding the Germans. Soon Whitman began sending patrols after dark to obtain information on enemy obstacles. After getting lost and separated, one Italian American was wounded by friendly fire when he couldn't respond in English to a guard from his Eighty-Second Division. "Me American!" he shouted after being shot. This was the All-American Division, so named for its ethnic diversity, whose leadership fruitlessly campaigned to have the non-native speakers transferred to the Service of Supply. Soon thereafter, a jittery American sentry killed Lt. Winston P. Anderson. On July 4, the chaplain held a memorial ceremony for Anderson, the first officer killed from the unit.[141]

The Germans scared Waring one night with a relentless bombardment of Saint-Jacques. He wrote his mother of the experience, with more candor than before, in a letter of July 3:

We are "in" now and believe me it is not what it is "cracked up" to be—we had quite some excitement one night. A battery of big guns behind us had been shelling the Germans all day—that night about the time everyone was in bed they opened up on us. I was in bed most sleep when I heard the first shell (you can hear them coming for some distance) coming over us—I didn't move but when shrapnel started falling on the roof and I heard another coming—I jumped out of bed—grabbed my "Tin Lizzie" (Steel Helmet) gas mask and put on my shoes then I beat it to a dugout. Believe me I didn't waste a minute getting in the hole. The bombardment last about 45 minutes, but it broke up our sleep for the rest of the night. It certainly does make you uncomfortable to hear those "Whiz Bangs" and "High Explosives" [illegible] around overhead.[142]

Besides digging in and covering up, soldiers relied on superstition and ritual. Some of the boys had found a rabbit to keep as a pet. When the Germans launched a shell, the bunny's ears would go up. If he raced into a dugout, the shell was landing close. If he stood still, it was going long. The attack on Saint-Jacques wounded seven men in Waring's regiment, but the Rochester, New York family of another soldier, Walter F. Owens, heard nothing of these events in his letters.[143]

On Bastille Day, July 14, Waring was in a safe place on the side of a mountain in beautiful country. There were no civilians. He hadn't seen a pretty girl yet and wasn't interested in them "except one," he told his mother.[144] Waring followed the script of the displaced warrior paramour, loyal to his girl, respectful of French womanhood, and keeping fit to fight. Years later, Knud Olsen recalled a different version of the 325th's exploits in France, the one consuming the attention of military officials and unsettling the story of doughboy righteousness:

They boys went out with [a] lot of the women over there too. The rule was if you were with a woman you had to go to a certain place and get a shot. The only thing was you had to wonder if the shot was worth the woman.[145]

The shots helped Gen. Pershing honor his guarantee that no serviceman would return disgraced by disease. By September 1918, the rate of venereal infections among Americans in France was low, less than one per thousand. Statistical victories may have boosted home front morale, but the brass knew the behaviors they obscured.[146]

Waring noted in July that postal delivery became spottier closer to the front. For parties on both ends, weeks could go by without a letter. On July 2, Waring received mail dated June 6. When his family read of his condition—"I am well and getting along just fine"—it told them how he had been doing about a month ago. But Waring believed he would see his parents soon enough. He promised his mother he would be home for Thanksgiving dinner.[147]

Then, on July 18, 1918, over a year after setting the goal, Waring Huston received his commission. The next day, he wrote a rare letter addressed to both mother and father and framed the milestone in the vocabulary of parental pride. "Just a note to tell you all," he said, "that your son is now a 2nd Lt. in the U. S. Army." He called himself a "child that was glad to see it come" and felt lucky he and his friend Blanton would stay with the 325th rather than go to another regiment or division. The promotion would mean a larger allotment and new uniform. First, though, in a day or two, he would be moving to the front and be unable to write for eight days.[148]

MAIL FROM HOME HAD a tremendous effect on the doughboy's happiness. He had more fleeting pleasures and diversions, but letters were everything. Marine private Thomas Boyd devoted much of his correspondence cataloguing the arrival, departure, or disappearance of notes to his family, friends, and sweethearts. Later, in *Through the Wheat*, Thomas drew on his experiences in France to describe what the arrival of letters looked like over there.

Boyd has Sgt. Harriman stride down the street in a crumbling French town with a packet of letters. He approaches a building where the boys are resting. "'Mailo! Mailo-ho!'" he shouts. Partially dressed soldiers jump to their feet and rush into the road. This is the first mail in two months. Harriman looks through the letters, organizing them by rank, officers first. The busted William Hicks (who stands in for Boyd in the book) has to wait for mail with the privates. Harriman reads Hicks's name, sending him "all aflutter." The men part as he comes forward. Harriman calls another name, another man comes up, but puts the letter in his pocket unopened. Some of his comrades offer to read the note to the illiterate American. Others mock him for taking up the precious time of the mail clerks. Most leave the scene disappointed.[149]

BY THE END OF June, Lige Dees's Fifty-Third Infantry had traveled to Camp Mills, Long Island. Lige found the cool weather a relief.[150]

Mae's correspondence stops for a time after June 8, 1918. (Lige was sending her notes back for safe keeping, but they don't survive for reasons that will become clear later.) Lige's letters that summer reveal she was unleashing jealous accusations even before receiving news of other women. Lige suspected somebody back in Missouri, maybe a saboteur from his own family, was putting ideas in her head. To fight Mae's fears, the doughboy deployed a scattershot strategy of reassurance. He reminded her he'd had his pick of women. He promised to tell her if he strayed but denied he had. "How did you think that I love some other woman," Eliga wrote on June 25. "I haven't seen a woman well I mean to talk to one or have my hands on one since I have see you."[151] He showered Mae with compliments and bemoaned his lonesomeness. He wrote "SMAK" on envelopes to signify kisses and sent her a little "star"—perhaps jewelry—to take his place in her bed.[152] Lige told Mae about a new dream where she wanted to be a soldier. "[W]hen I woke up I was laughing at it all," Lige said, mirroring mainstream opinion on the subject, "but hon I wish it was true."[153] He apologized for angry letters, regretting hasty words that escaped irretrievably by post. Through these weeks before the Sixth's departure, Lige dropped hints about Mae's lackluster writing schedule but subdued his criticisms. He hoped she would take "pride enough" in him to send four notes a week.[154]

On July 2, 1918, in a good mood with delivery of five letters from Mae, Lige came as close as ever to explaining why he fought. "I am staying with the flag," he wrote to Mae, "that my baby can have freedom." Lige echoed much of what public culture, in the aggregate, encouraged Americans to think. His words hinted at the political ideals the CPI and other agencies prioritized as well as the personal angles some officials believed too prevalent. But if Lige's words merged home and nation, public and private, they ultimately favored the personal. The flag was a means to an end; that end was freedom, a theoretically political concept, but "baby" suggests that to Lige it meant something about everyday life and his cherished Mae. When she asked about his level of enthusiasm, Lige said he went to France eagerly and joked about killing the Kaiser himself.[155]

On the Fourth of July, the regiment moved toward New York. In his last letter before crossing, Lige traded his reassuring tone for a woeful one. Relief at receiving five letters had lasted forty-eight hours. "[A]s long as you haven't ritten me why there is no use for you to rite now," he wrote, "for I'll not get it and I don't guess you care anyway and don't rite any until you hear from me again and remember this you are doing me dirty and trying to spite some one but you are only spiting yourself by not riting to me."[156]

Just as this venom began its journey to Missouri, Lige's First Battalion boarded the British ship *Ulysses*. He listed his father, Willie Dees, not Mae, as the person to notify in case of emergency.[157] On July 6, the ship joined a convoy and took twelve uneventful days to traverse the Atlantic, during which time Mae began her teaching assignment. Edward Streeter, the author who had crossed in May, wrote about the besotted soldier in transit. "Joe Loomis has his girls pictur pasted on the back of his tin lookin glass," Streeter's fictitious doughboy Bill tells Mable. "He lies on his bunk all day gapin at it. Some fellow make awful asses of themselves about there girls."[158] Lige periodically admitted to Mae that his comrades saw him this way.

The men landed at Liverpool and boarded trains on July 19 bound for Winchester. Three days later, most of the regiment traveled to Southampton, then undertook an overnight crossing to Cherbourg.[159] Lige sent Mae two letters he wrote in July. "I have arrived safe over seas some place in England," he reported, "and I am having a very good time." Lige provided his wife a new address. Because Lige sent Mae this information in mid-August, it's unlikely he had heard from her since writing his resentful note before the Atlantic voyage. "I am anxious to hear from you," he submitted in temperate tones. He reminded Mae not to worry about him, to teach school as she pleased, to "make life sweet" while he was away, to know they would be reunited.[160]

LIGE CAME TO EUROPE in July, the peak month (306,350 men) of a summer that brought the vast majority of Americans into the war. The week he arrived, the German Empire reached its limit.[161] On July 10, Marshal

Ferdinand Foch enjoined Pershing, "The American army must become an accomplished fact." By August, Pershing had established the First United States Army and occupied the southeastern sector of the front. The divisions of Waring, Arthur, and Lige would join that colossal force. American soldiers in massive numbers, the Allies hoped, would help roll back the Germans. "History awaits you," the French premier Georges Clemenceau wired Pershing upon formation of his army. "You will not fail it."[162]

5

So Prepare, Say a Prayer

CAKED IN MUD AND steaming mad, Waring Huston finally sent his family a letter after a week at the front. His Eighty-Second "All-American" Division was training in the active though subdued Lagney sector of the French line south of the Saint-Mihiel salient. He had slept little at night that week, Waring wrote on July 28, 1918, and had a "world of things" to do in the daytime.[1] He didn't mention nighttime patrols carried out by units of the 325th Infantry Regiment that yielded little intelligence and no prisoners. Cpl. Fred Takes, in a different battalion just behind the lines, took a walk one day and encountered a grave with eighteen French soldiers buried together. Soon he rotated to the front, around the end of July, as Waring came back.[2]

The Alabama doughboy had his name called in a recent mail delivery, but it brought unsettling news from Carrie Goodwin. She confessed to taking a ride and seeing a picture show with a boy named Will. In a letter to Mama, Waring unleashed a tirade on the slacker's unmerited access:

Here I am facing the d__ Hun living in mud and water and there he is going with the girl that I love better than my soul. I wouldn't tell her this because I know she don't love him but it sure does hurt way

160

down in the dug-out five thousand miles away. Oh! Well—some day I will be back and then those that are too yellow to fight had better look out.

Eliga Dees had walked this path of scorn and jealousy. So had the fictional Bill Smith, as large audiences in the United States were learning with the release of Edward Streeter's *Dere Mable* that summer. Streeter of the Twenty-Seventh Division would soon develop the point in his book *"Same Old Bill, Eh Mable!"* with a letter from Bill to Mable Gimp:

> That certainly was interestin about that poor young fello Archie Wainwright. It must be awful to have a murmur in your heart when you want to go to war so bad. . . . Tell him not to worry about missin the war cause when I get back Ill show him so much about it hell feel like a veteran in half an hour an his family will be hangin out a service flag.[3]

Waring was rather more revealing about the emotional pain as well as physical discomfort that fed his frustration. To his way of thinking, the dirty dug-out and filthy body should buy home front loyalty, the wartime romantic bargain that Mae Dees supposedly broke whenever she didn't write enough for Lige's epistolary appetite. That was the compact millions of Americans read about in public culture, the one peddled in 1918's two soldiers' bride manuals, *Over Here* and *Silver Lining*, and the one pitched in the film *Hearts of the World* that spring.

Thomas Boyd of the Sixth Marine Regiment, resting in a lull between battles at this moment in July, later mourned these broken promises of wartime in *Through the Wheat*. During a similar respite from combat, Sgt. Harriman, the imperious distributor of mail earlier in the book, receives a letter from his girlfriend Ellen. The stamp is glued at an angle, a symbol of love in the postal routine of doughboys and sweethearts. "Dear Carl," it begins, "You poor dear boy!!" Ellen praises his bravery in the face of the frightful Hun. Like Mae, she worries about her man being taken prisoner. Ellen asks if he received the knitted helmet, six bars of chocolate, and tobacco she had arranged through a soldiers' charity. She doesn't like him succumbing to tobacco, but is "willing to sacrifice a mere prejudice for so great a cause as you boys are fighting for." Her mother keeps talking up a local boy named John Ryder. He's not a slacker, Ellen says, but a farmer growing food the government needs. The mother thinks Carl isn't coming home alive. "Would you forgive me if I did, Carl? I mean, became Mrs. John R. Ryder? You better hurry or I will. Your loving Ellen. P. S. The papers say that we must call you Sammies now. Are you my little Sammy?"

The crushed Sgt. Harriman beholds his future—bloody gas masks, helmets pierced by German bullets, combat packs and pieces of equipment scattered near holes hastily dug and pitiful in their protective qualities. He walks into the woods and shoots himself in the foot. "Court martial and disgrace," he thinks, suddenly coming back to the present and suddenly fearful of the home front shame that had concerned the demoted William Hicks earlier in the novel. "And he had only meant to get back home. He began to whimper."[4]

THE SUMMER ARRIVAL OF the American Expeditionary Forces (AEF) helped reverse the German spring offensives. In June 1918, Thomas Boyd and the Marines as well as black doughboys of the 369th Infantry counterattacked at Belleau Wood. From July on, the Western Front would creep back toward Belgium and Germany. At the Second Battle of the Marne, beginning July 15, the Germans made their last major assault of the war. The French and Americans arrested the advance, then launched the Aisne-Marne counteroffensive in July and early August, winning at Château-Thierry and Soissons, where the First and Second Divisions fought. Bells rang in celebration in New York, Washington, Cincinnati, Boston, Cleveland, San Diego, and Birmingham, Alabama.[5] The press told stories of chivalric liberation. Arthur Huebner's hometown paper reported an old woman crawling out of a cellar, the tearful octogenarian ecstatic to be rid of the invaders, crying "*Vivent les Americains!*" as she kissed her liberators.[6]

Boyd of the Second Division received a commendation for his actions at Soissons on a blazing hot July 19, which generated material for some of the combat scenes in *Through the Wheat*. In the book's rendition of Soissons, Boyd later focused on "unendurable" heat, a headless body clutching a pipe, itchy skin and the tightening of chin straps and glistening of bayonets. In one scene, he reversed wartime contrasts between American and enemy character:

Pugh, exploring one of the packs, drew forth a pair of baby stockings and a small knitted hood. Beside the pack lay a peaceful-looking, home-loving German who had passed his middle years.

"Here's an orphan, all right!" Pugh announced, and went to the next pack.[7]

In the real engagement at Soissons, Boyd's fellow Marine Martin Gulberg took machine gun fire to both legs. He survived to spend several agonizing weeks in hospitals before rejoining his unit in October.[8] After these actions, the Sixth Marines withdrew to the quiet Marbache sector near Nancy.

The summer campaigns swept up Waring Huston's friend Pressley Cleveland, serving with the 167th Infantry of the Forty-Second "Rainbow" Division. The regiment's success at Croix Rouge Farm on July 26 Douglas MacArthur attributed to "gallantry I do not believe has been surpassed in military history."[9] The British won a victory to the north at Amiens on August 8, with units of Arthur's Thirty-Third "Prairie" Division aiding in that rollback before vacating the British sector. To the German general Erich Ludendorff, August 8 was the "black day" of his army. Relying on fresh American troops, the Allies retook the Marne salient and pushed the Kaiser's forces into a defensive position.[10] When September came, the Allies were planning further incursions, although the role of Gen. John Pershing's First American Army in those plans remained undetermined.

A YOUNG SOUTHERNER HAD been shot through the lung and evacuated to Hospital 14 in Beauvais. In early June 1918, his nurse, Natalie Scott, called him a "lovable boy," handsome and confident. He reminded Natalie of kids she knew from home, and in turn, he wished he had a sister like her. Natalie asked if there was a girl she could help him write in America. After some thought, he dictated a short note to his aunt and family. They must miss him terribly, Natalie said. "They do. They do," he answered, then added, "This'll break their hearts." Natalie stayed up with him all night, then found him in bad shape the next day:

I took him some fruit and eggs and the sweetest little flowering red geranium about 6 inches high, all in my nice old basket which all of the boys know. . . . He watched the things come out of the basket, as interested as a child at Xmas. I saw him again Monday. He died Tuesday. Now I must hurry and go to his funeral this morning.

This was the second loss for Natalie in short order. Days earlier, she had gone out to dinner with a major—he insisted—instead of checking on a sick British patient named Nolan. She came back to the hospital to find he had died.[11] Neither Natalie's grief nor her renderings of doughboy suffering mitigated her fidelity, at least as she articulated her feelings to her mother, to the tenets of American civil religion. Love gave death meaning—love of country, love of God, love of family—quite apart from the specific objectives of America's Great War intervention. To make the point she quoted the ancient Roman warrior Horatius, but adapted him to the monotheistic and patriotic environment of 1918 America. Here was Horatius:

> To every man upon this earth
> Death cometh soon or late;
> And how can man die better
> Than facing fearful odds,
> For the ashes of his fathers
> And the temples of his Gods[12]

Natalie changed the last two lines for her mother to, "For glory of his country and the honor of his God." Of the Horatius passage she wrote, "Do you remember how I used to ring it out, and how excited I used to get over it? I still love its bold spirit and its buoyant virility. And I think of it often as I look at our boys who have found the 'best death.' "[13]

In the middle of June, Natalie's mother Martha sent her articles from stateside newspapers calling her the "Air Raid Heroine."[14] One day, British aviators saw the clippings and Natalie was mortified. Compared to the risks those fliers took, she told her mother, it hardly seemed brave to trot "some soldier-boys down some steps."[15] The doughboys likewise eclipsed her exploits. She eulogized them to Martha:

> I couldn't love these plain, fine old fellows any more no matter what happened. . . . Our politicians and "higher minds" may argue as to

whether or not we are really fighting for democracy, but our men never doubt it, nor do they argue as to what democracy really is. They feel it as something as holy and perhaps as mysterious as the Holy Grail. And I find them as fine . . . as the knights of old,—Launcelots, and Tristans, and Galahads, too.[16]

Natalie used the word "democracy" but her remarks implied something rather more profound and ethereal, something emotional. She imagined Americans fighting not out of dedication to a political system but as an expression of character, of chivalric commitment, even of piety. Fighting a war for democracy, in Natalie's expansive understanding, made the doughboy lovable.

Natalie celebrated her birthday on July 18 by stockpiling letters from home for a week and spending the day catching up on New Orleans. Then arrived more painful news. Quentin Roosevelt had been killed in action on Bastille Day. The flier who had joked to Natalie that aviation kept him out of danger had gone "down in flames," as she put it. "He was really quite a fine little American," Natalie mourned to her mother.[17] Natalie wouldn't have known it, but the Germans, discovering in his pockets who Quentin was, buried him with military honors in the village of Chamery. Gen. Pershing wrote Col. Theodore Roosevelt an official letter of notification in the tones of wartime gender politics, assigning combat the power to reveal personal, patriotic, and masculine virtue. The general's epistolary homage resembled stories Natalie Scott told her mother about the doughboys and the meaning of their service:

Quentin died as he had lived and served, nobly and unselfishly; in the full strength and vigor of his youth, fighting the enemy in clean combat. You may well be proud of your gift to the nation in his supreme sacrifice.[18]

However familiar and meaningful this language may have been to the former Rough Rider, he went into a deep depression over the death of his youngest son.

During the balance of July and August, Natalie had a number of experiences that testified both to the durability of war's romantic narrative and to its disruption. Part of that story held that women in the war zone would perform traditionally feminine duties—compassionately caring for, wholesomely entertaining, and faithfully admiring the soldiers. The Red Cross in general, and Natalie in particular, fulfilled these roles yet added to them a commitment to professionalism, stoicism, and competence. Pushing even further in that direction were the female doctors in the hospitals of France, in whose ranks served a good friend of Natalie's, Dr. Greenough.[19] These various patterns of meaning ran through a single evening's affair in early August. Dr. Greenough asked Natalie to entertain some Allied ambulance drivers at the American Club in Beauvais that night at 6:30. Natalie was exhausted and somber from her nursing tasks, but sitting in the middle of twenty men forced her to be "very gay." Although Dr. Greenough was present, Natalie reported to her mother she was the "only feminine fixture" in the room, the doctor a woman she admired but not a feminine one. They all proceeded to have much fun talking and telling jokes about the boys' hometowns. "It was great to listen to," Natalie said, "but I had to run away, like Cinderella, in the midst of it." She had patients to see.[20]

Another strand of the wartime romance held that American doughboys were sexual innocents and French women dangerous seductresses. This certitude of moral difference Natalie both affirmed and challenged in a couple of stories she told her mother. There was a French nurse who had left her husband for another man and had many affairs. This "scandalous" woman flirted with American men endlessly. Yet Natalie admired her "bold" attractiveness, her "cleverly" applied hair dye and makeup, and her compassion for her patients, with the notorious exception of a gassed Senegalese soldier whose suffering the French nurse found comic. Natalie, who called herself "modern," was "fascinated" by her but sensed her mother would be "less tolerant of her than I am."[21] More straightforward was Natalie's view of another French nurse, whom she found making out with a dying patient. "These poor French girls," she said to Muddie, "they are brought up in such a disastrous fashion! That one is a merry, kind hearted little thing and I hate to think of her cheapening herself so."[22]

IN THE BEGINNING OF August, the American command rotated Waring's regiment and the Eighty-Second Division from their portion of the front. In his diary, Fred Takes recorded the 325th's last week in the

Lagney trenches, long days of mud and rain and short minutes of stolen sleep under tin roofs. "[T]he earth was shivering," he wrote of German barrages, "and the sky was red with flashes." Men slipping and sliding out of the wet trenches made way for Great Plains draftees of the relieving Eighty-Ninth Division. Yet Col. Whitman, Second Lt. Huston, and Cpl. Takes all mocked the notion of rest. In villages behind the trenches, the soldiers drilled endlessly and Waring censored mail. He chose not to tell his family about a horrific volley of gas attacks, first American, then German, which inflicted heavy damage on the enemy and produced seven hundred casualties in the Eighty-Ninth. On August 15, the course of rest and drilling finished, Waring's All-Americans in turn relieved Thomas Boyd's Second Division in the Marbache area, like Lagney on the southern face of the bulge at Saint-Mihiel. Since advancing to the front in late June, the Eighty-Second had lost forty-four soldiers killed, one of them the officer accidentally shot by his own man, and 327 wounded by gas.[23] The Huston family wouldn't have known these numbers. But on any given morning, as they opened papers at breakfast, they might be faced with throat-tightening headlines. "Many Alabama Boys Killed in Action," cried the *Selma Journal* on August 5, "Two Are Selmians." Pressley Cleveland's Rainbow Division was the unit in question.[24]

Waring assured his mother Marbache was a relatively safe sector, although he only could say he was near a town sharing the name of his brother's wife (Nancy). He reported plenty of activity and overwhelming heat. "Enough is enough," he griped, his experience filling with what a later divisional history called with characteristic euphemism "intensive military education."[25] The Germans put sixty men of the 325th in the hospital after another gas barrage. One night, Waring watched Allied planes bombard a German train. On August 29, several soldiers went out on a patrol and never returned. One survived, only to be reunited with his countrymen after the armistice. "Believe me I sure wish this war was over," Waring wrote. "You have no idea what it is."[26] He didn't say much to enlighten his parents, the same approach taken by his comrade Walter Owens of Company C, who wrote letters home during that eventful August revealing nothing of military activity. Instead, they threw their attention to prosaic things. Waring asked his family not to wear out their new Dodge. A French vase he found would be making its way to her by post. Waring wondered if they were receiving allotment payments. Meanwhile, officers were being sent back for instruction, and Waring hoped to be let "in on the deal."[27]

Yet at the end of August, he was with the Eighty-Second Division when it officially joined Gen. Pershing's new First U. S. Army. Those days found Waring holding an outpost about a mile in front of the lines, the regiment's three battalions rotating between forward, support, and reserve positions. He occupied a dug-out recently vacated and made gas-proof by his pal Claiborne Blanton's platoon. He had just heard from Press Cleveland that a mutual friend had been killed and buried in France. "I will be back home soon," Waring wrote his family, "safe and sound." But he sent Carrie Goodwin's correspondence to Alabama for preservation and asked that if anything should happen to him, his mother must return all of it to her and never read a word. Other notes from Carrie were stashed in his bureau in Selma. These he also wished restored to their author upon his death.[28]

As Waring Huston's division moved forward and his letters arrived at the house on Church Street, an article in the *Selma Journal* taught mothers lessons on wartime emotion and behavior. Kathleen Norris's prescriptive essay, "A Mother's Promise to Her Son," syndicated in papers around the country since at least May 1918, urged motherly stoicism and home front productivity. But the piece took the form of a surprisingly revelatory letter she tucked into his pack, next to his army manual and Bible and passports and address book:

> I know—as I write this in the room you love—that your fingers may fumble for this little piece of paper in some dreadful hour, a month or two months or six months from now, just to read it over once more for the last time, just to feel in your fingers out there in a shell lighted battlefield something that I have touched—for goodbye.

The mother pledges busy domestic industry on behalf of her son. This work, she says, will sustain her even should the blackest news arrive. "Perhaps in God's goodness," the letter closes, "this note will come safely back to me in the olive drab pocket, and we will smile over it together."[29]

Just days later, the Selma paper ran a story teaching quite a different lesson about wartime love. A young woman in Chicago named Mae had married three husbands for the allotment payments. When Walter went to France, she wed John, when John went to France, she wed Nick. Then she made a mistake: "She introduced husband No. 3 to the mother of No. 1. War Risk Bureau investigators got busy."[30]

THE 124TH MACHINE GUN BATTALION had spent June traveling around the British sector and continued to serve there from July 2 to August 23, 1918.[31] Arthur Huebner and fellow Wisconsin natives Ben Fluegel, Daniel McCarthy, and Clayton Slack were connected to two battalions of the British Fourth Army. On the Fourth of July, elements of two Thirty-Third Division infantry regiments assisted the Australians in a successful assault on German positions at Hamel, a few miles east of Amiens, supposedly shouting "Lusitania!" as they charged. Later in the month, Arthur's Company C of the 124th occupied part of the line. Clayton Slack remembered bombs dropping and shrapnel flying. A few British soldiers died. "Those that weren't scared weren't there," he said of this early "baptism by fire."[32]

Arthur spent August 6–12 stationed by a prisoner of war camp at Baizieux, as the Thirty-Third Division endured frequent enemy shelling. One outfit, the 131st Infantry Regiment, found itself loaned to the British for an assault in Gressaire Wood on a hot August 9. Three days later, back at division headquarters in Molliens-au-Bois, Gen. Pershing and Gen. Tasker H. Bliss were on hand to receive a visit from King George V of Great Britain. That day, the King bestowed military honors on American officers for the action at Hamel.[33] Then, on the afternoon of August 22, the assistant secretary of the navy visited the Thirty-Third and had lunch with the divisional commander. Franklin Delano Roosevelt delivered a stirring address to the Prairie Division. The following day, its time with the British ended. On August 23, 1918, the Thirty-Third transferred to the area of the First American Army in the Toul sector. Arthur and the machine gunners of the 124th went to a place called Bar-le-Duc.[34]

CPL. ELIGA DEES AND his mates in Company D, Fifty-Third Infantry, Sixth Division, arrived at their training sector on July 26, 1918. At Colombey-les-Deux-Eglises, about 160 miles southeast of Paris, the regiment worked for a month on open warfare and trench fighting. By

August 30, Lige's unit was in La Bresse, which became the regiment's jumping off point for assignments to the southern front.[35] Sometime in August, the Missourian regular became a sergeant, though he never commented on the promotion. Not much happened in Lige's zone until September 16, when a German raid killed Pvt. Leo Brooks in Company K.[36] Little came of the unit's patrols into enemy lines. Lige's colleague Wayne Turner wrote a light-hearted letter home on September 18, speaking of visits to the dug-out dentist and cootie inspections and tobacco. Apparently mail was taking thirty-eight days to reach him. Fritz, as he called the Germans, tended to drop shells near one particularly unlucky though as yet unscathed corporal, but beyond that Wayne kept mum on combat.[37]

Lige Dees continued to feed his wife's episodic familiarity with his life. "I am in the front line trenches and have been for some time," he wrote in September, "and I like them fine." He discouraged Mae from worrying and guessed he would be home by Christmas. She was sending letters that Lige in turn sent back to her but don't survive. From his responses it is clear that Mae was feeling well and asking if her notes were censored. Lige only complained about "pets" in the trenches, rats "big enough to carry a man over the top ha ha." He asked for a few pairs of thick socks.[38]

THE SEGREGATED UNITS OSCILLATED between training and fighting that summer. After the violence of June's engagement at Belleau Wood, the 369th Infantry, part of the Ninety-Third Division and lodged with the French, acquitted itself favorably in mid-July in actions near Minaucourt. The white commander Col. Hayward was gratified to report that his "regiment of negroes" was all that stood between the Germans and Paris. "No German ever got into a trench with my regiment," he wrote, "who did not stay there or go back with the brand of my boys upon him." There were few black officers in the 369th, but one, Capt. Charles Fillmore, earned a commendation for his leadership. The musician-soldier James Reese Europe suffered a terrible gassing in these actions. His bandmate Noble Sissle visited him in the hospital, where Europe wrote "On Patrol in No Man's Land," later a stateside hit. After more than four months on the front line, the unit got a week off in August. Upon return it began preparing for a major offensive planned for late September. Another regiment in the division, the draftee 371st, earned French and American praise for its performance that summer.[39]

Meanwhile the all-black Ninety-Second Division, training with the French, wasn't combat-ready in the eyes of Gen. Pershing. Although all manner of problems with instruction and equipment had hampered the division from the start, Pershing pinned its failings on the "lower capacity" of blacks and absence of white officers. One of the division's engineer units, once in France, did heavy labor instead of working as engineers. At the end of August, the ill-equipped Ninety-Second was stationed in a peaceful part of the front in the Vosges Mountains.[40]

For a brief time, many black soldiers found an unfamiliar degree of social freedom. Some of them had read about colonial African troops serving with distinction in the French army, but the real shocks came upon arrival overseas. Stevedores at Saint-Nazaire flirted with or dated French women. Ely Green, the soldier who had exhorted black men to defend their women against whites in Waxahachie, Texas, in the fall of 1917, later recalled segregation in Saint-Nazaire's clubs but black doughboys mingling freely with white women in the "colored" establishments. For those seeking masculine confirmation from their service, such interactions seemed payback for their transatlantic mission of rescue. French women, by this way of thinking, were both the objects of protection and the sources of grateful love in return. A soldier in the Ninety-Second wrote in the *Cleveland Advocate* that their delivery of chivalric emancipation made the men feel like the "true sons of France." The French harbored their own racist preconceptions and had them verified by nervous white Americans, competitors for French female attention. But the local people sanctioned a fluidity of movement and intimacy that doughboys of color reported favorably.[41]

For white military men, liaisons between French women and African American men confirmed expectations of black sexual predation. But they particularly threatened to undermine the wartime version of those fantasies, the narrative of masculine mission that cast *white* soldiers as the saviors of French women and therefore the rightful beneficiaries of their romantic devotion. Leaders in the AEF weren't thrilled with any doughboys wooing the locals, but especially black ones. White officials believed, or wanted to believe, that white women couldn't possibly consent to black advances. Rumors of rape began flying. "The black

American troops in France have, by themselves," wrote a French official working with the Americans in an influential August memo, "given rise to as many complaints for attempted rape as all the rest of the army."[42]

William Buckner was a black Kentucky teenager serving with the 313th Labor Battalion near the French town of Arrentières. On the night of July 2, at around nine-thirty, William had sex with a French woman named Georgette Thiebaux in an oat field. He called the encounter consensual; she called it rape. William was arrested three days later. Officials scheduled a general court-martial for late July.[43]

MAE'S TEACHING JOB BEGAN in Missouri during Lige's ocean journey.[44] The *Greenville Sun* praised education and other manifestations of womanly contribution—caring for the sick, managing foodstuffs, shepherding children to adulthood. "Many young women would do well to fit themselves for teachers," read a published call to duty. "[H]ow can children be brought up right without an education? We need nurses badly, but young women who have a talent for teaching are also serving their country in that capacity." Here was confirmation of Mae's own tendency, as she framed it for Lige, to imagine teaching as a way of avoiding the slacker's shame. A week later, the paper reprinted an image of a woman throwing herself into the war effort by planting a home garden and saving food.[45]

Wayne County reporters, like those in Selma and Watertown and New Orleans and a thousand other places, kept a sort of delayed vigil that summer on local boys in the service. Eli Thornburgh learned in August that his son Roy, formerly a teacher at Mae Dees's high school in Williamsville, had been severely injured in July and missed his First "Big Red One" Division's part in the Aisne-Marne offensive.[46] Meanwhile, at a patriotic rally on a very hot day, a good crowd sang "Hang Bill Kaiser on a Sour Apple Tree."[47] An appeal for a new drive to sell war savings stamps, though, written by a local man living in a place broadly skeptical of the war, ignored cause and enemy and implored the public to "save the lives of our boys and end this bloody war."[48] This approach would intensify with American combat losses as summer turned to fall.

The next week, readers found out more from Roy's letter printed in the Greenville weekly. A German bullet had lodged itself in the right side of his abdomen. Surgeons went in through Roy's back to remove it.

Soon he was walking around and eager to rejoin his Eighteenth Infantry. He reassured his father, and the paper thereby reassured the public, that the government would immediately notify the family "should anything ever happen." Other doughboys had their upbeat letters printed in the newspaper. Walter Wilkinson joked that the Huns would be crying mercy by Christmas. He did take comfort, though, from the Twenty-Third Psalm: *Even though I walk through the valley of the shadow of death, I will fear no evil, for you are with me.* With the Lord as his shepherd, his soul secure whatever the Germans did to his body, Walter was "feeling dandy."[49]

A meeting of Wayne County teachers at the end of August, meantime, revealed how Missourians were incorporating war into home front life. Local educators held a tutorial on taking part in War Activities; a talk called "A Flag for Every School"; an address on the war by a former state legislator; and an honorary roll call of educators like Roy who had gone into the service ("War Teachers").[50] Percolating through the program were strains of Missouri's reluctance about the intervention. Various speakers hoped the war would end quickly and pledged devotion to America, but made few claims about broader purposes. The superintendent of schools chose Independence Day 1918 to publicly oppose a national trend requiring teachers take a loyalty oath. Instead, he argued for supplying flags to every school and assigning teams of students to raise them, though he missed the coercive elements of his own plan.[51] When this idea came to pass in Greenville, attorney Voltaire V. Ing spoke not about war but on "The Flag, Its Origin and History." A reporter covering the speech noted the war's rejuvenation of patriotism, sighing that the flag had become "somewhat neglected in recent years."[52] Drives for money, rallies for soldiers, and the teachers' conference all communicated determination rather than bellicosity, love of community over zeal for war—rather akin to the spirit of other, far more stressed warring populations across the ocean.[53]

While many Missourians appreciated the doughboy's unimpeachable public service to nation, their newspapers simultaneously acknowledged the unimaginable private costs to family. Those costs, pictured in 1917 in abstract and sentimental terms, became ever more tangible. Jesse Talley missed the funeral of his sister. An infant named Robert Benjamin was born on August 8 without his serviceman father present.[54]

In September, word came down a rural road near Williamsville that the Akes family had lost their son and brother Harve, a single draftee of twenty-five who'd worked for the Missouri Pacific Railroad. Serving with the Fourth Division, Harve had been killed in action on July 18, 1918, roughly the day the German Empire reached its zenith.[55] The paper expressed sorrow and longed for the day the "Hun is driven across the Rhine." Arthur Lee Clayton was a Wayne County son killed the day before Harve, though it was late September before his family heard from the War Department.[56] He had dependent parents but was conscripted nevertheless.[57] Other boys were severely wounded or killed. But Roy Thornburgh was back to fighting fit, reported the *Greenville Sun*.[58]

Toward the end of summer, a member of the Wayne County Dees clan, William Oda, left the state for basic training at Camp Funston, Kansas.[59] A few months earlier, in February and March, eleven hundred trainees there had come down with severe influenza. It then traveled with soldiers from camp to camp. Ten percent of troops at Camp Forrest, where Eliga Dees was stationed, fell ill. It then spread from the United States to Europe and Asia, sickening many though killing relatively few. By the time William left, in August 1918, infections had slowed down dramatically. New Wayne County draftees gathering at Camp Funston wrote back of happy adjustment, of singing "Home Sweet Home" on the banjo with boyhood friends.[60] The virus's dormancy heading into the fall led a British medical journal to declare it had "completely disappeared."[61]

AT BAR-LE-DUC IN AUGUST and September, Arthur Huebner's unit trained and rested. Clayton Slack remembered eating French rye bread and goat meat. The doughboys relaxed, had baths, got new clothes. They nonetheless continued to fight the scourge of body lice. For shaving, Clayton used a razor and mirror off a German corpse. The men received the American Vickers guns they would be using in battle.[62]

On September 5, 1918, the Prairie Division's leadership accepted orders to replace French forces in the Verdun sector, and the division moved into new positions over the next few days. Arthur's unit operated in a subsector known as Mort-Homme, or dead man. These grounds bore the scars and stories of almost a million French and German killed or wounded in 1916 in the long, costly, and ultimately unsuccessful

German attack at Verdun. In Clayton Slack's memory, the French forces there in late 1918 were happy to be relieved. This move put the Thirty-Third Division under French command, where it remained until September 14.[63]

HOWEVER QUIET THE MARBACHE sector was in late summer 1918, it put Waring Huston and the rest of the Eighty-Second Division into contact with the Germans. The experience prepared the division for a role in looming battle plans. And as August turned to September, the All-American Division judged battle-worthy after an inspection, Waring became pious in his letters home.

He was a member of First Presbyterian Church in Selma. Like many other Protestants in the AEF, Waring had grown up in a climate steeped in muscular Christianity. Far from viewing violence and faith as contradictory, these young men imagined war as a religiously redemptive and personally strengthening experience. God approved of the American war effort and thus even combat death meant salvation and the fulfillment of His wishes. That worldview fit well with the broader tendency to regard the Great War as an opportunity to protect American domestic safety and preserve gender roles and familial stability, all under peril from so many angles. Religion was a major note in the wartime hymn of regeneration.[64]

Whether they were regular churchgoers or not, lots of soldiers appealed to a higher power. With them traveled a developed spiritual architecture including chaplains, field services, YMCA huts, religious ceremony and burial, and frequent religious discourse in *Stars and Stripes, Trench and Camp*, and other stateside and war zone publications. Pronouncements from local and national leaders rang with references to the Almighty. The army chaplaincy drew overwhelmingly from Protestant denominations, but officials made efforts to facilitate worship across the sixty-seven religious groups represented in the doughboy population. Roman Catholic and Jewish chaplains eventually made their way to the front.[65]

Waring's newly vocal piety coincided with his knowledge that something was coming. The Eighty-Second had been gearing up for Gen. Pershing's war of movement during the Marbache interlude.[66] At the beginning of September, Waring informed his mother he was about to "go in," but said, "by the time you get this I will be out again, so don't worry about me." Here was the heartbreaking paradox of modern postal circuitry. It fired well enough to keep loved ones in contact but not well enough to stay current. Nellye Huston would read that Waring had survived a campaign he had no way of knowing he would survive. Meanwhile Waring sent home more Carrie Goodwin correspondence. He despaired that everyone he loved was so far away. Yet Waring acknowledged that his family had the harder job—"waiting and praying"—and he thought them braver than himself. "Mama we have not been in any big action yet," Waring wrote, "but by the time you get this I believe we will have—I have gone through with everything so far and have done my duty—I only pray that I can always be strong and that the Lord will give me wisdom in leading my men. I trust in Him to take care of me." Waring was adamant that no one other than his mother and father read this note.[67]

Rather paradoxically, the Alabamian declared in these first two weeks of September that he preferred danger at the front to life in the rear. There were even unexpected pleasures on the line. One day Waring spotted some fruit hanging in an orchard in No Man's Land, or what Edward Streeter had his doughboy jokester Bill Smith call "Nobodies Land."[68] He crept forward through an old trench and got himself a whole armful of apples, rock-hard but tasty. The Germans never fired a shot, he assured his parents, giving them a sense of the sector's temperature. Waring received more mail from home, now reaching the front a good month and half after departing Alabama. He heard from Press Cleveland in the Rainbow Division, veteran of the Aisne-Marne offensive and now marching under cover of darkness toward Waring's unit and the same imminent operation.[69] Three thousand "horny men," remembered a veteran from the division, improvised racy ditties to pass the time.[70] Waring returned to the hated reserve area around September 4 in a driving rain and low mood. Two weeks had passed since his last bath.[71] Fred Takes went up when Waring came back, leaving a reserve area bustling with the sounds of rats and owls. At the front, Fred waited for an enemy charge and tried to stay dry. There were gas attacks. When he could, Fred picked berries and wrote letters and prayed.[72]

On September 14, Waring sent his father a letter. "[T]he drive is still on and going fine—suppose you have been reading about it today and wondering if I am in it—Yes I am, but don't worry about me for the Lord will take care of me," he wrote. "I am trusting in Him."[73]

THE WESTERN FRONT HAD bulged southward to the city of Saint-Mihiel since 1914. The French tried and failed to take it back the next year. In 1916, the Germans used the salient to stage attacks against Verdun. But trenches along the projection had proven quiet since 1915, hence their selection as training grounds for Waring's Eighty-Second and other divisions in August 1918.

By that time, under dimming estimations of Saint-Mihiel's strategic value, the Germans had recommitted some troops to other fronts. But the region contained important railways and stood at the doorstep of the fortified German city of Metz. Allied commander Marshal Ferdinand Foch thought retaking the salient might be a good job for Gen. Pershing's new First Army. Then he changed his mind, sharing the Germans' reduced interest in Saint-Mihiel, and decided to attach American divisions to French ones in the Champagne and Meuse-Argonne regions. Pershing erupted, his chance to audition an independent force fading. Foch reconsidered, opting to mobilize the First Army for two operations: first, the "drive" on Saint-Mihiel that Waring mentioned, expected to succeed quickly, and second, the Meuse-Argonne offensive, planned for the end of September. To position the First Army for these campaigns, the command gave the Americans control of the frontage stretching around the Saint-Mihiel salient and westward to the Argonne Forest. Waring's friend Pressley marched overnight as part of this movement to the region, a logistical feat involving long, snaking lines of wet, muddy infantry, guns, wagons, trucks, and horses.[74] The attack against the Saint-Mihiel salient was scheduled for September 12, 1918.

THE LEADERS OF THE Eighty-Second Division had their own issues with horny men in Nancy. The man whose problem this became was Maj. John Paul Tyler, senior chaplain of the Eighty-Second and the same major who had commanded Nellye Huston and other mothers of the 325th Infantry to "put the sunshine in your letters." On September 11, Tyler received a note of concern from Maj. Gen. John Burnham, commander of the All-Americans:

> [I]t has been brought to the attention of the Senior Chaplain [of the AEF by the military police] that soldiers are openly solicited by lewd women on the streets of Nancy. It is requested that steps be taken to protect our men from this temptation.[75]

Besides the military implications, men visiting prostitutes posed a challenge to the story of upstanding men saving women from German violation. To protect it, the divisional commander cast the doughboys as victims in need of protection, a profound but useful reversal of their reputation. That the women in question were French, long held to lack virtue by the nurse Natalie Scott and many other Americans, made it easier for the division's leaders to claim American innocence. Flyers aimed at soldiers in France warned they would be "accosted many times by public women."[76] But vilification of the French never stopped officials from working to contain doughboy sexuality. Authorities in France continued to combat venereal disease, and the Eighty-Second saw lower rates along with the rest of the AEF by September 1918.[77]

Still, some Americans dated French women, others wanted to marry them. This trend worried home front sweethearts and wives like Mae Dees and Carrie Goodwin, as well as authorities in the AEF. The government and press had spent months by the summer of 1918 trumpeting the doughboy's chastity and loyalty. He was in France to rescue French women, not court them. By the end of 1917, Americans were already either marrying surreptitiously or asking their commanding officers for permission. Some French women and their families appealed directly to Gen. Pershing for approval, but the army lacked a policy on the issue. Late in 1917, the American judge advocate general declared marriage a private rather than military matter, but the AEF persisted in neither sanctioning nor barring marriages.

By the spring of 1918, requests for marriage permission had grown more frequent. Most AEF commanders opposed overseas romances of any kind, wanting their men focused on war, not love. For the same reason, soldiers' American wives, sweethearts, and sisters generally were banned from coming to France, even through the nursing corps. Yet some authorities argued that marriage was a right that should follow the AEF to Europe, that it was a symbol, in fact, of the family-loving, free society doughboys were fighting to protect. In the end, the judge advocate recommended a ban on marriages, but Pershing disagreed and left the ambiguous policy in place. Individual commanders denying leave requests, as well as the intricacies of French marriage law, continued to prove obstacles to marriages.

But this non-resolution generated a different problem: out-of-wedlock babies. The French wished the AEF would make it easier for honest men to marry the mothers of their Franco-American children. Local governments also objected to doughboys behaving nothing like their chivalric reputation would suggest, impregnating and abandoning French women. Moral disapproval ran in both directions in this transatlantic partnership. Just as Americans regarded French sexual attitudes suspiciously, the French considered Americans overly casual in their acceptance of divorce and common-law marriages. The presence of babies fathered by Americans conjured memories of German behavior during the invasion, although the circumstances were of course very different. The children of foreign soldiers inflamed existing French fears of national decline and familial decay, particularly if they were the product of prostitution, rape, or abandonment.

British and French authorities clamored for the AEF to make marriage legal, legitimate, and regulated. The Red Cross agreed to help French families investigate an American's reputation and family history, provided he approved. Other French families registered complaints with the AEF when they found their daughters pregnant and alone, or requested marriage permission when the doughboy had stuck around. News of out-of-wedlock births alarmed the Wilson administration, which had worked diligently to proclaim a moral army and feared what it would look like to discourage marriage. The secretaries of state and war urged soldiers in individual cases to honor new familial obligations. By the late summer of 1918, the AEF still had no official policy facilitating marriages, but leaders were coming to see that accommodating rather than blocking amorous pursuits better aligned with the war's chivalric dimensions.[78]

THE ARMY'S POSITION ON black soldiers mingling with French women was moving in exactly the opposite direction. Many officials could scarcely believe consensual romance between black men and white women possible—or were terrified it might be. Policies toward whites and blacks thus differed dramatically in character but overlapped in intention: to protect the white doughboy's virtuous mission and reputation. The distinctions came into clear view in the summer of 1918.

The trial of nineteen-year-old Pvt. William Buckner began on July 27. The woman accusing him of rape, Georgette Thiebaux, gave her version of what had happened almost a month earlier. She was walking down the road at half past nine when suddenly a man she had never met—William—grabbed her and pulled her into an oat field. To stifle her screams, the accused stuffed a handkerchief into the woman's mouth. Georgette went limp with fear as Pvt. Buckner raped her. She openly admitted being horrified by his race. "I say he is ugly," she sneered through an interpreter, "because he is a nigger and niggers are disgusting." Two French soldiers confirmed hearing the attack and seeing Georgette and William emerge from the field. She ran to her countrymen crying, "Kill him, he has raped me." The next morning, she reported the crime to the local *gendarme*. A doughboy alleged William had bragged about chasing and doing "business" to a French woman.

Pvt. Buckner recounted a story not of violation but romance. He told the court he had known Georgette for some time. They met at a grocery store, drank wine together, and exchanged presents. William testified under oath that the encounter of July 2 followed a string of consensual acts. Nothing contentious happened until that night, William said, when she grabbed his arm, somehow breaking a watch he had given her, so he snatched it back from her. This angered Georgette. "Me and you are finish," she said, and then repaired to the road where she flagged down the French soldiers. After he was arrested, William disclosed at trial, he told his military superiors (including his defense counsel) about the relationship and showed them where he had spent time with Thiebaux. The prosecution responded with alibi witnesses for Georgette. Her father testified she didn't speak English, as William maintained. Townspeople and family members disputed that Georgette had possessed gifts she supposedly gave Pvt. Buckner and denied she had met him in public places. The defense closed by pointing out inconsistencies in the young woman's story. A physician's examination didn't conclusively show rape. Several men in William's unit testified to his version.[79]

After deliberation, the court found William guilty as charged, rejecting his contention that a French woman would consort willingly with a black man. Two-thirds of the panel agreed to sentence Buckner to death by hanging. The Office of the Judge Advocate reviewed the sentence and upheld it. Gen. Pershing and President Wilson approved William's execution.

The verdict revealed the transportability of American sexual and racial politics. French women, otherwise viewed as lustful predators, became chaste victims when their sexual partners were black. The case likewise reflected the racial character of the war's chivalric dimensions. In popular and official culture, the doughboys saving womanhood were overwhelmingly white. When blacks wanted a share of masculine martial honor, the military largely shunted them into the labor battalions in which William Buckner served. African American soldiers consorting with French women leveled an explosive challenge to the narrative of white chivalry, for both arbiters of public discourse in the United States and policymakers in the AEF. In their view, black servicemen might even menace those innocents as Germans had, expanding the AEF's protective mandate to include shielding French women from its own soldiers. In the case of Pvt. Buckner, crossing the line meant death. Eight of the eleven Americans executed in France were black. All had been charged with rape.[80]

These were the most notorious examples of a larger effort to separate black men from French women. Soon after William Buckner's conviction, on August 7, 1918, Col. Louis Albert Linard issued the memorandum claiming a spike in rape allegations against soldiers of color. Linard was head of the French Mission and a liaison between the French Army and attached units of the segregated Ninety-Third Division. Just as the division's 369th Regiment was acquitting itself honorably in combat, the AEF command asked Linard to prepare a confidential report on how French officers should handle their African American charges. He set out to brief his countrymen on American race relations and help reproduce them in France. The blurred local color line offended white Americans, Linard said, many of whom held the black man to be "an inferior being" unable to suppress his sexual passions. Thus he implored officers to keep French women from black doughboys, lest the latter become "spoiled" by unfettered social movement and sexual access.[81]

Many American officials shared Linard's views and his willingness to believe rumors of black rape. The Ninety-Second endured so many allegations that white officers nicknamed it "the rapist division." Maj. Gen. Charles Ballou, the white divisional commander whose stateside Bulletin No. 35 had ordered black soldiers to avoid racial conflict, once again blamed them for their reputation. A couple weeks after Linard released his memo, Ballou mandated his officers keep tabs on their men's movements, drew an imaginary barrier around camp, and permitted excursions across the line only to soldiers of "reliability." Black Americans caught in French homes would face a day on bread and water and a hike of eighteen miles. On the Fourth of July, a white officer commanded an audience of French villagers and black soldiers to stay apart. If the troops continued to prove a "menace to women," Ballou warned in a directive, the entire division would be sent home or broken up into labor battalions. The Ninety-Third Division underwent a comparable experience. In August, divisional officials directed French authorities to keep local women segregated from black soldiers. Like Linard, these leaders predicted dire consequences not only for the French people but also for postwar Americans. These actions undercut whatever sense of masculine prerogative African Americans may have found in the socially fluid environment of France.[82]

Yet the restrictions failed to prevent black liaisons with white women, as William Buckner had shown and was about to pay for. On September 6, 1918, around six o'clock in the morning, the teenager ascended a scaffold near the town of Bar-sur-Aube. William had maintained his innocence the night before, vowing that Georgette had "consented to the intercourse," but now declined to make a statement. Executioners bound his legs and put a black cap over his head and a noose around his neck. The floor beneath him dropped away and he plunged down. Fourteen minutes later, the examiner declared William dead. He was buried in France with the rope and black cap still on his body.[83]

SIX DAYS AFTER THE hanging of William Buckner, at five in the morning on September 12, half a million Americans and 110,000 Frenchmen launched the attack on Saint-Mihiel. The job of Waring's Eighty-Second Division was to hold the right end of the line, with Waring's 325th the most rightward element of the division. In the 328th Infantry, Alvin York took part in the capture of the town of Norroy. The division acted as a pivot for a large, sweeping drive northeast, comprising I Corps and

IV Corps of the First American Army. French forces handled other parts of the triangle. In the Verdun area, to the northwest of the salient, Arthur Huebner's Thirty-Third Division laid down diversionary machine gun fire.[84] While Waring's unit sat to the east, elements of his buddy Pressley Cleveland's battle-tested Forty-Second Division jumped off to its left.[85]

The Germans were planning to evacuate the salient anyway and beat a hasty retreat, but the surprise attack netted fifteen thousand prisoners. Men of the Rainbow Division found four years' worth of concrete trenches, gun emplacements, and dug-outs, and advancing soldiers descended upon food still steaming on field stoves. Edwin L. James, a war correspondent traveling with the American army, described a massive cemetery with six thousand graves dating to 1914, some of the tombstones carved by artisans from Germany.[86] Alvin York and his comrades in the 328th found untouched food on German mess tables and Belgian hares raised for meat running loose. Meantime the townspeople of Saint-Mihiel reported four years of brutality and plunder. The mayor and a local priest, they disclosed, had been hauled away as the Germans withdrew.[87]

The offensive cleared the salient and straightened the front in four days, at a price of almost nine thousand casualties. Though the operation exposed logistical flaws—Pershing's gigantic divisions were unwieldy to move, coordinate, and supply—the leader of the AEF was ecstatic. His commanders had proven their ability to carry out a major operation. Pershing boasted to his intelligence chief that the victory revealed masculine greatness. Saint-Mihiel showed "we had developed a type of manhood superior in initiative to that existing abroad," he said, "which given approximately equal training and discipline, developed a superior soldier to that existing abroad."[88]

Observers in the American press submitted Saint-Mihiel for membership in the pantheon of historic military victories. "The road from Concord bridge to the heights above the Meuse is long," wrote military historian Frank H. Simonds in the *Atlanta Constitution*, "but it runs straight." He praised the doughboys' fighting spirit, their tenacity fed by "love of liberty and service of democracy."[89] Papers in Selma and Watertown reveled in American battlefield glory, though the smaller *Greenville Sun*, focused on local implications of the war, failed to mention Saint-Mihiel.[90]

These pieces and the balance of coverage, like much wartime culture, communicated a story of liberation more than victory, of righteous doughboys and cruel Germans. Onrushing Americans released the population, readers of the *Washington Post* learned, from a "nightmare." Under the rule of the "Boche," young boys had been deported, old people forced into labor. The eyes of local French people turned "radiant" with gratitude.[91] Media heralds of the Saint-Mihiel victory deployed the vocabulary of a morality play: *tyrants, heroes, conquerors, rescued, martyrdom, vengeance, bondage, deliverance, suppression,* the *battle line of civilization.*[92] Freed women and children lent Saint-Mihiel its dramatic pulse. They greeted the emancipators with a wild "emotional outburst," went a wire piece in the *San Francisco Chronicle*. Much public gratitude came "hysterically uttered." When women met the visiting Secretary of War Newton Baker, after figuring out who he was, they "kissed his hands and wept and then they joined in a chorus of thankfulness."[93] Saint-Mihiel fulfilled the promise of the draft registration and much else in 1917. A theoretical fight for the innocent had become, in the oft-told story of Saint-Mihiel, a real mission of chivalric rescue.

PRESSLEY CLEVELAND OF SELMA survived Saint-Mihiel, though his division took almost a thousand casualties, and the 167th Infantry spent the balance of the month preparing to fight in the Argonne Forest.[94] His friend Waring Huston wrote home on September 16 to say war "certainly is not any fun," but things had been fairly quiet.[95] His comrade in the 325th, Fred Takes, felt safe enough on September 13 to keep up his duties as doughboy barber in the thick of the offensive.[96] "The Boche did not molest us," Col. Whitman of the 325th Infantry later wrote, though other units in the division had a worse time of it. More than a thousand men of the Eighty-Second were killed, wounded, or missing.[97]

Waring's regiment stayed at the front until a French one relieved it on September 20. From the newspapers he learned the draft age had been raised to forty-five, and he wondered in a letter if that expansion would envelope his brother Harry. Austria wanted peace, Waring had read. "I have seen enough war to last me the rest of my days," he wrote.[98] Fred Takes occupied himself frying eggs he had purchased and writing in the rain. Upon its relief, the 325th marched back to the woods near Marbache and spent three days in thick mud. Fred went to Nancy one day and paid a franc for his first dish of ice cream in France.[99] Then came time to move to the Argonne. One hundred and fifty French trucks transported the regiment to the great forest. They had benches running down the sides and middle, nineteen men to a vehicle with no room to do anything but sit. Dusty roads and gasoline fumes gave the men sore eyes and headaches.[100] They unloaded in a place called Froidos and walked into the woods to camp. "Believe me I had <u>some</u> trip" was how Waring described it for his mother in Selma. Things were "lively," he reported, but as always she shouldn't worry.[101]

The Sixth Division and Lige Dees, meanwhile, had spent the month of September holding frontage near Alsace, more than one hundred miles to the southeast of the Saint-Mihiel salient and even further from the German-held territory between the Argonne Forest and the Meuse River.

AFTER THE INITIAL DRAFT registration of June 5, 1917, there had been another, a year later, for men like William Oda Dees who had turned twenty-one in the interim. In July 1918, in the thick of the Allied counterpunch, President Wilson and his General Staff agreed to ask Congress to enlarge the AEF. Military leaders, planning for a charge into Germany in 1919, wanted 3.2 million doughboys. The new draft Waring mentioned was to populate this expanded force.

To do so, Selective Service could withdraw exemptions among existing registrants or widen the draft-age range to incorporate new ones. Wilson and his advisers knew that deferrals for men with families helped people tolerate conscription, so discussion turned to the age brackets. The army wanted younger men, considered more pliable, fit, and audacious. But in many states, eighteen-year-olds weren't legally adults. Rural Americans in particular had long worried about exposing farm boys to the moral hazards of military life as well as losing their labor. Industrial leaders countered that increasing the upper age limit too far would thin the managerial class. After much back and forth, Secretary of War Baker announced the administration would ask Congress to draft younger *and* older men. Eighteen to forty-five was the proposal, though Baker suggested that if possible, older men without dependents or important jobs go before younger ones.[102]

If Congress took too long to decide, Selective Service urged, exempted husbands and fathers would be drafted. Few wanted that. The proponents of age expansion sought to maintain the social as well as industrial stability underwritten by the current system of dependent and work exemptions. Most boys of eighteen to twenty, the bill's advocates declared, were neither married nor part of the labor force. A few lawmakers countered by citing the physical immaturity of eighteen-year-olds. Sen. William Borah (R-Idaho) launched a campaign to keep the future lifeblood of the country from service. Boys who couldn't vote shouldn't fight. Older married men with working wives ought to go first. He exhorted the Senate, "Is it fair? Is it just? Is it manly? Is it noble? Is it in harmony with the supreme and sublime task before us?"[103] An unmoved chamber endorsed the new limits unanimously a few days after the House approved it 336 to two.[104]

Borah and other opponents grew convinced of the bill's military necessity and voted yes. As tragic as it would be to lose young men in war, conceded the winners of the debate, it would be worse to disrupt the home front by conscripting married and working men. "They can stand more hard work," reasoned Sen. Knute Nelson (R-Minn.) of American youth, "they have more energy, more vim; and, what is more, they can really be better spared from home than can any other class of men of whom I know." But wasn't it a greater personal tragedy to lose a boy of eighteen than a man of thirty? No, replied Sen. Porter McCumber (R-N. Dak.), particularly if the older man had children. The lawmaker argued against ranking tragedy:

> A mother who sends her boy of 18 years to death must suffer agony indescribable; but does she suffer any more than the wife who sends her husband to death, who sends to the trenches to be slaughtered the father of her children? Is not the death of the latter as serious a loss as the death of the former? It is hard to make any character of distinction between the death of one individual and the death of another.

Perhaps death knocked at the mature man's door more insistently, McCumber suggested. Young people recovered more reliably from wounds, and a healthier army would win and return home sooner. To those who cried corruption of youth, supporters maintained the modern armed forces had become a "perfect paradise" of moral training, whole-some diversion, and even good dental care.[105] Above all, legislators still hoped to protect family and safeguard innocence, but to do it by short-ening the war and exposing fewer boys to combat. President Wilson signed the bill on August 31, 1918. The third national registration was set for September 12, the day of the Saint-Mihiel offensive.[106]

A massive public relations program announced the new registration. Far from imperiling young people, President Wilson vowed, the draft expansion invited them into a society of permanent masculine honor. He spoke in terms of opportunity more than obligation. War promised to give boys a future of proud recollection and national gratitude:

> They covet not only the distinction of serving in this great war but also the inspiring memories which hundreds of thousands of them will cherish through the years to come, of a great day and a great serv-ice for their country and for mankind.

For the older men now vulnerable to conscription, Wilson returned to the war's narrative of protection. Fathers and husbands had spent years nurturing families and careers and communities, laboring to develop the rhythms of everyday life. They had built what Germany threatened to destroy—not a political system or commercial network but a way of life. The president therefore appealed to the mature man's yesterday rather than his tomorrow:

> [H]aving assumed at home the graver responsibilities of life in many spheres, looking back upon honorable records in civil and industrial life, they will realize as perhaps no others could, how entirely their own fortunes and the fortunes of all whom they love are put at stake in this war for right and will know that the very records they have made render this new duty the commanding duty of their lives.

These words came from the top, as it were, but in many ways contra-dicted what the Committee on Public Information was trying to do in 1918: turn public attention to the war's broadest geopolitical justi-fications. Wilson's new entreaties to the teenager and forty-something stoked personal rather than national aspirations.[107]

Military bands lent festivity to registration day at Jefferson Barracks, where Eliga Dees had enlisted. The air in Baltimore rang with band music, bugles, and church bells, heralding the campaign to finally vanquish "tribes of German barbarians who have tried to destroy the peace of the world."[108] Yet the atmosphere betrayed little of the prior year's innocence. Then, all manner of public spokespeople had associated registration with familial pride. Reporters had written winsome stories of mothers handing sons over to the state. The antiwar movement had been vocal enough, even if suppressed by law, to invite counter-claims of martial virtue. September 1918 was more sedate. News of registration shared space with Saint-Mihiel, and the government's *Official Bulletin* was filling with casualty lists. Slackers, with their power to draw retaliatory bluster, were nowhere to be found. Journalists credited the calm to a consensus around the war, though the Espionage Act of 1917, amended and strengthened with the Sedition Act, meant dissenters held their tongues or were held in jail cells. But the press attributed to the public a gritty will to finish the war. Nationwide coverage spoke of victory more than meaning. "America's man power will decide the battle in France," went an Atlanta newspaper. Words like patriotism and honor and duty still circulated but seemed ends in their own right rather than means to greater ends. The papers in Greenville, Watertown, and Selma soberly reported the new draft.[109]

Family members remained key figures in registration narratives. Journalists covered fathers and sons registering together. Women involved themselves in new and old ways. In Atlanta, the Daughters of the American Revolution, the United Daughters of the Confederacy, and the Colonial Dames marched in support of registrants.[110] Dr. Anna Howard Shaw of the Woman's Committee of the Council of National Defense urged women to prod men to designated stations. Her appeal echoed the new tone of the September registration. Women had done everything asked of them to this point—conserve food, sell Liberty Bonds, serve the Red Cross, join the nursing and auxiliary corps. Now all that mattered was winning the war "in the shortest possible time." A mélange of personal and quasi-political priorities should move women to help enlarge the army: *honor, love, justice, patriotism, peace.*[111] One group of women in St. Louis did seek to attach political ambitions to the occasion. A federal woman suffrage amendment had passed in the House of Representatives in January 1918 but remained lodged in the Senate. While many advocates used women's war work to justify expanding the electorate, the Missourians cited wartime sacrifice. "If you are going to fight," went their plea, "your wife or mother ought to have the right to vote."[112] In return for suffering, they wanted something more than familial pride and paeans to their womanly citizenship.

On September 12, 1918, the government registered 13.4 million new candidates for conscription.[113] "Whole country goes over top," bellowed a Chicago headline. Small papers in Wisconsin and Alabama and Missouri confirmed the scale of the commitment.[114] As Waring had suspected, stepping forward was his half-brother Harry Bill Huston, now living with his wife Nancy in Tennessee. Also among the registrants was forty-four-year-old John Bilbrey, Mae Dees's father.[115]

TWO DAYS LATER, ON September 14, 1918, the Thirty-Third Division officially passed from the Seventeenth French Corps to III Corps of Gen. Pershing's First Army. For fifteen days, Arthur Huebner and Company C of the 124th Machine Gun Battalion occupied positions in a subsector called Raffecourt. Other units in the Thirty-Third underwent additional training as the division readied itself for a big offensive. Traffic in artillery, vehicles, equipment, supplies, and men choked roads leading into and out of Fromeréville. Rainy weather compromised doughboy comfort but also German aerial observation. By September 25, companies of the 124th and the balance of the Thirty-Third Division were arrayed along a stretch of front. To their north was the Forges Creek bed, a marshy, muddy expanse separating the lines.[116] The French had tried and failed to cross this swamp two years earlier. It still lay studded with human and animal remains, tangled barbed wire, broken military hardware, and live grenades. To the northeast were imposing German and Austrian positions on the Heights of the Meuse, their artillery trained toward Arthur's sector.[117]

BACK IN WISCONSIN, READERS of the paper witnessed the ongoing pursuit both of an explanation for why doughboys were huddled in trenches as well as a measurement of what sort of men they were. The avowedly patriotic *Watertown News* took a somewhat different approach to these questions than Mae and Lige's Greenville paper.

In Missouri, local leaders downplayed the war's meaning but devoted themselves to seeing it through, marveling at the soldier's admirable dedication to nation but mourning the impact on his body and family. In Wisconsin, despite or because of the fact that many German Americans had opposed intervention, the Watertown paper persisted in broadcasting explanations of its purpose. In doing so, it reflected and amplified the summer's official oscillation between political and emotional appeals. The paper aired the government's shifting justifications yet reported local events and commentary that confirmed the narrative of a fight for love and family. Meanwhile the *News* printed updated lists of Watertown-area combat casualties, as well as a "Roll of Honor" of local men in uniform. It listed Ben Fluegel and Daniel McCarthy but erroneously left out Arthur Huebner throughout the summer and fall of 1918.

On a Sunday in the middle of August, a crowd of Watertown citizens traveled to Waterloo for a patriotic rally.[118] In the evening, a thespian group called the Liberty Sextet staged a performance of "The Girls Over Here," a one-act play depicting the patriotic transformation of a German American woman with Wisconsin roots named Dolly. Until she predictably sees the light at the end, Dolly is a maudlin, selfish, materialistic pacifist. She pouts at war's disruption of her domestic dreams. Women in the play who engineer her reversal range from traditional to modern in their outlook and occupations. There is a Civil War veteran's wife, a nurse, an ambulance driver bound for France, and a female letter carrier substituting for a man. They all knit sweaters for soldiers. One of the women hates that she can't fight in the trenches herself. Several of them have loved ones in the war. Vera speaks for people like Mae Dees and Carrie Goodwin when she says, "We've all experienced that crushing disappointment—the looked-for letter that did not come!" To convert Dolly, the group tries political arguments about democracy but also emotional ones about German violation of women and children. What finally works is the appeal of the postal worker, who delivers mail from Germany to relatives in America. Those letters testify to the suffering of civilians in the mother country, she says. Thus it's the cause of all humanity, both political freedom and everyday happiness, for which the doughboys are fighting. The play ends with a ringing endorsement of wartime civil religion. "A new light will shine," says the Civil War bride, "a world peace, blessed by the Prince of Peace, and safe for all nations, on the honor of the Stars and Stripes!"[119]

The Watertown newspaper published the words of officials and their allies voicing a comparable blend of politics and feeling, keying the war to everyday life as well as grander ambitions. Advertisements funded by the Department of Labor and contributions from local businesses called the Great War a fight to make the world "a decent place to live in," but also one linked to "the cause of Democracy," as well as a battle for a combination of the two, of principle *and* place—a battle for "Liberty and America."[120] The speakers at a huge war rally in Ben Fluegel's hometown of Lake Mills added civil religious tones to wartime understanding, conflating devotion to God, family, and country. The war, in this tradition, served personal, national, and spiritual masters. One orator blended these things by equating patriotism with "the love of a mother for her son."[121]

President Wilson's Labor Day remarks charted the official evolution in war aims from the emotional to political, from the initial fight to avenge "violated" Belgium to what was "now plain"—that Germany threatened democratic forms of government everywhere.[122] Nonetheless, he and other spokespeople for the war, readers of the Watertown paper learned, continued to warn of Germany's threats to family life and happiness. They weren't asking Americans to abandon emotional motivations, but to imagine the war's political dimensions in everyday terms, to use heart *and* mind. Anna Howard Shaw made this connection explicitly in a piece published in the *Watertown News*:

> Whatever mistakes we have made in the past, however we may have underestimated Germany's desire to crush the *democratic ideals* of the world, now that that purpose is known, it must be overcome if *womanhood and childhood* are to be saved anywhere.[123]

When the War Mothers of America issued a statement demanding unconditional German surrender, President Wilson responded with a public telegram to the organization: "Their sons are making America loved and honored wherever men love freedom and respect justice. Their heroism and sacrifices will make the whole world a happy and safer home for the wives and mothers of brave men in the days to come."[124]

With death coming to American homes or threatening to, the president put love and defense of those homes at the core of the doughboy's inspiration.

Wisconsin readers confronted as well the racial and moral elements of the wartime narrative of chivalric liberation. The day before the Saint-Mihiel attack, the *News* printed a piece by James Montgomery Flagg, creator of the "I Want You" recruiting image. This appeal to buy Liberty Bonds drew its persuasive power almost entirely from a racialized vision of American moral superiority. Only the united "white" powers, Flagg wrote, echoing Wilson, could crush the threat of German evil. He likened the enemy onslaught to an infestation of repellant, subhuman, but dangerous pests:

> The world is cleaning house. Its house is alive with crawling Teutonic vermin—vermin that if not destroyed will make the house uninhabitable and kill off its dwellers. . . . Your house is the United States; the vermin is Germany. We will not allow the vermin to overrun our house—as it will if not stamped out.[125]

And what of the troops charged with the Hun's extermination? The Lake Mills rally featured a comforting talk from a man attesting to the moral purity of the doughboys in the cantonments.[126]

In the thick of its war coverage that summer, the *Watertown News* published a presumably fictional column from the McClure Newspaper Syndicate called "In War Time."[127] The piece promulgated the redemptive elements of the wartime love story, particularly its assurance that conflict pushed men and women into proper roles, but revealed that story under strain. The gender-bending tale begins with Harriet Wynne, dressed in her absent brother's clothes and farming in the heat of noontime. Harriet looks "as nearly like a handsome, healthy boy as a girl could look." She breaks for lunch, pulling her hat down over her eyes, playfully falling to the ground and rolling through brush toward the gate at the road. At this point, a soldier in khaki with twinkling eyes, Sergeant Joe Ames, comes up the lane. Harriet is tempted to apologize for her "unladylike" behavior, but when he kids her about "rolling boys" gathering no moss, she stays in the role of her brother. Harriet quietly envies Ames's right, and the "right of every man," to wear the uniform. They talk over the lunch Harriet, still acting the boy, shares with him. After a time, Ames takes his leave and announces he is soon off to France. Harriet is smitten with him. The young woman "suddenly discovered that wherever this boy went her heart would go with him." Harriet's impersonation of a man reaches its boundary—irrepressible romantic attraction to a boy in uniform—but she keeps up appearances and they agree to trade correspondence. Ames ships out and writes of the thrill of combat. She sends him "courage-inspiring" letters, until she hears that Joe is in the hospital, then only silence.

Sometime later, Harriet is sitting on her porch knitting. A man walks up the steps. It's Joe Ames, one sleeve empty. "The pretty girl in the fluffy white dress had entirely forgotten her role as a boy," writes the author, and she hugs Ames, the return of her femininity announced not only by her dress and the knitting but also by an audible sob. It turns out that the wounded doughboy had unlocked the secret when Harriet's letters became more emotional. The revelation actually had helped him recuperate from his injuries, the nurses said. Harriet asks him: *now what?*

> "I don't know," he answered thoughtfully, "but work which will count for our side will be found for my good right arm, and if you will agree to help me continue to keep my faith and courage, I can still help to 'carry on.'"

In many ways a microcosm of wartime American culture—and rather like the play "The Girls Over Here"—the story showed the durability of ennobling war narratives as well as the adaptations an actual war demanded. The author granted women wartime functions beyond the explicitly "feminine," although she reduced Harriet's farming to so much mischief when she returned her to zones of domestic industry and emotional preoccupation. Harriet coveting Ames's soldierly honor pushed, though not too hard, at the male monopoly on martial virtue. The plot acknowledged the compromised masculinity of disabled men but assured readers they could recover productive capabilities. "In War Time" testified simultaneously to the power of tradition and the necessity of change, to war's damaging and hopeful possibilities for the individual, to the romantic appeal of a doughboy coming down a country road and the reality of life with him thereafter. In line with the Watertown paper's politics, though, regeneration provided the tale's parting lesson.

A different story, this one real and without a happy ending, demonstrated how far a young Watertown man might go to meet his familial obligations. R. Harder was a twenty-five-year-old farmer's son. His mother had died recently. Mr. Harder's responsibilities to cultivate family land and care for his invalid father exempted him from the draft, but for some reason, the paper called it "delusion," he believed himself vulnerable. On a Tuesday afternoon in July, he mixed two portions of a poison called paris green and told his father he meant for each of them to take a dose. The older farmer scoffed at the plan and directed his son to make dinner. The next morning, Harder tried again, and dad turned him down again. The son went outside, did his chores, then came in and took the poison and lay down on the floor. In the other room, the senior Harder, unable to move, listened to his boy struggling as the toxic substance killed him in the afternoon. That night, a neighbor came by and discovered the scene. Local people recalled the dead youngster as a good son.[128] R. Harder obviously had his demons, but the war and its pressures on family had given shape to the man's misery and converted it to disaster.

WARING HUSTON'S JOSTLING BY truck on September 24, the traffic bottleneck near Arthur Huebner's position, the packing and unpacking of gear, endless miles walked and ridden, the dragging of equipment across rutted roads—these and a million other small vibrations formed the mobilization for a big operation. To hit the vulnerable Germans, their stock of reserves exhausted and some leaders seeking an armistice, the Allies planned a series of attacks for the end of September. The largest would be the first, the Meuse-Argonne offensive against the Hindenburg Line, or *Kriemhilde Stellung*, scheduled to begin September 26 with a million Americans and the French Fourth Army. The next day, the British would attack in the Cambrai sector, and the day after that, in Flanders, along with French and Belgian forces. On September 28, the French and British would strike the Hindenburg Line at Saint-Quentin in the Somme region. Edward Streeter's Twenty-Seventh Division, as well as the Thirtieth, were still attached to the British and would take part in that assault. Lige Dees and the Sixth Division remained in the

Vosges sector on the border with Alsace. Arthur's Thirty-Third and Waring's Eighty-Second Divisions had done time with the British but now served in Gen. Pershing's First Army. Both would play significant roles in the Meuse-Argonne offensive. Nine American divisions in three corps would make up the force, with others in reserve. The AEF mobilized 600,000 doughboys into the area and 220,000 out, moving things men and armies need.[129]

The territory in question was a well-defended, twenty-mile stretch of land between the Meuse River to the east and the Argonne Forest to the south and west. Terrain offered Pershing much to worry about. The Heights of the Meuse gave the Germans commanding positions from which to fire artillery into the battlefield. In the forest, largely unmolested by war, deep ravines, streams, and heavy woods presented major challenges to mobility, communication, supply, and attack. The Aire River, on the eastern side of the Argonne, featured bluffs similarly advantageous to those along the Meuse.[130]

Everybody was more or less in position by the evening of September 25. At 11:30 p.m., artillery opened up on the German positions. Doughboys in the trenches watched in awe as a second, much bigger salvo pounded the enemy for three hours or so before dawn. At 5:30 a.m., they began walking north across Nobodies Land.[131]

6

——◦◦◦◦◦——

Yankee Doodle Do or Die

ARTHUR HUEBNER'S DAY STARTED in the middle of the night. At 2:30 a.m. on September 26, he waited in the trenches for the artillery bombardment to lift.[1] Before him lay the grotesque muck of Forges Creek, full of rotting bodies and old barbed wire, water-logged holes and dense thickets of vegetation and mud. It was the job of engineers in the Thirty-Third "Prairie" Division to navigate a way across this inhospitable ground. In the dark of night, they crept out to forward trenches to retrieve stored wooden planks and twelve thousand fascines, bundles of sticks lashed together to fill in and stabilize marshy ground. Under a heavy mist and occasional enemy fire, these men ran tape and ropes to guide the infantry toward nine passages made of "duckboards," wooden decking laid four abreast.

At 5:30 a.m., Arthur Huebner's Company C and Clayton Slack's Company D of the 124th Machine Gun Battalion opened a barrage of fire to cover the infantrymen's approach to the walkways. The first doughboys forward served in the 131st and 132nd Infantry Regiments, which together with the 124th comprised the Sixty-Sixth Brigade. These infantrymen were veterans of labor battles in Chicago, working-class intimidators of midwestern farm boys at Camp Grant back in 1917. It took longer than expected to negotiate the swamp, and soon the artillery outpaced the advancing Americans. When the fog lifted, German shells and machine gun bullets poured into the ranks and sent soldiers diving off the duckboards. Some crawled toward German positions and disabled them with grenades. The line moved forward. When Arthur and Clayton's companies concluded their volley, they cleaned their guns, loaded their belts, and proceeded north. With them were support battalions of the Chicago regiments. Once across the swamp, they ascended rough, wooded ground leading up to the Bois de Forges. Telling friend from foe was difficult in this terrain, and machine gun crews had few viable targets. The defenders, surprised at the charge across the swamp and suffering from low morale—many were unenthusiastic recruits from Alsace-Lorraine—surrendered quickly. Clayton Slack recalled meeting demoralized enemy soldiers emerging from dugouts. Neither Company C nor D reported casualties. The 132nd Infantry lost sixteen dead and seventy-two wounded. In the 131st, twenty were killed and 133 hurt.[2] Henry Weinberg, a private who had weathered a shrapnel wound to the face at Hamel and survived the costly action at Gressaire Wood, wrote in his diary, "[W]ent over to see the Germans again but did not lose so many men this time."[3]

By the afternoon, the Thirty-Third had accomplished its objectives, capturing the town of Forges and German positions in the surrounding woods and proceeding to the west bank of the Meuse. The division had captured fourteen hundred prisoners, a great deal of weaponry, and eight railway cars. "Went over the top," the 131st Infantry doughboy Selmar Waldermar told his journal, "and chased the Germans 5 miles over the Meuse River."[4] Arthur's Company C reached its position and stayed there until October 8, when it prepared to move east, across the Meuse.

THE MORNING THE MEUSE-ARGONNE offensive began, Waring Huston's Eighty-Second "All-American" Division was encamped in the woods south of the French city of Varennes, its job to wait in reserve behind the Thirty-Fifth, Twenty-Eighth, and Seventy-Seventh Divisions of I Corps. They were about fourteen miles southwest of Arthur's division (figure 6.1). Waring and the 325th Infantry heard an incredible bombardment against the German lines, as the regiment held itself in what Col. Walter M. Whitman called "constant readiness." At first, objectives fell quickly and the barrage cycled forward. Fred Takes noted in his

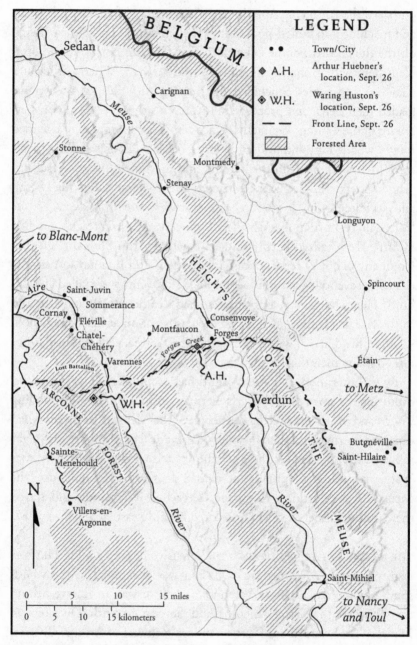

FIGURE 6.1 Map of the beginning of the Meuse-Argonne operation, September 26, 1918, with approximate positions of Waring Huston and Arthur Huebner. Cartographic Research Laboratory, University of Alabama.

journal the evening of September 26 that he could hardly hear it any more.[5] But enemy resistance soon stiffened. It became necessary to send a regiment of the Eighty-Second, the 327th Infantry, to support the faltering Twenty-Eighth Division. In a few days, the inexperienced Thirty-Fifth, including among its ranks Missourian Capt. Harry Truman, took heavy casualties, became disorganized, and withdrew. German prisoners streamed back in the same direction. Meantime, on October 1, the First "Big Red One" Division, veterans of operations at Cantigny, Saint-Mihiel, and Soissons, arrived to take over the Thirty-Fifth's sector. Back with the First was the injured former teacher from Mae Dees's high school, Roy Thornburgh.[6]

On September 29, as Col. Whitman awaited orders, Waring chastised his mother for withholding news that someone named Gordon had died—he didn't say how. Maybe Nellye had assumed he couldn't handle it, given his record of vulnerability. If so, he had changed. "I can stand anything now," he corrected her, "for I have <u>seen</u> some mighty bad things." Waring informed his mother the unit was poised and ready in the woods. It was cold and rainy. "C'est la guerre," he told his mother, then translated it for her. Waring promised to have a new picture of himself made the next time he found himself near a town.[7] Fred Takes, when he wasn't escaping the downpour in his tent, worked on payroll, drilled with his gas mask, and prayed.[8]

Back in Alabama, on the day Waring wrote his mother, the *Birmingham Age Herald*, published about ninety miles from Selma, ran an advertisement for the Fourth Liberty Loan picturing the Statue of Liberty and New York in flames as German planes fly overhead. The artwork by Joseph Pennell, and an accompanying essay, provided the broad field of vision in which government propagandists hoped the public understood the war. But the feature's terms weren't exclusively geopolitical. They perpetuated the mixture of emotional and ideological propaganda of 1918, authorizing chivalric outrage but casting Lady Liberty as the damsel in distress. The picture envisioned an apocalyptic sequel to that May's image of the Statue of Liberty in *Stars and Stripes* (see figure 4.4). It issued a warning about what would happen if the doughboys failed, by way of home front parsimony, in their mission of rescue and protection. Germany the *robber*, the *murderer*, the *enslaver* would menace home shores. Empty your pockets for the loan drive, the ad pleaded, or else "everything you possess is lost, and with it the American soul is lost." Much like registration day culture of two weeks earlier, the appeal banked on an emotional attachment to everyday values rather than an intellectual attachment to political ones. Somebody in the Huston household kept the piece in the family for decades.[9]

BLACK REGIMENTS IN THE Ninety-Second and Ninety-Third Divisions played rather different roles during the offensive, but all languished in a martial environment that both failed to prepare them for battlefield mettle and denounced them for allegedly lacking it.

Three of four infantry regiments in the Ninety-Third, like the Marine and future author Thomas Boyd's Second Division, operated during the Meuse-Argonne drive in the Champagne region with the French Fourth Army. The 371st, 372nd, and 369th "Harlem Hell Fighters" took part in the assault, while the 370th fought with the French in the simultaneous Oise-Aisne campaign. Men in the 369th, some led by the regiment's few black officers, charged forward in the opening attack and stayed in the line for nine days, taking heavy losses and inflicting severe ones on the enemy. Exhausted, the men failed only in their final attack. An officer on the Western Front and later historian of the war understood that this one blemish gave the regiment's "rear-area critics a chance to carp." The 369th Infantry spent the remainder of the war at rest in the Vosges Mountains. Individual Croix de Guerre awards went to 170 officers and enlisted men in the regiment, and the whole unit received one for a victory at Sechault in the opening thrusts of the Meuse-Argonne offensive.[10]

The 370th Regiment, formerly the Eighth Illinois Guard, had all black officers until it reached Europe in April 1918. The unit's first white officer was Col. T. A. Roberts, a man initially thought by the 370th's black chaplain to be a "traducer of the Negro soldier." In time, Roberts saw potential in his charges and condemned their marginalization by the army. The unit's attachment to five different French divisions galled Roberts and gutted regimental morale. But the soldiers did all right until the last days of September, when an attack on a German position disintegrated amid confused scattering. There followed a period of cross-cultural pointing of fingers. What seems clear is the 370th suffered from inconsistent leadership, cursory training, and ill feeling toward the white man suddenly put at its head. By October 6, the regiment was drawn from the front, but re-entered the war in November for a late chase of the Germans. Seventy-one men of the 370th won the Croix de Guerre from the French government. Another twenty-one received the Distinguished Service Cross.[11]

The 371st also had arrived in Europe in April. Most of its soldiers were drafted field hands from South Carolina, all their officers white. The American Expeditionary Forces (AEF) immediately threw them to the French, who immediately threw them into combat training at the front. The unit's French stewards and American officers praised its combat record that summer, but regimental leadership denied men access to the local population, once again citing the purported social preferences of French civilians as well as postwar Americans. The 371st began the Meuse-Argonne in reserve but came to the line when called. Despite typical obstacles—missing artillery support, stiff enemy resistance and counterattack, poison gas in the air—the former farm laborers fought courageously, earning a combined two hundred Croix de Guerre and Distinguished Service Crosses and losing about a thousand casualties before being pulled from the front in early October. Rumors of desertion surfaced as usual, but later regimental reports negated them.[12]

The Ninety-Third's last regiment, the 372nd Infantry, included National Guardsmen and both black and white officers. A mixture of incompetence and racism plagued the regiment's white leadership, generating low morale and occasionally the threat of violence among enlisted men. Black officers operated under constant threat of review or transfer. Still, the men battled in the Meuse-Argonne until being withdrawn to a quieter sector, like the division's other regiments, in early October. The unit took so many casualties that two battalions merged into one. Fifty-two boys of the 372nd earned Croix de Guerre and several won Distinguished Service Crosses. A Croix de Guerre with palm (a high decoration from the French government) went to the entire unit. Local villagers tried to mix with and congratulate the soldiers of the 372nd in their new post in Alsace, but white officers did everything they could to prevent it.[13]

Upward of 80 percent of officers were black in the other "colored" division at the outset of its war service. But in September 1918, just as it was moving to the front, military leadership reduced the percentage of black officers to fifty-eight. Then, toward the end of the month, the AEF hastily transferred the Ninety-Second to the Meuse-Argonne operation. One of its least experienced infantry regiments, the 368th, was to plug a hole in the advancing line and serve as a liaison between the French and American armies. Without proper wire cutters, maps, grenades, signal flares, or artillery support, the regiment moved forward, then back. After five days of death and confusion, leadership relieved the 368th and withdrew the division from the Argonne. Although it became clear over time that the failure owed to insufficient supply and training and the incompetence of the unit's white officers—later news reports revealed men had been ordered to retreat—the reputation of the African American soldier plummeted.[14] White officials called the men cowards, questioned their manhood, and condemned black officers to death in courts-martial (all eventually went free). One white officer confided to his diary that the 368th proved black men suited only to labor. Another impugned the division's military uselessness and sexual depravity—"they have in fact been dangerous to no one except themselves and women." No such opprobrium met the failures of white divisions such as the Thirty-Fifth.[15]

The shaming of the Ninety-Second showed that most white officials in the AEF could neither abide a prominent African American place in the war nor grant black servicemen the trappings of martial masculinity. Whatever feats of endurance, bravery, and patience black units accomplished came despite this hostile treatment. The aggregate impact of American wartime culture, official propaganda, and the words and actions of battlefield commanders, then, was to render the Great War a white mission of rescue. It was mainly in the 369th Infantry, suggests one important chronicle of the Great War, that the black soldier was "treated like a man and responded in a manly way."[16] For all the accomplishments of that unit and others in the Ninety-Third, it was the memory of the Ninety-Second that fueled white stereotypes of black military futility for years thereafter.[17]

THE DISINTEGRATION OF THE 368th Infantry had more immediate results as well. To the left of Waring Huston's Eighty-Second Division were the men of the Seventy-Seventh, whose orders were to push into the Argonne. German resistance opened a gap by October 2 between the Americans and the French to the west—the gap meant to be occupied in part by the 368th. The German infantry struck through it and trapped the First Battalion of the Seventy-Seventh's 308th Infantry. For five days the "Lost Battalion" languished in a ravine. Its food ran out the second day. The men had no clothing suited to the cold temperatures.[18]

Leading the battalion was Maj. Charles W. Whittlesey, an erudite man with leftist leanings and a college roommate of the socialist Max Eastman. Against those beliefs in Whittlesey's worldview worked other strains, faith in Theodore Roosevelt's Strenuous Life and indignation at German degeneracy. So motivated, Whittlesey had signed up to train in the Plattsburgh officers' camp and eventually made his way to Camp Upton. Now he found himself in the forest, its density helping the men withstand repeated German attacks, buying them time.[19]

ON THE MORNING OF October 3, while Whittlesey and the First Battalion remained lost, Waring Huston sent his mother a short note and another packet of letters. Waring repeated his demand that no one read them. In the mail that day, he received eleven new letters, six from his parents and five from Carrie Goodwin, which he spent the afternoon reading. Fred Takes used the time to visit an American hospital and graveyard. Dead doughboys lay in uncovered graves, others were piled in coffins awaiting burial. Late in the day, Waring wrote his mother a second time. Apparently the post office had sent word mail would stop after that night. Waring figured they must be about to leave their bivouac, so his family wouldn't hear from him for a few days. "Take care of these letters for me please," he asked again. "Take care of yourself. With love, Waring."[20]

THE SAME DAY, ABOUT thirty miles to the west, Thomas Boyd and the Sixth Marines, part of Maj. Gen. John A. LeJeune's Second Division, had been loaned to the French Fourth Army to operate in the Champagne region, to the left of the Americans in the Meuse-Argonne attack. The French from the west, the First American Army from the east—together these forces were to push the Germans from the Argonne Forest. The last four days of September saw both operations begin ferociously but then slow down. In the French sector, the German line held at Blanc-Mont ridge, a forbidding position held since 1915. On the morning of October 3, Thomas Boyd's Marine Brigade attacked there, though Martin Gulberg didn't make it back from his leg wounds in time to join the fight. The Second Division ultimately took the heights, where future Alabama author William March (*Company K*, 1933) fought his way to great distinction.[21] In *Through the Wheat*, Boyd has his alter ego William Hicks survive Blanc-Mont and contemplate the aftermath of victory:

> On the drab earth, beaten lifeless by carnage and corruption, drab bodies lay, oozing thin streams of pink blood, which formed dark, mysterious little pools by their sides. Jaws were slack—dark, objectionable caverns in pallid faces. Some men still moaned, or, in a tone into which discouragement had crept, called for help.

Next came a passage that rather upset domestic imagery of the meaningful death, of the sanctity of the body, of the symbolic inseparability of doughboy and nation: "Each body was alone, drawn apart from its companions by its separate and incommunicable misery. The bodies would remain alone until to-morrow or the day after to-morrow, when they would be furnishing a festival for the bugs which now only inquisitively inspected them."[22] Long before he crafted these scenes, Thomas Boyd was gassed in the real battle of Blanc-Mont on October 4. This was the end of combat for him.

AFTER A BRIEF TRIP to Paris to vacate her boardinghouse room, Natalie Scott returned on September 7 to the hospital in Beauvais.[23] In the capital, she had seen her friend "Press," a woman who "whooped like a boy" and to Natalie's delight startled conservative people in the Paris office.[24] Around this time, Natalie posed for a photograph that satirized gender roles and the chivalric tradition (figure 6.2).

A small number of women back in America, meanwhile, took such ideas beyond the realm of comedy. They formed shooting clubs, trained with rifles, and prepared to defend themselves, threatening the male monopoly on protective violence. Some of them had aligned these activities with preparedness campaigns preceding the war, though the movement persisted through intervention. For pushing at the boundaries of custom, these women faced backlash and scorn, a reaction consonant

FIGURE 6.2 Natalie Scott in France, 1918, from her scrapbook of World War I photographs and mementoes. Natalie Scott Papers, Louisiana Research Collection, Tulane University.

with popular and official efforts to reinvigorate the protective responsibilities of American men.[25]

Natalie could count herself among almost seventeen thousand women who went overseas either as members of the army, employees of it, or workers for affiliated welfare agencies in France. The majority worked as nurses, in canteens, or in clerical jobs. On the home front, at least twelve thousand women joined the navy and marines, while tens of thousands labored in military offices and hospitals. While some of these women hoped to break free of constraints through their war work, they faced constant pressures to fulfill domestic functions and to remain conventionally feminine. Part of the broader campaign to safeguard the doughboy's virtue entailed surrounding him with canteen workers and other "auxiliary women" to remind him of (not distract him from) his sweetheart at home. Soldiers' welfare workers were expected to offer companionship to men at army dances, just as nurses were expected to package emotional succor with medical care. Natalie Scott's calendar typically included both roles. Many war workers embraced these demands, seeing in their war service expressions of domestic and even Christian womanhood.[26] But those who invested their work with more transformative potential chafed under such expectations. Natalie oscillated between these conservative and progressive temperaments.[27]

In Beauvais, Natalie's war life continued to confront her with reward and tragedy, fun and sadness, social engagements and bedside heartbreak. Patients came in all stages of injury and illness. Ten or so French soldiers died every day from dysentery. In one case, a mother missed the morning train and lost the chance to see her son before he died that afternoon. Meanwhile, Natalie reconnected with Red Cross nurse Julia Stimson, soon named director of nursing for the entire AEF and someone who mirrored Natalie's traditional and modern impulses. To Natalie, Stimson's face was "strong and sweet and intelligent," embodying the Red Cross's evolving commitment to decorum as well as professionalism.[28] The two shared a commitment to expanding women's civic roles but behaving in what they considered ladylike fashion.[29] Natalie told her mother that her pride and curiosity led her to wish women could see combat, but confessed to relief that they couldn't.[30]

Natalie did want to get closer to the front, though, to treat boys from her own country, to escape the comforts of her nicely appointed office with its hanging portraits of American generals and President Wilson. While she awaited a transfer, she sat with dying Frenchmen, cradled their heads, and comforted their families. One day she visited an American cemetery. "I went to the places where are all of my different boys," she recalled to her mother around the time of the Saint-Mihiel campaign, "and greeted them once more, in spirit. I thought of all of their mothers, and wished that they could have just one glimpse of that beautiful spot."[31]

In September, a young man from Wisconsin named Otto came to Natalie's care with a terrible case of meningitis. He cried out in constant pain, she sponged his brow, he cuddled close to Natalie with child-like helplessness. A French soldier—"just a boy"—arrived in the same state and died quickly.[32] Otto improved for a time, but then worsened and died on a Monday night. Another nurse sat up all night consoling Natalie. She recounted to her mother, "He seemed to lapse from a living, breathing death to one more quiet and peaceful. The peace is his. But back in America, in Wisconsin, where he came from,— there is where the pain will be. I hate to think of that." Otto's friends came to his funeral, a moving ceremony steeped in religious, national, and martial symbolism. "The sun broke through the clouds," Natalie said, "and fell in a flood of brightness and warmth like a benediction on the colors, and their bearer. It was a beautiful thing." She exchanged letters with the Texas mother of another meningitis sufferer, tracing sinews of connection between war zone and home front. When this boy's prospects looked dark, Natalie wrote his mother for him and the local paper printed her note. He recovered and Natalie found herself touched by the mother's "worship" of her son.[33]

Natalie took a vacation in early October, hobnobbing with aristocratic French women and riding horses and hearing false news of an armistice. Back in Beauvais on October 23, she secured an assignment with the *Ambulance St. Paul*, a hospital in the shattered village of Resson-le-Long near the front. A French woman named Mlle. St. Paul ran the operation. Natalie left Beauvais after six months, sending her mother some shrapnel and "Boche" helmets and money she had accumulated.[34] People wept and told Natalie they loved her as she left.[35]

THE AMERICAN PART OF the great assault slowed in the beginning of October. More than nine German divisions vigorously defended the Argonne. Supplying the American force across the former No Man's Land was messy and slow. Field hospitals became macabre theaters of mangled bodies, blood, screaming shell-shock victims, and missing limbs. Doctors and nurses struggled to care for the nonstop stream of patients. Official statistics documented roughly twenty-six thousand

American casualties in the first week or so of the offensive.[36] By October 5, the cold and rain had contributed to an outbreak of influenza afflicting sixteen thousand men.[37] The first eleven days of the month, Pershing recalled, levied the "heaviest strain on the army and on me."[38] Logistical bottlenecks, hasty training, haphazard organization, imperfect communication, poor leadership, slow transportation, and low morale were worse for the black divisions but not exclusive to them.[39]

Pershing renewed the offensive on October 4, 1918, the day after Waring Huston wrote twice to his mother and Thomas Boyd suffered his gas wound. The Eighty-Second Division moved into Corps reserve, keeping just behind the advancing line.[40] Waring's 325th Infantry passed the damaged and withdrawing Thirty-Fifth Division. "There was no sign of revenge in that sorry looking bunch," remembered a disillusioned doughboy from Capt. Truman's outfit. "But, here we were fighting. Fighting for what?"[41] German trenches lay battered, caved in, the trees torn apart by artillery. Twisted wire lay everywhere. "The road was full of holes and there wasn't a tree around that wasn't cut to pieces by shrapnel," Fred Takes marveled in his diary on October 5, "and there wasn't even a blade of grass to be seen in some places."[42]

The new assault against the *Kriemhilde Stellung* called for the Seventy-Seventh, Twenty-Eighth, and First Divisions (I Corps) to take the Argonne bluffs. Roy Thornburgh's Eighteenth Infantry and other elements of the First made the deepest gains. But to relieve pressure on that division, rescue the Lost Battalion, and take the forest, First Army commanders decided on October 6 to send in a fresh American force. They gave the job to Waring's Eighty-Second Division, though unproven in major combat and just turned over to the aggressive leadership of Gen. George B. Duncan.[43] Plans called for the Eighty-Second to fill the gap between the Twenty-Eighth and First Divisions and attack west into the Argonne. On October 7, infantry regiments of the Eighty-Second (not Waring's) captured a couple hills but stopped short of the town of Cornay. By that evening, though, the Germans had withdrawn from the area around the Lost Battalion under pressure from attacks by the Eighty-Second as well as Twenty-Eighth Divisions. At 7:00 p.m., relief arrived. Of the 554 original members of the trapped unit, 144 couldn't walk, 194 could, and 216 were dead.[44] Maj. Whittlesey earned a quick promotion, but the forest siege would haunt him for years.[45]

Just a few hours later, during the night of October 7, Waring Huston's 325th Infantry marched to the town of Charpentry under German shelling. One blast produced a big cloud of smoke that had men diving for cover and scrambling for gas masks. No one was hurt. They arrived in Charpentry at two in the morning. A ruined building sheltered wounded doughboys of the Big Red One, moaning in agony. All day the 325th sat in the mud. "We sure were a fine looking sight this morning," Fred Takes wrote in his journal. "We were wet and full of mud from head to foot." The men could see corpses on a hill nearby, and two dead Americans lay outside the crumbling aid station. Takes found the grave of a German soldier killed seizing the area in 1914. Shrapnel from the Americans' own anti-aircraft fire, Takes said, "got some of the boys."[46] As predicted, Waring sent no letters home those days.

With Waring and Fred's regiment held in reserve, other elements of the Eighty-Second pressed German defenses in the Argonne. Maj. Gen. Hunter Liggett, commander of I Corps, ordered the All-Americans to push to the forest's western boundary. October 8 saw only sporadic progress in that direction, except for the mission of the 328th Infantry Regiment.[47] Alvin York's unit attacked the Germans at 6:10 a.m. near Châtel-Chéhéry, close to where the 325th waited at Charpentry. York's Company G got held up early in the attack by dense machine gun fire from Hill 223. The doughboys weren't moving in that direction but the guns had to be quieted if they were to advance. Seventeen men from one platoon set out to encircle the hill—four noncommissioned officers, including Cpl. York, and thirteen privates. As the Americans emerged from the brush, they surprised 250 Germans, some of whom quickly put up their hands, assuming the small American detachment led a bigger force. Machine gunners on the hillside, however, fired down into the ravine. Six Americans died and three were wounded. The only noncom standing was Alvin York. With privates nervously guarding the prisoners, the Tennessee marksman killed twenty-eight Germans and held off a charge with his pistol before the enemy surrendered. York and the others led the captives across the hill, picking up others as they went, and arrived in the American patrol camp with 132 prisoners. York later called October 8 the "awful morning."[48]

That night, Americans in the Eighty-Second could hear German vehicles abandoning the forest to cross the Aire River. On October 9,

Liggett ordered the 325th and 326th Infantry Regiments to advance toward Cornay. Fred Takes and the 325th met little opposition that foggy morning. He saw dead horses along the roads, a sky full of smoke, Americans killed and hastily buried.[49] Around that time, two other regiments of the Eighty-Second were locked down in a fight around Cornay with a German division temporarily unaware of the withdrawal plan. Finally trapped in several French houses, 166 soldiers of the 327th and 328th Infantry Regiments surrendered.[50] The rest of the men in those units, utterly exhausted and their ranks depleted, withdrew from Cornay on the night of October 9. Neither Waring Huston nor Alvin York was present for these developments. Waring's Company K had been sent across the Aire to serve as combat liaison between the Eighty-Second and First Divisions and in brigade reserve.[51] York, wracked with guilt and melancholy, received permission to return to the scene of his heroics to save any wounded left behind. There were none. So the pious York prayed for the dead men in his unit, including another boy named Waring, and for the Americans and Germans alike.[52]

By four in the morning on October 10, Fred Takes and the men of Col. Whitman's 325th Infantry Regiment were arrayed around Cornay. They attacked at 7:00 behind an artillery barrage, the regiment's first real assault. Before them lay a high ridge the enemy could have easily defended, Whitman later guessed, "had he stayed to defend it." Once again, the Germans had already decided to evacuate the town and retreat closer to the *Kriemhilde Stellung*. But they inflicted damage as they withdrew. In his journal, Fred Takes recorded hard going up a brushy, rough hill. The men wore combat packs with overcoats and heavy ammunition. Regular gas attacks kept uncomfortable and hot masks on faces. Corpses lay everywhere. Shells and bullets came screaming into the skirmish line. No one from his Company A was hit that day, though Fred saw other men fall.[53] By 9:00 a.m., Cornay was back in American hands. The woods nearby were full of dead doughboys and dead Germans. The after-action report listed the regiment's casualties of October 10, 1918, as "few."[54]

One of the dead from Company C was Walter Owens, the upstate New York boy who had written letters to his family about crops and weather and rarely the war. More than a month later, on November 15, readers of his hometown papers read the telegram his family had just received, a private message aired publicly: "Deeply regret to inform you that your son, Private Walter Francis Owens . . . was killed in action October 10."[55] Reports circulated among officers during the attack didn't mention Walter, though they did document a number of "accidents" and friendly artillery fire. One of those field messages, sent to a commanding officer at 9:20 a.m., read, "Congratulations on your fine advance."[56]

BY THAT MANEUVER AND a thousand others like it, and at enormous cost, the Allies had by October 10 pushed the Germans across the Aire River to the north and more or less discharged them from the Argonne Forest. Significant gains came of the efforts of the Big Red One and divisions of V Corps, which had crept within striking distance of the *Kriemhilde Stellung*. Hunter Liggett did regret, however, not getting Waring's division into action quickly enough to trap and destroy more of the Kaiser's army in the forest. The Germans were bent but not broken. And losses were appalling—6,314 in the First Division alone in the six days since October 4.[57]

Among the dead from that outfit was Roy Thornburgh. On October 9, his Eighteenth Infantry Regiment ran into a nightmare of machine gun and artillery fire in a wooded glen. "[I]t is doubtful if at any time the regiment passed through a more cruel ordeal than it endured under the rain of shells in this fatal valley," recalled the divisional history.[58] Despite his own reassurances to his father about rapid notifications back in July, it would be many weeks before his family in Missouri learned what happened to Roy.[59]

Taking the exhausted First's place at the front was the Forty-Second "Rainbow" Division, which included Pressley Cleveland's 167th Infantry. After fighting at Saint-Mihiel, Cleveland rested during the opening stages of the Meuse-Argonne. In this period, the local Selma paper printed a letter from Pressley to his father complaining about a lack of potable water and the abundance of wine, "the poorest excuse for a drink in the world."[60] Meantime another soldier in the Rainbow named George Browne wrote his fiancée Marty a letter voicing both sides of the wartime love story told in the correspondence of Mae and Eliga Dees. "Sometimes I despise this war and our separation Marty," he said, but then a few sentences later, "I'm glad I'm here anyway for

I wouldn't be satisfied or you couldn't be satisfied with me were I in the States now."[61] Press's regiment received orders to make its way on October 11 to the front. Pressley and his comrades relieved Roy's Eighteenth Regiment, which an officer from the 167th judged to have suffered "some most severe experiences." Meanwhile the Forty-Second got into the First's position for the next attack of the campaign. The men were rested but some suffered from dysentery. Doughboys heard rumors of German battle fatigue and peace talks.[62]

THE FEDERAL GOVERNMENT'S CALL to buy Liberty Bonds continued to surge outward to local papers. To capture the public's support and dollars, fundraisers mimicked the broader direction of national propaganda, shifting between political and emotional arguments. In some cases appeals imbued war with high meaning, subordinating personal loss to that meaning. In others, however, they did something rather different, asking people to contribute funds to save doughboy lives, not guarantee the victory of ideas or personal virtue of soldiers—to lend their support, that is, to preventing a single additional combat death. Amid reports almost every week of a local boy killed in France, the *Greenville Sun* ran ads for the Fourth Liberty Loan drive that fell into the latter category. One showed an image of warriors arrayed along a trench parapet, the text claiming, "The quicker we do it the less American blood will be shed." The emotional energy of the feature, and its bold-faced tagline, drew on filial more than patriotic obligations: "Don't Let the SON Go Down."[63] The next day, a *Watertown News* ad said nothing about redemptive meaning but asked people to help hasten victory and "save the lives of our sons."[64] Newspaper editors in Greenville, Missouri, their typical reader a more zealous advocate of family and nation than war in Europe, aired a simple bond drive image in mid-October. A grim doughboy strangles a German soldier above the demand, "FINISH THE JOB NOW!"[65]

The next page told the story of a writer in France coming upon an American soldier dead in the mud, his helmet stuck in the ground, a steady rain soaking his uniform but not yet obscuring the ink in a pocketed letter from his mother. "Your daddy sits by the fire at night," the mother disclosed, "and refuses to talk of anything but you and of the day you'll be back with us again." She hoped he was safe and healthy and dry. The reporter couldn't bear the contrast between those words and the drenched son with a bullet in his head. "The question left is a simple one," the piece ended. "How many of these have died and are going to die in vain because the people back home couldn't raise the money to crush the military power that made such things possible?" Even if you have to mortgage your future, implored another appeal, buy a bond.[66]

Other entreaties stoked a vision of patriotic sacrifice in which individual deaths marked the pinnacle of national experience. The *Watertown News* ran a Liberty Loan ad that quoted the dead American flier Dinsmore Ely. His last letter to his parents before he was killed in April 1918 read, "I want to say in closing, if anything happens to me let's have no mourning in spirit or in dress, for like a Liberty Bond, it is an investment, not a loss, when a man dies for his country."[67] The *Selma Journal* told Waring Huston's family and other readers that Liberty Loan dollars encouraged the boys fighting "for our common beliefs and principles." In a paean to martial-inflected multiculturalism, a testimony both to the assimilative benefits of military service and the sanctified character of sacrifice, the ad celebrated the diversity of names on America's casualty lists—"Gerondo and Norvich and Nowatny and all the other boys who are fighting shoulder to shoulder with Smith and Jones and Brown."[68] In a similar spirit the Wisconsin paper excoriated the bond-avoiding cheapskate for failing to support boys fighting for "freedom's cause."[69] One Liberty Bond appeal never mentioned soldiers at all, instead asking Watertown citizens to forego "earthly treasures" for "treasures that are godly"—life, liberty, happiness.[70] A final story appearing in both the *Watertown News* and Missouri's *Greenville Sun* zeroed in on what those terms actually meant, telling a familiar story of virtue and the sustaining influence of the auxiliary services: "Our boys are fighting for their homes. The Y. W. C. A. with its hostess work in this country and in France is helping to keep the ideal of American home life constantly before the men who are protecting it."[71] These linkages reflected a resilient impulse in American public life—to key efforts meant in part to keep servicemen out of trouble to a more edifying tale of doughboy righteousness.

Whatever sorts of appeals local papers ran, however diligently they worked to lend regenerative meaning to patriotic sacrifice, it was hard to escape the ghastly atmosphere of October 1918. Death always featured prominently in newspapers, war or no war. Now the overlapping stories of worldwide conflict and epidemic disease generated a ceaseless drumbeat of bad news. The influenza outbreak had entered a much deadlier second phase.[72] In Watertown, newspaper readers learned the contagion was so severe in training camps that the provost marshal had cancelled the call-up of 142,000 new draftees. The commander at Camp Grant, where Arthur had trained, killed himself on October 9 in a sleep-deprived and haggard state over the influenza crisis. A Watertown boy died of the disease in an Ohio camp around the same time.[73] Ben Fluegel of Arthur's Company C wrote his mother,

> Well you said that the sickness that is in the S[t]ates is taking the poor boys quite fast that is to[o] bad but I hope it stops very soon. One of our boys got a letter and he said that he heard there wear six hundred died in Camp Grant that is quite a few but we all over hear hope it will soon stop.[74]

In October, the flu was "taking hold" in Wayne County and "gaining way" in Selma.[75]

Local audiences continued to learn from their papers, if they didn't know it by epistolary exchange or official War Department notification, a bit about combat even amid censorship of the press. The edition of the normally upbeat *Watertown News* that reported a Francis Barnes severely wounded in France revealed a letter from a local doughboy saying, "This war is not what it's cracked up to be. The people in the U.S. don't realize what our boys are up against, for if they could see some of the things we have seen they would stop and think."[76] Opera star Geraldine Farrar harmonized the extremes of hope and tragedy when she wrote in a piece syndicated in the Watertown paper,

> At a theater the other day a box party was given in honor of half a dozen heroes disabled while fighting for that victory at the battle of Château-Thierry. Some were without arms and others without legs; others so badly injured by the deadly poison of the Germans they probably will not live more than a year. But from every one of them came a strange spirit of spiritual gladness. They held their heads erect and smiled as though to say, "It was fine to have done what we did."[77]

Accounts of battle in the paper in October likewise blended buoyant language with talk of gas wounds and waist-deep mud and withering German fire. "The Americans found the Germans and closed with them in a desperate bayonet hand-to-hand fight," went a piece on the Aire River fighting. "Rifles often were used as clubs and each man struggled to down his individual opponent."[78] The *Greenville Sun* in Wayne County, Missouri, reprinted letters from soldiers with fairly explicit descriptions of combat and the effects of gas wounds. One wished he could say more about war "as it really is" but knew the censors would never pass it.[79]

Some American war deaths were literally written onto the facades of homes made emptier by them, in the shape of the Service Flag. Losing thirty-year-old draftee farmer Asa Cradic of Missouri, said the local paper, changed yet another star in the "Service Flag of the county" to gold.[80] An article by Brig. Gen. Nathan William MacChesney in the Committee on Public Information's *Official Bulletin* had explained the guidelines for Service Flags in a May 1918 article, revealing the phenomenon's origins in the redemptive instinct. The idea came from a private citizen and army veteran, R. L. Queisser of Cleveland, who had sons serving in the National Guard. Queisser sought to design a symbol "which would be to their mother a visible sign of the sacrifice her sons were making." Any family with a member in the military (man or woman) could display a flag, but to honor women like Natalie Scott, serving in the Red Cross or other "auxiliary" roles, would be "contrary to the spirit and purpose" of the flag. As for the symbolic rather than logistical guidelines for the flag's deployment, MacChesney quoted Lincoln:

> The idea of the gold star is that of the honor and glory accorded the person for his supreme sacrifice in offering up for his country his "last full measure of devotion," and the pride of the family in it, *rather than the sense of personal loss*, which would be represented by a mourning symbol.[81]

However individual American families regarded or disregarded these pronouncements, they synchronized with the government's enduring commitment to minimizing or elevating, depending on one's perspective, the prospect of private loss. Local papers repeated that logic.

Watertown editors hoped the war's cause would "mitigate" the suffering of John Moriarty's family; Missouri ones thought it a "consoling factor" that Asa Cradic had died to bring a "brighter day" in the future.[82]

These patterns made up a conflicted war story in the fall of 1918. The war had rendered chivalric and personal justifications both more and less tenable—more because of the liberation of towns and dough-boy heroism, less because of the sobering reality of combat deaths and stateside heartbreak. Few publicly denied the intervention was worth those sacrifices, but the question of what they were buying continued to attract diverse and sometimes implicitly skeptical answers.

SLOWER THAN THE CONQUEST of the Argonne were efforts to the east to dislodge the Germans from the Heights of the Meuse. For nearly two weeks since charging across Forges Creek, Arthur Huebner's Thirty-Third Division had endured German shelling from the heights on the eastern side of the river, which here ran roughly north-south.[83] On the night of October 7, engineers built duckboard bridges across the river at Brabant-sur-Meuse and Consenvoye to attack the guns perched on long, sloping, imposing ground. The doughboys occupied the western-most part of an operation that included two American and two French divisions. Across the river, open fields and wooded inclines and ridges stood between these forces and the heights.

The attack began on the morning of October 8. Infantry from Arthur's division crossed the Meuse and walked into Consenvoye, cap-turing enemy prisoners and weapons. Clayton Slack's Company D was attached to the first wave of infantry from the 132nd Regiment. In the afternoon, he single-handedly captured Germans manning two machine guns and threatening the American lines.[84] Soon German fire from the Bois de Consenvoye and Bois de Chaume slowed the doughboy assault. October 8 ended with the Germans still dug into the Heights of the Meuse.[85]

The leadership held Arthur's Company C out of the action on October 8, attaching it the next day to a battalion in the 131st Infantry. A slew of orders and cancellations left the company in Forges Wood until October 10, when it went into reserve. Arthur's chaplain, C. M. Finnell, kept busy identifying the dead (figure 6.3). Thanks to Finnell, "no member of the 124th Machine Gun Battalion," went the later unit history, "sleeps in an

FIGURE 6.3 Chaplain C. M. Finnell, chaplain of the 124th Machine Gun Battalion, identifying the dead of the Thirty-Third Division in the Bois de Chaume, October 14, 1918. Records of the Signal Corps, National Archives and Records Administration.

unknown or unmarked grave." Soon Arthur and his comrades relieved another machine gun company in the line at Dannevoux Woods, which they held until October 20 without casualties.[86] But the broader experience of the Prairie Division was rather worse in those weeks. Before Gen. Pershing withdrew the division from the front on the 21st, most units fought a fierce battle east of the Meuse. Gas and artillery burst into the Allied lines with astonishing force and regularity, earning the Thirty-Third the notorious distinction of most-gassed American division. Exhaustion and scarce provisions made men miserable. They were out of the region before the silencing of the German guns.[87]

AFTER RETREATING NORTH OF the Aire River, Germans facing the Eighty-Second Division blew up bridges and set up defensive positions in the undulating farmland from Grandpré to Saint-Juvin and Sommerance. On October 11, the 325th Infantry received orders to advance with another regiment northward on the road from Fléville to Saint-Juvin, toward the eastern part of that line, wrongly thought to be empty of Germans. Into the teeth of enemy resistance came Fred Takes and the others. German and American artillery and machine guns killed many of the attackers. In a lull, Takes found a black loaf of bread on a dead "Boche" and shared it with some buddies. Soon enemy fire forced them off the road. Many Americans died, Fred confided to his diary, and the gutter ran red with blood. He played dead when a machine gunner trained his weapon on him. Finally, Fred joined up with other dough-boys and made a charge toward Saint-Juvin from the east. But pinned down and with darkness falling, they hunkered in a thicket. "There were some men hollering and murmuring all night," Takes wrote. "They were wounded and didn't get any care." Elements of the division captured Sommerance, while still others crossed the Aire to hit Saint-Juvin from the south but retreated in the face of German fire and a dissipating fog. By October 12, when the Eighty-Second earned a brief rest, the line held by the All-Americans wrapped around the tiny town, a "hot bed of machine guns," as a report soon put it.[88]

Waring Huston and Company K were still serving in the role of combat liaison during these operations, frustrating the company com-mander, Maj. Oliver Q. Melton. Waring Huston's superior, according to a report he soon wrote, found it excruciating to watch ambulances with wounded comrades rushing by the safe position of his company. While their fellow doughboys were "shot to pieces," Melton said, they were forced to cower behind a hill. There was no masculine honor in this role. His men felt *forgotten, overlooked, despondent*. Finally, they were ordered on October 12 to report back to their home in Col. Whitman's regiment. For many of the men, Maj. Melton reported, it was the hap-piest day of the war.[89]

ELIGA DEES'S SIXTH DIVISION remained to the southeast in September, eventually earning the nickname "Sight-Seeing Sixth" for a busy sched-ule of movement. Though far from the Meuse-Argonne, the Vosges sector had its dangers. On October 4, three hundred Germans with flamethrowers and machine guns raided a forward post manned by about thirty members of the Fifty-Third Infantry. The greatly outnum-bered force not only repulsed but also took prisoners from the raiding party. Nine men died and eighteen were injured in an action that earned the regiment commendations. Lige omitted the incident from a letter to his wife Mae the next day. On October 7, another tangle left one man from his company dead, one wounded and captured, several others hurt.[90] Once again, Lige mentioned to Mae only that he could hear "big guns." He urged her not to worry about him.[91]

Those letters revealed a rather transformed Lige, more forgiving of Mae's epistolary performance and more solicitous of her happiness. "SMAK," he scribbled on the place he licked the envelope containing his October 8 letter. He hoped her teaching was going well and appeared to have abandoned any objection to it. Without jealousy he congratulated her on staying busy and cheerful. Lige claimed that he was "ok" and "getting fat" and "having a very good time." He still mentioned that Mae seemed "very slow about ans[wering]." The imaginary Bill Smith, Edward Streeter's creation, captured something of Eliga's feeling and much of his spelling ability when he complained to Mable, "Ritin letters from here is like talkin to a fello over the fone that aint there."[92] In his collection of fictional letters Streeter lampooned the time lag that bedeviled correspondence:

> Well Mable at the rate Im not receivin mail I wont be able to tell wether its last winter or next winter that your talkin about when I finally get your letters. Im going to keep on ritin tho just to annoy the sensor.[93]

The new Lige of the trenches handled these delays with good humor. At long last he understood the concept of postal system delays. "I gess it takes a long time for them to come," he granted on October 8, so "ill not kick about them."[94]

By October 12, the French relieved Lige's regiment. A note he sent from the rear suggests Mae worried Lige had "forsaken" her, mainly, it appears, because the mail network was slowing down if not devouring his letters home. Like always, logistics had the power to disrupt romance. "I don't see why you don't get them," he wondered, though he admitted opportunities to write could be scarce, "for I get yours." One of his envelopes left the front on October 4 and was postmarked in Piedmont, Missouri, on November 4. Before she even received that letter, Lige promised his wife on October 22 that he was writing five letters a month. "I have just come out of the trenches and back for rest," Lige notified her, lying on the ground and using his mess kit as a table, "but ill rite you as often as I can."[95] Just a few days later, the Fifty-Third Infantry moved again.

WARING HUSTON AND THE men of Company K rejoined the 325th near Sommerance on October 12 to find comrades exhausted from the attack toward Saint-Juvin and a night of gas and artillery. That day, the Germans held their fire, the command reorganized, and soldiers looked for food and water. Sustenance arrived on October 13 along with enemy shelling. In the afternoon, the Germans launched an attack against the position but it was repulsed. Orders came to push northward in the morning toward Saint-Juvin across a series of ridges and ravines, part of a broader assault by the whole First Army. The Seventy-Seventh Division would be on Waring's left under orders to take the town itself, with the Rainbow Division on the right.[96] Three miles separated him from his buddy Pressley Cleveland that night.[97]

Waring's Third Battalion of the 325th Infantry began October 14 in support of the First Battalion. For a while, things went well. The attacking battalion achieved its objectives, and the Third trailed behind by about a thousand meters. According to the morning's traffic in messages, by eleven o'clock the First had advanced a kilometer and a half to the Saint-Juvin/Saint-Georges road and there were prisoners coming back. "Everything looks roseate," assured the First Battalion's commander, Capt. Castle. But an hour later, he reported German resistance from the ridge north of that road. Waring Huston and the Third Battalion were lagging, apparently, and Castle wanted them forward in case of counterattack. The regimental commander Col. Whitman sent orders to the Third's Maj. Thomas L. Pierce to get up to the road to support Castle and to put a company in if necessary. Over the next two hours, two companies from Third Battalion, including Waring's Company K, worked forward to the road while the two others stayed further behind. This move put the collective Third Battalion on a ridge behind Castle. At 2:00, Whitman ordered Pierce to forget about the trailing gap, stay on the ridge, and "hold to the last if attacked." Meanwhile the Seventy-Seventh hadn't taken Saint-Juvin and machine gun fire from the town harassed the Eighty-Second

Division's 326th Infantry. That unit took matters into its own hands and captured Saint-Juvin's eastern part in the early afternoon. To the right, the battalions of Waring's 325th had done what Whitman asked of them, holding their positions near the Saint-Juvin/Saint-Georges road. Throughout the afternoon, German artillery and machine gun fire pounded their ranks.[98] Toward the end of the day, the commanding officer of Waring's battalion sent a message saying friendly shellfire was hitting the Americans. In fact the accidental harassment and killing of Americans by their own comrades had been a frequent subject of Col. Whitman's field messages in October and a broader problem in the war. One urgent Whitman missive on the subject came in the thick of this October 14 operation.[99]

The divisional history later called October 14 one of the "outstanding days" of the Eighty-Second's war story.[100] By nightfall, the 325th Infantry Regiment had captured about a mile of hilly enemy territory. The forward battalion sat on an unprotected ridge north of the road, while American artillery continued to strike the area in front of the position. The men were terribly hungry, muddy, and wet. Rations arrived after dark, but German bombardment hampered their distribution. A chilly rain fell. Doughboys bedded down for the night in empty shell holes. Knud Olsen, the Danish immigrant who had been sentenced to clean his ship's decks of vomit during the Atlantic crossing, suffered a minor wound and was off to the hospital.[101] Pierce was injured for the second day running. Col. Whitman soon listed the dead officers in a report:

Killed.
1st Lieut. William P. Spratt.
1st Lieut. Norman A. Garrett.
2nd Lieut. George W. Huston.[102]

At some point in the day, a shell exploded near Waring and a fragment hit him in the neck. Maj. Melton eulogized these soldiers. "They went into the scrap with a smile on their lips," he said of George Waring Huston and the others in a report, "and every man of the company, who lies on the hills near St. Juvin still wears a smile beneath his cover of wild flowers."[103]

TWO DAYS AFTER WARING Huston died, on October 16, his Company K finally occupied the attacking position Maj. Oliver Q. Melton craved. "Many of the sergeants and both Lt. Long and Lt. Huston had been killed," he wrote soon thereafter of the unit's pre-attack condition. Weak from hunger and thirst and illness, the doughboys nonetheless charged over the top crying, "it's for Col. Whitman!" Melton reported the men proving their fighting spirit that day before giving up the ground won when flanking units failed to do their jobs.[104] Subsequent accounts of Waring's death would place it on October 16, a likely error that found its way to the casualty notification telegram, newspaper tributes, and eventually his tombstone. It's possible Waring died then, though the reports of Whitman and Melton suggest otherwise. The day Company K attacked, rather than the day it followed in support and took friendly as well as hostile fire, would be the day associated with his sacrifice.

The 325th Infantry and Eighty-Second Division were much depleted. When they entered the line, Waring's regiment had contained one hundred officers and 3,276 enlisted men. By October 23, these numbers were twenty-three and 513.[105] For the remainder of October, the division failed to gain much ground, facing ammunition shortages, exhaustion, leadership turnover, illness, miscommunication, cold and wet weather, and more injuries and death.[106] An officer from Company B termed these losses a "useless sacrifice of the lives of many of America's patriotic sons."[107] Low morale plagued the unit. "We were all disgusted," Fred Takes grumbled to his diary after being ordered to go over the top on October 18, "thinking they wanted to kill us all off. We were wet and cold as it had rained all night. The captain said he knew none of us was hardly able for any more scrapping."[108] The higher command finally replaced the Eighty-Second Division with the Eightieth on Halloween. The first of November, the All-Americans marched south for rest.[109]

THE EXPERIENCES OF ARTHUR'S Thirty-Third and Waring's Eighty-Second signaled a broader truth about the offensive by October 16: the First Army had achieved great gains but at an enormous cost. The Argonne had been cleared, the defenses along the Aire River broken. Many divisions had paid dearly in lives and fatigue, including the First, Third, Fourth, Fifth, Twenty-Ninth, Thirty-Second, Thirty-Third, Forty-Second, Seventy-Seventh, and Eighty-Second. The area east of the

Meuse River, where Arthur was until October 21, remained contested ground, the big German guns still in place.[110]

On October 16, Gen. Pershing handed command of the First Army to Hunter Liggett, about to be promoted to lieutenant general. A tour of the lines revealed to Liggett an exhausted, depleted, depressed, wet, hungry, thirsty, and disorganized army. A hundred thousand stragglers, 10 percent of the total force of more than a million men, wandered the French countryside. "Such endless hammering in bad weather was a terrific strain on young troops," he reasoned. "There was serious need for rest and reorganization." Pershing wanted Liggett to pressure the breached *Kriemhilde Stellung*, but the new commander of First Army got his way. He asked for two weeks to reconstitute his forces and assimilate the reserve divisions into plans for a new offensive at the end of the month. That operation called for clearing the Germans from forests and strong points in the middle of their defenses.[111]

AFTER RESTING FOR A few days south of Verdun, the 124th Machine Gun Battalion marched eighteen miles overnight on October 24–25 to the Troyon sector. Arthur's comrade Ben Fluegel, still writing on Camp Upton stationery from buildings formerly occupied by Germans, explained the pattern of relief on November 3 to his mother in Watertown: "one division realeaves another from a bad to a good sector and from a good to a bad sector." She had asked how he was sleeping and he replied quite well, finally shed of clothes so dirty and "lousy" he could hardly rest. Ben asked after a "big baby" named August he knew from home, who should buy a bond or else be sent to France to "be a man." Ben thought the war would be over soon.[112] The 124th held its part of the line without incident except for German gas attacks at Avillers in the first week of November that afflicted Watertown doughboy Daniel McCarthy.[113] On November 10, Arthur and Ben's Company C along with elements of the 131st and 132nd Infantry advanced after the retreating Germans to a small, partially ruined town called Saint-Hilaire.[114]

ELIGA DEES BOARDED A rail car on October 26, bound for the Argonne, his Fifty-Third Infantry coming forward to pursue the Germans. Lige arrived in Villers-en-Argonne on the twenty-seventh, and then the Sixth embarked over several weeks on what its historian guessed was the longest march by any division in the AEF. Pvt. Sol Arouesty estimated no man in the unit would ever forget it. A fifteen-mile walk brought the men to Camp Chillaz, where they could hear action from the front, the division now in reserve for the First Army as it hit the German lines on November 1. Over charred and barren land the troops marched by night, slept by day, reaching the old Siegfried line on November 2, Grandpré on the fourth, Stonne on the sixth. "For a desolate place," wrote Lige's comrade Wayne Turner, "I never saw anything to equal it." Cold downpours and bombed-out roads depressed the men. It was just warm enough to keep the sometimes waist-high mud from freezing. Mercifully, the Fifty-Third stayed in Stonne more than forty-eight hours, where the doughboys found refugees living in a church with unexploded ordnance and heard about armistice talks.[115]

THE CENTRAL POWERS HAD unraveled rapidly since the commencement of the Meuse-Argonne offensive. Bulgaria and Turkey surrendered by Halloween, with Austria-Hungary following days later. The Kaiser departed Germany for a resort town in Belgium on October 30, the government, population, and army he left behind teeming with dissent and war-weariness. Recharged Allied armies surged ahead on November 1, 1918. The Heights of the Meuse fell to the French XVII Corps and the American Twenty-Sixth and Seventy-Ninth Divisions. Into the center of the old *Kriemhilde Stellung*, the Second, Eighty-Ninth, Ninetieth, and Fifth Divisions made advances. And on the left, the Eightieth, Seventy-Seventh, and Seventy-Eighth formed the long edge of the large, sweeping, northeastward pivot. The late Missourian Roy Thornburgh's First Division, and Pressley Cleveland's Forty-Second, whose 167th Infantry had fought in the costly victory at Côte de Châtillon, both followed in reserve.[116] Soon Pressley saw action in the offensive, which quickly invited alternately redemptive and tragic assessments. One commander in the Forty-Second Division called the late assault a "useless slaughter," another pronounced it emblematic of "an era of adventure and romance."[117]

As these divisions did their last work, and amidst outbursts of mutiny in German cities and the military, the Germans sent a peace delegation to France on November 7. By the ninth they were negotiating an armistice in a railway carriage in the Compiègne Forest. The Kaiser abdicated his throne the next day, and a little after five a.m. on November 11, negotiators signed an armistice to end the Great War. The fighting would stop at eleven that morning.

With the Germans and their allies weakening, the stateside press showed them in a degraded and unmanly light. Audiences in Alabama, Wisconsin, and Missouri read the Austrians were *on their knees*, Bulgaria was in *complete surrender*, the Huns *begged terms* but were suspected of *trickery*, the Teutons were *in retreat*, the Ottoman Empire *quits*, the Turks *give up*, and Emperor Charles of Austria had *fled*.[118] The German "ravishes old women as well as young," wrote the *Selma Journal* in October, "he carries away to unspeakable slavery the young maidens who fall into his hands." Selma's Charles Lamar Hoomes had died to shield America from the "ravages of the Hun."[119] In the *Greenville Sun*, a local doughboy spoke of refugees traumatized by "the tortures of four years." The stories made Sgt. Frank Stephens want to "wipe the Hun from the face of the globe."[120]

AS THE ARMISTICE TALKS drew to a close, on November 8, Lige's Fifty-Third Infantry continued its long walk around the Western Front. In an overnight rain the unit trudged off from Stonne toward Verdun. On November 10, the divisional commander presented the Distinguished Service Cross to three men, two alive and one posthumously, for their gallantry during a German raid. "Then came word of the armistice," reported the regiment's Wayne Turner. "It reached us about 9 a.m. but it didn't sound much like truth for the artillery all along the line were giving Fritz all they had as a parting souvenir. Then at 10:55 every gun stopped, and it was really uncanny after the fearful racket."[121] The end of the war didn't mean the end of the march—Lige and the Fifty-Third left quickly for Châtel-Chéhéry, where Alvin York's feats of October 8 had begun.[122]

Edward Streeter's Twenty-Seventh Division had been with the British all along. The New Yorkers had seen heavy fighting in the Somme region during the big Allied push beginning in late September. At the end of October, they pulled back for rest and spent the remainder of the war buying fruit from destitute French civilians and finding entertainment in the division's theatrical troupe. On November 10, in rare sunny weather, the division held a memorial parade in Corbie for its fifteen hundred dead. Bands played "Nearer, My God, To Thee." When the doughboys of the New York Division heard of the armistice, five thousand of their comrades remained in hospitals. "There were no cheers and there was no excitement of any sort," the commander Maj. Gen. John F. O'Ryan later wrote in a history dedicated to "The Mothers."[123]

The Great War held a few final indignities for African Americans of the AEF. After being withdrawn from the Argonne in early October, the Ninety-Second Division spent a month on patrols and lost almost five hundred dead and wounded. Still, the men attracted unfounded epithets like "worthless" and "unreliable." Lt. Gen. Robert Lee Bullard, commander of the newly created Second Army of which the division was a part, called it a "failure." More sympathetic observers occasionally noted the success of the division's units, including a once-raw regiment of Alabama draftees. Then, the division found itself part of a late push on November 10. The black regiments advanced effectively at great cost, but Bullard couldn't bring himself to praise them. To his diary he confided Arthur's Thirty-Third Division and others had done alright. The Ninety-Second had gained ground yet done the enemy "little harm."[124]

IN THE FIRST WEEK of November, Mrs. J. C. Hayward of Selma received a letter from her son Jack in France. He was a member of Waring Huston's Third Battalion. His note, dated October 17, 1918, had crossed the Atlantic relatively quickly. "We have some very sad news," Jack told his mother. "Lieut. Waring Huston was killed in action. A shell struck him on the neck." Mrs. Hayward immediately contacted the Hustons. They wired their congressman, Fred Blackmon, in search of confirmation from the War Department. As of the time the *Selma Journal* printed this story on Wednesday, November 6, the family hadn't heard back from Washington. The paper recounted Waring's story of early voluntarism, temporary physical setback, enlistment in the army, and cherished commission. He exemplified "the finest type of young manhood."[125]

In France, Jack Hayward and the remainder of the 325th Infantry were spending November pulling back from the front and reorganizing what Col. Whitman called their "shattered forces." They heard about the armistice during a march and met the news with relief. Whitman soon hailed his men for doing their bit in the fight for "human liberty" and pledged they would return to their families "better fitted physically and morally."[126] In the Eighty-Second Division, the unit's great losses muted any feeling of merriment.[127]

AFTER BEING GASSED ON October 4, Thomas Boyd had moved from hospital to hospital, unable to write until late in the month. He imagined his mother Alice beside herself with fear, he now told her, and surely the dread accumulated further in the weeks it took for this letter to reach her. From his hospital bed on October 27, he raved about unfamiliar comforts:

> I ate a good breakfast and this noon I had <u>chicken</u> for dinner! And tapioca pudding! Can you beat that? It wouldn't have been so surprising if some beatific celestial being in a long flowing white robe had passed it out for then I would have known I was in heaven, but to have a common orderly give me <u>chicken</u> and tapioca pudding—such things don't happen in France.

Thomas closed by promising he would see his mother soon, guessing the war had "run its course."[128] Around the same time, Martin Gulberg found himself in a gas attack and separated from his mask. He held his breath but too late. As his unit in the Second Division jumped off on November 1, Martin couldn't talk. He made his way to a base hospital in southern France near Bordeaux. Unsatisfied with the medication supply, he went absent without leave in the city. There the man who'd had trouble eating celebrated the armistice with a case of "cognac fever." Then Thomas Boyd rejoined the Marines on November 16, after the Great War was over.

TWO DAYS OF SLOW travel brought Natalie Scott in late October from Beauvais to the French field hospital at Resson-le-Long.[129] All the "sorry panoply of war" cycled past her train window—ruined buildings, trenches, lone children, barbed wire, cannons, troops. Then, closer to her destination, Natalie reported with surprise to her mother, she saw "American soldiers (colored!)." The hospital occupied a small château. It had a little room for Natalie crammed with a bed, chair, and nightstand. She tended right away to the wounded in tents outside the house. These included two "little black Singali," one of whom, she told Muddie without comment or embarrassment, she had bathed that morning. Here Natalie's professional commitments overrode the prevailing racial sensibilities of her country, where bathing a black man was about the last thing a respectable white woman would have confessed to doing. One day, the wife of President Wilson's adviser Colonel House came to visit, but wouldn't tour the hospital for fear of catching something. "I never before met the idea that a wound was contagious," Natalie snickered to her mother. She liked the woman in charge, Mlle. St. Paul, who was "attractive in the French vivacious way."[130]

Yet Natalie did have one gripe about Mlle. St. Paul. It revealed the boundaries of her racial tolerance and more broadly exposed the ways black service riled up white people. The black "Singalis" were unfamiliar foreigners and posed no threat to American race relations. When Natalie arrived at Resson-le-Long, however, she was disappointed to learn a black doughboy regiment was quartered there. Mlle. St. Paul behaved scandalously in her view by receiving black officers socially. One lieutenant "leans over and sings sentimentally in her very ear," Natalie fumed to her mother, "and she coquettes with him happily!" One day this man had the temerity to "breezily" flirt with Natalie. The French and British nurses seemed charmed by him. Such intercourse was precisely what many white American military officials and soldiers found dangerous and endeavored to prevent. It reinforced their stereotypes about black sexual predation and French moral failure while violating their sense of white sexual entitlement. Many Americans in the AEF, including Natalie, worried African American veterans might convert their service into emboldened masculine pride and imperil the racial status quo. Natalie, for her part, was as bothered by the "colored" dentist in the unit as by the flirtatious lieutenant. "Just imagine the time we shall have with these people after the war," she fretted. "Our country has done us a great wrong to give us such a problem to cope with, I think."[131] The wartime romance of white men protecting women and accruing masculine credibility had room for neither black dentists nor paramours. Natalie challenged that story in some of her behaviors and reinforced it in others.

In early November, Natalie heard the armistice had been signed. This time it was only slightly premature, and she recorded her mixed feelings in a note home. Natalie thought of the hearts "too heavy with the price they have paid to rejoice wholly." Nothing she saw during the war had eclipsed her upbeat perspective, but news of its ending did. "To-night," she wrote to her mother,

the war seems to me horrible in a way that I have never felt before in all the time that I have been here. Little wizened faces of men, torn flesh, mutilated limbs, faces twisted with suffering,—as though I had never been in a hospital before. I hope that the sun will shine to-morrow and do away with the picture. I can't be rid of it to-night.[132]

Natalie didn't recite her usual slogans charging war with chivalric purpose, martial virtue, or spiritual meaning. The silencing of the guns, or perhaps the looming end to Natalie's busy preoccupation, allowed her to breathe in the devastating impact of combat on individual lives, personalities, and families.

IT WAS THE MORNING before the Great War ended, November 10, about 130 miles to the east of Natalie Scott. Arthur Huebner's Third Platoon of Company C, led by Lt. Allan R. Goodman and comprising four guns and their crews, joined Company F of the 131st Infantry in an unopposed occupation of Saint-Hilaire.[133] By the afternoon, infantry from the 132nd had also arrived in the damaged town. Saint-Hilaire lay in a broad valley in front of the Troyon sector, surrounded by hills and escarpments and woods. The marshy ground was crisscrossed by small streams, making it tough to move troops and equipment.[134] When the doughboys entered Saint-Hilaire, the German 439th Infantry withdrew less than a mile down the road to the tiny village of Butgnéville. Late in 1916, this regiment had been formed with Alsatian recruits and sent to fight on the Eastern Front. Two years later, with the Russians out of the war, the 439th moved west with the Ninety-Fourth Division.[135] The unit was likely to have lost men to desertion along the way to Butgnéville. Alsatians and other minorities suffered marginalization and abuse in the German army and many resented fighting.[136]

On November 10, the Thirty-Third Division's commander, Maj. Gen. George Bell, Jr., had orders from Lt. Gen. Bullard of the Second Army to press the Germans while negotiators talked, and these orders traveled by mounted messenger down to the company level by nine that evening. Very early the next morning, officers in Saint-Hilaire learned, they would be expected to attack Butgnéville after a heavy barrage of artillery fire scheduled for five o'clock. "We had received no water and rations since coming to St. Hilaire," Goodman soon reported, "and had very little water and one days iron rations." Arthur Huebner and other members of his platoon camped in the ruins that night.[137] Other soldiers of the Thirty-Third Division, arrayed along the front, likewise slept before their part in the assault ordered by Bell, eager to show his division's mettle.[138]

The next morning, the hungry and thirsty men in Saint-Hilaire awoke before five to watch the barrage. Fewer than ten shells screamed toward Butgnéville, some falling short, and then, quickly, it was over. Officers debated whether to wait for more artillery. At about that moment, negotiators signed the armistice, effective at eleven that morning.

A decision made, the men set out at 5:20 a.m., on November 11, 1918, advancing the short distance toward the town across flat terrain. Two platoons from the 131st Infantry went in the first wave, two in the second, with two platoons from the 132nd in support and Arthur's machine gun platoon on the flanks. The force totaled 150 infantry and four machine gun crews, with eight foot soldiers assigned to carry ammunition. It was cold, foggy, and dark, with visibility of about three hundred feet. Five hundred yards short of the village, the attackers received machine gun and rifle fire. They crept ahead by echelon. At a hundred yards' distance from Butgnéville, everyone got held up at a line of barbed wire that looked like it was mined. They fought from this position for about thirty minutes. The Americans, aware of the war's direction though not its scheduled ending, wrongly expected the Germans to put up brief resistance and evacuate. Pinned behind the wire, the doughboys could not move forward and began to withdraw. The machine crews that hadn't been compromised covered the retreat, raking the German machine gun positions with fifteen hundred rounds throughout the course of the operation. In his report a few days later, Lt. Goodman singled out Pvt. Albert V. Vahl, Cpl. Homer Bale, and Pvt. Edwin Stensaas for manning their guns after the infantry had retreated, while the reduction of two machine crews to one man had forced the unit to disable and abandon those weapons. The force made its way back across the farmlands by 9:00 a.m. to Saint-Hilaire. Ten Americans had died and fifty-two were wounded along the short roadway to Butgnéville. Six of the dead and five of the injured came from the 124th Machine Gun Battalion.[139]

Officers were getting ready to attack again when they heard Gen. Bell was terminating the Thirty-Third Division's advance. He had received confirmation of the armistice from Bullard just before eight o'clock and sent out messages to his brigade commanders to stop.[140] The infantry came back and artillery stopped firing, but the Germans responded to an assault many of them knew to have come after the signing of the armistice. Thus in Arthur's division, twenty Americans died in one very late shell blast, another fourteen in a soup kitchen. A historian of the field artillery brigade operating in the area soon divulged that regimental commanders had intercepted messages attesting to the armistice just after five o'clock. In his estimation, the doughboys nevertheless asked to go forward that morning and to suffer German retaliation considered their losses "useless and little short of murder."[141] Maj. Gen. Liggett later defended the decisions to attack that morning before a House investigation committee, explaining that failure to do so would have left two divisions vulnerable to the enemy. He also called it "remarkable" that staff had succeeded in getting out the word of the eleven o'clock armistice to far-flung detachments along the front.[142]

Not all divisional commanders chose to cease as Bell did, even with verification of the imminent armistice in hand. Bullard's orders were vague—he announced only that the firing would stop at eleven. In fact, Bullard went out to the front that morning to watch the war's ending, wishing to "see the last of it, to hear the crack of the last guns in the greatest war of all ages. . . . Our men showed great zest in the striking of the last blows against the enemy."[143]

The zestful striking of last blows against little Butgnéville had produced two bullet wounds in the chest of Arthur Huebner, spending the last minutes of the Great War back in Saint-Hilaire (figure 6.4). Blood seeped through his uniform and stained the pages of his pocket Book of Psalms and New Testament. Ben Fluegel saw him that day. Arthur looked pale but Ben expected him to survive.[144]

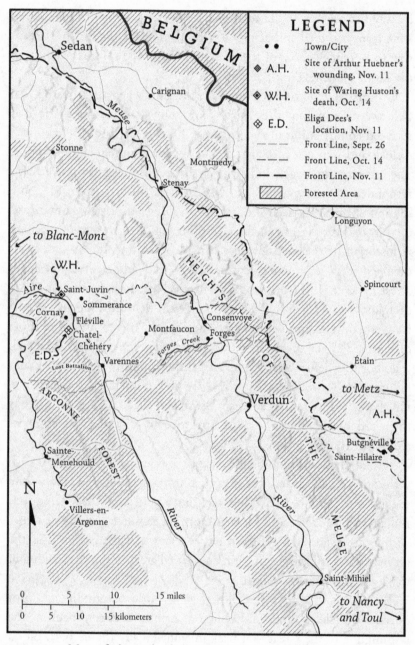

FIGURE 6.4 Map of the end of the Meuse-Argonne operation and the war, November 11, 1918, with approximate positions of Waring's death (Saint-Juvin), Arthur's wounding (Butgnéville), and Lige's encampment (Châtel-Chéhéry). Cartographic Research Laboratory, University of Alabama.

7

It's Over Over There

IN SIX WEEKS, 26,277 Americans died in the million-man Meuse-Argonne offensive, 95,786 were wounded.[1] On November 11, 1918, it was uncertain which column would claim Arthur Huebner.

At about eleven that morning, as fighting quieted across the front, the men of Company C withdrew from Saint-Hilaire and returned to Longeau Farm, where they had been in late October. While his comrades went to work cleaning up that area, then training and drilling at Doncourt after November 20, Arthur lay convalescing somewhere in France.[2] Although he had been shot twice in the chest, Arthur was feeling well enough to send his father Christian a letter saying he was recovering.[3] In the hospital on November 23, he turned twenty-seven.

NATALIE SCOTT FINALLY HAD good information the third time she heard the war ended.[4] On November 11, while workers packed up the field hospital run by Mlle. St. Paul, Natalie traveled to Paris to check in with the Red Cross. She arrived to unmistakable celebration and spent several exuberant days visiting with friends from New Orleans, co-workers from the Red Cross, and people in town from Beauvais. Her next assignment brought her to an American hospital in Nantes, France, far to the southwest of Paris and near the port at Saint-Nazaire. Late in November, she reported for work at American Evacuation Hospital 36. She undertook clerical duties, counseled patients, and planned activities. Recovering doughboys unburdened themselves of stories of romantic rejection by home front sweethearts. Those still corresponding with girlfriends or wives could visit the writing room, furnished daily with a thousand envelopes and two thousand sheets of paper, or dictate letters to Red Cross workers if unable to write.[5] Natalie reported spending days drafting homeward bound sentences for convalescing soldiers. She started a library for the hospital and brought books to wounded men. One day, a recuperating patient commandeered Natalie's typewriter while she was out of the room and inserted a word of thanks into the middle of a letter to her family. "We fellows were at a loss for some recreation," he typed, until Natalie came along with her "dandy library."[6]

Natalie's low mood at word of the armistice lifted once she became busy. She found energy and motivation and purpose, Natalie explained to her mother, in her patients. The war hadn't ended for them, so why should it end for her? "I don't want to forget the old song I have hummed along (considerately low) with the boys, but with great feeling and earnestness," she wrote, " 'And we won't be back till it's over over there.' "[7]

PATTERNS GOVERNING PUBLIC AND official campaigns to assign the war meaning persisted across the divide between war and peace. Rhetoric on the intervention's purpose continued to pivot from personal to political, from individual redemption to global transformation, from the safety of families to enduring peace for a planet. The tones of civil religion, the assuredness that God was on America's side and that war cleansed the nation's soul, rang through the vocabulary of victory as it had the words of wartime. Political, grandiose, global, and spiritual justifications had conditioned public support from the beginning, but initially had shared space with promises war would renovate American familial virtue and personal character. As in the last few months of the intervention, those prosaic elements proved durable though now increasingly muted. With the arrival of private tragedy and the end of the draft's motivational mandates, explanations for the war continued to drift from what it could do for families to what it promised to do for peoples. The story of redemptive war persisted, then, but with the terms and beneficiaries of redemption pushed outward. President Woodrow Wilson gestured at the enlargement when he said to Congress, "It is international justice that we seek, not domestic safety merely."[8] He sailed for the peace conference in France soon thereafter.

Following the armistice, the war's expansive implications reverberated through church services, town squares, city streets, and print culture. The victory marked the *greatest day in the history of nations*, had *for all time cast down the ambition of despots*, delivered *the most thrilling Thanksgiving in the history of the world*, and ensured American ideals would become *the fixed philosophy of all nations*.[9] Grief-stricken families should know their sacrifices guaranteed the survival of *civilization, rights of mankind, international law, the spirit of God*, the *security of the world*, the *cause of liberty*, and *world democracy*, and contributed to the defeat of *the militaristic classes, militarism and autocracy*, and *violations of international law*.[10] These were many of the outcomes upon which the advocates of April 1917 had predicated their calls for intervention. Meanwhile, though rather overwhelmed by grander stuff, stories percolated on simple things the war bought, stories of liberation and emotion and the return of everyday blessings. A reporter with British soldiers wrote in the *New York Times*,

> And the women and children came running to them with Autumn flowers, mostly red and white chrysanthemums, and they put them in their tunics and in the straps of their steel helmets.

One little girl told the writer in a high voice of scary machine guns and scattered dead men. "She spoke like an old woman," wrote the correspondent, "this child of seven in the town of Mons."[11] The men who had accomplished the mission, whether framed in spectacular terms of global rescue or poignant tones of personal emancipation, not only had channeled but also restored masculine character. Heralds of this redemption story could claim to have promised its fulfillment in the days surrounding Wilson's war address, to have invested conscription with its assurances, and to have remained loyal to it as Americans arrived at the front. To believers in regenerative war, especially if they imagined the army in the aggregate, as most did, the intervention had delivered. The day of the armistice, the *New York Times* declared the war had offered an "education" and a "salvation to the young men of America assembled in her armies," the discipline, clean living, and physical fitness of military life generating better men.[12] A preacher in Nashville swore from the pulpit that the doughboy "presents the highest type of manhood that ever drew sword on any battlefield since the beginning of time."[13] Even the mortally wounded man, Americans read in the papers, had died well, had died with home on his mind, had shown himself to be a good boy by being a good soldier. "As they die," intoned a piece in a big Kentucky sheet,

> these multitudes of men are thinking never of self, but of suffering chums and loved ones at home. With their lips murmuring the names of their womankind, mothers, sisters, sweethearts, wives, speaking tenderly of God, men go over the top for the long good-bye, their feet planted firmly upon the way as though to victory.[14]

Such accounts offered a bookend to the testimonials of May 1917, with boys and mothers parting ways to do the bidding of God and nation and family, and with womenfolk at the heart of the war's purpose. In this durable vision, soldiering and even death didn't so much destroy the family as reveal its strength.

The vignette also reassured stateside audiences that doughboys had fixated on home and faith, particularly at the moment of reckoning, and not French women or other degraders of reputation. With the war over, reformers put soldierly virtue at the heart of a persistent chivalric narrative. The United War Work Campaign sought donations to fund activities for men like Eliga Dees to "keep them clean in body and clean in thought."[15] Although venereal disease rates had crept low, it was only by preventing the infected from boarding transports that Gen. John Pershing kept his pledge that no sickened man would set foot in America.[16]

Men wounded in more conventionally honorable ways were abundant and coming home by the thousands. Their arrival challenged the regeneration narrative, which assigned personal benefit to combat wounds and promised government help to restore the breadwinner's earning power. Prophets of that story could keep telling it if they considered wounded veterans in abstract terms or zeroed in on disabled veterans of extraordinary pluck.[17] Newspaper headlines reinforced the views of Theodore Roosevelt and other war injury romantics when they reported *maimed* though *heroic* men, the nation's *sons*, casting away their crutches, *cured at the sight of America*, of men *proud of scars* and even *gay*, who could *smile, though wounded*.[18] Reports on the December arrival of seven thousand men spoke of boys returned as men, whether wounded or not, and of a veteran missing both feet but glad to have made the sacrifice. Journalists tempered frightful disclosures with comforting sentimentality: "Here was a man with a jaw shot away—and happy in his expectation of rejoining his wife and children."[19] President Wilson, visiting injured troops at a hospital in France, found the men cheerful and the conditions sure to please their mothers.[20] Believers in the bright prospects of government rehabilitation plans for the wounded, optimistic advocates of the War Risk Insurance Act (WRIA), could still say of the disabled veteran in December 1918, as one official did in the periodical *Outlook*,

> His family will not suffer by reason of an inadequate income supplied only by the pension; they are comfortably supported and living under proper conditions. His children are not compelled at an early age to find employment with which to eke out the family revenue, thereby jeopardizing their education and prospects of the right mental training to insure a fair chance in life's struggle.[21]

Here was the allure of the WRIA, which had promised minimal disruption of domestic arrangements should the doughboy forfeit his wage-earning capabilities to the state's demands. To make the injured veteran "A MAN among MEN in spite of his physical handicap"—this was the mantra of the main government rehabilitation journal, *Carry On*.[22]

Yet quickly, the inadequacies of government plans and experiences of families undercut such reassurances. The story of romantic injury absorbed dissonant counter-narratives of war's obvious degenerative consequences. Even newspaper stories headlined by the rhetoric of pride and resilience painted sober pictures of empty sleeves, deaf ears, torn muscles, missing feet, gas wounds, blindness, and tuberculosis. Only a few days separated those columns from stories announcing the public's first taste of *grim tragedy* and *war tragedies*.[23] Wilson grew "tired and worn" by his visit to the Neuilly Red Cross hospital. He asked one doughboy why there were no men injured above the waist. They had "gone on," said the soldier.[24] Journalists and commentators wondered what would happen once the wounded man turned from a jawless veteran meeting a reporter to one seeing his children. As social welfare advocate Sophie Irene Loeb asked in the *Washington Post*, "Yet what about him after he has put aside his patriotic garb and limps about in civilian clothes?"[25]

AS AMERICANS CELEBRATED THE war's end and contemplated its costs, Waring Huston's parents in Selma remained unaware of their son's fate. On Monday, November 18, local editors put Waring's picture in the paper and reviewed his story (figure 7.1). He was unofficially reported killed in a doughboy letter, his family was awaiting news, and everyone hoped there had been a mistake.[26] A telegram from the War Department,

FIGURE 7.1 Photograph of Waring Huston appearing in the *Selma Journal* on November 18, 1918. Alabama Department of Archives and History.

dated that evening and addressed to Waring's mother, ended those hopes (figure 7.2).

In a eulogy the next day, the *Selma Journal* described Waring as a popular young figure in the Selma business and social scene, now mourned by "hundreds and hundreds" of local friends. In the prime of life, he was engaged to be married, the piece reported, something he never said in his surviving letters home. "The name of Lieut. George W. Huston will be emblazoned upon the annals of Selma's history," the *Journal* concluded, "as one of the greatest heroes who gave his life that others might live."[27]

The last weeks of 1918 saw the arrival at the Selma house of condolence notes from military officers and soldiers and friends and family. Together, the correspondence testified to the cross-pollination of private and public mourning culture. Perhaps unsurprisingly, the brass saw grandiose accomplishments in Waring's death, the friends more personal outcomes. But all the writers pictured his service as an expression of character, tracing the range of ways Americans had been encouraged

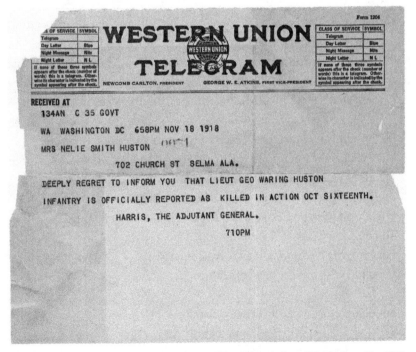

FIGURE 7.2 Western Union telegram to Waring's mother, November 18, 1918. Huston Family Papers, University of Alabama Libraries Special Collections.

to think of military service since April 1917. They had the effect, that is, of making salutary the sacrifice of loved ones to national purposes, although they materialized in an environment of personal sympathy rather than persuasive appeal. Almost all the consoling notes went to Waring's mother.

From France, Gen. George B. Duncan, commander of the Eighty-Second Division, offered a classic sermon on sacrifice and civil religion, assuring Nellye of her son's good and courageous death and his burial by a Christian chaplain in the soil he had "died to free." World freedom was brought closer by Waring's demise.[28] The day after Christmas, Col. Walter Whitman of the 325th Infantry sent his regrets that good men like Waring should be sacrificed "even for so just a cause." Whitman added weight to the good death narrative when he reported to Mrs. Huston her son had died "instantly and swiftly—in the height of a bitter contest—and in the flush of enthusiasm over an assured victory." He called the ten days in the middle of October "that awful period," when many officers had died leading their men into the teeth of machine gun and artillery fire. Waring had perished setting "an example of fearlessness."[29]

Other than a letter from Waring's buddy William Harper associating the war with "political freedom," people close to the family keyed the boy's death to purposes more modest though no less revealing of his character.[30] Waring's brother-in-law John Lapsley wrote a commemorative poem that saw the world's "happiness" driving Waring's war:

He loved his life; each hour, each breath, was sweet;
His eyes laughed out upon the world; the cup
He lifted would not hold what Youth held up, —
So sparkling with delight, —to make complete
His dream of happiness. He did not try
To count the years, nor measure what Life stored
For him; the end, like some far eagle, soared
Beyond his sight, lost in a golden sky.

Suddenly came war's challenge o'er the sea
To him! The happiness of all mankind
Trembled before the world's great tragedy!

Mother and sweetheart—all—he left behind,
And fell at dawn of glorious victory!
Now, all things beautiful bring him to mind.[31]

More explicit on Waring's chivalric virtue was a co-worker of his father Walter's at the City National Bank in Selma.[32] Robert Blakey Cater, an ambulance driver in the French-led *Convois Automobiles*, noted key elements of Waring's military biography—the early enlistment, the combat service, the "supreme sacrifice" to save flag and country—but imagined his friend's achievement in terms circulated for months and likely to resonate with Walter. Waring had died

> to help keep the dirty Hun those educated Barbarians from doing to his mother and sister what we have seen done to these poor French women.

To Rob Cater, a witness to wartime death and suffering, Waring had literally protected his family from degenerate Germans. "We Americans have a mighty lot to be thankful for," he said, flipping the *over there* motif from his post in Europe, "that this war was never fought over there." Rob thought Waring had been buried near Toul and offered to photograph his grave.[33]

A card from Waring's buddy Blanton lent visual testimony to the chivalric impulse, depicting an American handing a Christmas gift to a little French girl. Blanton reported on December 1, 1918, that he was headed off on leave to Paris, Nice, and Monte Carlo, a trip he had planned to take with Waring. He told Nellye he was putting Waring in for a Distinguished Service Cross.[34] Then she heard from Waring's best friend. Pressley Cleveland told Nellye he had found himself near the 325th and sought out Waring, only to learn of his death. Press's paean rested on Waring's masculine character and capacity for love, intertwining those qualities with his martial virtue in the way Waring's brother Harry had done in a letter many months earlier:

> Mrs. Huston, my heart simply is broken over the loss of my best friend, he was not only a friend at all times, a comrade at all cost, and a brother to me, a man who during my years of associations with

him, I have always found a Gentleman, a man who was a man, a man whom was loved by all of his Fraternity men, a man whom all liked and respected at college. "No knew him but to love him."

Press hoped to fill a part of the vacant place in Nellye's heart. He couldn't ease her pain, but echoed Gen. Duncan in reminding her Waring had died "like a man, like an American."[35]

MEDICAL WISDOM IN 1918 held that chest wounds should be treated with bed rest. Arthur Huebner likely lay flat from the time he entered the hospital around November 11 through his birthday on the twenty-third. Lying down suppresses coughing and allows bacteria to multiply in the lungs rather than be expelled. The pain drug morphine aggravates these problems by making breathing shallow and inhibiting coughing. A merging of these factors likely facilitated the buildup of bacteria in Arthur's lungs, which led to pneumonia, the disease that took his life on November 26.[36] The next day, Arthur was buried in the American cemetery at Toul, perhaps near Waring Huston, thirty-five miles from where he had fallen at Butgnéville.[37]

Without Arthur and other casualties, Ben Fluegel and Clayton Slack marched from France to Germany, then Germany to Luxembourg.[38] These moves were part of the Allied push to occupy the industrial and transportation centers of western Germany. The goal was to confront the vanquished foe with a disincentive to scuttle peace talks scheduled to begin in January 1919. Occupying the Rhineland would afford the Allies advantage in any resumption of hostilities.[39]

In mid-December, just as the Wisconsin boys were leaving France, Christian Huebner received a telegram informing him his son had died. The German-language *Watertown Weltbürger* published a sparse biography of Arthur, noting his conscription, training, and deployment. Joining their father in mourning were Arthur's brothers Otto, Walter, and Carl, and his sisters Martha, Johanna, and Alvina.[40] At this moment, Arthur finally showed up in the *Watertown News's* "Roll of Honor" listing area boys in the service. Five days later, he appeared in the paper's casualty list, next to another Huebner, both having "died of disease."[41] Then, *after* hearing word of his son's death, Christian received Arthur's letter hopeful of recovery.

A different cruelty awaited the family of Watertown's Daniel McCarthy. On November 24, his parents received a telegram reporting he had died from gas wounds on November 10. In the middle of December, they got a letter from a doughboy in France dated November 16 saying Daniel had been wounded. "That there may be a mistake," went a local newspaper piece, "is the belief of his parents."[42] Official sources disagree on how this story ended. The history of the 124th Machine Gun Battalion published in 1919 listed Daniel as dead, but Arthur as only wounded. The history of the Thirty-Third Division published in 1921 listed neither as fatalities, but the 1920 compendium *Soldiers of the Great War* put them both in that category.[43] If the most finely grained account, the unit history, is the accurate one, Daniel's family was devastated twice.

ELIGA DEES AND THE Fifty-Third Infantry spent the first day after the armistice marching from Châtel-Chéhéry to the battered town of Montfaucon. More walking brought the men to an area east of Verdun, where they spent a week salvaging equipment and receiving liberated prisoners from German representatives. By December 6, Lige's company had marched to Quemignerot, France, for training. Since arriving at Villers-en-Argonne on October 27, the Fifty-Third Regiment of the "Sight-Seeing" Sixth Division had walked almost five hundred kilometers, crossing five French departments and entering 110 towns.[44] As for hiking, Lige's comrade Wayne Turner wrote his brother, "Have had enough to last me a life time."[45]

Meantime, back in Missouri Mae Dees may have read in the paper that Roy Thornburgh had been killed. The *Greenville Sun* could summon no redeeming words about his death. For Roy's family, "nothing can be said which would soften the final, cruel blow." Nearby on the front page, the paper reported that a fire had destroyed Williamsville High School, where Mae had graduated and Roy had taught. Classes were in session but no one was hurt.[46]

From Quemignerot, Lige erupted, again, over Mae's purportedly lackluster letter-writing schedule, apparently forgetting, again, the difficulties with the mail. What few notes he did receive from her are lost. By January, he was counting his outgoing letters and her incoming ones and complaining about the discrepancy. "I cant understand," he fumed,

unless you have learn to love some slacker and if so I would rite and
say so anyway for I am always wondering what my sweet mama is
doing and you are all the world to me without you I wouldn't want to
live so please rite to me this is my 11 letter and only got 2 in 3 weeks
and all of the other boys gets 2 a week and I feel so bad to think that
I am slited so don't get mad at this for you cant imagine what I have
got to go through with[47]

Soon thereafter he had the temerity to backtrack, writing that he hadn't
gotten much from her but wouldn't "kick about it like you did."[48] Yet
later he painted this pitiful scene:

I started to rite your letter and when the bugler sounded mail call
I got up in front and listened for them to say Dees. But when they
said all gone I drop my head and walk down to my quarters and layed
down on my bed and went to sleep[49]

It seems Mae was equally worried about Lige's own commitment, so he
reminded her he couldn't speak French and she was the only one he
wanted to speak with anyway.[50] "Don't worry about me for these frogs
don't look good to me," he assured her.[51] Freed of wartime censorship
restraints, Lige supplied Mae with a guidebook to his movements over the
past months, when he had been to the "Alsas Section" and the "Argonne
Park" and near the "rhyne river" and to "Virdone" and "another place
that I cant think of."[52] Lige predicted in December he would be home
in one month. In early 1919, he anticipated it would be three or four.[53]

IN THE NEW YEAR, the remainder of the 124th Machine Gun Battalion
spent a quiet Luxembourg winter training and exercising and watching
entertainers. Ben Fluegel divulged to his mother in January that the
boys went to a dance every Saturday night but he couldn't wait to dance
with American girls again. To break the monotony, he secured a position taking care of foals in a stable. Ben then updated his mom about
two boys she apparently knew:

Say you asked about Dan MacCarthy well he is dead alright to bad
poor kid. I heard about it last week from headquarters so it must be

true. Some of the boys that got wounded the last day of fighting came back and one told me that Arthur Hubener is dead too I didn't think he would die but it was worse than I thought it was. I think I told you he was shoot twice thro the lung he looked white wen I saw him last and we shure can be thank and shake hands with our self that we are here it was and awful bad place I'll never forget it.[54]

Although headquarters may have had bad information, this note adds another source to the case that Daniel had died. It is also the only known description of Arthur's wounding. After sending the letter, Ben stayed in Luxembourg through the spring. In May, almost a year after they had left for France and with the peace conference nearing conclusion, Ben Fluegel and Clayton Slack and the Thirty-Third Division reversed the steps of that journey. From Brest they sailed on May 9 for the United States, traveling on the *Mount Vernon* again. The battalion chronicler, drafting the unit's history from the vessel, praised men who had given up "homes and vocations to help make the world safe for democracy. . . . Our task is now completed and we are returning to our homes and loved ones happy in the knowledge that we have contributed in no small degree towards the triumph of that cause."[55] These words hinted at the private costs of war but subsumed them to a political project, making no claims for the veteran's personal benefit other than his happiness.

The men of the 325th Infantry Regiment and Eighty-Second Division stayed in Europe several months after Waring Huston's death. In February, during an elaborate review of the division, the corps commander fêted Alvin York. Another ceremony saw York receive the Medal of Honor for the October 8 action. In April 1919, the division sailed from Bordeaux to New York. By June 1, most of the unit had been demobilized, and this iteration of the Eighty-Second, according to its chronicler, "passed into history."[56]

NATALIE SCOTT SPENT THE holiday season caring for twelve hundred soldiers in Hospital 36. There were gift packages to be prepared for every doughboy, Christmas trees to be positioned, and a program of entertainment to be planned. To recreate domestic holiday comforts, Natalie and other Red Cross workers distributed candy and nuts and cigarettes and socks and razors. They passed out decorations so the boys could dress up their own spaces. Even the hardest and "saddest" cases, men living in Ward 130, wrapped medical equipment in tin foil. Natalie thought she perceived "renewed interest" in their faces. A quartet of black singers performed ragtime hits in the "raggiest way," making the boys wild, Natalie delighted in telling her mother.[57]

Into 1919, Natalie kept up her work in the Red Cross hut and library, then took a March vacation with two officers and a girlfriend through France and Spain. In May, she wrote a history of the Red Cross at Nantes. Wounded doughboys were recovering and heading home, the last of them leaving in June 1919, seven months after the armistice. The Nantes hospital closed. Natalie traveled to the front in Belgium, France, and Germany. By July, she was back in Paris, helping account for and allocate Red Cross hospital supplies.[58] She sat in the grandstands near Gen. John Pershing to watch a track and field meet in the Paris stadium named after him. Natalie spent romantic evenings with officers in the city's bistros and drinking establishments. One night she found herself with a Captain Finley at the gleaming new Basilica of Sacré-Coeur in Montmartre.[59] Into the envelope with her letter home on these happenings, she pressed a small flower, still preserved a century later in a Louisiana archive. Before her family in New Orleans, Natalie dangled the mystery of something keeping her in France through the fall of 1919.

LIGE'S REGIMENT PASSED FIVE busy months earlier that year in Quemignerot, which he got unusually close to spelling correctly when he wrote "Quemignyrot." The men could take college courses and remedial ones. There were shooting competitions. Regiment members played baseball, football, basketball, and ran track. Lige bragged to Mae that his company had the best football players and that he played on a baseball team. In snowy conditions the baseball games ran to scores like 27–33.[60]

Early in 1919, Lige received a despairing letter from Mae about his devotion to her, or at least his response suggests as much. He urged her not to worry, to trust in his affection, to appreciate the difficulties of maintaining a romantic relationship at a distance of four thousand miles while carrying out his commitment to army and nation. Together they navigated the irony that fighting a war keyed to everyday happiness, familial stability, and sexual virtue was making Mae and Lige miserable, destabilizing their union, and introducing opportunities for infidelity. "I am doing all in my power," Lige wrote with desperation, "to make you happy and be happy myself for you know what it is to serve our country." He dedicated his loyalties to both family and nation, and hung on to the hope, reiterated often in American home front culture, that he could fulfill his responsibilities to both. Lige in fact understood his obligations to home and country equally as duties. "I know it is hard to be apart," he reasoned, "but duty call [and] some day duty will call and your dada will be with his sweet one."[61] But deeper into his postwar time in France, Lige craved domestic rather than martial recognition of his masculine virtue. He was just a "good man," he submitted to Mae in March, who wasn't where he was supposed to be.[62] The separation created awkward situations for their families as well. Lige's mother wrote him to say Mae should come visit his people, but Mae didn't think it her place to do so without her husband.[63]

Through the late winter and spring, Lige mingled jealous admonitions with romantic fantasies and loving words. He reminded Mae of their wedding anniversary in February, off by a month. The premature realization nonetheless stirred Lige's nocturnal imagination:

> I was thinking of you so strong when I went to bed and o mama you cant guess what I dream of that night I cant tell you now but some day ill be able to tell you all of it[64]

Another Lige fantasy had the pair taking a bath together.[65] He longed to lie in bed with her in the morning and to attend a "good old country dance," which the social conservatives of Wayne County had only recently stopped considering a crime.[66] Lige asked about her physical appearance after a year apart. In one letter he confirmed his approval of Mae's plan to have her teeth "fixed" and asked if she'd gotten fat, but closed with cuddly talk and x's and o's.[67] For his part, Lige's hair had gone gray and he planned to send her a picture once stateside to ease her shock.[68]

Lige hated France and the French. There were no toilets, he griped, and you could watch people squat by the road any time of day.[69] Mae sent Lige pictures of herself and he would have done the same except these "frogs" hardly knew what a picture was and only sold postcards. The cards and the population alike made him sick:

> All they think of is asking a soldier is he pollivou Francais when they ask me I say do you compry? Shit ha ha God they get on my nerves Well ill let the frogs up and you seem to think that ill

take up with one of them I may but if I do ill be crazy or some
thing rong[70]

Lige repeatedly addressed mutual jealousies. "Listen honey," he wrote,
"as far as me flirting with the girls and having a good time I am a married man and living true and listen you flirting with soldiers boy ill be
jealous for I know more about soldiers than you do and I know what it
takes to satisfy a soldier boy so you must lay off of them."[71] Lige again
expressed regret for sending letters to Mae from another woman before
he had left for Europe.[72]

Mae and Lige negotiated the trials of separation and looked forward to reunion. The situation called for concessions. In one letter, Lige implicitly accepted Mae swimming by asking her to teach
him once he got back to Missouri, but then soon reversed himself
and decreed that she not go in the water "with them old boys" until
he returned.[73] Lige grudgingly admitted his reduced authority over
Mae's social calendar and work decisions. "Do as you wish about
teaching while I am gone," he wrote, clarifying several times that his
tolerance owed only to his unavoidable absence. Then periodically
he would backpedal and "beg" her, as Mae later put it, not to return
to her profession.[74] He put similar conditions on her movements,
approving of some engagements but then fretting over how her solo
presence might look.[75]

Sometimes these negotiations implicated contemporary political and
social debates. Lige asked in March how the states had voted on prohibition and clarified what Mae could expect from him as far as liquor
was concerned. With hilarious and defensive repetition, Lige sought to
distance himself from the soldier's ribald reputation:

> I like one or 2 drinks and that will not hurt any one but I don't get
> any more than I need but I do take one or 2 drinks and I want you to
> know it but don't get excited for I don't take but one or 2 drinks and
> that is all and I don't care for you knowing it[76]

Otherwise they talked about their domestic life, speaking of future
babies and the home they would make and work he would do. In

February, he asked Mae to pick out a place to live and think about what job he should get. Lige was open to farming or "public works" and also possessed haircutting skills.[77] Finally, in April, as Congress prepared to reconsider woman suffrage, Lige wrote Mae hopefully that he didn't think "my pet wants to vote will you honey[?]," but vowed that either way they would not "fall out" about it.[78] In these cases and many others, Mae and Lige worked at a great distance and slow pace to get to know each other, to adjust their feelings and expectations to a situation inhospitable to romance.

The reappearance of Mae Dees in the epistolary record—a twenty-five-page missive dated April 13, 1919—took up all these matters and more. She said she loved and missed Lige and looked forward to his return in just about every way imaginable. He had talked of her being sick in preceding weeks. She had caught the influenza virus, currently killing 675,000 Americans and up to 100 million people worldwide and likely sickening President Wilson in France at the moment Mae was writing.[79] She kidded Lige about getting their wedding anniversary wrong, which suggested to her friends that "French girls are making him buggy." She confessed that she had indeed torn up some of the letters involving other women that Lige had sent from France, particularly those originating with the "little idiot girl" still writing him in May 1918 not knowing he was married. But Mae was more or less over the episode. Contrary to his worries, she hadn't taken up with any "slacker" and only loved her "brave soldier boy."[80]

For the rest of April 1919, Mae and Lige wrote back and forth, sometimes confident and reassuring, sometimes insecure and despairing. He got in a fistfight. She was living at home in Chaonia and quarreling with her sister Clara and quilting and washing dishes. Both reported more dreams about each other but Mae was afraid to describe hers in much detail for fear of prying eyes. It made her terribly sad to see other returned soldiers with their sweethearts and wives, though she realized some couples would never be reunited:

Dearie, I guess you know it though—that Raymond Moss was killed. Ella wrote him a letter quite a long time ago and the other day it came back to her unopened with the words "killed in action" wrote on it.

Soon Mae herself received a terrifying envelope marked "Night Message," mistaking it for a telegram about Lige.[81] Meanwhile Mae mocked the "<u>brave</u> fellows" who pretended to be sorry they avoided fighting and proposed they relieve soldiers in the postwar army. And she addressed Lige's comments about legislative debates. As Congress passed woman suffrage and prepared to send it to the states, Mae staked out a zigzagging position:

> Honey why don't you want your wife to vote. I think that is just the time the men come to their senses when they voted in woman suffrage. Don't you? Ha! ha! I didn't mean that. I am honest I really think women haven't any right to vote, I mean I think they are out of place at the polls but of course if all the others vote why I guess I shall too ha! ha!

Here Mae upheld her broader tendency to both genuflect before and push against Lige's traditional views. She pushed again when she told Lige she favored the country going dry. Mae had seen Lige drunk in their past, but believed him when he promised her (three times) that he wouldn't repeat it. As for her general state of mind, Mae wrote in April 1919, "I'm not living now, I'm just existing."[82]

FOR PROGRESSIVES WHO HAD attached hopes for reform to the European intervention, woman suffrage and prohibition made for satisfying tales. But the two cases together showed war could both stabilize and unsettle family life and gender roles.

The anti-liquor and woman suffrage lobbies had by 1917 secured dry legislation in nineteen states and the vote for women in seventeen, with rumblings of constitutional amendments in both movements. The war pushed the issues further along toward that resolution. Reformers who guarded doughboy morality in the cantonments had gotten the War Department to limit liquor traffic in their vicinity and bar men in uniform from partaking. Making beer and liquor wasted grains that could be put to better purpose at a time of worldwide deprivation. And the big brewers were unmistakably German—Pabst, Schlitz, Busch. In the summer of 1917, Congress temporarily banned the manufacture of alcohol, and by the time Mae and Lige spoke about the matter, the amendment had been ratified. The Volstead Act took effect several months later, in January 1920.[83] Advocates of woman suffrage sensed in war a chance to destabilize essentialist certitude about women's civic capacity. Except for Alice Paul's National Woman's Party, which opposed war in 1917 and endured physical assaults outside the White House for it, suffrage organizations used their support for war to make the case for the ballot. President Wilson saw opportunity to attract future Democratic voters and corroborate claims of a war for democracy. Woman suffrage won ratification a few months after passage of the Volstead Act.[84]

Promoters of the war for family, of an intervention congenial to personal virtue, thus had things to boast about. Prohibitionists spoke with pride about soldiers' support for their cause, despite reports of mass doughboy displeasure with the new law.[85] "The war has advanced our lines against the liquor traffic and the social evil," said a Baptist preacher in Connecticut after the armistice. "And the understanding of the misery and unhappiness that are the result of the social evil, will make for a greater sanctity of the home and for cleaner communities in which to live."[86] Some suffragists, in fact, made similar arguments, vowing that female voters would prioritize household stabilization and matters concerning women and children. The wife of Secretary of the Navy Josephus Daniels, speaking to a gathering chaired by Carrie Chapman Catt of the National American Woman Suffrage Association (NAWSA), keyed her demand for the vote to women's obligation to and expertise in making the world "a safe place in which the boys and girls may live." NAWSA passed a resolution recommending female representation at the French peace table because women possessed "special and peculiar interests" in areas like the protection of innocents. A male southerner even switched his view on the subject because "chivalry demands it."[87]

Many proponents of suffrage, including some of these same people, forged more disruptive arguments. A postwar issue of the NAWSA newsletter *Woman Citizen* based its case on women's record in wartime occupations not typically coded as feminine, including doctors and munitions workers.[88] President Wilson publicly urged Congress to "make [women] the equals of men in political rights as they have proved themselves their equals in every field of practical work they have entered."[89] Nurses like Natalie Scott had upset expectations of women's behavior and performance. A representative of the Red Cross proclaimed at the NAWSA convention, "Martial courage has in many of our minds been held as a masculine attribute, but the nurses who have served in the front line hospitals and evacuation tents, with the whistle of the shells always overhead, have helped establish a new tradition for bravery in action."[90] These figures wanted suffrage rooted in objective merit and fairness, not chivalric gratitude.

In the longer view, the Great War accelerated prohibition to passage but it didn't last. Woman suffrage did, along with the expanding realms of civic engagement upon which it rested. Thus could the war both reinforce a narrative of national strength deriving from virtuous families with clear spheres but also stimulate modifications to that narrative.

IF REFORMERS CELEBRATED THE war's nationally redemptive benefits, any notion of its personally redemptive ones suffered with the arrival of War Department telegrams, or soon, disinterred corpses, at the doorsteps of American homes.

Modern warfare produced bodies on a mass scale. The Graves Registration Service (GRS) had been created to manage combat fatalities, but no one predicted the enormity of that task. GRS staff worked to identify and put underground thousands of Americans in plots across the battlefields, some organized into cemeteries, some isolated. Yet by 1919, the War Department still had no coherent policy for what to do with these scattered remains. Some in the government, military, and public thought it respectful to leave doughboys in ground they had helped free, others that they should be returned to their families. Meanwhile the French were refusing to allow exhumations for a three-year period, citing the complex and macabre spectacle of decomposing bodies crisscrossing their country and the insulting prospect of American families receiving remains before French families did.

Amid this circulation of uncertainties, the War Department gauged the wishes of America's Gold Star families. Beginning in early 1919, the office sent letters and a ballot to next of kin asking whether they wished their loved one's remains repatriated to the United States, and, if so, whether they preferred him to come home or be buried in a national cemetery. According to the letter accompanying the ballot, if the dead doughboy was unmarried, his father held the authority to make this decision. Although popular culture had long assigned mourning to mothers (or *because* of that), the War Department granted the repatriation decision to the allegedly more clear-eyed head of household, as the Census Bureau labeled husbands. Also, facing the enormous costs and logistical challenges of return, some in official circles wished to discourage it. Indeed, a congressional committee traveled to France just as the ballots were being distributed and concluded that foreign burial would be best. Like-minded members of the Senate soon voted for a half-million-dollar appropriation to build serene American cemeteries in France.

Two developments moved the debate along. First, the majority of families opted to bring loved ones home for local bereavement rather than leave them overseas for patriotic symbolism. Congress had apportioned five million dollars for repatriation in the expectation constituents would register that preference. Then, in December 1919, the French lifted their opposition to disinterment. The path was clear for the return of thousands of war dead to American hometowns.

But that resolution ignited a further debate. Many loved ones wished to confirm the identity of corpses or see what kind of death they had experienced. Authorities in the military were deeply uncomfortable with this possibility. Clergy and officers had written thousands of letters and telegrams describing noble deaths, quick deaths, peaceful deaths, painless deaths—above all, symbolic and distant deaths charged with high purpose and generated in a war invested with personal benefit. Threatening such pictures of "the good death," a cherished element of American mourning culture, would be boxes filled with unrecognizable, mutilated, un-embalmed, decomposing, incomplete, or fragmentary remains. Authorities also likely wished to shield mothers, fathers, siblings, spouses, and children from seeing what had become of their soldier boys. A "gruesome spectacle" was what one official thought awaited viewers of open caskets. Some suggested the Public Health Service issue a warning about the risks of the practice. Ultimately, though, Americans wanted their dead back and wanted to see them.

They got their way on both counts. At the government's expense, about 70 percent of American war dead came home. Bodies were disinterred, put into new coffins, and sent by truck or boat or rail to European ports. Ships brought them to the United States. As the flow of returning cadavers peaked in mid-1921, voices in the press began questioning whether they were who the government said they were. Unmarked graves and distorted corpses hindered identification. A significant number of families, some reports claimed thirteen thousand, changed their minds about repatriation when they imagined the wrong soldier resting in family plots. However military and government officials tried to discourage it, people opened caskets.

By the early 1920s, the GRS reported something like forty-five thousand dead doughboys repatriated to the United States. It all cost about thirty million dollars. For some people it took half a decade for their fallen relative to return.[91]

CHRISTIAN HUEBNER RECEIVED THE burial ballot in early 1919. His son Arthur's name and serial number were typed at the top. In the space for "organization," a clerk had incorrectly entered, "129 MG BN." Below, Christian wrote down his relationship to the deceased, his address, and his signature. In between were questions reducing Arthur to "the remains":

Do you desire the remains brought to the United States? *Yes.*

If remains are brought to the United States, do you wish them interred in a national cemetery? *No.*

If you desire the remains interred at the home of the deceased, give full information below as to where they should be sent.[92]

Christian's desire was that Arthur come home to be buried next to his mother. Since Louise's death in March 1918, Christian had met a German American woman from church named Johanna, who'd had an affair with the family chauffeur and left the old country in shame. The resulting marriage produced several children and ended when the man died in 1910. Around the time he filled out the ballot, Christian married Johanna. They lived in a new and bigger house on Dewey Avenue in Watertown purchased with Arthur's life insurance money.[93] After returning the form, the family waited. Christian availed himself of a service provided by the government and received a photograph of his son's grave (figure 7.3).[94]

FIGURE 7.3 Arthur Huebner's grave, Toul, France. The cross wrongly reads "109 M. G." Author's collection.

MAE REVEALED TO LIGE in May 1919 she was saving his correspondence and organizing it into bundles from Camp Forrest, Camp Wadsworth, Camp Mills, and Europe. She read these many pages again and again, for months, filling in the long spaces between new letters.[95]

But her own notes covering almost a year, those Lige had returned to her from abroad, she burned. Mae didn't say why, but in April she apologized for being "jealous and silly," suggesting she may have wished to purge her collection of embarrassing content. She also worried aloud several times, as Waring Huston had done, that unauthorized people would peek at her correspondence.[96] Waring had been vague about who might invade his privacy, but Mae and Lige complained about nosy acquaintances and family members who gossiped or otherwise threatened their relationship. They also may have feared the exposure of sexual innuendo. Somebody, in fact, most likely Mae or Lige, took a pair of scissors to his letter of March 21, 1919. Its last section began, "I am ready to go to bed and I only wish that you"—and then stopped abruptly at the edge of a snipped-away rectangle of paper, lost to history. The text picked up in the midst of kisses, then the line, "I love you for ever and ever Mae."[97]

These episodes suggest that Mae and Lige, in 1919 or later, not only valued letters for their own purposes but also anticipated a broader audience for them, whether it was snooping provocateurs or family members finding them in an attic. One doubts they foresaw their record in an archive, but they seem to have expected the exposure of private emotion.

LIGE'S COMRADE IN THE Fifty-Third Infantry, Wayne Turner, had to smile at his mother's suggestion that he marry a French girl. "There are very few of the boys marrying French girls," he wrote, "but imagine it would be different were we in England and Scotland."[98] Mae Dees heard similar reassurances from a veteran at a Wayne County "egg roast" in April 1919. To her questions about girls in the war zone, a returned serviceman comforted Mae, "Well girlie don't worry about them because if French girls look to your soldier boy like they do to me there isn't any danger."[99] Doughboy Fred Leach wrote home to his fiancé, rather in the spirit Lige often did, to say, "I don't think much of the French girls. Any young man is a darn fool who would take up with them."[100]

Those private exchanges aligned with wider suspicions about the character of Americans who did marry foreign women, including those from England and Scotland. After its earlier vagueness, and under pressure from Allied governments, the AEF by early 1919 accommodated and facilitated such unions. Veterans eventually brought five thousand wives back to the United States. But European women who had in 1917 inflamed the American protective imagination now generated derision among policymakers, aid workers, and journalists, whether stemming from sexual jealousy, stereotypes about French moral poverty, or the xenophobia of Red Scare America. More electric bitterness awaited the doughboy with a patient home front sweetheart. In the summer of 1919, Wanda Drewes of Chicago filed a breach of promise lawsuit against her fiancé—Fred Leach, in fact—for bringing home a French bride. Drewes told the court, "The day before the Fourth I received a letter . . . saying Fred was home with a French bride—a woman who had nursed him in France. I could have killed her. He hadn't written, hadn't breathed a word of it to me. I love him—love him—ah, but it's no use now."[101] Here as elsewhere, it was the foreign wife who shouldered blame, not the wayward soldier.

In this environment, many war brides endured an entrance ritual of humiliation, inconvenience, and condemnation. At first, the Young Women's Christian Association (YWCA) arranged to house outgoing war wives in quarters established for AEF women in European ports. Workers at these facilities quickly grew overwhelmed by their guests, some of whom spoke no English, were sick or pregnant, had children or pets, or furnished unreliable evidence of marriage. Unfounded rumors circulated of prostitutes taking advantage of free passage to the United States. The Red Cross insisted at one point on testing war brides for venereal disease before they would assist them. There were problems with brides arriving in New York only to go "unclaimed" by husbands.

The AEF thus had issued new orders by the middle of 1919. A foreign wife had to produce a sworn statement from her husband's commanding officer affirming her "reputable character." Port officials in Europe were to prevent venereal disease-afflicted women from boarding vessels. Doughboys should travel with their wives. The Service of Supply established emigration camps in Brest and Bordeaux and Saint-Nazaire to replace the homier houses. Women in these barracks underwent embarrassing inspections and physicals and lived under military discipline. Many Americans in AEF welfare agencies harbored low opinions of matrimonial migrants. Some blamed the marriages on sexual immorality or opportunism, rarely aiming those assumptions at soldiers. They found the women unhygienic and uncouth, promiscuous or criminal. German wives attracted particular venom. A YWCA worker found it galling that "enemy" women shared space on ships with American war dead. Stateside newspapers ran headlines like, "New Order Refuses to Take Girls Unless They're Ladies."[102]

Although the foreign woman had served as a motivational symbol, some Americans wanted nothing to do with her as a human being. As the nation negotiated its postwar relationship with the world, commentators invested war brides with symbolic meaning. Immigration restrictionists, long active but reinvigorated by postwar migration, held up the allegedly disreputable war bride as a sign of threats to American familial health, morality, and racial purity. Those wary of international obligations converted stereotypes about "gold digging" women who wanted to "get into bed" with doughboys to cautionary tales about the dangers of entangling alliances with European states. Soon both analogies would feed into major policy victories.

AS THE PEACE TALKS progressed in 1919, rumors of a move circulated among Lige Dees's mates in Quemignerot, France. One week they heard America was the destination, the next Germany. Lige and fellow Fifty-Third Infantry member Wayne Turner asked their families to scour the papers for information.[103] When Gen. John Pershing, a "nice old chap" in Lige's opinion, reviewed the Sixth Division in April, the Missouri doughboy took it as a sign he was homeward bound. Lige and Wayne wrote home to say their movements depended on the peace resolution.[104]

Then, on April 26, Lige sent Mae a quick note and departed by rail for Trier, Germany. The trip put Lige into the American Army of Occupation, the force that had held the Rhineland since late 1918 to encourage German compliance at the peace table. His First Battalion guarded bridges and tunnels while others in the Sixth Division took sightseeing tours through the Rhineland. Lige found this unspoiled part of Germany more hospitable than France. He preferred American girls to any others he had encountered, including German and French and "Russen" and Mexican ones. But this "cleaner" country had working toilets, less rain and mud, pretty hills, and good railroads.[105] Wayne Turner of the Fifty-Third Infantry wrote his mother,

> There is a world of difference in the country and the people here than in France. These people seem to be well off. Better in fact than the French and also seem to be more industrious and their morals are certainly much better than the French. Am living in a house here where

there are five girls and three boys in the family and they all work. Seems as tho they should all be rich soon.[106]

The views of Lige and Wayne mirrored a broader reversal of sympathies among the Rhineland occupiers. Doughboys who'd accumulated resentments against French price-gouging reveled in German baked goods and accommodations. Popular hearsay in the AEF taught soldiers that French troops were mistreating, displacing, stealing from, and destroying property of German villagers. An American military official told another that such abuse "was the very thing that America went to war for the purpose of exterminating."[107] These shifting allegiances threatened the intervention's foundational contrast of wicked, hypermasculine Germans against the supine, victimized French. Allied leaders undertook (ultimately fruitless) investigations to see if German hopes for diplomatic leniency lay behind the charm offensive. The American brass labored as well to ban fraternization with locals, as Wayne Turner informed his mother.[108] The commander of the occupation force in Germany, Maj. Gen. Henry Allen, worried German families were offering up daughters for war marriages and took steps to prevent them.[109] The flipping of doughboy loyalties so concerned Allied officials, in fact, that some wondered if the American rank-and-file would fight on the right side should war resume.

Then, rather suddenly in May, the Fifty-Third learned it was scheduled to return home. Lige wrote to surprise Mae but she already had read the Sixth Division would be released in June.[110] "Needless to say," recalled the regiment's historian, "the morale of the 53rd Infantry was high."[111]

Lige nevertheless wrote bitterly to Mae about rumors she reported to him. People at home were charging he'd tried to quit the army and had only enlisted because his father needed a way to support him. These threats to his reputation as a soldier and man infuriated Lige. "Every body hates me and think I am a bum," he seethed. Sometimes, he confessed to Mae, it felt like he didn't have a friend in the world. He aimed to finish the enlistment that showed he had "the nerve to stand up for the good old USA."[112] Other rumormongers predicted Lige's military career would be prolonged. After church one day, a soldier home from France saw Mae wearing a blue star to denote Lige's service. She disclosed her husband's unit, and the man regretted to tell her those boys still faced three years in the reserve. Mae didn't believe it but vowed if Lige stayed in the army past his three-year enlistment she'd live with him at camp.[113]

Lige and the other men frantically returned equipment as their superiors completed paperwork. The days seemed long to him "until I step off the boat and then step in my little wifie house."[114] On May 24, Lige boarded a train at Trier, bound for Camp Pontanezen, where the regiment spent several days, then steamed off on the *Leviathan* on June 5, 1919. Seven days at sea brought Lige to Hoboken, New Jersey. The men gathered as a regiment for the last time for the rail journey to Camp Mills, Long Island, where they had assembled a year earlier for the crossing. Lige reminded Mae that his enlistment ran until November. But he would apply for a month-long furlough or a discharge if the army expected him to finish it. How this washed with his earlier pledge to honor his word Lige didn't say, nor did he address the prospect of a three-year reserve hitch.[115]

The army demobilized the Fifty-Third Infantry at Camp Mills and shuffled its men into various units. Lige found himself in mid-June 1919 on the way to Camp Grant, in Rockford, Illinois, where Arthur Huebner's journey had begun in October 1917. It was scorching hot but Lige preferred that to the constant rain of France.[116] And Rockford, Illinois, was "not so awful far from home" and Mae Dees in Wayne County, Missouri.[117]

TWO WEEKS AFTER LIGE DEES set foot in America, the Versailles delegates signed a peace treaty stripping the Germans of colonial possessions, forcing them to admit war guilt, imposing steep reparation payments, and granting German territory to surrounding states. Out of the crumbling empires of Europe and the Middle East, some areas became independent entities, others protectorates of Britain and France. President Wilson had arrived in France hoping to charge the treaty with the spirit of the Fourteen Points he had articulated in January 1918—self-determination for nations and an international organization to secure peace, among others. In the long view, much of what came out of Versailles set up more than a century of violence. But Wilson persuaded the signatories to include the covenant for a League of Nations.

Opponents of the treaty in the Republican-held Senate thundered about entrapping the United States in future wars. Even some of Wilson's allies turned against him. To progressives and liberals, the president's peace program and the League had promised to give tangible shape to the vague hopes driving their support in 1917—that war could bring a just peace, that America and the world could be regenerated through the defeat of militarism and secrecy. When the treaty and the League's terms were watered down or made punitive, their power to bring peace undermined, liberals at the *New Republic* and elsewhere split with the administration. Editors at that journal sighed, "national promise [remained] still unredeemed."[118] Unlike in the case of prohibition, in the eyes of some disappointed observers, the war failed to deliver greater stability for nations and communities. But to those opposed to League membership—the eventual winners of the debate—*they* were the ones safeguarding the security of future generations.[119]

One of the territories the treaty granted France was the Alsace-Lorraine region, which it had lost in the Franco-Prussian war. This transfer meant the Alsatian recruits of the 439th Infantry who had shot Arthur Huebner on November 11, 1918, now found themselves citizens of France. These Alsatians, regarded warily by many ethnic Germans yet fighting for Germany, had killed Arthur, a German American regarded warily by many Americans yet fighting for America.

LIGE DEES WROTE WITH rare elegance in late June 1919 that he was "dying by degrees" to see Mae, now four hundred rather than four thousand miles away. Lige thought by July he could travel to Missouri or Mae could visit him at Camp Grant. But he had a new problem. Lige didn't have cash to buy clothes he thought befitting a regular army man and wasn't yet eligible for the sixty-dollar separation bonus. Joining his sense of self-worth to his sartorial standards, Lige dreaded looking like a "bum" and being confused with "these drafted men." Mae replied she'd take him in overalls. She even offered to send him allotment money he had been providing her, precisely revealing what some people were pointing out: the deductions meant to shore up a doughboy's family disrupted his breadwinner's credibility. Lige resisted such disruptions whenever he could and politely rejected his wife's proposal.[120]

Mae's regard for the conscripted men veered as low as her husband's. She impugned their courage and resented the fanfare meeting their arrival. She called them "slouches" and "slackers" without irony and "princes and heroes" with it. Mae seethed when they talked "smart" to her and claimed to shut them up with the question, "Was you drafted?" She held area soldiers' brides and sweethearts in equal contempt. It sickened Mae (as she said to Lige) to see women in dresses bought with allotment money flirting with home front shirkers. Then it embittered her further to watch those women reunite with conscripted returnees ahead of regulars in the demobilization queue.[121] All this social critique added up to a jaundiced view of a popular wartime narrative, the story of virtuous men fighting while stateside wives, stabilized by diverted army pay, waited loyally. Mae and Lige aspired to live that story, but around them saw it replaced with violated bargains, undeserved admiration, and unmerited early homecomings.

In June and July, Mae and Lige went back and forth about whether he could get a pass, whether she should come to Rockford on the train, and even whether he should ditch the army. Mae, staying with her family, watched for Lige to arrive several times. Taking care of children convinced her she didn't want any babies.[122] Lige told Mae stories about men he'd killed at war and wondered if he would be called to quell labor strikes, while she reported a friend decapitated in a sawmill.[123] In July, Lige lost patience with the furlough process and gave Mae instructions on traveling to Rockford. He found a place for her to stay and said he'd meet every train.

Then Mae stopped writing, and Lige worried because he'd changed his mind. An army camp was "no place for a woman." He threatened to go absent without leave.[124] This letter, dated July 17, 1919, is the last one in the record for the summer. Mae must have packed her bags at first mention of train schedules. Upon her arrival in Rockford, the couple immediately conceived a baby.

ON MARCH 11, 1919, THE mother of William Buckner, the laborer from Kentucky hanged for rape in September 1918, wrote the army about her son. "I have been informed," she said, "that the circumstances surrounding the death of my son . . . was such as to cancel the insurance. I wrote . . . and asked . . . to tell me the circumstances. In reply, they refer me to you. Will you please write to me at once, telling me about it?" There is no record that Mary Buckner ever heard what happened to William. Workers dug up his body in February 1922, his legs still bound, a hood over his head, the noose around his neck. Mary or someone else in the family made a different decision than Christian Huebner about the remains and requested interment in France. Today he lies buried in the Saint-Mihiel American Cemetery, Plot D, Row 20, Grave 16, his date of death listed ten days after his execution.[125]

William Buckner never came home. For his black comrades who did, it took a while. There were the same delays and false hopes that plagued Lige's division and others, but racial injustices amplified the burdens. Some segregated units moved into Germany as occupiers. Tales of black rape circulated in venues like the German film "Black Shame," a departure from the Kaiser's wartime leaflets dropped on African American soldiers urging them to reconsider their commitment to a racist and undemocratic country.[126] Officials quickly jerked black occupation units back to France, where many performed brutal jobs. Six thousand found themselves assigned to the Graves Registration Service to dig up bodies for the Meuse-Argonne National Cemetery, possibly including Missouri teacher Roy Thornburgh. Just as taxing if less nauseating, they built the stadium where Gen. Pershing and Natalie Scott watched track and field in Paris. Meanwhile an Allied victory parade and French war mural both excluded African American troops, although French charities welcomed their 300,000 francs for orphans in rather tangible gestures of chivalric virtue. As for the Atlantic crossings, Service of Supply troops, with their heavy proportion of black men, were last in the order of departure. Some ship commanders refused to board African American doughboys. The Harlem Hell Fighters' band kept silent in Brest for fear of breaking a regulation and losing its place in the queue.[127]

Freed from such concerns, James Europe's famous musicians found appreciative crowds in New York in February 1919, as the battle-tested 369th Infantry proceeded solemnly to French marches up Fifth Avenue. The black press and its audiences showered the returning units with adulation. Henry Johnson and Needham Roberts became national heroes to many African Americans and some whites, Johnson earning praise from that self-appointed judge of masculine mettle, Theodore Roosevelt.[128] But these were bright spots in an otherwise dark period. A bandmate murdered James Europe in May 1919. Johnson and Roberts continued to suffer from their wounds, and worse fates awaited them. The generalized black doughboy couldn't shake his reputation as a rapist. In 1919, Sen. James Vardaman (D-Miss.), played to two stereotypes when he authorized white violence against "those military, French-woman-ruined negro soldiers." Out of the dangerous pride or sexual license white people claimed to sense in black veterans came a wave of lynchings, sometimes with victims wearing the uniform of the army. Several of the almost forty race riots during that Red Summer of 1919 involved veterans fed up with Jim Crow humiliation. Of course some relished the new militancy. One black woman said of violence in the nation's capital, "The Washington riots gave me the thrill that comes once in a lifetime. I was alone when I read between the lines of the morning paper that at last our men had stood like men, struck back, were no longer dumb, driven cattle." But if the war energized black resistance, white counterforces held fast. President Wilson never condemned the violence against former doughboys' families just miles from the White House. After Washington came the bloody riots in Chicago that began with the stoning and drowning of a black boy. The Ku Klux Klan enjoyed a revival in the 1920s, though its scapegoats of racial decline expanded to include immigrants.[129]

In the early 1930s, the federal government paid for Gold Star mothers to make pilgrimages to Europe to visit the graves of their loved ones. If Mary Buckner went to sit with William at Saint-Mihiel Cemetery, she traveled in segregated accommodations with other black women. Even at the stage of mourning, it was a white man's war.[130]

ON SEPTEMBER 6, 1919, NATALIE VIVIAN SCOTT attended the ceremony keeping her in Paris. For courage under bombardment in Beauvais, Natalie received the Croix de Guerre with Bronze Star, the only American woman so honored (figure 7.4). After one last trip around Europe, she sailed in October for New York City. It was "thrilling" for Natalie to see immigrants aboard as they "shrieked and shouted" at the sight of land. Among them were a handsome American soldier bringing his mother and grandfather from Italy, one of the countries soon to find its quota of migrants curtailed.[131]

FIGURE 7.4 Natalie Scott with Croix de Guerre, 1919. Natalie Scott Papers, Louisiana Research Collection, Tulane University.

From New York she went by rail to New Orleans, arriving to a throng of family, friends, and reporters on October 25, 1919. "Hello folks. Glad to see you again," she reportedly greeted the crowd. The newspaper used the words *hero, honor, bravery,* and *valor* to characterize the local citizen who'd made good, the woman who had flipped the chivalric narrative and saved men under fire. Natalie purportedly refused to discuss the feats that made her famous.[132]

AFTER THREE MONTHS TOGETHER at Camp Grant, Mae and Lige wrote each other the same late October day from Illinois and Missouri. Lige devoted his attention to parlaying Mae's pregnant condition into some sort of reprieve from the army, she dedicated hers to making sheets and quilts for their domestic future and complaining about living at home. Lige needed her to secure a doctor's note testifying she was "in a family way."[133] He wanted out of the service on account of his coming dependent, but barring that outcome they spoke of her returning to Rockford.

Mae spent a lachrymose Thanksgiving in Chaonia. Her mother would have killed one of the old gobblers if Lige had come home, she sighed, but settled for two guinea hens and a duck.[134] December arrived, and Mae again looked in vain for her husband to come up the walkway. She had a disappointing dream her baby was a boy. In her letter of December 7, 1919, Mae wrote, "Honey I am crazy to be with you all the time. We will not leave each other any more, will we dearie?" It appears they didn't, as this is their last surviving letter.[135]

On the nineteenth of January 1920, the census taker came by the barracks at Camp Grant. Among the long list of single soldiers he recorded a "Mae Dees, wife." A few other brides also resided on the base.[136] Lige moved to a Military Police company late in 1919, then went on furlough, and then rode an honorable discharge to the reserves on February 2, 1920.[137] Back in Missouri, the couple welcomed Helen Mae Dees on March 17, 1920, a child the calendar suggests arrived prematurely.[138] By December, Mae was pregnant again.

OF THE GREAT WAR's 224,000 wounded doughboys, about 120,000 had begun the army's rehabilitation regimen by May 1919. A quarter returned to military service and 5 percent were discharged for disability. Although a successful if expensive program, fewer than half of disabled veterans finished their course of rehabilitation within a year of the armistice. More than three hundred thousand veteran-applicants failed to demonstrate that their disabilities kept them from working, so the government denied them training.[139]

The pitiful condition of wounded warriors and the chaotic network of agencies to care for them drew intense public scrutiny. Into the early 1920s, newspapers ran hundreds of stories on jobless, hungry, or injured veterans. Scholars issued reports predicting crime waves. The architecture of veterans' care promised by the WRIA had devolved into a clutter of mismanaged or overwhelmed programs. Public critics and a 1920 congressional study reported tens of thousands of neglected, poverty-stricken former doughboys, shell-shocked veterans sitting in jails or waiting in endless queues for government help. As President Warren Harding took office early the next year, ex-soldiers testified in public hearings on the bureaucratic nightmares of injury. Sympathy for the disabled veteran reached a crescendo when Gen. Pershing spoke in April 1921 in New York City on "Justice for the Wounded," excoriating the neglect of soldiers who had "protected us" and calling for a central agency devoted to veterans' affairs. Gold Star mothers, who'd sacrificed their sons to the war and now sacrificed their time to aid the wounded, spoke the following day. They issued tearful pleas for greater care for these men. Some declared hospital conditions so bad they preferred their sons' deaths over the agonies of survival.[140]

In the summer of 1921, the campaign to centralize care won an important victory with Congress's establishment of the United States Veterans' Bureau, a single agency to which veterans could appeal for compensation, medical care, or vocational training. The thirty-thousand-employee bureau amounted to an admission that the welfare of ex-doughboys and their families would become a permanent fixture in the government's stable of obligations. But the American Legion and Veterans of Foreign Wars (VFW) sought a greater prize for Great Warriors: monetary payment for their service. Ironically, veterans complained that the wartime payroll deductions for allotments and insurance—the familial stabilizers of the WRIA—left them financially behind men who'd stayed home and earned inflated wages. By 1919, some advocates were campaigning for retroactive adjusted compensation beyond the sixty dollars demobilized men already received. The next year, seventy-five thousand veterans marched in New York City in support of such a bonus.[141]

The debates and reforms of the 1920s exposed war's radiating impact on individual families in the age of mass conscription and industrial warfare. The government theoretically pledged to keep families stable through new legislation, agencies, and programs. Supporters of the war also had promised since April 1917 that deeper benefits awaited the soldier: the admiration of loved ones and community, the bolstering of masculinity, the gratitude of a nation. But in practice neither the programs nor the intangibles were enough. Veterans wanted compensation for the disruption of their domestic lives. They campaigned for a general bonus over the opposition of those who continued to claim—and they included Wilson as well as the Republican presidents of the 1920s— that patriotic pride, not a cash payout, should satisfy the Great War doughboy.

IN FEBRUARY 1921, ABOUT two years after registering his request, Christian Huebner received word from the Quartermaster's office that his son's body would soon arrive in Watertown.[142] Befitting the confusion of repatriation, this message was wrong. In fact, Arthur was still in the ground in Toul.

The beginning of his journey home came on March 29, 1921, after almost three years in Europe, when workers dug up his body and prepared it for shipment. A month later he arrived in Antwerp, Belgium. The ship *Wheaton* left that port on May 3 with the remains of Arthur and five thousand others. The papers said they represented every state and every division in the AEF and comprised the largest shipment of disinterred bodies to date. Two weeks at sea brought Arthur to Hoboken, where he stayed another two weeks. The army held memorial services on the piers for big clusters of men. There were two hundred dead from Pressley Cleveland's Forty-Second Division, a handful from Edward Streeter's Twenty-Seventh, and many from Roy Thornburgh's First. He wasn't among them, though, as his family in Missouri had opted to leave Roy's remains in Europe. Big crowds came to services for New York and New Jersey doughboys. Reporters wrote that some Gold Star mothers stayed through all the ceremonies.[143] The writer Owen Wister, a critic of repatriation, claimed that scores of bodies went unclaimed from the piers at Hoboken, but the Graves Registration Service denied it.[144]

Representatives of the Watertown undertaker and furniture dealership Kohls and Knaak received Arthur's body in New Jersey. From there it was three days by rail before he arrived in Watertown, Wisconsin, on Saturday, June 4, 1921.[145] Arthur's teenaged brother Walter remembered going down to the railroad station with his older brother Otto and their father Christian to identify the body. Carl, the brother who had been with his mother when she collapsed, was too young to come along and maybe thought to have seen enough trauma for a short life. Walter recalled Arthur in uniform and still recognizable. The returned doughboy likely then spent eight days at the Kohls and Knaak funeral home on Main Street in Watertown.

Walter turned eighteen on Sunday, June 12, the day of Arthur Huebner's second funeral. It began at 1:30 p.m. at Christian and Johanna's house on Dewey Avenue. Mourners then proceeded for the service a few blocks to St. Mark's Lutheran Church, where somebody wrote in the funeral record that Arthur had "*gefallen im Krieg in Frankreich*" (fallen in the war in France) and would be laid to rest in the church cemetery a few miles away.[146] Everyone continued to the plot where Arthur's mother Louise was buried. His grave lay a few feet away from hers on an embankment built into the sloping ground. His headstone read, "*Gest. in Frankreich*"—died (*gestorben*) in France (figure 7.5). The monument company got Arthur's unit right. The *Watertown Weltbürger* reported a burial with full military honors. He was liked and respected by everyone, the paper said in German, because he was quiet.[147]

Among Arthur's effects returned to Christian were the small books he had received in basic training. In the front of the New Testament, below small blots of Arthur's blood, were the words, "The blood of Jesus Christ His Son cleanseth us from all sin." And in the back: "For God so loved the world that He gave His only begotten Son, that who believeth in Him should not perish but have everlasting life." Far larger stains bloodied the pages of Arthur's Book of Psalms.

FIGURE 7.5 Arthur Huebner's second and final grave, Watertown, Wisconsin. Author's collection, courtesy of James Huebner.

THE WIDESPREAD SUSPICION OF war brides, with their alleged threats to American moral health, fed into a long-standing campaign to permanently restrict immigration. Fears of familial decline, or perhaps the exploitation thereof, had undergirded the restrictionist position for decades. The end of the Great War amplified this strain of anti-immigrant thinking. Many vocal Americans and their leaders imagined a dystopian future of poor immigrant hordes dragging down the national economy and way of life. Old-stock Protestants continued to perceive, dread, and portend an assault on their moral traditions. Many groups, Asians as well as southern and eastern Europeans, were suspicious precisely because, in the xenophobic mind, they raised their children or got married or behaved in ways threatening to the cherished values of many white, middle-class Americans. Nativism found reinforcement and legislative success in the wake of the Russian Revolution, postwar strike wave, and Red Scare. A temporary congressional measure in 1921 and an enduring one in 1924 placed the first numerical limits on immigration in American history. The Immigration Act of 1924 applied those limits to the most "exotic" peoples of southern and eastern Europe and excluded Asians entirely.[148]

So while advocates of intervention in 1917 had keyed the nation's masculine and familial resolve to the protection of European innocents, now restrictionists kept them out. Abstract objects of mercy turned into harbingers of national decline. Populations briefly envisioned as victims of war and militarism now "swarm[ed] like flies at every European port of embarkation," said former Committee on Public Information head George Creel in 1921.[149] In fact both impulses, the protective and the exclusionary, supposedly safeguarded American moral health and family values, the same ambition woven into the prohibition of alcohol and, for some advocates, the woman suffrage movement. Such vilification of immigrants wasn't so much a reversal as a return, then, demonstrating both the flexibility and durability of arguments about how to protect the American family. European innocents played a role in the validation of masculine courage and familial strength in 1917, but once the war ended, they would have to prove their moral virtue to join the American body politic.

Thus when Christian Huebner, father of the dead doughboy Arthur and a German immigrant from the former Russian empire, applied for citizenship in 1920, he had to swear two things: he was neither an anarchist nor a polygamist. The government took familial deviants as seriously as those who favored no government at all.[150]

IN AUGUST 1921, MAE DEES gave birth in Stoddard County, Missouri, to a little boy the couple called William Clifford. He lived two months, dying just after noon on October 28 of congestion of the stomach and bowels. Lige and Mae buried William two days later. Acting as undertaker was John Bilbrey, Mae's father, who worked as a farmer. The family laid William to rest in Dees Chapel Cemetery, founded by his ancestors in the nineteenth century.[151]

AROUND THE TIME OF William Dees's birth, George Waring Huston arrived, like Arthur Huebner and Lige Dees before him, in the New Jersey port at Hoboken.[152] It took about a month before his body's homeward trip from the hills around Saint-Juvin culminated in Selma, Alabama. On the afternoon of September 3, 1921, around five o'clock, members of the American Legion and other local military organizations marched from the armory to Nellye and Robert Huston's house on Church Street. From there they escorted Waring's body a few blocks to the First Presbyterian Church. A clergyman led the services and a choir serenaded the cortege. A line of marchers then proceeded less than a mile to Live Oak Cemetery. First came men bearing the American flag, then a group called the Selma Rifles, then the hearse and pall-bearers, six men from Waring's unit including Jack Hayward, who had written to his mother of his fellow Selmian's fate, then the Legionnaires, then family and friends. At the graveside, a chaplain pronounced the benediction, the company fired a volley, taps were sounded. It had been almost three years since Waring's death.

The flat grave marker that lay over Waring's body reported that date as October 16, 1918, repeating the official telegram. The *Selma Times-Journal's* account of the funeral also used October 16, the day Waring's company had attacked after several days in support:

He was a friend of the soldier and when he led his Platoon "over the top" in the Argonne in the afternoon of October 16th, his men stuck to him like glue. When the men were ordered to seek shelter from the enemy fire, he was the last to seek a place of safety. It was here that he gave his life for his country, at the age of 22.

Waring's marker read, "Greater Love Hath No Man Than This," the first line of John 15:13. The line suggested Waring had died to save comrades he loved:

> Greater love hath no man than this,
> That a man lay down his life for his friends.

People in Waring's orbit confirmed the sentiment ran in both directions. A sergeant in the 325th Infantry wrote, "He was new to the men but soon they all learned to love him."[153] Pressley Cleveland said the same thing in his 1918 letter to Nellye. Such language reinforced what Americans had been hearing for many months: fighting wars summoned and revealed one's personal character, one's capacity to love, one's commitment to family and community and platoon. Selecting the biblical verse signaled Robert and Nellye's piety as well as their admiration of their son's love for those around him, of his very personal and prosaic feeling for his friends. Even if "friends" is taken in a more broadly symbolic way, the narrative on his tombstone invested George Waring Huston's death with personally redemptive meaning. In some venues, the war story could still be told as a love story, though this was love for virtue over ideology, friends over country, family over politics.

Apparently the pattern repeated at reburials around the country, where one scholar of the subject has noted the "virtual disappearance" of Wilsonian rhetoric.[154] On the occasion of the burial of the Unknown Soldier two months after Waring's funeral, H. G. Wells surmised the doughboy had died for "no narrow devotion to the 'glory' or 'expansion' of any particular country but a wide spirited hostility to wrong and oppression."[155] A poet writing in the same moment called the Unknown, in part, "all brothers dead, all lovers lost/All sons and comrades resting over there/The symbol of the knightly, fallen host."[156]

But for some Americans, redeeming or chivalric narratives proved unconvincing. In the spring of 1920, Carrie Goodwin commiserated by letter with Waring's mother Nellye, framing her grief in domestic terms. "I see all of the boys and girls so happy together with their plans for the future," she wrote Nellye, "and I dare not face even the thought of tomorrow with all of its aching <u>longing</u>, <u>loneliness</u>, <u>emptiness</u>, <u>unfulfillment</u>." In April 1917, many newspapermen, federal officials, songwriters, and regular citizens had hoped war would strengthen family, clarify the roles of men and women, stoke pride in mothers, protect the innocent, and inflame "khaki-mad" passions in young women. The prospect of individual loss had hardly registered. Three years later, voices in public culture still asked families to face empty chairs with pride, to invest sacrifices with transcendent national import. The citizens, soldiers, and officers who wrote Nellye after Waring's death sought comfort in what he had died for. None of this was working for Carrie. Nothing offered explanatory power or emotional relief. "Oh, Nell," she wrote, "<u>why, why, why</u>!!" She couldn't assign redeeming value to her loss. To Carrie, that failure amounted to a rejection of contemporary reassurances. She called her feelings "the terrible *rebellious* questionings of my crushed soul."

Carrie Goodwin closed with apologies for her moroseness. She wished to say something more upbeat to Waring's mother, to help her, but she understood there was "<u>no</u> way." Each season was bringing new reminders and new anguish, and all she could offer was her love. Carrie ended by saying she would always be Nellye's little girl.[157]

SOMETIME IN THE 1920s, local officials in Watertown, Wisconsin, added a plaque commemorating veterans of the Great War to a memorial plaza downtown. Lying flat in the shadow of a tall Civil War monument, it features a quotation by "RHL," probably the war correspondent Richard Henry Little.[158] His eulogy for the doughboys related love and death with greater anguish than most words etched so permanently:

To you men who spent weary months in barren gloomy training camps in remorseless drudgery.

To you who went overseas and under murderous fire and sickening torturing gas, never faltered nor failed.

To you lads who defied submarines and a nameless grave in the ocean and landed our army in France.

To those who are still suffering from wounds and gas, shell shock and disease.

To those who died.

Our prayers our love and our tears.

EPILOGUE

━━━━◦◦◦◦━━━━

ALTHOUGH THE INTERVENTION OF 1917–18 generated uncountable war stories, one prominent organizing narrative for that war held that it benefitted the family literally and figuratively, restored or bolstered personal virtue, and allowed Americans to express devotion to home by devotion to nation. Many mainstream commentators envisioned white people as both agents and beneficiaries of this story of love and rescue. This was hardly the first time such a tale had been told in the United States, but it offered special explanatory and motivational power as concerns over the white family coursed through American political, social, and cultural life.

Yet as the story of familial redemption proliferated during the Great War, the lives of Americans at home and in France upended its certainties. The characters in this book testified at times to the power of that story, at times to its destabilization. Waring Huston and his family required no coercion to align their personal and patriotic obligations, but Waring often doubted whether the national purposes were worth the private sacrifices. Mae Dees found her husband Eliga's service simultaneously intoxicating and intolerable. The government's efforts to steady domestic gender arrangements could not prevent Mae from working nor Lige from hating it. Public appreciation of collective chivalry failed to stop the Missouri regular from agonizing over his forfeiture of individual chivalry. Natalie Scott scrambled traditional assignments of courage when she saved injured doughboys at Beauvais and, along with thousands of other wartime workers, pushed at civic boundaries and helped secure woman suffrage. Yet Natalie also recoiled at the breaching of the color line that got William Buckner killed. His death attested to the explosive sexual politics of African Americans in the war zone, to a concurrent widening and shutting down of black access to martial honor. The moral campaigns of stateside cantonments exposed an embarrassing problem with doughboy virtue as well as efforts to preserve it. Many of Waring's conscripted trainees, and one in five servicemen in the whole military, were born outside the United States, ineligible for the privileges of whiteness yet members of a force almost wholly white in popular culture. War took Arthur and Waring from their families, however well-wishers may have tried to reassure the Huebners and Hustons that those deaths had meant something.

These modifications to the American war story rehearsed, anticipated, or directly led to decades of subsequent revision and debate. Contests pivoted around questions of who served, what it meant, what it did to soldiers and families, what they expected from the state, and how architects of culture represented the experience. Answers to those questions never pulled in a single direction. Instead they comprised a dynamic reimagining of relationships between war, military, state, and family. The next hundred years ultimately left very little of the Great War story of family and conflict intact, with ensuing wars and domestic developments contributing to its ongoing amendment.

That tale's whiteness and maleness reasserted themselves after the war but weakened in the longer view, roughly paralleling and constituting part of the greater, incomplete struggles for equality of race and gender. Although the army issued a dim and biologically racist postwar appraisal of black service in 1925, and the shrunken military of the period enlisted few blacks and fewer black officers, the experiences of African Americans in the First World War propelled the interwar civil rights movement and set precedents for the activism of the Second. Jim Crow followed the army to war again, then desegregation came, barely in time for Korea. The United States fought the Vietnam War with a more fully integrated force, but that intervention saw disproportionate black casualties early on and racial violence later. After 1973, in the era of the All-Volunteer Force (AVF), African Americans found in the military an avenue for social advancement and claims for citizenship rights but remained overrepresented in the army. By the end of the century and into the twenty-first, black disproportionality in recruiting classes had declined, and many young enlistees had availed themselves of job training and money for education.[1]

In the 1920s, the military retreated from its inclusion of women. The navy barred them until World War II, and the army failed to invite a single woman to a 1923 conference on moral training. The prize of nurses' rank, with amenities of commission and pay, wouldn't come until after 1945. Yet the Great War fired the ambitions of thousands of individuals committed to professional engagement. Women had launched important wartime campaigns to protect women and children from violence and challenged the chivalric narrative. The fight for rank galvanized nurses, attracted powerful allies, and foreshadowed battles for recognition, inclusion, and remuneration. World War II saw the creation of the Women's Army Auxiliary Corps, which was disestablished in the 1970s just as the army was starting to incorporate women into its regular units. By the early twenty-first century, women had gained access to almost every military occupation, although they weathered ongoing discrimination, sexual assault, and popular associations of soldiering with masculinity. The military labored with particular zeal, meanwhile, to police sexual orientation and gender identification. LGBTQ soldiers confronted violence, discrimination, and humiliating compromises along the road to (albeit perhaps tenuous) inclusion.[2]

Although the military supported immigration restriction in 1924, nothing could undo the assimilative but also empowering experience of wartime service.[3] By the Second World War, children of immigrants filled the American ranks, and propagandists made much of how GIs embodied the diversity and unity of the war effort. That moment pushed forward the broader incorporation of many previously suspect groups into the tent of white entitlement. But wars involving Japanese, Korean, and Vietnamese enemies and allies—and the ways Americans talked about and treated them—testified to the strength of racialized ways of conducting and seeing war. Many Cold War Americans likewise remained enthralled with adventures of cowboys and Indians on radio and the small and silver screens. During and after the Vietnam War, a conflict with explosive reporting of war crimes and no victory, narratives of martial and racial superiority may have lost their galvanizing power for a time, but wars in the Middle East showed they didn't die.[4] A twenty-first century chronicler of American empire found soldiers at its far-flung edges speaking of "Injun country."[5]

One of the most dramatic adaptions to the war story of 1918 lay in the way citizen-soldiers regarded military service in the era of mass conscription. Most First World War veterans had not chosen to serve, even if they did so willingly once called. That fact shaped how they saw their contract with the state. At war's end, the government pursued rehabilitation for the wounded over a pension for the broader population of servicemen, sending federal funds to the medical infrastructure rather than veterans' pockets—already emptied by withdrawals from army paychecks for wartime dependent care and insurance. Dissatisfied with payback in masculine gratification or patriotic standing, veterans wanted compensation for lost wages and the disruption of their lives. They won a 1924 measure promising them a bonus, not a pension, payable in 1945 as an interest-bearing bond. President Calvin Coolidge vetoed the bill but was overridden. Despite his assurance that veterans didn't want a monetary prize for their service, 4.1 million veterans applied for the certificate. Meanwhile an extension of the deadline for and liberalization of the terms of disability pensions dramatically expanded the number of First World War veterans garnering them. Postwar claimants soon made up 80 percent of all beneficiaries of government disability programs. The administrations of the 1920s, even with the Civil War generation dying out, allocated roughly 20 percent of the federal budget to veterans' benefits.[6]

When the Depression put men out of work, forty thousand Great War veterans marched on Washington in 1932 demanding early payment of the bonus. The army drove them and the families they couldn't support out of the capital. Marchers came year after year. In 1933, Franklin Roosevelt maintained Herbert Hoover's general position on the issue when he cut veterans' benefits, including disability pensions and hospitalization expenses. Eventually Congress and public opinion—and the lobbying of Great War veterans' groups—pushed Roosevelt to reinstate much of what had been cut. By the mid-1930s, the administration was offering bonus marchers expedited access to positions in the Civilian Conservation Corps, although Roosevelt, like Coolidge, vetoed a bill accelerating bonus outlays. Congress overrode the veto in 1936, and soon almost all veterans received the full value of their certificates.[7]

Former doughboys then helped engineer management of the next, far bigger, reintegration of veterans. The Servicemen's Readjustment Act of 1944, or GI Bill, had less to do with rewarding citizens for their service and more to do with compensating them for the interruption of their domestic lives. Although also showered with public veneration, World War II veterans enjoyed unprecedented access to education, housing, medical care, and jobs. They got a bond issue, too, but could convert it to cash as early as 1947. The monumental law created a special set of citizens with its own social welfare infrastructure, thus swelling the middle class and making prosperity as much as pride the repayment for military service. What Great War veterans had wanted, and what government programs of 1917–18 had in part endeavored to provide, had come to pass on a far larger scale—the trading of wartime sacrifice for enduring financial and familial stability.[8] Unfortunately, although restrictions weren't written into the bill, some women, homosexuals, and African Americans faced blockages to this aid from the local agencies administering it. Then, Vietnam-era veterans suffered from diminished budgets in the 1970s, lagging behind their Greatest Generation fathers in the provision of benefits.[9]

When the United States abandoned conscription in 1973, the brass handled a different problem—how to entice recruits into service—with a similar solution: extend them a long-term social safety net of benefits, skills training, medical care, housing assistance, and other stabilizers of domestic life. This model served the troops and their families well in the late 1970s and 1980s. But in the Clinton era, military welfare programs underwent privatization and shrinkage together with comparable changes to civilian entitlements. The overextended military of the War on Terror taxed this pinched support network. Some help for the injured and their stateside families came in George W. Bush's second term, but an ethos of self-reliance persisted. "Army Family Strong" joined "Army Strong" as the slogans of tough independence in the face of adversity. Meanwhile scandal rocked the increasingly privatized Walter

Reed Hospital in the mid-2000s. Into the Barack Obama administration, miraculous tales of recovery and rehabilitation shared space with stories of neglect, incompetence, and outsourcing of care.[10]

The American war story through 1918 hawked regenerative potential in at least three registers. Redemptive war would deliver broad social benefit; protect innocents literally; and stimulate personal growth for soldiers, whether by clarifying gender roles, building character, or providing a venue for expressing love of home and family. The first of those ideas, that war brought societal enhancement, seems to have receded, while the other two endured in subsequent decades, if in amended form.[11] Reformers, officials, and pundits continued to politicize the American family and imagine it in crisis—through debates over gay rights, abortion, poverty, the black "underclass," suburbanization, feminism, labor politics, entitlement spending, divorce, family values, immigration, crime, gender identification, and more—but it became rare for anyone to claim that war could fix anything.[12] The prospect that war could protect families, daily life, and cherished American values, however, reappeared during World War II and the Cold War and then again in the aftermath of 9/11. And Americans still hear about war—or more precisely, military service—as an incubator of personal betterment. Much like shifts in veterans' benefits, the redeeming qualities of service have increasingly sprung from skills training, character building, and the admiration of one's family or community as much as the promise of ennobling combat or even patriotic fulfillment. At the White House Correspondents' Association Dinner in 2013, President Obama honored members of the armed forces. His answer to why they served offered a way of ranking obligation: "They do it because they love their families and they love their neighborhoods and they love their country."[13]

American political and popular culture, though, grew increasingly likely to reveal the damaging as well as edifying impact of combat on soldiers and families. Even amid efforts to glorify the Great War, the 1920s and 1930s witnessed biting satire on the myth of redemptive conflict. College students joined groups like the "Veterans of Future Wars" and "Future Gold Star Mothers." Minnesotans in the former group vowed that next time the state called them to "defend our wives and sweethearts" they would do so—by staying home.[14] Marine general

Smedley Butler, who vilified the nation for turning its back on veterans, published *War Is a Racket* in 1933, charging that profiteers got rich and doughboys "paid with heartbreaks when they tore themselves away from their firesides and their families."[15] The same year saw the appearance of Alabama veteran William March's *Company K*, a brutal montage of war as "the ultimate irredeemable social evil," according to one literary scholar.[16] Early opinion polling in 1937 revealed that 70 percent of Americans thought intervention in the Great War had been a mistake. The same year, congressional commemorations of the twentieth anniversary of entrance included rituals honoring members who had voted against it.[17] Before World War II, there was significant support for a constitutional amendment requiring public referenda before future wars. It came close but never passed, although the Neutrality Acts moved successfully through Congress between 1935 and 1937 to great approval.[18]

William March's fellow Marine and Blanc-Mont veteran Thomas Boyd embodied the tug between romantic and critical renderings of war. The 1923 publication of *Through the Wheat* made him a literary star (F. Scott Fitzgerald championed it) and offered a grim view of personal breakdown in combat. It ended with the line, "The soul of Hicks was numb."[19] Yet Boyd's publisher marketed the book as a tale of heroic toughness. The author himself wrote other works that valorized the Marines, even contributing stories to the patriotic *American Legion Monthly* before his death at thirty-seven of a cerebral hemorrhage. The unsettled and contradictory nature of Boyd's writings mirrored a broader pattern of Great War remembrance on the commemorative and literary landscape.[20] Over the course of the next three American wars, popular and media culture offered consistent strains of antimilitarism, but they mingled with durable and sometimes overpowering romantic renderings of war. Even the Good War, like the Great one, followed no single script in American life. The public seems to find war alternately seductive and repellant.[21]

These zigzagging plotlines of the post-1918 war story offer clues about the First World War's quiet presence in American collective memory. Its immediate and long-range effects on the family and state are overshadowed, obscured, or complicated by subsequent conflicts, nonlinear in their trajectories, or difficult to summarize in digestible sound bites. But with hindsight it's clear the American war story has shed some of its exclusions of race and gender, revealed more of the damaging impact of war, and pushed the state into a position of greater sensitivity to that impact. We can appreciate those revisions. Or we can mourn that they came slowly, expensively, and unevenly. We can mourn that they accompanied, abetted, or did nothing to prevent a militarized and interventionist foreign policy that shows no evidence of modification. As salutary as parts of the new war story may be, they signify a nation that has been, and expects to be, perpetually at war. The costs of *that* development for many American families—and millions more around the world—are beyond comprehension.

WARING HUSTON'S FATHER WALTER died a little more than a decade after his son, on April 10, 1929, and was buried a few feet away.[22] His tombstone reads, "Some Day, Some Time, We'll Understand." The next year's census had Nellye living in the house at 702 Church Street with her sister Mamie and a servant. About two blocks away resided Waring's best friend Pressley Cleveland and his wife Tyler. In the spring of 1930, they welcomed a child they named Waring Huston Cleveland. One imagines they brought the infant around to see Nellye, but soon the family moved to Georgia. There the boy died right around his third birthday. Press and Tyler brought Waring Cleveland back to Live Oak Cemetery in Selma to be buried. He lies near his namesake and near Walter Huston, near Confederate generals and senators Edmund Pettus and John Tyler Morgan, and near the big memorial to Robert E. Lee and smaller one to the defender of Selma, Nathan Bedford Forrest.[23]

Meanwhile Nellye stayed on at Church Street, living with her stepdaughter Helen, son-in-law John Lapsley, and their children until she died at eighty in 1955.[24] That was the year John donated Waring's letters to the special collections library at the University of Alabama. He and Helen also named a son after Waring—George Waring Huston Lapsley, born in 1919 almost a year to the day after his uncle's death. This boy followed his ancestors into the service, joining the navy during World War II.[25] The 1957 Selma directory showed the veteran living in the Church Street house with his parents and older brother John Jr., one of the "little brats" Waring had referred to in his Great War letters.[26]

Christian Huebner's remaining children never particularly liked their new stepmother Johanna, and the older ones kept their distance from her in the years following Arthur's re-burial in 1921. Christian preceded her in death in August 1943 and it's unclear what she or anyone else did with Arthur's war letters. But photographs and mementoes, including the New Testament and Book of Psalms, went to Arthur's brother Otto and then in the 1960s to James Huebner, son of Arthur's brother Walter. The youngest brother in the family, Carl, settled in Sheboygan, Wisconsin, and married Doris Hultgren. They had a son, John, in 1944. He met and married Wendy Walthers, and they had a son, me, in 1973.

Mae and Lige Dees appear to have stayed in Missouri the rest of their lives. In 1930, their daughter Helen Mae was ten, a boy named Raymond Eliga seven, and Mary Alice, called "Teenie," was four. The family was renting a farmhouse, with Lige's occupation listed as "none" but then crossed out. Ten years later, the census takers labeled Lige "head" of a $300 house they now owned, but recorded Mae as the "farmer," left Lige's vocation blank, and answered "no" to the question of his employment for pay. Apparently he was "unable to work," a mysterious and ironic turn for a couple whose epistolary dialogue on wage-earning generated such resentment.[27] Lige died just after the Tet Offensive in Vietnam of early 1968. Mae went on to write nostalgic essays on her beloved Wayne County before her own death in 1973.[28] One of their grandchildren provided the only image of the couple in my possession (figure E.1). To my mind, that she's looking at the camera and he's looking at her utterly captures the Mae and Lige I've come to know. Sometime after Mae's death, her wartime correspondence with Lige ended up at an antique dealership. Their grandson couldn't shed light on how the letters left the family. They found their way to a collector of memorabilia who happened to be a student of mine. She gave me the collection, which now resides at the State Historical Society of Missouri.

Natalie Scott became an important figure in the artistic and literary scene of 1920s New Orleans, establishing a French Quarter community playhouse and forging friendships with Sherwood Anderson and William Faulkner. Later she established a school and medical facility in an impoverished town in Mexico called Taxco. She suddenly fell ill with uremic poisoning in November 1957 and died in a Mexico City hospital. When her body returned to Taxco, the roads were lined with children and other friends. For the two-day visitation, a villager placed

FIGURE E.1 Eliga and Mae Dees, c. 1930s. Author's collection, courtesy of Raymond Dees.

the Croix de Guerre and additional medals she had won during World War II on her casket. She is buried in Taxco, her stone reading, "Rest in Peace Near the Little Ones You Loved."[29]

Edward Streeter continued writing comedy, hitting it big with the 1949 bestselling novel *Father of the Bride*. Spencer Tracy and Elizabeth Taylor played the leads in the Hollywood feature of the same name, which earned several Academy Award nominations in 1950.

COMBAT HEROISM FAILED TO shield Henry Johnson and Needham Roberts from the punishing lives of black people after the war. Both Harlem Hell Fighters found fame, marched in parades, and secured speaking engagements, but both also felt sharply the limits of patriotic credibility bought by their service. Johnson met national reproach when he called white soldiers bigots and cowards. The government investigated him for subversion and for wearing his uniform past the three-month limit from discharge. Roberts went to federal prison in 1924 for the same offense—for daring to stretch his association with the uniform and thus his wartime feats. They also both suffered from war wounds. Johnson's kept him from resuming work as a railroad porter. He struggled to support his wife and son with a small disability pension and a problem with alcohol. She left him in 1923, and by the end of the decade the family had lost touch. Johnson died alone in 1929 in an Albany veterans' hospital. He was buried at Arlington but his family wasn't notified. Needham Roberts likewise had trouble holding down a job back home in New Jersey. He was in and out of prison in the 1920s, once convicted of "sexual abuse." Roberts soon married and had a daughter, but in the late 1940s was arrested again, this time for allegedly "bothering" an eight-year-old girl in a theater in Newark. Knowing his record and prospects, Needham and his wife Idia hung themselves together in their bathroom. She left a note claiming his innocence, and the molestation charge went unconfirmed.[30] In 2015, Henry Johnson posthumously received the Congressional Medal of Honor from President Obama.

It took until 1939, when witnesses came forward, for Albert Vahl of the 124th Machine Gun Battalion to win a Distinguished Service Cross for covering retreating comrades at Butgnéville on the morning of the armistice. A wire story in the *New York Times* didn't mention Arthur Huebner, but reported that two decades later Vahl's "deepest impression" of the day remained "one of futility, of soldiers sagging under their wounds, not knowing that the terms of peace already had been agreed upon."[31]

Others' awards came more quickly. Alvin York of Waring's division and Clayton Slack of Arthur's machine gun battalion both earned the Medal of Honor for their exploits of October 8, 1918, and Charles Whittlesey of the Lost Battalion won that distinction for actions taken just days earlier. Alvin's story became immortalized in the film *Sergeant York* (1941). Slack likewise parlayed his military record into a lucrative career in government films and public speaking. Photographs of Slack with Gen. John J. Pershing and Presidents Franklin Roosevelt and John Kennedy fill out his collection of papers at the Wisconsin Historical Society. Whittlesey found comparable if unwanted celebrity. Requests for public appearances poured in even as he grew to believe the war "a bloody and unnecessary business." He sensed a betrayal of the intervention's redemptive promise in postwar vilification of immigrants and the failure of America to join the League of Nations. And well aware of the war's horrific impact on individual men, he continued to fund-raise for veterans and speak on behalf of the Red Cross.[32]

Just after serving as a pallbearer at the burial of the Unknown Soldier in late 1921, Whittlesey embarked by ocean liner to Havana, Cuba. After a convivial evening with the ship's captain, he jumped overboard. In his cabin, the veteran had left a note for his law partner vowing, "I shall not return." The press attributed Whittlesey's suicide to grief over the war and the painful ceremonies at Arlington. Charles left his Medal of Honor, by the terms of a revised will, to his mother.[33]

ACKNOWLEDGMENTS

This is a book about family so I'd like to begin there, with my wife Lisa Davis and our daughter Sofia. Beyond understanding when the project required sacrifices, Lisa was a loving and patient listener through every twist and turn it took. Sofia has grown up with the book, understanding vaguely that I was working on "the battle back then." Her bottomless curiosity about and sympathy for her doughboy relative Arthur Huebner never failed to touch me. But more importantly, Lisa and Sofia have made my life richer than I ever could have imagined. My love and appreciation for them made writing about family poignant every day. For making this book possible—and for making life good—I dedicate it to them.

My parents, John and Wendy, continue to be unswerving supporters of my career and cherished presences in our lives. Together with my brother Min and his family, as well as my Mississippi family on Lisa's side, we've shared lots of fun, exuberant, and memorable occasions over the course of this book's life. For all the love and good times, thank you to Alberto, Brandon, Dylan, Gaby, Girlesa, Isaac, Maria, Rachel, Tiffany, Tyler, and Veronica.

Keeping things in the family, this book's origins, like the deeper roots of my interest in history, lay in stories my father's cousin Jim Huebner told me about Arthur, his Great Warrior uncle. Jim began gathering material on Arthur decades before he knew it would form part of a book. As the main custodian of our genealogy, he has fielded countless questions from me. We took trips together to European battlefields and family history sites in Wisconsin. This book aims in part to faithfully record Arthur's story, but also pays tribute, I hope, to Jim's lifelong project of documenting the Huebners' story. I cannot thank him enough.

Love and Death in the Great War also owes its existence to the kindness of my former student, Caitlin DeAngelis Hopkins, who gave me the set of letters between Mae and Eliga Dees she had acquired as a collector of historical material. Their grandson, Raymond Dees, generously provided the one photograph of the couple in my possession. It was an honor to bring the existence of the letters to the attention of his family.

Over many years, meals, conferences, and conversations, I've developed the ideas in this book within a circle of outstanding scholars of war and society. Beth Bailey, Susan Grayzel, Jennifer Keene, Michael Neiberg, Stephen Ortiz, and Kara Dixon Vuic have supported and encouraged me and shaped the book in uncountable ways. These great friends and historians also helped facilitate chances to audition arguments at meetings and in print. I learned much from the "Interchange" Jennifer Keene and I conducted for the *Journal of American History*, which included Christopher Capozzola, Julia Irwin, Ross Kennedy, Mike Neiberg, Steve Ortiz, Chad Williams, and Jay Winter. Credit for that conversation goes to Ed Linenthal, who believed in the idea and gave us the venue. I was honored to take part in an Oxford University Press podcast hosted by Thomas Zeiler that included Christopher Capozzola, David Ekbladh, and David Kennedy, whose seminal book got me interested in the Great War many years ago.

Many of these historians shared space and expertise on roundtables and panels, instrumental in rehearsing my ideas, at meetings of the American Historical Association, Organization of American Historians, Society for Military History, and Institute for Political History. I benefitted enormously from symposia organized by Beth Bailey at Temple University in 2013; Kara Dixon Vuic at High Point University in 2014 and Texas Christian University in 2017; and Susan Grayzel, John Neff, and April Holm at the University of Mississippi in 2015. For other opportunities to present my research in talks, I thank the ROTC and Department of History at the University of Alabama, where I joined my colleagues John Beeler and Harold Selesky for an event at Harold's urging; and Gary Iams, chair of the Warren G. Harding Symposium at The Ohio State University at Marion. Gary's invitation came late in the manuscript's development and put me on a program with Sheryl Smart Hall, Michael Kazin, and David Steigerwald. My talks with them led to some last-minute edits and also new friendships. Finally, at a much earlier point in the book's life, my dear friend Woody Register gave me a platform to speak on the project at the University of the South. I'm indebted to Woody and his colleagues at Sewanee for their feedback at a key moment.

Kara Dixon Vuic, once again, as editor of *The Routledge History of Gender, War, and the U.S. Military*, asked me to contribute an essay that sharpened my thinking for this book. The same is true of a piece I wrote called "The War for Family" at the behest of Carla Walker for the Fall 2014 edition of the *Oklahoma Humanities* magazine. I appreciate both invitations, and some content here is adapted from those articles.

I am lucky to be part of a supportive and intellectually rich department at the University of Alabama. For helping me think through ideas, I'm grateful to Bart Elmore, Kari Frederickson, Larry Kohl, George Rable, Dan Riches, and Josh Rothman. I subjected John Giggie and George McClure to more than their fair share of talk about the project, and they provided consistently good counsel and much-needed comic relief. Holly Grout and Jenny Shaw showed steadfast patience and support across years of reading and discussing my work, and I hope they know how much I appreciate them for it. Glenn Brasher and Chuck Clark answered key questions about topics in their areas of expertise. Thanks as well to all the colleagues and graduate students who read an early chapter for our departmental workshop. My PhD students Blake Ball, Mark Folse, Jonathan Merritt, and Margaret Montgomery patiently endured meetings on their work that veered to talks on my own. I am indebted to graduate students in various seminars, as well as undergraduates in my yearly course on war and culture, not only for tolerating similar digressions but also for teaching me so much about history. Every student in those courses contributed something to this volume. And in our departmental office, Christina Kircharr, Ellen Pledger, and Morta Riggs not only helped handle the bureaucracies of research but also make our department a congenial and fun place to work.

Several friends, relatives, and other scholars read portions of the manuscript or gave advice: Jonathan Boff, Miles Eddins, William Gillis, Jonathan Gumz, Rob Guthrie, Jim Huebner, John Huebner, Lee Huebner, and Wendy Huebner. My earliest friend from graduate school, Robert Fleegler, has influenced my understanding of history for two decades. And my dissertation director many years ago, James Patterson, graciously read an early and *very* rough partial draft. I'm continually grateful to Jim for taking me on as a graduate student and for all the support he's offered since I graduated. Nothing I've done would have happened without him.

For arranging time off from teaching to complete the manuscript, I'd like to thank Dean Robert Olin of the College of Arts and Sciences and Kari Frederickson of the Department of History. Judge Quentin Brown extended great generosity in supporting my work. During research trips to Europe, I was hosted by dear friends and family: Lee and Berna Huebner in France, and Theo Kilgert, Dagmar Hauser-Kilgert, Katja Kilgert-Grashey, and Rupert Grashey in Germany. I'm so happy this book has reconnected us with our German friends.

I was fortunate to receive the research assistance of many undergraduate and graduate students at the University of Alabama. My deepest gratitude goes to Blake Ball, Daniel Bush, Lewis DeHope, Taylor Hermann, Hilary Jones, Jonathan Merritt, Adam Seltzer, and James Yerby. Their work is everywhere in these pages. Thanks as well to Dr. Bruce Fleegler and Georgia Sylke, RN, who taught me a bit about early twentieth-century medicine.

Much appreciated assistance came from the staff at various libraries and archives: the Ohio Historical Society; St. Mark's Lutheran Church in Watertown, Wisconsin; the Watertown Public Library; the Wisconsin Historical Society; the Military History Institute in Carlisle, Pennsylvania; Becky Nichols and Mary Morrow at the Selma-Dallas County Public Library; John Bradbury and Kathleen Seale at the State Historical Society of Missouri; Sean Benjamin at the Louisiana Research Collection at Tulane University; Russell Horton of the Wisconsin Veterans Museum Research Center; Meredith McDonough at the Alabama Department of Archives and History; and Jessica Lacher-Feldman, Allyson Holliday, Marina Klarić, Kevin Ray, Brett Spencer, and Donnelly Lancaster Walton at the University of Alabama. Mike

Constandy did meticulous work gathering material from the National Archives. Craig Remington and Alex Fries of the Cartographic Research Laboratory at Alabama created wonderful maps for the book.

As *Love and Death in the Great War* wound its way toward publication, many people provided invaluable advice about the publishing landscape. They included many of the colleagues listed above, as well as Jonathan Ebel, Mike Foley, Lesley Gordon, David Greenberg, Karl Jacoby, John Kinder, and George Thompson. At Oxford University Press, Susan Ferber believed in the book early on and proved an outstanding editor. On matters of copyediting, production, design, and marketing, it has been a pleasure working with Elyse Bailey, Maya Bringe, Suzanne Copenhagen, Holly Haydash, and Julie Mullins. I am deeply grateful, finally, to the anonymous readers at OUP, whose comments helped shape the book's trajectory and improve the final product.

So: thanks to everyone mentioned here and apologies to those I omitted. Of course, in the end, responsibility for whatever is wrong, undercooked, or oversold in this book is all mine.

NOTES

Prologue

1. Several studies share my interest in how the American public came to accept, understand, or reject intervention in the European war, including Michael S. Neiberg, *The Path to War: How the First World War Created Modern America* (New York: Oxford University Press, 2016); Christopher Capozzola, *Uncle Sam Wants You: World War I and the Making of the Modern American Citizen* (New York: Oxford University Press, 2008); Jonathan H. Ebel, *Faith in the Fight: Religion and the American Soldier in the Great War* (Princeton: Princeton University Press, 2010); Michael Kazin, *War Against War: The American Fight for Peace, 1914–1918* (New York: Simon and Schuster, 2017).

2. For models of such a microhistorical approach see Martha Hanna, *Your Death Would Be Mine: Paul and Marie Pireaud in the Great War* (Cambridge: Harvard University Press, 2006); Thomas Childers, *Soldier From the War Returning: The Greatest Generation's Troubled Homecoming from World War II* (New York: Mariner Books, 2009); Stephen Ash, *A Year in the South: 1865* (New York: Perennial, 2004); Richard Rubin, *The Last of the Doughboys: The Forgotten Generation and Their Forgotten World War* (Boston: Houghton Mifflin Harcourt, 2013); Peter Englund, *The Beauty and the Sorrow: An Intimate History of the First World War* (New York: Knopf, 2011); David Laskin, *The Long Way Home: An American Journey from Ellis Island to the Great War* (New York: Harper Perennial, 2010).

3. For these subjects, among many other works, see Susan Zeiger, *In Uncle Sam's Service: Women Workers with the American Expeditionary Force,*

1917–1919 (Ithaca: Cornell University Press, 1999); Jennifer D. Keene, *Doughboys, the Great War, and the Remaking of America* (Baltimore: Johns Hopkins University Press, 2001); Lynn Dumenil, *The Second Line of Defense: American Women and World War I* (Chapel Hill: University of North Carolina Press, 2017); David Kennedy, *Over Here: The First World War and American Society* (New York: Oxford University Press, 2004 ed.); Chad L. Williams, *Torchbearers of Democracy: African American Soldiers in the World War I Era* (Chapel Hill: University of North Carolina Press, 2010); Adriane Lentz-Smith, *Freedom Struggles: African Americans and World War I* (Cambridge: Harvard University Press, 2009); Lisa Budreau, *Bodies of War: World War I and the Politics of Commemoration in America* (New York: New York University Press, 2010). In Andrew J. Huebner, "Gee! I Wish I Were a Man: Gender and the Great War," in Kara Dixon Vuic, ed., *The Routledge History of Gender, War, and the U.S. Military* (New York: Routledge, 2018), I explored the implications for gender history in this scholarship and the broader literature on America in World War I, and therefore rehearsed ideas that appear in revised form throughout this book.

4. For his sensitivity to language and meaning, I am influenced by Paul Fussell, *The Great War and Modern Memory* (New York: Oxford University Press, 1975).

5. See Kristin Hoganson, *Fighting for American Manhood: How Gender Politics Provoked the Spanish-American and Philippine-American Wars* (New Haven: Yale University Press, 1998); Stephen Berry, *All That Makes a Man: Love and Ambition in the Civil War South* (New York: Oxford University Press, 2003); Aaron Sheehan-Dean, *Why Confederates Fought: Family and Nation in Civil War Virginia* (Chapel Hill: University of North Carolina Press, 2007); Robert Westbrook, *Why We Fought: Forging American Obligations in World War II* (Washington: Smithsonian Books, 2010); Mary Louise Roberts, *What Soldiers Do: Sex and the American GI in World War II France* (Chicago: University of Chicago Press, 2013); Heather Marie Stur, *Beyond Combat: Women and Gender in the Vietnam War Era* (New York: Cambridge University Press, 2011).

6. A sampling of scholarship on Great War home fronts includes Michael S. Neiberg, *Dance of the Furies: Europe and the Outbreak of World War I* (Cambridge: Belknap Press of Harvard University Press, 2011); Neiberg, *Path to War*; Adrian Gregory, *The Last Great War: British Society and the First World War* (Cambridge: Cambridge University Press, 2008); Susan R. Grayzel, *Women's Identities at War: Gender, Motherhood, and Politics in Britain and France during the First World War* (Chapel Hill: University of North Carolina Press, 1999); Hanna, *Your Death Would Be Mine*; Benjamin Ziemann, *War Experiences in Rural Germany, 1914–1923* (Oxford: Berg, 2007), 137–54; Helen B. McCartney, *Citizen Soldiers: The*

Liverpool Territorials in the First World War (Cambridge: Cambridge
University Press, 2005); Desmond Morton, *Fight or Pay: Soldiers' Families
in the Great War* (Vancouver: University of British Columbia Press, 2004);
Michael Roper, *The Secret Battle: Emotional Survival in the Great War*
(Manchester: Manchester University Press, 2009); Erika Kuhlman, *Of
Little Comfort: War Widows, Fallen Soldiers, and the Remaking of the Nation
after the Great War* (New York: New York University Press, 2012); Michelle
Moyd, "Centring a Sideshow: Local Experiences of the First World
War in Africa," *First World War Studies* 7 (July 2016): 111–30; Kathryn
M. Hunter, "Australian and New Zealand Fathers and Sons during the
Great War: Expanding the Histories of Families at War," *First World War
Studies* 4 (Oct. 2013): 185–200; Erika Quinn, "Love and Loss, Marriage
and Mourning: World War One in German Home Front Novels," *First
World War Studies* 5 (July 2014): 233–50.

7. William G. Rosenberg, "Reading Soldiers' Moods: Russian Military
Censorship and the Configuration of Feeling in World War I," *American
Historical Review* 119 (June 2014): 714–40.

8. In 2011, Jay Winter called for such a blend of emotions history and the
study of war. See Jay Winter, Review of Steven Trout, *On the Battlefield of
Memory* and John Bodnar, *The "Good War" in American Memory*, *American
Historical Review* 116 (June 2011): 755–58.

9. For challenges to the "Lost Generation" argument see Steven Trout, *On
the Battlefield of Memory: The First World War and American Remembrance,
1919–1941* (Tuscaloosa: University of Alabama Press, 2010); Ebel, *Faith in the
Fight*; Mark Meigs, *Optimism at Armageddon: Voices of American Participants
in the First World War* (New York: New York University Press, 1997).

10. Historians of gender across national experiences have noted war's
simultaneously liberating and limiting impact. See Susan R. Grayzel and
Tammy M. Proctor, eds., *Gender and the Great War* (New York: Oxford
University Press, 2017); Grayzel, *Women's Identities at War*; Mary Louise
Roberts, *Civilization without Sexes: Reconstructing Gender in Postwar
France, 1917–1927* (Chicago: University of Chicago Press, 1994);
Kimberly Jensen, *Mobilizing Minerva: American Women in the First World
War* (Urbana: University of Illinois Press, 2008); Margaret Randolph
Higonnet, Jane Jenson, Sonya Michel, and Margaret Collins Weitz,
eds., *Behind the Lines: Gender and the Two World Wars* (New Haven: Yale
University Press, 1987).

11. For race and war's regenerative value see Richard Slotkin, *Regeneration
through Violence: The Mythology of the American Frontier, 1600–1860*
(Middletown, Conn.: Wesleyan University Press, 1973); Gail Bederman,
*Manliness and Civilization: A Cultural History of Gender and Race in the
United States, 1880–1917* (Chicago: University of Chicago Press, 1995);
Gary Gerstle, *American Crucible: Race and Nation in the Twentieth Century*

(Princeton: Princeton University Press, 2001), 3–13; Jonathan H. Ebel, *G.I. Messiahs: Soldiering, War, and American Civil Religion* (New Haven: Yale University Press, 2015); Jackson Lears, *Rebirth of a Nation: The Making of Modern America, 1877–1920* (New York: HarperCollins, 2009); Michael C. C. Adams, *The Great Adventure: Male Desire and the Coming of World War I* (Bloomington: Indiana University Press, 1990).

12. See Berry, *All That Makes a Man*; Sheehan-Dean, *Why Confederates Fought*; Drew Gilpin Faust, *This Republic of Suffering: Death and the American Civil War* (New York: Knopf, 2008); George C. Rable, *God's Almost Chosen People: A Religious History of the American Civil War* (Chapel Hill: University of North Carolina Press, 2010); Gary W. Gallagher, *The Confederate War* (Cambridge: Harvard University Press, 1997); Gary W. Gallagher, *The Union War* (Cambridge: Harvard University Press, 2011); Chandra Manning, *What This Cruel War Was Over: Soldiers, Slavery, and the Civil War* (New York: Knopf, 2007).

13. For the debate on the timing, character, and venues of sectional reconciliation see David W. Blight, *Race and Reunion: The Civil War in American Memory* (Cambridge: Belknap Press of Harvard University Press, 2001); Caroline E. Janney, *Remembering the Civil War: Reunion and the Limits of Reconciliation* (Chapel Hill: University of North Carolina Press, 2013). See also Gaines M. Foster, *Ghosts of the Confederacy: Defeat, the Lost Cause, and the Emergence of the New South* (New York: Oxford University Press, 1987 ed.).

14. See Hoganson, *Fighting for American Manhood*.

15. For the investment of women's domestic activities with patriotic or political meaning see Linda K. Kerber, *Women of the Republic: Intellect and Ideology in Revolutionary America* (Chapel Hill: University of North Carolina, 1980). See also Susan Zeiger, "She Didn't Raise Her Boy to be a Slacker: Motherhood, Conscription, and the Culture of the First World War," *Feminist Studies* 22 (Spring 1996): 7–39; Cecilia Elizabeth O'Leary, *To Die For: The Paradox of American Patriotism* (Princeton: Princeton University Press, 1999), 226. For a philosopher's take on the "gender binary" that encourages male warriors and female nurturers, see Tom Digby, *Love and War: How Militarism Shapes Sexuality and Romance* (New York: Columbia University Press, 2014). Mahan quoted in Hoganson, *Fighting for American Manhood*, 36–7. For doldrums see Jensen, *Mobilizing Minerva*, 16–17.

16. For the nineteenth-century military see Edward M. Coffman, *The Regulars: The American Army, 1898–1941* (Cambridge: Belknap Press of Harvard University Press, 2004), 1–2, 96–104; John M. Kinder, *Paying with Their Bodies: American War and the Problem of the Disabled Veteran* (Chicago: University of Chicago Press, 2015), 39.

17. Stephen Crane, *The Red Badge of Courage* (New York: Modern Library, 2000), 11.

18. See Nancy Bristow, *Making Men Moral: Social Engineering during the Great War* (New York: New York University Press, 1996); 4–6; Susan J. Matt, *Homesickness: An American History* (New York: Oxford University Press, 2011), 5.

19. For the antimilitarist tradition see Kazin, *War Against War*, 1–16; Kinder, *Paying with Their Bodies*, 22–5, 41–3; Michael S. Sherry, *In the Shadow of War: The United States since the 1930s* (New Haven: Yale University Press, 1995), 1–11; David Mayers, *Dissenting Voices in America's Rise to Power* (New York: Cambridge University Press, 2007), 201–6.

20. Quoted in Hoganson, *Fighting for American Manhood*, 259, n. 33.

21. For this paragraph see Kennedy, *Over Here*, 30; Hoganson, *Fighting for American Manhood*, 33; Robert H. Zieger, *America's Great War: World War I and the American Experience* (Lanham, Md.: Rowman and Littlefield, 2000), 138–39. Addams quoted in Geoffrey R. Stone, *Perilous Times: Free Speech in Wartime from the Sedition Act of 1798 to the War on Terrorism* (New York: W. W. Norton, 2004), 140. Preamble quoted in Jensen, *Mobilizing Minerva*, 19.

22. See Kinder, *Paying with Their Bodies*, 28–39. For Trumbull see Lears, *Rebirth of a Nation*, 27.

23. See Lears, *Rebirth of a Nation*, 40; Williams, *Torchbearers of Democracy*, 29; Coffman, *Regulars*, 7.

24. See Nancy Cott, *Public Vows: A History of Marriage and the Nation* (Cambridge: Harvard University Press, 2000), 136–42; Roger Daniels, *Guarding the Golden Door: American Immigration Policy and Immigrants since 1882* (New York: Hill and Wang, 2004), 14, 17, 29, 40, 46.

25. See Madison Grant, *The Passing of the Great Race or The Racial Basis of European History* (New York: Charles Scribner's Sons, 1916), 81; Jacob A. Riis, *How the Other Half Lives* (New York: Dover Publications, 1971 ed.), 44–153.

26. See Michael McGerr, *A Fierce Discontent: The Rise and the Fall of the Progressive Movement in America* (New York: Oxford University Press, 2003), 269–71; Beth Linker, *War's Waste: Rehabilitation in World War I America* (Chicago: University of Chicago Press, 2011), 31, 47.

27. For this material and quotations see Linda Gordon, *Pitied But Not Entitled: Single Mothers and the History of Welfare, 1890–1935* (New York: The Free Press, 1994), 24–29, 41; Theda Skocpol, *Protecting Soldiers and Mothers: The Political Origins of Social Policy in the United States* (Cambridge: Belknap Press of Harvard University Press, 1992), 371.

28. See Linker, *War's Waste*, 12–19; Kinder, *Paying with Their Bodies*, 26.

29. Lears, *Rebirth of a Nation*, 101.

30. See Lears, *Rebirth of a Nation*, 21–22, 28–29, 101–2; Bederman, *Manliness and Civilization*, 25; Lentz-Smith, *Freedom Struggles*, 82–9; Bristow, *Making Men Moral*, 23–8; Celia Malone Kingsbury, *For Home and Country: World War I Propaganda on the Home Front* (Lincoln: University

of Nebraska Press, 2010); Christina Gier, "Gender, Politics, and the Fighting Soldier's Song in America during World War I," *Music and Politics* 2 (Winter 2008): 1–20; Michael Kimmel, *Manhood in America: A Cultural History* (New York: Oxford University Press, 2012 ed.); Hoganson, *Fighting for American Manhood*; Cott, *Public Vows*, 143.

31. Danielle L. McGuire, *At the Dark End of the Street: Black Women, Rape, and Resistance—A New History of the Civil Rights Movement from Rosa Parks to the Rise of Black Power* (New York: Vintage Books, 2010), 27.

32. For gender and racial violence see Lentz-Smith, *Freedom Struggles*, esp. 82–83; Glenda Elizabeth Gilmore, *Gender and Jim Crow: Women and the Politics of White Supremacy in North Carolina, 1896–1920* (Chapel Hill: University of North Carolina Press, 1996); Joel Williamson, *A Rage for Order: Black/White Relations in the American South Since Emancipation* (New York: Oxford University Press, 1986), 83–86; Nancy MacLean, *Behind the Mask of Chivalry: The Making of the Second Ku Klux Klan* (New York: Oxford University Press, 1994).

33. McGerr, *Fierce Discontent*, xiv.

Chapter 1: Johnny Get Your Gun

1. *Congressional Record*, Senate, 65th Congress, 1st sess., Apr. 2, 1917, 104.

2. See "High School Notes from Williamsville," *Greenville* (Mo.) *Sun*, Apr. 5, 1917; Mae Bilbrey to Eliga Dees, Apr. 12, 1917, Eliga and Mae Dees Letters (Dees Letters), Collection R1453, State Historical Society of Missouri, Columbia, Mo. (SHSM).

3. See John Bilbrey; p. 6B, line 82, Enumeration District 163, St. Francois Township, Wayne County, Mo. Census of Population; *Thirteenth Census of the United States, 1910* (National Archives Microfilm Publication [NAMP] T624, roll 827); Records of the Bureau of the Census, Record Group 29 (RG 29); National Archives Building, Washington, D.C. (NAB). John L. Bilbury [sic]; p. 5A, line 11, Enumeration District 178, Lost Creek Township, Wayne County, Mo. Census of Population; *Fourteenth Census of the United States, 1920* (NAMP T625, roll 965); RG 29; NAB. Minnie Bilbrey; p. 11B, line 67, Enumeration District 150, Black River Township, Wayne County, Mo. Census of Population; *Twelfth Census of the United States, 1900* (NAMP T623, roll 907); RG 29; NAB.

4. See Elijah [sic] Dees; p. 9A, line 8, Enumeration District 150, Black River Township, Wayne County, Mo. Census of Population; *Twelfth Census of the United States, 1900* (NAMP T623, roll 907); RG 29; NAB. The family doesn't appear in 1910 or 1920, so it's possible Lige had additional younger siblings.

5. Mae Bilbrey to Eliga Dees, [May ?] 19, July 6 and 15, 1917, Dees Letters, SHSM.

6. Eliga Dees Service Record; Missouri Digital Heritage; Soldiers' Records: War of 1812–World War I, *sos.mo.gov/archives/soldiers* (Aug. 16, 2012).

7. Mae Bilbrey to Eliga Dees, April 12, 1917, Dees Letters, SHSM.

8. For the army in this period see Edward M. Coffman, *The Regulars: The American Army, 1898–1941* (Cambridge: Belknap Press of Harvard University Press, 2004), 96–104, 199.

9. See Eliga Dees; p. 2A, line 21, Enumeration District 112–5, Cowan Township, Wayne County, Mo. Census of Population; *Sixteenth Census of the United States, 1940* (NAMP T627, roll 2163); RG 29; NAB.

10. See Beth L. Bailey, *From Front Porch to Back Seat: Courtship in Twentieth-Century America* (Baltimore: Johns Hopkins University Press, 1988), 20.

11. Mae Bilbrey to Eliga Dees, Apr. 12, 1917, Dees Letters, SHSM.

12. See *Congressional Record*, Senate, 65th Congress, 1st sess., Apr. 2, 1917, 103, 104.

13. "Impose" quotation from John Milton Cooper, Jr., "The World War and American Memory," *Diplomatic History* 38 (Sept. 2014): 729. Some scholars find in Wilson's war rhetoric grand terms of national and international regeneration, including Susan A. Brewer, *Why America Fights: Patriotism and War Propaganda from the Philippines to Iraq* (New York: Oxford University Press, 2009), 46; Jackson Lears, *Rebirth of a Nation: The Making of Modern America, 1877–1920* (New York: HarperCollins, 2009), 328–39. In contrast, John Milton Cooper, Jr., argues for Wilson's more limited ambitions in "The World War and American Memory," while two other works privilege Wilson's desire for security: Michael S. Neiberg, *The Path to War: How the First World War Created Modern America* (New York: Oxford University Press, 2016) and Ross A. Kennedy, *The Will to Believe: Woodrow Wilson, World War I, and America's Strategy for Peace and Security* (Kent: Kent State University Press, 2009).

14. See *Congressional Record*, Senate, 65th Congress, 1st sess., Apr. 4, 1917, 201, 208, 215, 219, 223, 253.

15. *Congressional Record*, House, 65th Congress, 1st sess., Apr. 5, 1917, 307–8.

16. See *Congressional Record*, Senate, 65th Congress, 1st sess., Apr. 4, 1917, 222.

17. For German atrocities and their media coverage see Larry Zuckerman, *The Rape of Belgium: The Untold Story of World War I* (New York: New York University Press, 2004); John Horne and Alan Kramer, *German Atrocities, 1914: A History of Denial* (New Haven: Yale University Press, 2001); Ruth Harris, "'Child of the Barbarian': Rape, Race and Nationalism in France during the First World War," *Past and Present* 141 (Nov. 1993): 170–206; Neiberg, *Path to War*, 25–31; Susan R. Grayzel, *Women's Identities in War: Gender, Motherhood, and Politics in Britain and France during the First World War* (Chapel Hill: University of North Carolina Press, 1999),

50–85; Julia F. Irwin, *Making the World Safe: The American Red Cross and a Nation's Humanitarian Awakening* (New York: Oxford University Press, 2013), 56.

18. "A Woman Put to Death," *New York Times*, Oct. 23, 1915.

19. Quoted in Mary L. Dudziak, "How War Lost Its Politics," *Dissent* (Summer 2016).

20. For the Zimmermann telegram see Neiberg, *Path to War*, 221; Michael Kazin, *War Against War: The American Fight for Peace, 1914–1918* (New York: Simon and Schuster, 2017), 164–66.

21. See *Congressional Record*, Senate, 65th Congress, 1st sess., Apr. 2, 1917, 102; "Noted Men of Europe Praise the War Message of President Wilson," *St. Louis Post-Dispatch*, Apr. 29, 1917.

22. See Richard Slotkin, *Regeneration through Violence: The Mythology of the American Frontier, 1600–1860* (Middletown, Conn.: Wesleyan University Press, 1973); Tom Engelhardt, *The End of Victory Culture: Cold War America and the Disillusioning of a Generation* (Amherst: University of Massachusetts Press, 1995), 24.

23. See Neiberg, *Path to War*, 11–12; Modris Eksteins, *Rites of Spring: The Great War and the Birth of the Modern Age* (Boston: Houghton Mifflin, 1989), 70–80; Matthew Frye Jacobson, *Whiteness of a Different Color: European Immigrants and the Alchemy of Race* (Cambridge: Harvard University Press, 1998), 46–47; John Higham, *Strangers in the Land: Patterns of American Nativism, 1860–1925* (New York: Atheneum, 1970), 25. Frederick C. Luebke, *Bonds of Loyalty: German Americans and World War I* (De Kalb: Northern Illinois University Press, 1974), 57–78.

24. Prof. Sam Chambliss Rigney ("The Kaiser's Impeachment") to U.S. Secretary of War, Dec. 23, 1917, folder 1, box 5; Correspondence of Guy Stanton Ford; Records of the Committee on Public Information, Record Group 63; National Archives at College Park, Md.

25. See, for example, "Says We Will Obey if Germany Wins," *New York Times*, June 22, 1915; Emile Verhaeren, "The Uncivilizable Nation," in *The European War*, vol. 4, July–Sept. 1915, *Current History* (New York: The New York Times Company, 1915), 777–79; "Calls Germans Brutal," *New York Times*, Jan. 25, 1915; "Germans as Exponents of Culture," *New York Times*, Sept. 20, 1914; "Hollanders Beg American People to Save Belgians," *Atlanta Constitution*, Dec. 12, 1916.

26. For Grant and Hall see Higham, *Strangers in the Land*, 201–2, 218.

27. *Congressional Record*, Senate, 65th Congress, 1st sess., Apr. 4, 1917, 222, 251, 256–58, 260.

28. *Congressional Record*, House, 65th Congress, 1st sess., Apr. 5, 1917, 310.

29. *Congressional Record*, Senate, 65th Congress, 1st sess., Apr. 4, 1917, 249.

30. See John W. Scott, *Natalie Scott: A Magnificent Life* (Gretna, La.: Pelican Publishing Co., 2008), 17–46.

31. Quotations from Scott, *Natalie Scott*, 32, 35.

32. Wyeth Scott to Natalie Scott, undated letter of early 1917, folder 5, box 1, Correspondence, Natalie Scott Papers, Manuscripts Collection 123, Louisiana Research Collection, Tulane University, New Orleans, La.

33. Physical description from George Huston draft registration card, Dallas County, Ala.; *Draft Registration Cards, 1917–1918* (Family History Library Microfilm [FHL] roll 1509378); Records of the Selective Service System (World War I), 1917–1939, Record Group 163 (RG 163); National Archives and Records Administration–Southeast Region, Morrow, Ga. (NARA-Southeast). For the family's military background see Biographical Memoranda in Reference to George Waring Huston; Alabama Department of Archives and History; World War I Goldstar Database, *archives.alabama.gov/goldstar/info.html* (Aug. 16, 2012); George Waring Smith membership application, Sons of the American Revolution, *U.S., Sons of the American Revolution Membership Applications, 1889–1970* (Provo: Ancestry.com Operations, Inc., 2011), *Ancestry.com* (July 27, 2013).

34. Some correspondents spelled her name "Nellie," but it is "Nellye" on her tombstone. See Robert W. Huston family; p. 14B, lines 93–100, Enumeration District 0043, Selma City, Dallas County, Ala. Census of Population; *Twelfth Census of the United States, 1900* (NAMP T623, roll 14); RG 29; NAB; Marie Whaley McLaughlin and Carolyn Ward Vintson, comps., *Dallas County Alabama Marriage Records, 1818–1918* (Selma, Ala.: Prestige Research and Publishing, 1992), 105. For Walter's first wife's death see *Dallas County, Alabama Genealogical Records, Vol. 3: Inscriptions—Live Oak Cemetery, Selma, Alabama Prior to June, 1968* (Selma, Ala.: The Sturdivant Museum Association, 1969), 115. For Walter's insurance agency see Advertisement for Huston and Monk, *Sel-Ala, 1914* (Selma High School Yearbook), Edwin Condie Godbold Local History Collection (Godbold Collection), Selma-Dallas County Public Library, Selma, Ala. (SDCPL).

35. Report card for George Waring Huston, Dallas Academy, Dec. 26, 1902, folder 11, box 1080; Huston Family Papers (Huston Papers), W. S. Hoole Special Collections Library, University of Alabama, Tuscaloosa, Ala. (UASC).

36. *Sel-Ala, 1914*, pp. 17–34, Godbold Collection, SDCPL.

37. Selma High School Graduation Program, June 2, 1914, folder 11, box 1080, Huston Papers, UASC.

38. See George Waring Huston to Robert Huston, Nov. 3, 1914, folder 8; Peter Hamilton to Nell Huston, Sept. 26, 1916, folder 12; M. H. S. to Nell Huston, Oct. 30, 1914, folder 12; box 1080, Huston Papers, UASC.

39. President George H. Denny to George Waring Huston, June 19, 1916, folder 10, box 1080, Huston Papers, UASC. See also "Four Hundred Students Sign for Military Work," *Crimson White* (Tuscaloosa, Ala.), Oct. 19, 1916.

40. Edward M. Coffman, *The War to End All Wars: The American Military Experience in World War I* (Lexington: University Press of Kentucky, 1998 ed.), 55.

41. For these three antiwar impulses see David M. Kennedy, *Over Here: The First World War and American Society* (New York: Oxford University Press, 2004 ed.), 21–23.

42. *Congressional Record*, Senate, 65th Congress, 1st sess., Apr. 2, 1917, 103.

43. *Congressional Record*, Senate, 65th Congress, 1st sess., Apr. 4, 1917, 209, 214, 220.

44. *Congressional Record*, Senate, 65th Congress, 1st sess., Apr. 4, 1917, 223.

45. La Follette quoted in David Mayers, *Dissenting Voices in America's Rise to Power* (New York: Cambridge University Press, 2007), 239.

46. *Congressional Record*, House, 65th Congress, 1st sess., Apr. 5, 1917, 312.

47. *Congressional Record*, House, 65th Congress, 1st sess., Apr. 5, 1917, 333, 379.

48. "Seek to Explain Miss Rankin's 'No,'" *New York Times*, Apr. 7, 1917.

49. *Congressional Record*, Senate, 65th Congress, 1st sess., Apr. 4, 1917, 237.

50. *Congressional Record*, Senate, 65th Congress, 1st sess., Apr. 4, 1917, 250.

51. For antiwar and "safe war" impulses see John M. Kinder, *Paying with Their Bodies: American War and the Problem of the Disabled Veteran* (Chicago: University of Chicago Press, 2015), 52–56, 60–63. Susan J. Matt, in *Homesickness: An American History* (New York: Oxford University Press, 2011), 176, astutely notes the antiwar songs privileged the family's claim to the individual over the state's.

52. *Congressional Record*, Senate, 65th Congress, 1st sess., Apr. 4, 1917, 219. See also Kazin, *War Against War*, 152–53; Kennedy, *Over Here*, 23.

53. George Waring Huston to Commanding General, Governors Island, Apr. 9, 1917; E. W. Pettus to Honorable Newton D. Baker, Secretary of War, Apr. 16, 1917; Marian E. Martin to John W. Lapsley, Apr. 19, 1917, folder 11; Robert Huston to Nellye Huston, Apr. 9, 1917, folder 12; box 1080, Huston Papers, UASC. Information on Waring's brother-in-law from State of Alabama Department of Archives and History, *Alabama Official and Statistical Register, 1915* (Montgomery: Brown Printing Company, 1915), 11–12.

54. See "Orders to Report at Camp are Sent," *Atlanta Constitution*, May 10, 1917; "Three States Represented at Fort McPherson Training Camp," *Atlanta Constitution*, May 12, 1917.

55. George Waring Huston to Nellye Huston, May 26, 1917, folder 6, box 1080, Huston Papers, UASC.

56. For Boyd and Gulberg's movements see Thomas Boyd, *Through the Wheat: A Novel of the World War I Marines* (Lincoln: University of Nebraska Press, 2000), v–vi; Martin Gus Gulberg, *A War Diary* (Chicago: The Drake Press, 1927), 1–5.

57. Thomas Alexander Boyd to Aunt Mattie, July 24, 1917, folder 1, box 1, Thomas Boyd Papers (Boyd Papers), Ohio Historical Society, Columbus, Ohio (OHS).

58. Thomas Alexander Boyd to Mother, May 25, 1917, folder 1, box 1, Boyd Papers, OHS.

59. See Thomas Alexander Boyd to Aunt Mattie, July 24, 1917; Thomas Alexander Boyd to Aunt Marion, Summer 1917 (undated); Thomas Alexander Boyd to Mother, July 17, 1917; folder 1, box 1, Boyd Papers, OHS.

60. Thomas Alexander Boyd to Mother, Aug. 10, 1917, folder 1, box 1, Boyd Papers, OHS.

61. This paragraph relies on Coffman, *War to End All Wars*, 8–9, 17–18, 22; Ian F. W. Beckett, *The Great War* (London: Pearson Longman, 2007 ed.), 288–89.

62. Clark quoted in Lears, *Rebirth of a Nation*, 340.

63. Reed quoted in David Laskin, *The Long Way Home: An American Journey from Ellis Island to the Great War* (New York: Harper Perennial, 2011), 124.

64. *Congressional Record*, House, 65th Congress, 1st sess., Apr. 25, 1917, 1092.

65. Quoted in John Whiteclay Chambers II, *To Raise an Army: The Draft Comes to Modern America* (New York: The Free Press, 1987), 154.

66. See Jeanette Keith, *Rich Man's War, Poor Man's Fight: Race, Class, and Power in the Rural South during the First World War* (Chapel Hill: University of North Carolina Press, 2004), 33–54; Jennifer D. Keene, *Doughboys, the Great War, and the Remaking of America* (Baltimore: Johns Hopkins University Press, 2001), 10; Chambers, *To Raise an Army*, 155.

67. Wilson quotation and "coercive voluntarism" from Christopher Capozzola, *Uncle Sam Wants You: World War I and the Making of the Modern American Citizen* (New York: Oxford University Press, 2008), 8. See also "President Warns Those Who Flee From Draft Law," *New York Times*, June 2, 1917; "Jail for Slackers," *Washington Post*, June 5, 1917.

68. Capozzola, *Uncle Sam Wants You*, 23; Keene, *Doughboys*, 9.

69. See Coffman, *War to End All Wars*, 27.

70. Thomas Alexander Boyd to Mother, July 24, 1917, folder 1, box 1, Boyd Papers, OHS.

71. Arthur Huebner draft registration card, June 5, 1917, Jefferson County, Wisc.; *Draft Registration Cards, 1917–1918* (FHL roll 1674737); RG 163; NARA-Southeast. For his personality see *Watertown Weltbürger*, June 11, 1921.

72. Arthur Huebner; p. 13A, line 17, Enumeration District 0125, Ixonia, Jefferson County, Wisc. Census of Population; *Thirteenth Census of the United States, 1910* (NAMP T624, roll 1714); RG 29; NAB.

73. Watertown population from Bureau of the Census, *Thirteenth Census of the United States, 1910, Volume III: Population, Nebraska-Wyoming* (Washington: U.S. Government Printing Office, 1913), 1057. Family information from Christian Huebner to Ernstine Finkelday, Feb. 6, 1924, author's collection; Interview with James R. Huebner, Aug. 4, 2012, Fish Creek, Wisc.

74. See Laskin, *Long Way Home*, 102.

75. "Mass Meeting of German-Americans," *Watertown* (Wisc.) *Gazette*, Nov. 11, 1915.

76. *Congressional Record*, Senate, 65th Congress, 1st sess., Apr. 4, 1917, 224; Apr. 3, 1917, 133.

77. Wallman, *German-Speaking 48ers*, 24; *Watertown* (Wisc.) *Weltbürger*, May 12, 1917.

78. William H. Thomas, Jr., *Unsafe for Democracy: World War I and the U.S. Justice Department's Covert Campaign to Suppress Dissent* (Madison: University of Wisconsin Press, 2008), 110–45.

79. *Congressional Record*, Senate, 65th Congress, 1st sess., Apr. 3, 1917, 131–33.

80. See Mayers, *Dissenting Voices in America's Rise to Power*, 241.

81. "Watertown Will Hustle Money for Uncle Sam," *Watertown* (Wisc.) *News*, May 28, 1917.

82. "Turn Verein 'Opens Its Doors,'" *The Reveill-E: Official Organ Company E*, Fifth Wisconsin Infantry, Aug. 4, 1917.

83. "Roll Call," *Watertown* (Wisc.) *Daily Times*, May 14, 1917.

84. See Brewer, *Why America Fights*, 57.

85. "Memorial Day," *Watertown* (Wisc.) *News*, May 28, 1917.

86. "'America' Fails to Thrill 4,000 at Peace Meet," *Chicago Daily Tribune*, May 28, 1917.

87. "'Support the Nation,' Rabbi Schulman Calls," *New York Times*, June 3, 1917. As David Kennedy puts it, "Many American citizens felt uncertain about the causes and aims of American belligerency." See Kennedy, *Over Here*, 62.

88. See Lears, *Rebirth of a Nation*, 341; Kennedy, *Over Here*, 49–53; Brewer, *Why America Fights*, 53.

89. "America at War in Self-Defense," *Atlanta Constitution*, June 5, 1917.

90. "Why I Will Be Ready on June 5th," *Boston Globe*, June 3, 1917.

91. "Over There," *War Facts and Patriotic Songs*, 23, William L. Ashton Papers, 82nd Division, 325th Infantry Regiment, Veterans Survey Collections, U.S. Army Heritage and Education Center, Military History Institute, Carlisle, Penn. (USAHEC).

92. See Christopher C. Gibbs, *The Great Silent Majority: Missouri's Resistance to World War I* (Columbia: University of Missouri Press, 1988), 24–49.

93. Stone quoted in *Congressional Record*, Senate, 65th Congress, 1st sess., Apr. 4, 1917, 210.

94. *Congressional Record*, House, 65th Congress, 1st sess., Apr. 5, 1917, 413.

95. See Gibbs, *Great Silent Majority*, 34; "Large Crowd Attends Flag Raising Here," *Greenville* (Mo.) *Sun*, Apr. 19, 1917.

96. "Babies Starve in the Streets," *Greenville* (Mo.) *Sun*, Apr. 26, 1917.

97. "Sheriff's Proclamation to Foreign Born Residents," *Greenville* (Mo.) *Sun*, May 24, 1917.

98. Quoted in Gibbs, *Great Silent Majority*, 37.

99. See "Hustling, Bustling City of 2,500 Springs Up at Fort McPherson," *Atlanta Constitution*, May 13, 1917; "Not a Place Left at Training Camp for U.S. Officers," *Atlanta Constitution*, May 14, 1917; George Waring Huston to Nellye Huston, May 14, 1917, folder 6, box 1080, Huston Papers, UASC.

100. Quoted in Coffman, *War to End All Wars*, 55.

101. "Training Begins Wednesday," *Atlanta Constitution*, May 15, 1917.

102. George Waring Huston to Nellye Huston, no date, folder 4; George Waring Huston to Nellye Huston, May 14, 19, and 21, 1917, folder 6; box 1080, Huston Papers, UASC.

103. George Waring Huston to Nellye Huston, May 21, 1917, folder 6, box 1080, Huston Papers, UASC.

104. George Waring Huston to Nellye Huston, May 21 and 22, 1917, folder 6, box 1080, Huston Papers, UASC.

105. George Waring Huston to Nellye Huston, May 14, 1917, folder 7; box 1080, Huston Papers, UASC.

106. "Hustling, Bustling City of 2,500 Springs Up at Fort McPherson," *Atlanta Constitution*, May 13, 1917.

107. "United States Will Never Turn Back Until Peace Is Made . . . ," Committee on Public Information, *Official Bulletin*, June 7, 1917, vol. 1, no. 24, p. 7.

108. See Brewer, *Why America Fights*, 57; "Functions of the Official Bulletin," Committee on Public Information, *Official Bulletin*, May 22, 1917, vol. 1, no. 11, p. 4; James R. Mock and Cedric Larson, *Words That Won the War: The Story of the Committee on Public Information, 1917–1919* (Princeton: Princeton University Press, 1939), 92–96. Mock and Larson wrote that the CPI "both mobilized and expressed the thoughts and emotions supporting these extraordinary dislocations of peaceful life" (p. 5).

109. George Creel's "Preliminary Statement" on press censorship of May 28, 1917, established restrictions on publishing sensitive military news and a procedure for submitting stories for CPI approval. These rules were technically "voluntary," but legal means stood ready to enforce them. And the CPI encouraged civilians to report treasonous language. The CPI's best weapon was to produce and disseminate the government's view through the *Official Bulletin*, press releases, syllabi, and advisory pamphlets for cartoonists and advertisers. See Mock and Larson, *Words That Won the War*, 77–84; Robert H. Zieger, *America's Great War: World War I and the American Experience* (Lanham, Md.: Rowman and Littlefield, 2000), 78–84.

110. See "American Manhood Responds to Country's Call," *Racine* (Wisc.) *Journal-News*, June 5, 1917; "Patriotic Meetings Mark Registration," *New York Times*, June 6, 1917; "They Answer, Uncle Sam, about 10,000,000 Strong," *Atlanta Constitution*, June 6, 1917; "Registration Day

in Georgia Marked by Sincere Patriotism," *Atlanta Constitution*, June 6, 1917; "Whole Nation Answers Call to Registration," *Christian Science Monitor*, June 6, 1917; Chambers, *To Raise an Army*, 210–11.

111. Quoted in "Appeal to Women to Aid in Making Registration Day a Public Festival," Committee on Public Information, *Official Bulletin*, May 25, 1917, vol. 1, no. 14, p. 5.

112. "The Democracy of Motherhood," *Eau Claire* (Wisc.) *Leader*, June 5, 1917.

113. "Enthusiasm Marks Great Celebration at Capitol," *Montgomery* (Ala.) *Advertiser*, June 6, 1917.

114. For this paragraph see "Tennessee Women and Registration," *Christian Science Monitor*, June 5, 1917; "Many Register for Uncle Sam," *Watertown* (Wisc.) *News*, June 6, 1917; "Registration Day Features," *Christian Science Monitor*, June 2, 1917; "Great War Message to Be Distributed at Polling Places," *Atlanta Constitution*, June 3, 1917; "Women to Post Wilson War Call at Draft Booths," *Chicago Daily Tribune*, June 5, 1917; "Personals," *Nashville Tennessean*, June 3, 1917; "Whole Nation Answers Call to Registration," *Christian Science Monitor*, June 6, 1917; Gerald E. Shenk, *"Work or Fight!" Race, Gender, and the Draft in World War One* (New York: Palgrave Macmillan, 2005), 23.

115. "Patriotic Meetings Mark Registration," *New York Times*, June 6, 1917.

116. "Appeal to Women of Nation to Purchase Liberty Bonds," Committee on Public Information, *Official Bulletin*, May 31, 1917, vol. 1, no. 18, p. 1.

117. "This is YOUR War as Well as HIS," *Emmetsburg Palo Alto* (Iowa) *Tribune*, June 6, 1917.

118. CPI quoted in Kennedy, *Over Here*, 55. For children see Celia Malone Kingsbury, *For Home and Country: World War I Propaganda on the Home Front* (Lincoln: University of Nebraska Press, 2010), 169–217.

119. "Maryland Musings," *Baltimore Sun*, June 6, 1917. Emphasis added.

120. "Georgia Will Do Her Part," *Atlanta Constitution*, June 4, 1917.

121. Quoted in Capozzola, *Uncle Sam Wants You*, 33.

122. Quoted in Richard Slotkin, *Lost Battalions: The Great War and the Crisis of American Nationality* (New York: Henry Holt, 2005), 47. See also Shenk, *"Work or Fight!"*; Keith, *Rich Man's War, Poor Man's Fight*.

123. Quoted in Chad L. Williams, *Torchbearers of Democracy: African American Soldiers in the World War I Era* (Chapel Hill: University of North Carolina Press, 2010), 31–32.

124. See Slotkin, *Lost Battalions*, 47–51; Williams, *Torchbearers of Democracy*, 23–26; Arthur E. Barbeau and Florette Henri, *The Unknown Soldiers: Black American Troops in World War I* (Philadelphia: Temple University Press, 1974); Adriane Lentz-Smith, *Freedom Struggles: African Americans and World War I* (Cambridge: Harvard University Press, 2009), 7, 38–41, 82–83; Mark Whalan, *The Great War and the Culture of the New Negro* (Gainesville: University Press of Florida, 2008).

125. "Negro Is Loyal to His Country," *Kansas City Advocate*, June 8, 1917.

126. "Race Man, Wake Up," *Chicago Defender*, Oct. 6, 1917.

127. See "Sammies in War to Win," *Cleveland Gazette*, July 7, 1917; Slotkin, *Lost Battalions*, 49–50; Lentz-Smith, *Freedom Struggles*, 39–42.

128. For brief coverage of the Great War fostering reconciliation see Blight, *Race and Reunion: The Civil War in American Memory* (Cambridge: Belknap Press of Harvard University Press, 2001), 258.

129. All quotations from "Cheered by Dixie Men," *Washington Post*, June 5, 1917.

130. "Rebel Yell Raised by Dixie Veterans to Honor Wilson," *Atlanta Constitution*, June 6, 1917.

131. A woman at one gathering thanked "you grand old men who guarded with your lives the virgin whiteness of our Georgia." See Gaines M. Foster, *Ghosts of the Confederacy: Defeat, the Lost Cause, and the Emergence of the New South* (New York: Oxford University Press, 1987 ed.), 136; Aaron Sheehan-Dean, *Why Confederates Fought: Family and Nation in Civil War Virginia* (Chapel Hill: University of North Carolina Press, 2007).

132. "Rebel Yell Raised by Dixie Veterans to Honor Wilson," *Atlanta Constitution*, June 6, 1917.

133. Quoted in "Views of Capital Visitors on Interesting Current Events," *Washington Post*, June 5, 1917. For elites supporting the war, see Keith, *Rich Man's War, Poor Man's Fight*; "Registration Day in Georgia Marked by Sincere Patriotism," *Atlanta Constitution*, June 6, 1917; "Registration Holds Governor in Georgia," *Atlanta Constitution*, June 6, 1917; "Confederate Veteran Urges Full Registration Today," *Atlanta Constitution*, June 2, 1917.

134. See "Favorable Report Made for U. of A. Training Corps," *Crimson White* (Tuscaloosa, Ala.), Sept. 21, 1916. For preparedness see Kennedy, *Over Here*, 30–36; Coffman, *War to End All Wars*, 14–18.

135. Enlistment number from Keith, *Rich Man's War, Poor Man's Fight*, 43.

136. *Congressional Record*, House, 65th Congress, 1st sess., Apr. 5, 1917, 374.

137. *Congressional Record*, House, 65th Congress, 1st sess., Apr. 5, 1917, 350.

138. *Congressional Record*, House, 65th Congress, 1st sess., Apr. 5, 1917, 373.

139. See Keith, *Rich Man's War, Poor Man's Fight*, 34–36; "Debate Lasted 16 ½ Hours," *New York Times*, Apr. 6, 1917; *Congressional Record*, House, 65th Congress, 1st sess., Apr. 5, 1917, 413; Apr. 28, 1917, 1557.

140. Eighty percent figure from Keith, *Rich Man's War, Poor Man's Fight*, 1.

141. See "Great Wave of Patriotism Sweeps Over City," *Montgomery* (Ala.) *Advertiser*, June 6, 1917; "Is Your Boy in the War?", *Selma* (Ala.) *Mirror*, June 15, 1917.

142. George Waring Huston to Robert Huston, May 25, 1917, folder 6; George Waring Huston to Nellye Huston, June 10, 1917, folder 5; box 1080, Huston Papers, UASC.

143. George Waring Huston to Nellye Huston, May 26, 1917 (first ltr.), folder 6, box 1080, Huston Papers, UASC.

144. George Waring Huston to Nellye Huston, June 10, 1917, folder 5, box 1080, Huston Papers, UASC.

145. See Luebke, *Bonds of Loyalty*, 225–59; quotation on 234.

146. "Roosevelt Would Ostracize Slackers," *New York Times*, June 8, 1917.

147. "Antidraft Revolt Is Under Control," *Selma* (Ala.) *Mirror*, Aug. 3, 1917.

148. "Comment on Passing Events Heard in Washington Hotels," *Washington Post*, June 6, 1917.

149. Quoted in Thomas, *Unsafe for Democracy*, 120.

150. "Man Who Hid to Resist Conscription Is Killed," *Washington Post*, June 6, 1917; "Draft Opponent Shot to Death," *Atlanta Constitution*, June 6, 1917.

151. Theodore Roosevelt, "American Preparedness," in *The European War*, vol. 4, July–Sept. 1915, *Current History* (New York: The New York Times Company, 1915), 841. See also Slotkin, *Lost Battalions*, 32.

152. See Theda Skocpol, *Protecting Soldiers and Mothers: The Political Origins of Social Policy in the United States* (Cambridge: Belknap Press of Harvard University Press, 1992).

153. "Quiet Registration Gratifies Freschi," *New York Times*, June 6, 1917.

154. "Young Americans Expected to Rally for Registration," *Atlanta Constitution*, June 4, 1917.

155. "Registers in Prison Cell as His Sister Sobs Plea," *Washington Post*, June 6, 1917.

156. See "Columbia Student Is Arrested Again," *New York Times*, June 6, 1917; "Draft Slackers Must Face Trial," *New York Times*, June 7, 1917; "The Slacker," *Nashville Tennessean*, Oct. 7, 1917.

157. See Zieger, *America's Great War*, 137.

158. "Troops Quell Antidraft Demonstration in Butte," *Washington Post*, June 6, 1917.

159. "Antidraft Mob Riots," *Washington Post*, June 5, 1917.

160. "Billy Sunday Wins 1,000 Bluejackets," *Daily Independent* (Harrisonburg, Va.), June 6, 1917.

161. See Kathleen Kennedy, *Disloyal Mothers and Scurrilous Citizens: Women and Subversion during World War I* (Bloomington: Indiana University Press, 1999); Susan Zeiger, "She Didn't Raise Her Boy to Be a Slacker: Motherhood, Conscription, and the Culture of the First World War," *Feminist Studies* 22 (Spring 1996): 7–39; Rebecca Jo Plant, *Mom: The Transformation of Motherhood in Modern America* (Chicago: University of Chicago Press, 2010); Brewer, *Why America Fights*, 67; Zieger, *America's Great War*, 137.

162. See "Near Riot Over Draft," *Baltimore Sun*, June 5, 1917.

163. See Paul L. Murphy, *World War I and the Origin of Civil Liberties in the United States* (New York: W. W. Norton, 1979), 212; Geoffrey R. Stone, *Perilous Times: Free Speech in Wartime from the Sedition Act of 1798 to the War on Terrorism* (New York: W. W. Norton, 2004), 146; Mayers, *Dissenting Voices in America's Rise to Power*, 240.

164. Quoted in Stone, *Perilous Times*, 172.
165. See Kennedy, *Disloyal Mothers and Scurrilous Citizens*, 18–19.
166. See Stone, *Perilous Times*, 164–68.
167. "War Time Weddings and How They Are Celebrated Abroad," *Atlanta Constitution*, July 1, 1917.
168. Statistic from Capozzola, *Uncle Sam Wants You*, 28. George Huston draft registration card, June 5, 1917, Dallas County, Ala.; *Draft Registration Cards, 1917–1918* (FHL roll 1509378); RG 163; NARA-Southeast.
169. See Luebke, *Bonds of Loyalty*, 48, 202; Neiberg, *Path to War*, 85–86.
170. Arthur Huebner draft registration card, Jefferson County, Wisc.; *Draft Registration Cards, 1917–1918* (FHL roll 1674737); RG 163; NARA-Southeast.

Chapter 2: Make Your Daddy Glad

1. See Mae Bilbrey to Eliga Dees, July 6 and 15, 1917, Eliga and Mae Dees Letters (Dees Letters), Collection R1453, State Historical Society of Missouri, Columbia, Mo. (SHSM).
2. "Oglethorpe Has Grown More than Three-fold," *Trench and Camp* (Fort Oglethorpe ed.), Oct. 8, 1917.
3. See Eliga Dees Service Record; Missouri Digital Heritage; Soldiers' Records: War of 1812—World War I, *sos.mo.gov/archives/soldiers* (June 10, 2014); *The Gold Chevron: A History of the Fifty-Third U.S. Infantry*, p. 5; box 12; Records of the 6th Division, 53rd Inf. Regt.; Combat Divisions, 1917–1919; Records of the American Expeditionary Forces (World War I), Record Group 120; National Archives and Records Administration, College Park, Md.
4. "Expansion Camp Named in Honor of Gen. Forrest," *Trench and Camp* (Fort Oglethorpe ed.), Jan. 28, 1918.
5. Mae Bilbrey to Eliga Dees, July 15, 1917, Dees Letters, SHSM.
6. See Susan J. Matt, *Homesickness: An American History* (New York: Oxford University Press, 2011), 3.
7. For comparative censorship see Martha Hanna, *Your Death Would Be Mine: Paul and Marie Pireaud in the Great War* (Cambridge: Harvard University Press, 2006), 9; Martha Hanna, "War Letters: Communication between Front and Home Front," in Ute Daniel et al., eds., *1914–1918 Online: International Encyclopedia of the First World War* (Berlin: Freie Universität Berlin, 2014); Eberhard Demm, "Censorship," in Ute Daniel et al., eds., *1914–1918 Online: International Encyclopedia of the First World War* (Berlin: Freie Universität Berlin, 2014); William G. Rosenberg, "Reading Soldiers' Moods: Russian Military Censorship and the Configuration of Feeling in World War I," *American Historical Review* 119 (June 2014): 714–40.
8. See Mary L. Dudziak, *War-Time: An Idea, Its History, Its Consequences* (New York: Oxford University Press, 2012), 21.

9. Mae Bilbrey to Eliga Dees, Apr. 12, 1917, Dees Letters, SHSM.

10. George Waring Huston to Nellye Huston, June 15, 1917, folder 5, box 1080, Huston Family Papers (Huston Papers), W. S. Hoole Special Collections Library, University of Alabama, Tuscaloosa, Ala. (UASC).

11. George Waring Huston to Nellye Huston, June 3, 1917, folder 5, box 1080, Huston Papers, UASC.

12. George Waring Huston to Nellye Huston, June 1, 1917, folder 6, box 1080, Huston Papers, UASC.

13. Harry Huston to Nellye Huston, May 29, 1917, folder 12, box 1080, Huston Papers, UASC.

14. See "Williamsville Gives Nine to Uncle Sam," *Wayne County* (Mo.) *Journal*, Apr. 26, 1917; "Williamsville News," *Greenville* (Mo.) *Sun*, May 3, 1917.

15. See Susan Zeiger, "She Didn't Raise Her Boy to Be a Slacker: Motherhood, Conscription, and the Culture of the First World War," *Feminist Studies* 22 (Spring 1996): 7–39.

16. See "Songwriters Doing Their Bit in War," *New York Times*, July 29, 1917; Cecilia Elizabeth O'Leary, *To Die For: The Paradox of American Patriotism* (Princeton: Princeton University Press, 1999), 227.

17. "Patriots—Meet the Mother of the Chicago Gracchi," *Chicago Daily Tribune*, Aug. 3, 1917.

18. "Woman Has 4 Sons and 2 Daughters in War Service," *St. Louis Post-Dispatch*, Aug. 20, 1917.

19. "Savannah Father Gives '24 Feet of Fighting Manhood' . . . ," *Atlanta Constitution*, Aug. 5, 1917; "A Wisconsin War Mother," *Watertown* (Wisc.) *News*, Dec. 7, 1917.

20. "Mother's Plea to Mother Adds a Son to the Army," *Chicago Daily Tribune*, July 7, 1917.

21. "To What End, O God?", *Greenville* (Mo.) *Sun*, July 12, 1917.

22. "Bringing the War Home to an Ozark Suffragist," *St. Louis Post-Dispatch*, July 8, 1917.

23. "A Mother and Her Sons," *Chicago Daily Tribune*, Sept. 8, 1917.

24. See "Life's Uncertainty in Peace or War," *Atlanta Constitution*, Sept. 9, 1917; "Tragedy of Ruthlessness," *Washington Post*, Sept. 9, 1917.

25. "Why Misfortune Makes a Man Want His Mother . . .," *Nashville Tennessean*, Sept. 16, 1917.

26. See "End This War, Addams Party Plea to Women," *Chicago Daily Tribune*, Aug. 13, 1917; Zeiger, "She Didn't Raise Her Boy to be a Slacker," 7–39; Kimberly Jensen, *Mobilizing Minerva: American Women in the First World War* (Urbana: University of Illinois Press, 2008), 33.

27. "The Business of Living," *Eau Claire* (Wisc.) *Leader*, June 6, 1917.

28. "The Business of Living," *Eau Claire* (Wisc.) *Leader*, June 6, 1917.

29. "The Business of Living," *Eau Claire* (Wisc.) *Leader*, June 16, 1917.

30. "The Business of Living," *Eau Claire* (Wisc.) *Leader*, June 15, 1917.

31. "Former Greenville Boys in U.S. Service," *Greenville* (Mo.) *Sun*, Aug. 23, 1917.

32. "The Business of Living," *Eau Claire* (Wisc.) *Leader*, June 16, 1917.

33. See John Whiteclay Chambers II, *To Raise an Army: The Draft Comes to Modern America* (New York: The Free Press, 1987), 185; Jennifer D. Keene, *Doughboys, the Great War, and the Remaking of America* (Baltimore: Johns Hopkins University Press, 2001), 18.

34. See Jeanette Keith, *Rich Man's War, Poor Man's Fight: Race, Class, and Power in the Rural South during the First World War* (Chapel Hill: University of North Carolina Press, 2004), 10, 63.

35. See Gerald E. Shenk, *"Work or Fight!" Race, Gender, and the Draft in World War One* (New York: Palgrave Macmillan, 2005); Kennedy, *Over Here*, 162; Chambers, *To Raise an Army*, 225–26. For black draftees see Arthur E. Barbeau and Florette Henri, *The Unknown Soldiers: Black American Troops in World War I* (Philadelphia: Temple University Press, 1974), 36.

36. Ninety percent figure from Susan A. Brewer, *Why America Fights: Patriotism and War Propaganda from the Philippines to Iraq* (New York: Oxford University Press, 2009), 55. For changes to the draft see Keene, *Doughboys*, 18–19.

37. Quoted in Keene, *Doughboys*, 18.

38. Broadly speaking, in France, Germany, and Austria-Hungary, where the overrunning of homelands was a fact or real possibility, men with families had much to lose, and the state pursued maximum participation for total war, married men faced conscription. But in Canada, parts of Russia, and even Britain, the drafting of married men in particular proved controversial. For these and other belligerent states see Ian F. W. Beckett, *The Great War* (London: Pearson Longman, 2007 ed.), 93, 282–89; Susan R. Grayzel, *Women's Identities at War: Gender, Motherhood, and Politics in Britain and France during the First World War* (Chapel Hill: University of North Carolina Press, 1999), 35–6; David Stevenson, *Cataclysm: The First World War as Political Tragedy* (New York: Basic Books, 2004), 161–67.

39. Quoted in Nancy K. Bristow, *Making Men Moral: Social Engineering during the Great War* (New York: New York University Press, 1996), 2. See also Kristin L. Hoganson, *Fighting for American Manhood: How Gender Politics Provoked the Spanish-American and Philippine-American Wars* (New Haven: Yale University Press, 1998), 189.

40. For this paragraph and Baker quotation see Bristow, *Making Men Moral*, 7, 15.

41. "Real Life Starts at Training Camp," *Atlanta Constitution*, May 16, 1917.

42. "Training Camp Where Future Funstons Are Being Formed," *Atlanta Constitution*, May 20, 1917.

43. "Holiday Is Enjoyed by Student Officers, *Atlanta Constitution*, May 31, 1917. For Waring see George Waring Huston to Nellye Huston, May 30, 1917, folder 6, box 1080, Huston Papers, UASC.

44. See "Hours Are Fixed for Visiting Fort," *Atlanta Constitution*, May 19, 1917.

45. See "M'Pherson Y.M.C.A. Dedicated Tonight," *Atlanta Constitution*, May 27, 1917; "In the Social Whirl," *Atlanta Constitution*, June 10, 1917.

46. See Zeiger, "She Didn't Raise Her Boy to Be a Slacker," 7–39.

47. "Hostess House at Camp Devens," *Christian Science Monitor*, Apr. 19, 1918.

48. See George Waring Huston to Nellye Huston, June 17, 1917, folder 5, box 1080, Huston Papers, UASC; Selma City Directory, 1916–1917, vol. 3, p. 43, *U.S., City Directories, 1822–1995* (Provo: Ancestry.com Operations, Inc., 2011), *Ancestry.com* (July 28, 2016).

49. See Willis Brewer, *Alabama, Her History, Resources, War Record, and Public Men: from 1540 to 1872* (Montgomery, Ala.: Barrett & Brown, 1872), 207–8.

50. Marriage and Birth Certificates of the Huston family, 1800s, folder 21, box 1080, Huston Papers, UASC; S [*sic*] Waring Smith family; p. 16B, lines 53–56, Enumeration District 0096, Selma, Dallas County, Ala. Census of Population; *Thirteenth Census of the United States, 1910* (National Archives Microfilm Publication [NAMP] T624, roll 11); Records of the Bureau of the Census, Record Group 29 (RG 29); National Archives Building, Washington, D.C. (NAB); Nellie [*sic*] Huston; p. 14B, line 94, Enumeration District 0043, Selma City, Dallas County, Ala. Census of Population; *Twelfth Census of the United States, 1900* (NAMP T623, roll 14); RG 29; NAB; George Waring Smith death record, *Alabama, Deaths and Burials Index, 1881–1974* (Provo: Ancestry.com Operations, Inc., 2011), *Ancestry.com* (July 26, 2013); Peter Hamilton family; p. 628, lines 11–16, Mobile, Mobile County, Ala. Census of Population; *Eighth Census of the United States, 1860* (NAMP M653, roll 17); RG 29; NAB.

51. See Guide to Huston Papers, UASC, *www.lib.ua.edu/content/findingaids/pdf/ms_0724.pdf* (Aug. 8, 2014); William Stanley Hoole, *Historical Sketch of the Fifth Alabama Infantry Regiment, C. S. A.* (University, Ala.: Confederate Publishing Co., 1985), Alabama Collection, UASC. See Marriage and Birth Certificates of the Huston family, 1800s, folder 21, box 1080, Huston Papers, UASC; W. H. Huston service record, 1 Class Alabama Militia; William Huston service record, 5th Alabama Cavalry Regiment; *U.S., Civil War Soldiers, 1861–1865* (Provo: Ancestry.com Operations, Inc., 2007), *Ancestry.com* (Aug. 7, 2013).

52. See Brewer, *Alabama, Her History, Resources, War Record, and Public Men*, 209–10; Walter M. Jackson, *The Story of Selma* (Birmingham, Ala.: Birmingham Printing Co., 1954), 197–219; Ona Stewart Morrison, *The Battle of Selma* (pamphlet) and "Wilson's Selma Raid," from *Civil War Times*, Battle of Selma folder, Edwin Condie Godbold Local History Collection, Selma-Dallas County Public Library, Selma, Ala.

53. Wm. H. Huston family, p. 405B, lines 21–29, Mobile, Mobile County, Ala. Census of Population; *Ninth Census of the United States, 1870*

(NAMP M593, roll 31); RG 29; NAB; W. H. Huston family, p. 468C, lines 22–31, Enumeration District 072, Selma, Dallas County, Ala. Census of Population; *Tenth Census of the United States, 1880* (NAMP T9, roll 11); RG 29; NAB; Robert W. Huston family; p. 14B, lines 93–100, Enumeration District 0043, Selma, Dallas County, Ala. Census of Population; *Twelfth Census of the United States, 1900* (NAMP T623, roll 14); RG 29; NAB; Marie Whaley McLaughlin and Carolyn Ward Vintson, comps., *Dallas County Alabama Marriage Records, 1818–1918* (Selma, Ala.: Prestige Research and Publishing, 1992), 105.

54. See Alston Fitts III, *Selma: Queen City of the Black Belt* (Selma, Ala.: Clairmont Press, 1989), 85–104.

55. George Huston draft registration card, June 5, 1917, Dallas County, Ala.; *Draft Registration Cards, 1917–1918* (Family History Library Microfilm [FHL] roll 1509378); Records of the Selective Service System (World War I), 1917–1939, Record Group 163 (RG 163); National Archives and Records Administration-Southeast Region, Morrow, Ga. (NARA-Southeast).

56. See John W. Scott, *Natalie Scott: A Magnificent Life* (Gretna, La.: Pelican Publishing Co., 2008), 22.

57. See Scott, *Natalie Scott*, 48–50.

58. "War Time Weddings and How They Are Celebrated Abroad," *Atlanta Constitution*, July 1, 1917.

59. "Send Me Away with a Smile," *www.firstworldwar.com* (Aug. 30, 2013).

60. Mae Bilbrey to Eliga Dees, July 6, 1917, Dees Letters, SHSM.

61. Mae Bilbrey to Eliga Dees, July 15, 1917, Dees Letters, SHSM.

62. Mae Bilbrey to Eliga Dees, July 15, 1917, Dees Letters, SHSM.

63. Mae Bilbrey to Eliga Dees, Apr. 12 and July 6, 1917; Mar. 8, 1918; Dees Letters, SHSM.

64. Mae Bilbrey to Eliga Dees, July 6, 1917, Dees Letters, SHSM.

65. See p. 203A, lines 21, 30, 34, 40, Enumeration District 101, Wayne County, Mo. Census of Population; *Seventh Census of the United States, 1850* (NAMP M432, roll 421); p. 631, lines 9, 15, 23, 29, St. Francois Township, Wayne County, Mo. Census of Population; *Eighth Census of the United States, 1860* (NAMP M653, roll 660); p. 217B, lines 7, 17, St. Francois Township, Wayne County, Mo. Census of Population; *Ninth Census of the United States, 1870* (NAMP M593, roll 825); RG 29; NAB. See also Rose Fulton Cramer, *Wayne County, Missouri* (Cape Girardeau, Mo.: Ramfre Press, 1972), 480; Mae Bilbrey Dees, *Wayne County, Missouri: A Little Bit of God's Country* (1968), p. 24; Publication f. 103, Russell and Bernadine How Collection, State Historical Society of Missouri, Columbia, Mo.

66. See Cramer, *Wayne County*, 139–88, 229; James McPherson, *Battle Cry of Freedom: The Civil War Era* (New York: Oxford University Press, 1988), 290–93, 783–88.

67. Draft officials noted Elijah was "Enrolled in Militia." See Elijah Dees draft registration record, Wayne County, Mo.; *Consolidated Lists of Civil War*

Draft Registrations, 1863–1865 (NM 65, entry 172); Records of the Provost Marshal General's Bureau (Civil War), Record Group 110 (RG 110); NAB. Jonathan Dees survived service with the Seventh Kansas Cavalry and is buried in Dees Cemetery. See *freepages.genealogy.rootsweb.ancestry.com/ ~wcmc/dees_chapel/dees_jonathan_1.JPG* (May 28, 2014); Dees, *Wayne County*, 25; Cramer, *Wayne County*, 188, 554.

68. Quoted in Christopher C. Gibbs, *The Great Silent Majority: Missouri's Resistance to World War I* (Columbia: University of Missouri Press, 1988), 6.

69. See John, Ida, and Minnie Bilbrey; p. 11B, line 65–67; William, Sarah, and Elijah [Lige] Dees; p. 9A, lines 1, 2, 8; Enumeration District 150, Black River Township, Wayne County, Mo. Census of Population; *Twelfth Census of the United States, 1900* (NAMP T623, roll 907); RG 29; NAB; Cramer, *Wayne County*, 316, 378–82, 621–30.

70. See Keene, *Doughboys*, 10–11; Edward M. Coffman, *The War to End All Wars: The American Military Experience in World War I* (Lexington: University Press of Kentucky, 1998 ed.), 28; Shenk, "*Work or Fight!*" 4–5.

71. For army organization see Keene, *Doughboys*, 8–16.

72. See Barbeau and Henri, *Unknown Soldiers*, 75.

73. See Frederic Louis Huidekoper, *The History of the 33rd Division, A. E. F.*, Vol. 1 (Springfield, Ill.: Illinois State Historical Library, 1921), 1; Chad L. Williams, *Torchbearers of Democracy: African American Soldiers in the World War I Era* (Chapel Hill: University of North Carolina Press, 2010), 32–39; Barbeau and Henri, *Unknown Soldiers*, 26–32.

74. See Adriane Lentz-Smith, *Freedom Struggles: African Americans and World War I* (Cambridge: Harvard University Press, 2009), 39–42; Richard Slotkin, *Lost Battalions: The Great War and the Crisis of American Nationality* (New York: Henry Holt, 2005), 48–51; Williams, *Torchbearers of Democracy*, 80–1; Keene, *Doughboys*, 20–23.

75. "Young College Men Show Pluck," *Cleveland Gazette*, June 9, 1917.

76. Quotations from Lentz-Smith, *Freedom Struggles*, 52, 70, 76–77.

77. See Robert V. Haynes, "The Houston Mutiny and Riot of 1917," *Southwestern Historical Quarterly* 76 (Apr. 1973): 418–39; "Soldiers Pay for Grime [*sic*] With Lives" and "South Best Place for the Negro," *Selma* (Ala.) *Mirror*, Dec. 14, 1917.

78. See Williams, *Torchbearers of Democracy*, 67, 80–81; Keene, *Doughboys*, 23.

79. See Barbeau and Henri, *Unknown Soldiers*, 71–75; Nimrod T. Frazer, *Send the Alabamians: World War I Fighters in the Rainbow Division* (Tuscaloosa: University of Alabama Press, 2014), 41; Slotkin, *Lost Battalions*, 51–71.

80. See "More Registrants Are Summoned," *Jefferson County* (Wisc.) *Union*, Aug. 17, 1917; "180 Men Called in Second Draft," *Watertown* (Wisc.) *News*, Aug. 10, 1917; Daniel McCarthy; p. 3A, line 16, Enumeration

District 158, Watertown Town, Jefferson County, Wisc. Census of Population; *Twelfth Census of the United States, 1900* (NAMP T623, roll 1793); RG 29; NAB.

81. "Only 16 Registers Rejected on Saturday," *Watertown* (Wisc.) *News*, Aug. 6, 1917.

82. Quoted in Keene, *Doughboys*, 25–26.

83. See Roger Daniels, *Guarding the Golden Door: American Immigration Policy and Immigrants since 1882* (New York: Hill and Wang, 2004), 9; Frederick C. Luebke, *Bonds of Loyalty: German Americans and World War I* (De Kalb: Northern Illinois University Press, 1974), 28; Charles J. Wallman, *The German-Speaking 48ers: Builders of Watertown, Wisconsin* (Madison: Max Kade Institute, 1992), 3–4; Elmer C. Kiessling, *Watertown Remembered* (Watertown, Wisc.: Watertown Historical Society, 1976), Kindle electronic ed., loc. 139 and 818.

84. For Old Lutherans and the Braunschweigs see Wilhelm Iwan, *Die Altlutherische Auswanderung um die Mitte des 19. Jahrhunderts* (*The Old Lutheran Emigration at the Middle of the 19th Century*), Vol. 2 (Ludwigsburg: Eichhorn Publishing, 1943), 281–83. See also Luebke, *Bonds of Loyalty*, 37–43; Wallman, *German-Speaking 48ers*, 7–8, 82–91; Kiessling, *Watertown Remembered*, Kindle ed., loc. 1352–68; James S. Pula, *The Sigel Regiment: A History of the Twenty-Sixth Wisconsin Volunteer Infantry, 1862–1865* (Campbell, Calif.: Savas Publishing Co., 1998), 8–13.

85. See Christian Huebner to Ernstine Finkelday, Feb. 6, 1924, author's collection; Luebke, *Bonds of Loyalty*, 29.

86. For Christian's date of arrival, June 17, 1887, see Pauline Roge to Ernstine Dey, July 18, 1887, author's collection.

87. See William H. Thomas, Jr., *Unsafe for Democracy: World War I and the U.S. Justice Department's Covert Campaign to Suppress Dissent* (Madison: University of Wisconsin Press, 2008), 111–12; David Laskin, *The Long Way Home: An American Journey from Ellis Island to the Great War* (New York: Harper Perennial, 2011), 100.

88. George Waring Smith death record, *Alabama, Deaths and Burials Index, 1881–1974* (Provo: Ancestry.com Operations, Inc., 2011), *Ancestry. com* (July 26, 2013); S [*sic*] Waring Smith family; p. 16B, lines 53–56, Enumeration District 0096, Selma, Dallas County, Ala. Census of Population; *Thirteenth Census of the United States, 1910* (NAMP T624, roll 11); RG 29; NAB.

89. "Their Boy," *Selma* (Ala.) *Mirror*, Aug. 3, 1917.

90. Halstead Dorey to George Waring Huston, Aug. 10, 1917, folder 11, box 1080, Huston Papers, UASC.

91. "How U.S. War Insurance Will Provide for Soldiers' Families . . . ," *St. Louis Post-Dispatch*, Aug. 19, 1917.

92. Quoted in "Proposed System of Government Insurance . . . ," Committee on Public Information, *Official Bulletin*, Aug. 10, 1917, vol. 1, no. 78, p. 8.

93. See "McAdoo Urges Quick Action on War Insurance Bill . . . ," *Baltimore Sun*, Aug. 19, 1917; "Insurance for Families of Those Fighting Our War . . . ," *Washington Post*, Aug. 19, 1917.

94. Quoted in "Women Aid War Insurance Bill," Committee on Public Information, *Official Bulletin*, Aug. 23, 1917, vol. 1, no. 89, p. 4.

95. See Paul H. Douglas, "The War Risk Insurance Act," *Journal of Political Economy* 26 (May 1918): 461; Keene, *Doughboys*, 73; Linker, *War's Waste*, 1–9, 29–33; Stephen R. Ortiz, *Beyond the Bonus March and GI Bill: How Veteran Politics Shaped the New Deal Era* (New York: New York University Press, 2010), 14–15; Erika Kuhlman, *Of Little Comfort: War Widows, Fallen Soldiers, and the Remaking of the Nation after the Great War* (New York: New York University Press, 2012), 79–81.

96. Quoted in Scott, *Natalie Scott*, 50.

97. Quoted in Scott, *Natalie Scott*, 59–60.

98. For the voyage to France see Scott, *Natalie Scott*, 51–61.

99. Thomas Alexander Boyd to Mother, Aug. 10, 1917; Thomas Alexander Boyd to Aunt Marion, Sept. 13, 1917; folder 1, box 1, Thomas Boyd Papers (Boyd Papers), Ohio Historical Society, Columbus, Ohio (OHS).

100. See Thomas Boyd, *Through the Wheat: A Novel of the World War I Marines* (Lincoln: University of Nebraska Press, 2000), vi–vii; Martin Gus Gulberg, *A War Diary* (Chicago: The Drake Press, 1927), 5–8.

101. See "Eighteen Men Are Called in Third Draft," *Watertown* (Wisc.) *News*, Sept. 28, 1917; "Those Passed by District Board," *Greenville* (Mo.) *Sun*, Sept. 6, 1917.

102. Arthur Huebner to Otto Huebner, Oct. 1917, author's collection.

103. "Enfilade from the 331st 'M.G.'," *Trench and Camp* (Camp Grant ed.), Nov. 19, 1917; Interview with James R. Huebner, Aug. 4, 2012, Fish Creek, Wisc.

104. "I Can't Go to the Front—But—," *Watertown* (Wisc.) *News*, Oct. 22, 1917.

105. Christian Huebner to Ernstine Finkelday, Feb. 6, 1924, Orange Co., Calif., author's collection.

106. See George Waring Huston to Nellye Huston, Sept. 8, 1917, folder 5, box 1080, Huston Papers, UASC; "War of 1917," *Trench and Camp* (Fort Oglethorpe ed.), Nov. 12, 1917.

107. See Walter M. Whitman, *The Story of the 325th* (Bordeaux: Saugnac and Drouillard, 1919), 4; G. Edward Buxton, Jr., *Official History of Eighty-Second Division, American Expeditionary Forces, 1917–1919* (Indianapolis: Bobbs-Merrill Co. Publishers, 1920), 1; "Contractors Rush Cantonment Work on Eve of Opening," *Atlanta Constitution*, Sept. 3, 1917.

108. Statistic from Coffman, *War to End All Wars*, 31; the number was 687,000 according to "Final Draft Oct. 17," *Watertown* (Wisc.) *News*, Oct. 3, 1917. Buxton, Jr., *Official History of 82nd Division*, 1, lists Ga., Ala., and Tenn.;

mention of Fla. draftees in "Young Officers Assigned to Commands," *Atlanta Constitution*, Sept. 4, 1917.

109. Quoted in Coffman, *War to End All Wars*, 20.

110. "Weather Prophecy," *Atlanta Constitution*, Sept. 9, 1917.

111. R. H. Agee to George Waring Huston, Sept. 3, 1917, folder 11, box 1080, Huston Papers, UASC.

112. George Waring Huston to Nellye Huston, Sept. 8, 1917, folder 5, box 1080, Huston Papers, UASC.

113. *Trench and Camp* (Camp Grant ed.), Oct. 14, 1917.

114. George Waring Huston to Robert Huston, Sept. 1915[?], folder 7, box 1080, Huston Papers, UASC.

115. George Waring Huston to Nellye Huston, Sept. 9 and 10 (second ltr.), 1917, folder 5, box 1080, Huston Papers, UASC.

116. "Young Officers Assigned to Commands," *Atlanta Constitution*, Sept. 4, 1917.

117. "Great Draft Army Begins Gathering for War Lessons," *Atlanta Constitution*, Sept. 6, 1917.

118. George Waring Huston to Nellye Huston, Sept. 8, 1917, folder 5, box 1080, Huston Papers, UASC.

Chapter 3: Tell Your Sweetheart Not to Pine

1. See "Resistance to Draft," *Greenville* (Mo.) *Sun*, Aug. 23, 1917; "Wayne County Has Full Quota," *Greenville* (Mo.) *Sun*, Sept. 27, 1917.

2. "Day of Bachelor," *Greenville* (Mo.) *Sun*, Aug. 9, 1917.

3. See "Wayne County Boys off for Training Camp," *Greenville* (Mo.) *Sun*, Sept. 27, 1917; "Demonstration for Soldier Boys," *Greenville* (Mo.) *Sun*, Aug. 23, 1917; "Williamsville High School Notes," *Greenville* (Mo.) *Sun*, Sept. 27, 1917; "Second Contingent leaves for Camp Funston, Kansas," *Greenville* (Mo.) *Sun*, Oct. 4, 1917.

4. *Trench and Camp* (Fort Oglethorpe ed.), Oct. 29, 1917.

5. Mae Bilbrey to Eliga Dees, Apr. 12, 1917, Eliga and Mae Dees Letters (Dees Letters), Collection R1453, State Historical Society of Missouri, Columbia, Mo. (SHSM).

6. See "Y. M. C. A. Rally at Christian Church" and "Williamsville High School Notes," *Greenville* (Mo.) *Sun*, Nov. 15, 1917; "About $6,000 Raised in County Y. M. C. A. Drive" and "From Wayne County Boys at Camp Funston," *Greenville* (Mo.) *Sun*, Nov. 22, 1917.

7. "Camp Gordon Will Welcome 5000 New Draft Men Today," *Atlanta Constitution*, Sept. 19, 1917; "Regiments to Full War Strength Will Be Mustered in Wednesday," *Atlanta Constitution*, Oct. 5, 1917.

8. Quotation and information on transfers from "Georgia and Alabama Men in 325th Infantry Go First to Wheeler," *Atlanta Constitution*, Oct. 13, 1917; Walter M. Whitman, *The Story of the 325th* (Bordeaux: Saugnac and Drouillard, 1919), 4; G. Edward Buxton, Jr., *Official History of*

Eighty-Second Division, American Expeditionary Forces, 1917–1919 (Indianapolis: Bobbs-Merrill Co. Publishers, 1920), 1–2.

9. See Jennifer D. Keene, *Doughboys, the Great War, and the Remaking of America* (Baltimore: Johns Hopkins University Press, 2001), 37; Edward M. Coffman, *The War to End All Wars: The American Military Experience in World War I* (Lexington: University Press of Kentucky, 1998 ed.), 66–67.

10. See Keene, *Doughboys*, 28.

11. See George Waring Huston to Nellye Huston, Sept. 10, 1917 (second ltr.), folder 5, box 1080, Huston Family Papers (Huston Papers), W. S. Hoole Special Collections Library, University of Alabama, Tuscaloosa, Ala. (UASC); "News Notes from Camp Gordon," *Atlanta Constitution*, Sept. 9, 1917.

12. "News Notes from Camp Gordon," *Atlanta Constitution*, Sept. 9, 1917.

13. See Keene, *Doughboys*, 20.

14. See Buxton, Jr., *Official History of 82nd Division*, 2; Nancy Gentile Ford, *Americans All! Foreign-born Soldiers in World War I* (College Station: Texas A&M University Press, 2001), 3, 67–87.

15. "Linguist, Sleuth, Actor, Cuban, Chinaman, All Are Among Friday's Soldier Arrivals," *Atlanta Constitution*, Nov. 10, 1917.

16. "Scores of New York's Most Prominent . . . ," *Atlanta Constitution*, Nov. 1, 1917.

17. See Christopher M. Sterba, *Good Americans: Italian and Jewish Immigrants during the First World War* (New York: Oxford University Press, 2003); Ford, *Americans All!*

18. Buxton, Jr., *Official History of 82nd Division*, 2.

19. Quoted in David Laskin, *The Long Way Home: An American Journey from Ellis Island to the Great War* (New York: Harper Perennial, 2011), 137.

20. Whitman, *Story of the 325th*, 2.

21. Richard Wheeler, ed., *Sergeant York and the Great War: His Own Life Story and War Diary* (San Antonio: Vision Forum, 2011), 76.

22. George Waring Huston to Nellye Huston, Nov. 18, 1917, folder 5, box 1080, Huston Papers, UASC.

23. See "Billy Sunday Salutes Soldiers in Audience," *Atlanta Constitution*, Nov. 19, 1917; Thekla Ellen Joiner, *Sin in the City: Chicago and Revivalism, 1880–1920* (Columbia, Mo.: University of Missouri Press, 2007), 196.

24. George Waring Huston to Nellye Huston, Nov. 18, 1917, folder 5, box 1080, Huston Papers, UASC.

25. George Waring Huston to Nellye Huston, Sept. 10, 1917, folder 5, box 1080, Huston Papers, UASC.

26. "Why I Will Be Ready on June 5th," *Boston Globe*, June 3, 1917.

27. R. Walter Huston to George Waring Huston, Dec. 20, 1917, folder 9, box 1080, Huston Papers, UASC.

28. For the course of the war in 1917 see Martin Gilbert, *The First World War: A Complete History* (New York: Henry Holt, 1994), 333–34, 363–86.

29. See Coffman, *War to End All Wars*, 149–51; Arthur E. Barbeau and Florette Henri, *The Unknown Soldiers: Black American Troops in World War I* (Philadelphia: Temple University Press, 1974), 75, 111; Richard Slotkin, *Lost Battalions: The Great War and the Crisis of American Nationality* (New York: Henry Holt, 2005).

30. Thomas Boyd, *Through the Wheat: A Novel of the World War I Marines* (Lincoln: University of Nebraska Press, 2000), vii–ix.

31. Thomas Alexander Boyd to Aunt Marion and Mother, Nov. 15, 1917, folder 1, box 1, Thomas Boyd Papers (Boyd Papers), Ohio Historical Society, Columbus, Ohio (OHS).

32. See Edward G. Lengel, *To Conquer Hell: The Meuse-Argonne, 1918* (New York: Henry Holt, 2008), 44.

33. Boyd, *Through the Wheat*, 1–2.

34. Boyd, *Through the Wheat*, 14–15. Emphasis in original.

35. Martin Gus Gulberg, *A War Diary* (Chicago: The Drake Press, 1927), 8, 10.

36. See Allan M. Brandt, *No Magic Bullet: A Social History of Venereal Disease in the United States Since 1880* (New York: Oxford University Press, 1985), 99–103.

37. Gulberg, *War Diary*, 10.

38. Thomas Alexander Boyd to Mother and Aunt Marion, Jan. 28, 1918, folder 1, box 1, Boyd Papers, OHS.

39. Thomas Alexander Boyd to Mother, Feb. 22, 1918, folder 1, box 1, Boyd Papers, OHS.

40. Boyd, *Through the Wheat*, 30.

41. See Julia F. Irwin, *Making the World Safe: The American Red Cross and a Nation's Humanitarian Awakening* (New York: Oxford University Press, 2013), 58–87.

42. Natalie Scott to Martha Scott, Dec. 18, 1917, folder 5, box 1, Correspondence, Natalie Scott Papers (Scott Papers), Manuscripts Collection 123, Louisiana Research Collection, Tulane University, New Orleans, La. (LaRC).

43. Natalie Scott to Martha Scott, Sept. 25 and 26, 1917, folder 2, box 1, Scott Papers, LaRC.

44. Quoted in Scott, *Natalie Scott*, 65.

45. Natalie Scott to Martha Scott, Sept. 26, 1917, folder 2, box 1, Scott Papers, LaRC.

46. Natalie Scott to Martha Scott, Dec. 25, 1917, folder 5, box 1, Scott Papers, LaRC.

47. Quoted in Scott, *Natalie Scott*, 70–71.

48. See John W. Scott, *Natalie Scott: A Magnificent Life* (Gretna, La.: Pelican Publishing Co., 2008), 63–89.

49. See John Ellis and Michael Cox, *The World War I Databook* (London: Aurum Press, 2001), 146; *The Gold Chevron: A History of the*

Fifty-Third U.S. Infantry, p. 5; box 12; Records of the 6th Division, Fifty-Third Inf. Regt.; Combat Divisions, 1917–1919; Records of the American Expeditionary Forces (World War I), Record Group 120 (RG 120); National Archives and Records Administration, College Park, Md. (NACP).

50. See "Regulars Begin Trench Session," *Trench and Camp* (Fort Oglethorpe ed.), Oct. 8, 1917; "For Kaiser Bill," *Trench and Camp* (Fort Oglethorpe ed.), Oct. 22, 1917.

51. See "Chickamauga Park Is No Back Number When It Comes to Building Cantonments," *Trench and Camp* (Fort Oglethorpe ed.), Oct. 22, 1917; "So Those at Home May Know Just What We Have Here at Chickamauga Park," *Trench and Camp* (Fort Oglethorpe ed.), Oct. 29, 1917.

52. For this assertion see Coffman, *War to End All Wars*, 61.

53. "Only a Volunteer," *Trench and Camp* (Fort Oglethorpe ed.), Nov. 26, 1917. A slightly different version of the verse is quoted in Keene, *Doughboys*, 15.

54. Mae Dees to Eliga Dees, May 9, 1918, Dees Letters, SHSM.

55. Wayne Turner to Mother, July 4, 1918, Wayne O. Turner Papers, 6th Division, Fifty-Third Infantry Regiment, Veterans Survey Collections, U.S. Army Heritage and Education Center, Military History Institute, Carlisle, Penn. (USAHEC).

56. "The Regular Army Man," *Trench and Camp* (Fort Oglethorpe ed.), Nov. 5, 1917.

57. "Mess Hall Gossip," *Trench and Camp* (Camp Grant ed.), Oct. 22, 1917.

58. "The Other Fellow," *Trench and Camp* (Fort Oglethorpe ed.), Dec. 10, 1917.

59. Jennifer D. Keene, *World War I: The American Soldier Experience* (Lincoln, Neb.: University of Nebraska Press, 2011), 45.

60. Coffman, *War to End All Wars*, 35, 64–65.

61. Clayton K. Slack interview (sound recording), Oct. 12, 1964, UC box 22, Wisconsin Historical Society, Madison, Wisc. (WHS). Edward M. Coffman conducted the interview.

62. "Private A. W. Krueger Writes from Camp to Friends at Home," *Watertown* (Wisc.) *News*, Sept. 26, 1917.

63. See postcard, undated, call no. M82–499, Bernhard (Ben) Fluegel Papers, WHS.

64. Nancy K. Bristow, *Making Men Moral: Social Engineering during the Great War* (New York: New York University Press, 1996), 236.

65. Army Service Experiences Questionnaire, William L. Helberg Papers, 33rd Division, 124th Machine Gun Battalion, Veterans Survey Collections, USAHEC.

66. See "Camp Grant War Whoops," *Trench and Camp* (Camp Grant ed.), Oct. 7, 1917; Keene, *Doughboys*, 29.

67. See Keene, *Doughboys*, 20, 31, 33.

68. See Keene, *World War I*, 13.

69. "Fall In," *Trench and Camp* (Fort Oglethorpe ed.), Nov. 26, 1917.

70. See Keene, *Doughboys*, 13–14.

71. For the camp routine see Keene, *World War I*, 42–43; Coffman, *War to End All Wars*, 65–66.

72. See "Rookie Writes Home to His Chums," *Trench and Camp* (Camp Grant ed.), Oct. 7, 1917; Clayton Slack interview, WHS.

73. Coffman, *War to End All Wars*, 66.

74. See images in *Trench and Camp* (Camp Grant ed.), Oct. 7 and 22, 1917; Nov. 12, 1917.

75. "Get First Workout with Machine Guns," *Trench and Camp* (Camp Grant ed.), Nov. 12, 1917.

76. Clayton Slack interview, WHS.

77. "New Machine Guns Arrive," *Watertown* (Wisc.) *Daily Times*, Oct. 28, 1917.

78. "What Is This Y. M. C. A. War Work," *Watertown* (Wisc.) *News*, Nov. 14, 1917.

79. See Bristow, *Making Men Moral*, 4–11, 35–38; Michael McGerr, *A Fierce Discontent: The Rise and the Fall of the Progressive Movement in America* (New York: Oxford University Press, 2003), 79.

80. Mark Meigs, *Optimism at Armageddon: Voices of American Participants in the First World War* (New York: New York University Press, 1997), 74.

81. See Bristow, *Making Men Moral*, 36.

82. "High Class Shows Will Be Staged at Every Camp," *Trench and Camp* (Camp Grant ed.), Nov. 5, 1917.

83. "Athletics Booming in Rockford Camp," "Boxing Hailed at Rockford," "About the Camp," *Trench and Camp* (Camp Grant ed.), Oct. 7, 1917.

84. "Machine Gunners Entertain" and "Interest Is Shown in Camp's Mass Singing," *Trench and Camp* (Camp Grant ed.), Nov. 5, 1917.

85. Draft of pamphlet, "The Girl You Leave Behind," p. 1; Records of the Commission on Training Camp Activities (CTCA), box 85; General Correspondence, 1918–1921; Records of the War Department General and Special Staffs, 1860–1952, Record Group 165; NACP.

86. Bristow, *Making Men Moral*, 30–35, 92.

87. Quoted in Elizabeth Alice Clement, *Love for Sale: Courting, Treating, and Prostitution in New York City, 1900–1945* (Chapel Hill: University of North Carolina Press, 2006), 156.

88. See Bristow, *Making Men Moral*, 14, 34–35; Clement, *Love for Sale*, 118.

89. See Keene, *Doughboys*, 24–25; Bristow, *Making Men Moral*, 107–19, 206.

90. Quoted in Brandt, *No Magic Bullet*, 97.

91. See Clement, *Love for Sale*, 115–43; Bristow, *Making Men Moral*, 30–31, 119–36; quotation on p. 31.

92. George Waring Huston to Nellye Huston, Oct. 30, 1917, folder 5, box 1080, Huston Papers, UASC.

93. George Waring Huston to Nellye Huston, Nov. 17, 1917, folder 5, box 1080, Huston Papers, UASC.

94. George Waring Huston to Nellye Huston, Nov. 30, 1917, folder 5, box 1080, Huston Papers, UASC.

95. "Mother Will Like It!" *Trench and Camp* (Fort Oglethorpe ed.), Nov. 26, 1917.

96. "A Letter from the Commander-in-Chief," *Trench and Camp* (Fort Oglethorpe ed.), Oct. 8, 1917.

97. "American Army Camps Not Plague Spots," *Trench and Camp* (Fort Oglethorpe ed.), Dec. 24, 1917; "A Word for the Y's Is Sufficient," *Trench and Camp* (Fort Oglethorpe ed.), Dec. 3, 1917; "Men Are to Be Protected from the Wild, Wild Women," *Trench and Camp* (Fort Oglethorpe ed.), Dec. 24, 1917.

98. "U.S. Soldiers' Christmas Today in Strong Contrast with Cold, Cheerless Yuletides Their Forefathers Spent in Field," *Trench and Camp* (Fort Oglethorpe ed.), Dec. 24, 1917.

99. "The Army Y.M.C.A. From A Soldier's Standpoint," *Trench and Camp* (Fort Oglethorpe ed.), Dec. 3, 1917.

100. "Men Are to Be Protected from the Wild, Wild Women," *Trench and Camp* (Fort Oglethorpe ed.), Dec. 24, 1917.

101. "The Frightfulness of Peace," *Trench and Camp* (Fort Oglethorpe ed.), Oct. 29, 1917.

102. "Our Thanksgiving," *Trench and Camp* (Fort Oglethorpe ed.), Nov. 26, 1917.

103. "Soldiers Come Back Clean," *Trench and Camp* (Fort Oglethorpe ed.), Dec. 10, 1917.

104. "Maj. Wieser Entertains Men of 11th Infantry," *Trench and Camp* (Fort Oglethorpe ed.), Dec. 24, 1917.

105. "Frank Hines, 122 F. A. Band, Wins Cartoon Contest," *Trench and Camp* (Fort Oglethorpe ed.), Nov. 26, 1917.

106. "Rookies Devise Many Ruses to Visit Home," *Trench and Camp* (Camp Grant ed.), Oct. 7, 1917.

107. "A Soldier's Letter to His Sweetheart," *Gas Attack*, Nov. 27, 1917.

108. See finding aid for Streeter's papers: *http://dlib.nyu.edu/findingaids/html/fales/streeter2/bioghist.html* (Aug. 28, 2014); "Edward Streeter, Humorist, Dies at 84," *New York Times*, Apr. 2, 1976; "Rookie Books," *Atlanta Constitution*, May 11, 1919; "Display Ad 30," *San Francisco Chronicle*, July 23, 1919.

109. "A Soldier's Letter to His Sweetheart," *Gas Attack*, Nov. 27, 1917.

110. "A Soldier's Letter to His Sweetheart," *Gas Attack*, Dec. 29, 1917.

111. Florence Elizabeth Summers, *Dere Bill: Mable's Love Letters to Her Rookie* (New York: Frederick A. Stokes Co., 1918, 1919), 2.

112. "A Soldier's Letter to His Sweetheart," *Gas Attack*, Dec. 29, 1917.

113. "Soldiers at Camp Gordon Resume Training Program This Morning," *Atlanta Constitution*, Dec. 26, 1917.

114. Request for pass from Sergeant Major Huston to Commanding Officer M. N. Patton, Dec. 27, 1917, folder 1, box 1080, Huston Papers, UASC.

115. Clayton Slack interview, WHS.
116. *Gold Chevron*, p. 5; box 12; Records of the 6th Division; RG 120; NACP.
117. "Christmas, 1917," *Trench and Camp* (Fort Oglethorpe ed.), Dec. 24, 1917.
118. "Williamsville High School Notes" and "Mississippi Important Objective for Invader," *Greenville* (Mo.) *Sun*, Dec. 6, 1917.
119. Mae Bilbrey to Eliga Dees, Mar. 8, 1918, Dees Letters, SHSM.
120. "Did You Write to Your Soldier Boy?" *Watertown* (Wisc.) *Daily Times*, Oct. 27, 1917.
121. Mae Bilbrey to Eliga Dees, Mar. 8, 1918, Dees Letters, SHSM.
122. "A Soldier's Letter to His Sweetheart," *Gas Attack*, Jan. 12, 1918.
123. "A Soldier's Letter to His Sweetheart," *Gas Attack*, Jan. 19 and Feb. 9, 1918.
124. "A Soldier's Letter to His Sweetheart," *Gas Attack*, Feb. 16, 1918.
125. "A Soldier's Letter to His Sweetheart," *Gas Attack*, Feb. 23, 1918.
126. See "Over There," *War Facts and Patriotic Songs*, p. 23, William L. Ashton Papers, 82nd Division, 325th Infantry Regiment, Veterans Survey Collections, USAHEC.
127. Mae Bilbrey to Eliga Dees, Mar. 8, 1918, Dees Letters, SHSM.
128. "German Airmen Kill Numbers of Women and Children," *Selma* (Ala.) *Journal*, Jan. 1, 1918.
129. George Waring Huston to Nellye Huston, Jan. 3, 1918, folder 1, box 1080, Huston Papers, UASC.
130. George Waring Huston to Nellye Huston, Jan. 3 and 5, 1918, folder 1, box 1080, Huston Papers, UASC.
131. See George Waring Huston to Nellye Huston, Jan. 6 and 18; Feb. 14 and 25; Mar. 4 and 13; Apr. 5, 1918; folder 1, box 1080, Huston Papers, UASC.
132. Pressley W. Cleveland to Mrs. Walter Huston, Mar. 7, 1918, folder 1, box 1080, Huston Papers, UASC.
133. Letter from John Paul Tyler, Chaplain, 325th Infantry, Camp Gordon, Atlanta, Ga., to "those who have loved ones in this regiment," Mar. 27, 1918, folder 1, box 1080, Huston Papers, UASC.
134. George Waring Huston to Nellye Huston, Apr. 5 and 9, 1918; Western Union telegram, George Waring Huston to Mrs. R. W. Huston, Apr. 10, 1918; folder 1, box 1080, Huston Papers, UASC.
135. Telephone interview with Dodge/Jefferson Counties Genealogical Society, May 29, 2014. Arthur traveling from Camp Grant is documented in *Watertown* (Wisc.) *Weltbürger*, June 11, 1921.
136. Denninger's advertisement, *Watertown* (Wisc.) *News*, July 30, 1917.
137. Coffman, *War to End All Wars*, 59.
138. Interview with James R. Huebner, Aug. 4, 2012, Fish Creek, Wisc.
139. "The Thrill That Comes Once in a Lifetime," *Trench and Camp* (Camp Grant ed.), Nov. 19, 1917.
140. Eligah [sic] Dees marriage record, *Missouri, Marriage Records, 1805–2002* (Provo: Ancestry.com Operations, Inc., 2007), *Ancestry.com* (June 23, 2014).

141. Eliga Dees to Mae Dees, Mar. 21, 1918; Mae Dees to Eliga Dees, Mar. 22, 1918, Dees Letters, SHSM.

142. "A Soldier's Letter to His Sweetheart," *Gas Attack*, Mar. 2, 1918.

143. Summers, *Dere Bill*, 97–98.

144. Mae Dees to Eliga Dees, Mar. 22, 1918, Dees Letters, SHSM.

145. Eliga Dees to Mae Dees, Mar. 21, 1918, Dees Letters, SHSM.

146. John M. Barry, *The Great Influenza: The Epic Story of the Deadliest Plague in History* (New York: Viking, 2004), 169.

147. Eliga Dees to Mae Dees, Apr. 3, 1918, Dees Letters, SHSM.

148. "A Soldier's Farewell," World War I Sheet Music Collection, Library of Congress, *www.loc.gov/collection/world-war-i-sheet-music* (Sept. 8, 2014).

149. Mae Dees to Eliga Dees, Apr. 11, 1918, Dees Letters, SHSM.

150. Mae Dees to Eliga Dees, Apr. 18, 1918, Dees Letters, SHSM.

151. Eliga Dees to Mae Dees, Apr. 16, 1918; Mae Dees to Eliga Dees, Apr. 18, 1918; Dees Letters, SHSM. For war and religion see Jonathan H. Ebel, *Faith in the Fight: Religion and the American Soldier in the Great War* (Princeton: Princeton University Press, 2010).

152. Eliga Dees to Mae Dees, May 2, 1918, Dees Letters, SHSM.

153. "Hearts of the World" advertisement, *Variety*, Mar. 29, 1918.

154. See Susan A. Brewer, *Why America Fights: Patriotism and War Propaganda from the Philippines to Iraq* (New York: Oxford University Press, 2009), 68.

155. See Committee on Public Information, *German War Practices, Part I: Treatment of Civilians*, Jan. 1918, p. 5; David M. Kennedy, *Over Here: The First World War and American Society* (New York: Oxford University Press, 2004 ed.), 62.

156. See "For the Fathers and Mothers of Soldiers," *New York Times*, Mar. 17, 1918.

157. R. W. F., *Silver Lining: The Experiences of a War Bride* (Boston: Houghton Mifflin Co., 1918); Ethel M. Kelley, *Over Here: The Story of a War Bride* (Indianapolis: Bobbs-Merrill Co., 1918).

158. Frederic Louis Huidekoper, *The History of the 33rd Division, A. E. F.*, Vol. 1 (Springfield, Ill.: Illinois State Historical Library, 1921), 3–7.

159. "Lend Him a Hand," *Watertown* (Wisc.) *News*, April 10, 1918; "Honor Flag Is Presented to Dallas County," *Selma* (Ala.) *Journal*, Apr. 5, 1918.

160. Clayton Slack interview, WHS.

161. Huidekoper, *History of the 33rd Division, A. E. F.*, Vol.1, 27.

162. *History of the 124th Machine Gun Battalion, 66th Brigade, 33rd Division, A. E. F.* (pub. unknown, 1919), 5–6, 47.

163. Huidekoper, *History of the 33rd Division, A. E. F.*, Vol.1, 30–31.

164. George Waring Huston to Nellye Huston, Apr. 20, 1918 (first ltr.), folder 2, box 1080, Huston Papers, UASC.

165. Transcribed diary, p. 1, Fred H. Takes Papers, 82nd Division, 325th Infantry Regiment, Veterans Survey Collections, USAHEC.

166. Slotkin, *Lost Battalions*, 72; Edward A. Gutiérrez, *Doughboys on the Great War: How American Soldiers Viewed Their Military Experience* (Lawrence: University Press of Kansas, 2014), 76; Whitman, *Story of the 325th*, 5; George Waring Huston to Nellye Huston, Apr. 21, 1918, folder 2, box 1080, Huston Papers, UASC.

167. George Waring Huston to Nellye Huston, Apr. 20, 1918 (first ltr.), folder 2, box 1080, Huston Papers, UASC.

168. Quoted in Chad L. Williams, *Torchbearers of Democracy: African American Soldiers in the World War I Era* (Chapel Hill: University of North Carolina Press, 2010), 86–87.

169. See Slotkin, *Lost Battalions*, 148. "Coon," "dago," and "wop" were also on the list.

170. George Waring Huston to Nellye Huston, Apr. 20, 1918 (second ltr.), folder 2, box 1080, Huston Papers, UASC.

171. See Keene, *Doughboys*, 88; Williams, *Torchbearers of Democracy*, 85.

172. George Waring Huston to Nellye Huston, Apr. 23, 1918, folder 2, box 1080, Huston Papers, UASC.

173. See Whitman, *Story of the 325th*, 5–6; Buxton, Jr., *Official History of 82nd Division*, 5; Transcribed diary, pp. 1–2, Takes Papers; Second Army Services Experiences Questionnaire, p. 6, George H. Anderson Papers, 82nd Division, 325th Infantry Regiment; Veterans Survey Collections, USAHEC.

174. See Williams, *Torchbearers of Democracy*, 80–81.

175. See Western Union telegram, Eliga Dees to Mae Dees, May 2, 1918, Dees Letters, SHSM; *Gold Chevron*, p. 5; box 12; Records of the 6th Division; RG 120; NACP.

176. See *http://ny.ng.mil/27bct/Pages/History.aspx* (Aug. 28, 2014).

177. "A Soldier's Letter to His Sweetheart," *Gas Attack*, May 4, 1918.

178. See *History of the 124th Machine Gun Battalion*, 9; Clayton Slack interview, WHS; "Give Watertown Soldier Boys a Mother's Care," *Watertown* (Wisc.) *News*, May 15, 1918.

179. "The Weather," *New York Times*, May 16, 1918; *History of the 124th Machine Gun Battalion*, 9.

Chapter 4: The Yanks Are Coming

1. See Edward M. Coffman, *The War to End All Wars: The American Military Experience in World War I* (Lexington: University Press of Kentucky, 1998 ed.), 227; Walter M. Whitman, *The Story of the 325th* (Bordeaux: Saugnac and Drouillard, 1919), 6–7; Transcribed diary, May 1–3, 6, 7, 1918, pp. 1–2, Fred H. Takes Papers (Takes Papers); Reminiscences, pp. 1–2, Knud J. Olsen Papers (Olsen Papers); Eighty-Second Division, 325th Infantry Regiment, Veterans Survey Collections, U.S. Army Heritage and Education Center, Military History Institute, Carlisle, Penn. (USAHEC).

2. Coffman, *War to End All Wars*, 227.

3. See Whitman, *Story of the 325th*, 7; Transcribed diary, May 8–10, 1918, p. 2, Takes Papers, Veterans Survey Collections, USAHEC.

4. Western Union Telegram from George Waring Huston to Nellye Huston, May 9, 1918, folder 2, box 1080, Huston Family Papers (Huston Papers), W. S. Hoole Special Collections Library, University of Alabama, Tuscaloosa, Ala. (UASC).

5. See "King Reviews Americans," *New York Times*, May 12, 1918; Whitman, *Story of the 325th*, 7–14; Transcribed diary, May 11, 1918, pp. 2–3, Takes Papers, Veterans Survey Collections, USAHEC.

6. See "King Reviews Americans," *New York Times*, May 12, 1918; Whitman, *Story of the 325th*, 9–14; "U.S. Troops Praised by London Press," *Watertown* (Wisc.) *News*, May 18, 1918; "With Bared Head Britain's Ruler Receives Troops," *Selma* (Ala.) *Journal*, May 12, 1918.

7. "King Reviews Americans," *New York Times*, May 12, 1918.

8. See Susan R. Grayzel, *Women and the First World War* (London: Longman, 2002), 12; Mark Meigs, *Optimism at Armageddon: Voices of American Participants in the First World War* (New York: New York University Press, 1997), 122.

9. See "King Reviews Americans," *New York Times*, May 12, 1918; Meigs, *Optimism at Armageddon*, 122.

10. See Susan Zeiger, *Entangling Alliances: Foreign War Brides and American Soldiers in the Twentieth Century* (New York: New York University Press, 2010), 14–24.

11. Transcribed diary, May 12, 1918, p. 3, Takes Papers, Veterans Survey Collections, USAHEC.

12. George Waring Huston to Nellye Huston, May 13, 1918, folder 2, box 1080, Huston Papers, UASC; Whitman, *Story of the 325th*, 15.

13. "Latest Racers for the Atlantic Speedway," *New York Times*, Aug. 11, 1907.

14. "German Liner Cecilie in Port at Bar Harbor," *Christian Science Monitor*, Aug. 4, 1914.

15. See *History of the 124th Machine Gun Battalion, 66th Brigade, 33rd Division, A. E. F.* (publisher unknown, 1919), 9; Clayton K. Slack interview (sound recording), Oct. 12, 1964, UC box 22, Wisconsin Historical Society, Madison, Wisc. (WHS).

16. *History of the 124th Machine Gun Battalion*, 10; Maj. Gen. John F. O'Ryan, *The Story of the 27th Division*, Vol. 1(New York: Wynkoop Hallenbeck Crawford Co., 1921), 148.

17. Edward Streeter, *Love Letters of Bill to Mable: Comprising Dere Mable, "That's Me All Over, Mable," and "Same Old Bill, eh Mable!"* (New York: Frederick A. Stokes Co., 1918, 1919), 194–95, 220.

18. See "Book Reviews," *St. Louis Post-Dispatch*, June 1, 1918.

19. Laurence Stallings, *The Doughboys: The Story of the AEF, 1917–1918* (New York: Harper and Row, 1963), 175.

20. See Allan M. Brandt, *No Magic Bullet: A Social History of Venereal Disease in the United States Since 1880* (New York: Oxford University Press, 1985),

96–121; Coffman, *War to End All Wars*, 132–34; Meigs, *Optimism at Armageddon*, 107–8; Zeiger, *Entangling Alliances*, 14–24.

21. See Steven D. Collins to David A. Keough, Oct. 23, 1997, James E. Collins Papers, 33rd Division, 124th Machine Gun Battalion, Veterans Survey Collections, USAHEC.

22. See Whitman, *Story of the 325th*, 15; G. Edward Buxton, Jr., *Official History of 82nd Division, American Expeditionary Forces, 1917–1919* (Indianapolis: Bobbs-Merrill Co. Publishers, 1920), 11; Transcribed diary, May 13–15, 1918, p. 3, Takes Papers, Veterans Survey Collections, USAHEC.

23. This material and quotation from Richard Wheeler, ed., *Sergeant York and the Great War: His Own Life Story and War Diary* (San Antonio: Vision Forum, 2011), 113–15.

24. George Waring Huston to Nellye Huston, May 30 and June 5, 1918, folder 2, box 1080, Huston Papers, UASC.

25. George Waring Huston to Nellye Huston, May 30, 1918, folder 2, box 1080, Huston Papers, UASC.

26. Transcribed diary, May 20, 1918, p. 4, Takes Papers, Veterans Survey Collections, USAHEC.

27. George Waring Huston to Nellye Huston, June 20, 1918, folder 2, box 1080, Huston Papers, UASC.

28. George Waring Huston to Nellye Huston, May 30, June 5, 11, and 13, 1918, folder 2, box 1080, Huston Papers, UASC.

29. For these movements see *History of the 124th Machine Gun Battalion*, 10–14; Clayton Slack interview, WHS.

30. See Martin Gus Gulberg, *A War Diary* (Chicago: The Drake Press, 1927), 12–21.

31. See Thomas Boyd, *Through the Wheat: A Novel of the World War I Marines* (Lincoln: University of Nebraska Press, 2000), ix; American Battle Monuments Commission, *2d Division: Summary of Operations in the World War* (Washington: U.S. Government Printing Office, 1944), 4.

32. Gulberg, *War Diary*, 22.

33. See Mark Ethan Grotelueschen, *The AEF Way of War: The American Army and Combat in World War I* (New York: Cambridge University Press, 2007), 72–83; Hew Strachan, *The First World War* (New York: Penguin Books, 2003), 298; Coffman, *War to End All Wars*, 156–58, 212–20, 262–63, 291; Martin Gilbert, *The Routledge Atlas of the First World War*, 3rd ed. (London: Routledge, 2008), 110, 112. Edward G. Lengel, *To Conquer Hell: The Meuse-Argonne, 1918* (New York: Henry Holt, 2008), 44–45.

34. John W. Scott, *Natalie Scott: A Magnificent Life* (Gretna, La.: Pelican Publishing Co., 2008), 91–93.

35. "Paris Asylum Is Victim of German Gun," *Selma* (Ala.) *Journal*, Apr. 12, 1918.

36. For Natalie in this period and for Hugh Young, see Scott, *Natalie Scott*, 81–82, 89–150.

37. Natalie Scott to Martha Scott, Dec. 18, 1917, folder 5, box 1, Correspondence, Natalie Scott Papers (Scott Papers), Manuscripts Collection 123, Louisiana Research Collection, Tulane University, New Orleans, La. (LaRC).

38. Natalie Scott to Martha Scott, Mar. 4, 1918, folder 3, box 2, Scott Papers, LaRC.

39. Natalie Scott to Martha Scott, Mar. 19, 1918, folder 3, box 2, Scott Papers, LaRC.

40. Natalie Scott to Martha Scott, Mar. 25, 1918, folder 3, box 2, Scott Papers, LaRC.

41. Natalie Scott to Martha Scott, Apr. 1, 1918, folder 3, box 2, Scott Papers, LaRC.

42. See Richard Slotkin, *Lost Battalions: The Great War and the Crisis of American Nationality* (New York: Henry Holt, 2005), 146; Michael S. Neiberg, *The Path to War: How the First World War Created Modern America* (New York: Oxford University Press, 2016), 101–2.

43. Natalie Scott to Martha Scott, May 5, 1918 [incorrectly dated 1917], folder 5, box 2, Scott Papers, LaRC.

44. See Arthur E. Barbeau and Florette Henri, *The Unknown Soldiers: Black American Troops in World War I* (Philadelphia: Temple University Press, 1974), 81.

45. See Barbeau and Henri, *Unknown Soldiers*, 111–13.

46. See Slotkin, *Lost Battalions*, 138–51; Chad L. Williams, *Torchbearers of Democracy: African American Soldiers in the World War I Era* (Chapel Hill: University of North Carolina Press, 2010), 124–27; Barbeau and Henri, *Unknown Soldiers*, 116–17.

47. See "Henry Johnson and Needham Roberts . . . ," *Cleveland Gazette*, July 27, 1918; "Hero's Relative Resides in Savannah," *Savannah Tribune*, Aug. 3, 1918; "Doing Their Duty," *Washington Bee*, Dec, 12, 1918; "Large Crowd Honors Relatives of War Heroes," *Chicago Defender*, July 6, 1918; "Courage and Cowardice," *Chicago Defender*, June 1, 1918.

48. See untitled ads in *Chicago Defender*, June 29, July 6, and Aug. 3, 1918.

49. See "The Negro Under Fire," *Atlanta Constitution*, June 26, 1918; "Privates Bill and Needham," *New York Times*, May 22, 1918; "Private Who Beat 22 Germans," *New York Times*, Oct. 31, 1918; "Southern White Daily Becomes Conscience Stricken," *Chicago Defender*, June 22, 1918.

50. Letter reprinted in "Croix de Guerre," *Washington Bee*, Sept. 14, 1918.

51. "Hero's Relative Resides in Savannah," *Savannah Tribune*, Aug. 3, 1918; "Honor Negro War Heroes," *New York Times*, June 28, 1918; "Large Crowd Honors Relatives of War Heroes," *Chicago Defender*, July 6, 1918.

52. "Woman Lynched by Brooks Co. Mob," *Atlanta Constitution*, May 20, 1918; Slotkin, *Lost Battalions*, 144–45.

53. "Courage and Cowardice," *Chicago Defender*, June 1, 1918.

54. "Southern White Daily Becomes Conscience Stricken," *Chicago Defender*, June 22, 1918.

55. Adriane Lentz-Smith, *Freedom Struggles: African Americans and World War I* (Cambridge: Harvard University Press, 2009), 43–79.

56. "The Negro Under Fire," *Atlanta Constitution*, June 26, 1918.

57. "Privates Bill and Needham," *New York Times*, May 22, 1918.

58. See reprint of the piece in *Louisville Courier-Journal*, Aug. 28–30, 1918.

59. See Slotkin, *Lost Battalions*, 142–51.

60. See Barbeau and Henri, *Unknown Soldiers*, 116–18, 139–40; Williams, *Torchbearers of Democracy*, 122.

61. See Eliga Dees to Mae Dees, May 5 and June 23, 1918, Eliga and Mae Dees Letters (Dees Letters), Collection R1453, State Historical Society of Missouri, Columbia, Mo. (SHSM).

62. Mae Dees to Eliga Dees, May 7 and 15, 1918, Dees Letters, SHSM.

63. Mae Bilbrey to Eliga Dees, July 15, 1917; Mae Dees to Eliga Dees, May 7, 1918; Dees Letters, SHSM.

64. Mae Dees to Eliga Dees, Apr. 18, 1918; Eliga Dees to Mae Dees, May 11, 1918; Dees Letters, SHSM.

65. See David M. Kennedy, *Over Here: The First World War and American Society* (New York: Oxford University Press, 2004 ed.), 284–87; Robert H. Zieger, *America's Great War: World War I and the American Experience* (Lanham, Md.: Rowman and Littlefield, 2000), 143–51.

66. See Scott, *Natalie Scott*, 45.

67. See Christopher Capozzola, *Uncle Sam Wants You: World War I and the Making of the Modern American Citizen* (New York: Oxford University Press, 2008), 83–103.

68. Mae Dees to Eliga Dees, May 15, 1918, Dees Letters, SHSM.

69. "When We Come Back," *Gas Attack*, May 4, 1918.

70. Mae Dees to Eliga Dees, May 31, 1918, Dees Letters, SHSM.

71. Streeter, *Love Letters of Bill to Mable*, 146.

72. Mae Dees to Eliga Dees, May 7, 1918, Dees Letters, SHSM.

73. Mae Dees to Eliga Dees, May 17, 1918, Dees Letters, SHSM.

74. Mae Dees to Eliga Dees, June 8, 1918, Dees Letters, SHSM.

75. "When We Come Back," *Gas Attack*, May 4, 1918.

76. See Nancy K. Bristow, *Making Men Moral: Social Engineering during the Great War* (New York: New York University Press, 1996), 2; Geoffrey R. Stone, *Perilous Times: Free Speech in Wartime from the Sedition Act of 1798 to the War on Terrorism* (New York: W. W. Norton, 2004), 172.

77. See "Report of Informal Conference on Morale," Apr. 12, 1918, pp. 1–2; folder 1, box 5; Correspondence of Guy Stanton Ford; Records of the Committee on Public Information, Record Group 63 (RG 63); National Archives at College Park, Md. (NACP); Susan Zeiger, "She Didn't Raise Her Boy to Be a Slacker: Motherhood, Conscription, and the Culture of the First World War," *Feminist Studies* 22 (Spring 1996): 7–39; Jennifer D. Keene, *Doughboys, the Great War, and the Remaking of America* (Baltimore: Johns Hopkins University Press, 2001), 76–77.

78. George Creel, *How We Advertised America* (New York: Harper and Brothers, 1920), 99–100.

79. Memorandum for Assistant Secretary of War on "Necessity of Systematic Effort to Generate and Sustain the Fighting Morale of American Forces," undated, p. 5; folder 1, box 5; Correspondence of Guy Stanton Ford; RG 63; NACP.

80. Col. E. L. Munson, Memorandum for the Surgeon General, Mar. 2, 1918, p. 1; folder 1, box 5; Correspondence of Guy Stanton Ford; RG 63; NACP.

81. See Keene, *Doughboys*, 77.

82. Committee on Public Information, *War Information Series*, "Why America Fights Germany," Mar. 1918, no. 15, p. 13.

83. James R. Mock and Cedric Larson, *Words That Won the War: The Story of the Committee on Public Information, 1917–1919* (Princeton: Princeton University Press, 1939), 12.

84. See Col. E. L. Munson, Memorandum for the Surgeon General, Mar. 2, 1918, p. 4; folder 1, box 5; Correspondence of Guy Stanton Ford; RG 63; NACP.

85. See Keene, *Doughboys*, 77–78; Delivery to Training Camps of Pamphlets of Committee on Public Information for the First Three Months of 1918, undated; folder 1, box 5; Correspondence of Guy Stanton Ford; RG 63; NACP.

86. Creel, *How We Advertised America*, 109–10.

87. John Milton Cooper, Jr., "The World War and American Memory," *Diplomatic History* 38 (Sept. 2014): 729.

88. "This Is Mother's Day," *New York Times*, May 10, 1914; "Mothers' Day Is Observed in State Today," *Nashville Tennessean*, May 12, 1918. See also Linda K. Kerber, *Women of the Republic: Intellect and Ideology in Revolutionary America* (Chapel Hill: University of North Carolina, 1980).

89. "Secretaries Baker and Daniels Pay Tribute to Heroism of Nation's Women . . . ," Committee on Public Information, *Official Bulletin*, May 11, 1918, vol. 2, no. 307, p. 2.

90. " 'Mother's Letter' Plan Gives Every Man in A. E. F. . . . ," *Stars and Stripes*, May 3, 1918.

91. "The Man and His Mother," *Atlanta Constitution*, May 10, 1918.

92. Natalie Scott to Martha Scott, May 5, 1918 [incorrectly dated 1917], folder 5, box 2, Scott Papers, LaRC.

93. "Secretaries Baker and Daniels Pay Tribute to Heroism of Nation's Women . . . ," Committee on Public Information, *Official Bulletin*, May 11, 1918, vol. 2, no. 307, p. 1.

94. "Every Soldier's Duty to Write Home Often," Committee on Public Information, *Official Bulletin*, June 10, 1918, vol. 2, no. 331, p. 4.

95. "President Asks Nation to Honor Mothers' Day," *St. Louis Post-Dispatch*, May 12, 1918. Emphasis added.

96. "One 'Mother's Letter'," *Stars and Stripes*, May 10, 1918.

97. "Mothers' Mail to Soldiers," *Washington Post*, June 1, 1918.
98. "Mothers' Day Is Observed in State Today," *Nashville Tennessean*, May 12, 1918.
99. "Help the Greatest Mother When Honoring Them All," *Baltimore Sun*, May 12, 1918; Julia F. Irwin, *Making the World Safe: The American Red Cross and a Nation's Humanitarian Awakening* (New York: Oxford University Press, 2013), 86.
100. "They Come to Me—I Come to You," *Selma* (Ala.) *Journal*, May 16, 1918.
101. "When the Flag Goes Over," *Greenville* (Mo.) *Sun*, May 16, 1918.
102. *War Facts and Patriotic Songs*, p. 3, William L. Ashton Papers, 82nd Division, 325th Infantry Regiment, Veterans Survey Collections, USAHEC.
103. Mae Dees to Eliga Dees, May 9, 1918, Dees Letters, SHSM.
104. "This, That, and the Other," *Nashville Tennessean*, May 12, 1918.
105. Kathleen Kennedy, *Disloyal Mothers and Scurrilous Citizens: Women and Subversion during World War I* (Bloomington: Indiana University Press, 1999).
106. See R. W. F., *Silver Lining: The Experiences of a War Bride* (Boston: Houghton Mifflin Co., 1918), 41; Jonathan H. Ebel, *Faith in the Fight: Religion and the American Soldier in the Great War* (Princeton: Princeton University Press, 2010), 130–31.
107. Ethel M. Kelley, *Over Here: The Story of a War Bride* (Indianapolis: Bobbs-Merrill Co., 1918), 259.
108. " 'Mother's Letter' Plan Gives Every Man in A. E. F. . . . ," *Stars and Stripes*, May 3, 1918.
109. "Mother's Day: Say It with Flowers," *Watertown* (Wisc.) *News*, May 8, 1918.
110. "To Those Who Fail to Grasp War's Meaning," *Watertown* (Wisc.) *News*, June 12, 1918.
111. "Why We Fight," *Watertown* (Wisc.) *News*, June 5, 1918.
112. "New Phase of Hun Brutality," *Selma* (Ala.) *Journal*, June 5, 1918.
113. See Mae Dees to Eliga Dees, May 9 and 17, 1918, Dees Letters, SHSM.
114. See "Wayne County Over The Top," *Greenville* (Mo.) *Sun*, Apr. 25, 1918; "St. Francis River Goes Over the Top," *Greenville* (Mo.) *Sun*, May 16, 1918; "How Williamsville Went Over The Top," *Greenville* (Mo.) *Sun*, May 30, 1918; Mae Dees to Eliga Dees, May 7 and 15, 1918, Dees Letters, SHSM.
115. See "Licensed to Wed," "Wayne County Over the Top," and "New Swindle Takes Money from Parents of Soldiers," *Greenville* (Mo.) *Sun*, Apr. 25, 1918.
116. Eliga Dees to Mae Dees, May 17, 1918, Dees Letters, SHSM.
117. Mae Dees to Eliga Dees, May 21, 1918, Dees Letters, SHSM. Emphasis added.
118. Mae Dees to Eliga Dees, May 17, 1918, Dees Letters, SHSM.

119. Florence Elizabeth Summers, *Dere Bill: Mable's Love Letters to her Rookie* (New York: Frederick A. Stokes Co., 1918, 1919), 1–2, 15.

120. Boyd, *Through the Wheat*, 8–9.

121. "Dance with the Home Guards at the Armory Thursday Eve," *Watertown* (Wisc.) *News*, June 19, 1918.

122. Eliga Dees to Mae Dees, May 24 and 25, 1918, Dees Letters, SHSM.

123. Eliga Dees to Mae Dees, May 31, 1918, Dees Letters, SHSM.

124. Mae Dees to Eliga Dees, May 31, 1918, Dees Letters, SHSM.

125. See Scott, *Natalie Scott*, 128–58.

126. Natalie Scott to Martha Scott, May 10, 1918, folder 5, box 2, Scott Papers, LaRC.

127. Natalie Scott to Martha Scott, May 27, 1918, folder 5, box 2, Scott Papers, LaRC.

128. "Teuton Fliers Kill Doctors and Patients in Hospital," *Washington Post*, June 1, 1918.

129. Coffman, *War to End All Wars*, 286.

130. See Whitman, *Story of the 325th*, 16–17; Buxton, Jr., *Official History of 82nd Division*, 12; Transcribed diary, June 16–18, p. 9, Takes Papers, Veterans Survey Collections, USAHEC; George Waring Huston to Nellye Huston, July 14, 1918, folder 2, box 1080, Huston Papers, UASC.

131. George Waring Huston to Nellye Huston, June 18, 20, and 22, 1918, folder 2, box 1080, Huston Papers, UASC.

132. Eliga Dees to Mae Dees, May 29, 1918, Dees Letters, SHSM.

133. Mae Dees to Eliga Dees, May 31, 1918, Dees Letters, SHSM.

134. Mae Dees to Eliga Dees, June 8, 1918, Dees Letters, SHSM.

135. Mae Dees to Eliga Dees, June 8, 1918, Dees Letters, SHSM.

136. Eliga Dees to Mae Dees, June 13, 1918, Dees Letters, SHSM.

137. Eliga Dees to Mae Dees, June 15, 1918, Dees Letters, SHSM.

138. Eliga Dees to Mae Dees, June 16, 1918, Dees Letters, SHSM.

139. Eliga Dees to Mae Dees, June 18 (first and second ltrs.) and June 19, 1918, Dees Letters, SHSM.

140. Eliga Dees to Mae Dees, June 18, 1918 (first and second ltrs.), Dees Letters, SHSM.

141. See James J. Cooke, *The All-Americans at War: The 82nd Division in the Great War, 1917–1918* (Westport, Conn.: Praeger: 1999), 41, 45–46; Whitman, *Story of the 325th*, 17.

142. George Waring Huston to Nellye Huston, July 3, 1918, folder 2, box 1080, Huston Papers, UASC.

143. See Whitman, *Story of the 325th*, 19; Reminiscences, p. 4, Olsen Papers; Walter F. Owens to Edd, June 1918, Walter F. Owens Papers, 82nd Division, 325th Infantry Regiment; Veterans Survey Collections, USAHEC.

144. George Waring Huston to Nellye Huston, July 14, 1918, folder 2, box 1080, Huston Papers, UASC.

145. Reminiscences, p. 2, Olsen Papers, Veterans Survey Collections, USAHEC.

146. See Coffman, *War to End All Wars*, 133; Bristow, *Making Men Moral*, 206.

147. George Waring Huston to Nellye Huston, July 11, 1918, folder 2, box 1080, Huston Papers, UASC.

148. George Waring Huston to Nellye Huston, July 19, 1918, folder 3, box 1080, Huston Papers, UASC.

149. Boyd, *Through the Wheat*, 10–12.

150. Eliga Dees to Mae Dees, June 29, 1918, Dees Letters, SHSM.

151. Eliga Dees to Mae Dees, June 25 and 30, 1918, Dees Letters, SHSM.

152. Eliga Dees to Mae Dees, July 2, 1918, Dees Letters, SHSM.

153. Eliga Dees to Mae Dees, June 23 ["smak"] and 25, 1918, Dees Letters, SHSM.

154. Eliga Dees to Mae Dees, June 21, 1918, Dees Letters, SHSM.

155. Eliga Dees to Mae Dees, July 2, 1918, Dees Letters, SHSM.

156. Eliga Dees to Mae Dees, July 4, 1918 (second ltr.), Dees Letters, SHSM.

157. Eliga Dees travel record, *Lists of Outgoing Passengers, 1917–1938*; NAI number 6234477; box 601; Records of the Office of the Quartermaster General, 1774–1985, Record Group 92; NACP.

158. Streeter, *Love Letters of Bill to Mable*, 204.

159. *The Gold Chevron: A History of the Fifty-Third U.S. Infantry*, pp. 5–9; box 12; Records of the 6th Division, 53rd Inf. Regt.; Combat Divisions, 1917–1919; Records of the American Expeditionary Forces (World War I), Record Group 120; NACP.

160. Eliga Dees to Mae Dees, Aug. 16, 1918, Dees Letters, SHSM.

161. See Strachan, *First World War*, 298; statistic on July arrivals from Coffman, *War to End All Wars*, 227.

162. See Coffman, *War to End All Wars*, 263; John Ellis and Michael Cox, *The World War I Databook* (London: Aurum Press, 2001), 146.

Chapter 5: So Prepare, Say a Prayer

1. George Waring Huston to Nellye Huston, July 28, 1918, folder 3, box 1080, Huston Family Papers (Huston Papers), W. S. Hoole Special Collections Library, University of Alabama, Tuscaloosa, Ala. (UASC).

2. See James J. Cooke, *The All-Americans at War: The 82nd Division in the Great War, 1917–1918* (Westport, Conn.: Praeger: 1999), 46–47; Walter M. Whitman, *The Story of the 325th* (Bordeaux: Saugnac and Drouillard, 1919), 19–20; Transcribed diary, July 22 and 31, 1918, pp. 13–14, Fred H. Takes Papers (Takes Papers), 82nd Division, 325th Infantry Regiment, Veterans Survey Collections, U.S. Army Heritage and Education Center, Military History Institute, Carlisle, Penn. (USAHEC).

3. Edward Streeter, *Love Letters of Bill to Mable: Comprising Dere Mable, "That's Me All Over, Mable," and "Same Old Bill, eh Mable!"* (New York: Frederick A. Stokes Co., 1918, 1919), 236.

4. See Thomas Boyd, *Through the Wheat: A Novel of the World War I Marines* (Lincoln: University of Nebraska Press, 2000), 144–49.

5. See "U.S. Celebrates Victory," *Watertown* (Wisc.) *News*, July 19, 1918.

6. "On Heels of the Huns," *Watertown* (Wisc.) *News*, July 22, 1918.

7. See Boyd, *Through the Wheat*, xi, 175–92.

8. Martin Gus Gulberg, *A War Diary* (Chicago: The Drake Press, 1927), 38.

9. Quoted in Nimrod T. Frazer, *Send the Alabamians: World War I Fighters in the Rainbow Division* (Tuscaloosa: University of Alabama Press, 2014), 125.

10. See Edward M. Coffman, *The War to End All Wars: The American Military Experience in World War I* (Lexington: University Press of Kentucky, 1998 ed.), 212–61; Martin Gilbert, *The Routledge Atlas of the First World War*, 3rd ed. (London: Routledge, 2008), 112; Hew Strachan, *The First World War* (New York: Penguin Books, 2003), 316.

11. Natalie Scott to Martha Scott, June 6, 1918, folder 6, box 2, Correspondence, Natalie Scott Papers (Scott Papers), Manuscripts Collection 123, Louisiana Research Collection, Tulane University, New Orleans, La. (LaRC).

12. Thomas Babington Macaulay, *Lays of Ancient Rome* (London: George Routledge and Sons, 1888), 73.

13. Natalie Scott to Martha Scott, June 6, 1918, folder 6, box 2, Scott Papers, LaRC. For the "good death" see Drew Gilpin Faust, *This Republic of Suffering: Death and the American Civil War* (New York: Knopf, 2008).

14. See Scott, *Natalie Scott*, 166–69.

15. Natalie Scott to Martha Scott, June 25, 1918, folder 6, box 2, Scott Papers, LaRC.

16. Natalie Scott to Martha Scott, July 17, 1918, folder 7, box 2, Scott Papers, LaRC.

17. Natalie Scott to Martha Scott, July 17, 1918, folder 7, box 2, Scott Papers, LaRC.

18. Letter available at *www.theodorerooseveltcenter.org* (June 15, 2016).

19. For female physicians see Kimberly Jensen, *Mobilizing Minerva: American Women in the First World War* (Urbana: University of Illinois Press, 2008), 77–97.

20. Natalie Scott to Martha Scott, Aug. 5, 1918, folder 8, box 2, Scott Papers, LaRC.

21. Natalie Scott to Martha Scott, July 28, 1918, folder 7, box 2, Scott Papers, LaRC.

22. Natalie Scott to Martha Scott, Aug. 21, 1918, folder 8, box 2, Scott Papers, LaRC; John W. Scott, *Natalie Scott: A Magnificent Life* (Gretna, La.: Pelican Publishing Co., 2008), 159–90.

23. See G. Edward Buxton, Jr., *Official History of 82nd Division, American Expeditionary Forces, 1917–1919* (Indianapolis: Bobbs-Merrill Co. Publishers, 1920), 15–17; Whitman, *Story of the 325th*, 20–21; Cooke, *All-Americans at War*, 52; George Waring Huston to Nellye Huston, Aug. 2,

1918, folder 3, box 1080, Huston Papers, UASC; Transcribed diary, Aug. 4, 6, and 9–13, 1918, p. 15, Takes Papers, Veterans Survey Collections, USAHEC.

24. "Many Alabama Boys Killed in Action, Two Are Selmians," *Selma* (Ala.) *Journal*, Aug. 5, 1918.

25. George Waring Huston to Nellye Huston, Aug. 23 and 24 (to Nellye and Robert Huston), 1918, folder 3, box 1080, Huston Papers, UASC; Buxton, Jr., *Official History of 82nd Division*, 14.

26. Whitman, *Story of the 325th*, 21; Buxton, Jr., *Official History of 82nd Division*, 18; George Waring Huston to Nellye Huston, Aug. 21 and 24 (to both parents), 1918, folder 3, box 1080, Huston Papers, UASC.

27. George Waring Huston to Nellye Huston, Aug. 23 and 24 (to Nellye and Robert Huston), 1918, folder 3, box 1080, Huston Papers, UASC; Walter F. Owens to Edd, Aug. 24, 1918, Walter F. Owens Papers, 82nd Division, 325th Infantry Regiment, Veterans Survey Collections, USAHEC.

28. See Buxton, Jr., *Official History of 82nd Division*, 13, 17; George Waring Huston to Nellye Huston, Aug. 24 (to Nellye and Robert Huston) and Aug. 30, 1918, folder 3, box 1080, Huston Papers, UASC.

29. "A Mother's Promise to Her Son," *Selma* (Ala.) *Journal*, Aug. 18, 1918.

30. "Girl Marries Too Many Soldier Husbands," *Selma* (Ala.) *Journal*, Aug. 22, 1918.

31. *History of the 124th Machine Gun Battalion, 66th Brigade, 33rd Division, A. E. F.* (publisher unknown, 1919), 12–15.

32. Clayton K. Slack interview (sound recording), Oct. 12, 1964, UC box 22, Wisconsin Historical Society, Madison, Wisc. (WHS); Frederic Louis Huidekoper, *The History of the 33rd Division, A. E. F.*, Vol. I (Springfield, Ill.: Illinois State Historical Library, 1921), 37–44, 322n. 35.

33. Huidekoper, *History of the 33rd Division*, 44–51.

34. *History of the 124th Machine Gun Battalion*, 12–5; Huidekoper, *History of the 33rd Division*, 52–56; Clayton Slack interview, WHS.

35. *The Gold Chevron: A History of the Fifty-Third U.S. Infantry*, pp. 11–13; box 12; Records of the 6th Division, 53rd Inf. Regt.; Combat Divisions, 1917–1919; Records of the American Expeditionary Forces (World War I), Record Group 120 (RG 120); National Archives and Records Administration, College Park, Md. (NACP).

36. Diary from July 5, 1918 to June 4, 1919, p. 1, Sol J. Arouesty Papers, 6th Division, 53rd Infantry Regiment, Veterans Survey Collections, USAHEC; *Gold Chevron*, p. 28; box 12; Records of the 6th Division; RG 120; NACP.

37. Wayne Turner to Mother, Sept. 18, 1918, Wayne O. Turner Papers, 6th Division, 53rd Infantry Regiment, Veterans Survey Collections, USAHEC.

38. Eliga Dees to Mae Dees, Sept. 19 and 29, 1918, Eliga and Mae Dees Letters (Dees Letters), Collection R1453, State Historical Society of Missouri, Columbia, Mo. (SHSM).

39. Richard Slotkin, *Lost Battalions: The Great War and the Crisis of American Nationality* (New York: Henry Holt, 2005), 186–87; Arthur E. Barbeau and Florette Henri, *The Unknown Soldiers: Black American Troops in World War I* (Philadelphia: Temple University Press, 1974), 118–19, 133–34.

40. See Barbeau and Henri, *Unknown Soldiers*, 141–42; Coffman, *War to End All Wars*, 315.

41. Adriane Lentz-Smith, *Freedom Struggles: African Americans and World War I* (Cambridge: Harvard University Press, 2009), 106–8; Chad L. Williams, *Torchbearers of Democracy: African American Soldiers in the World War I Era* (Chapel Hill: University of North Carolina Press, 2010), 160–67.

42. Williams, *Torchbearers of Democracy*, 160.

43. See Fred L. Borch III, "Anatomy of a Court-Martial: The Trial and Execution of Private William Buckner," *The Army Lawyer* (Oct. 2011), 1–6; Williams, *Torchbearers of Democracy*, 170–72; Lisa M. Budreau, *Bodies of War: World War I and the Politics of Commemoration in America, 1919–1933* (New York: New York University Press, 2010), 59.

44. Mae Dees to Eliga Dees, May 7, 1918, Dees Letters, SHSM.

45. "Piedmont News," *Greenville* (Mo.) *Sun*, Aug. 29, 1918; "Uncle Sam's Partner," *Greenville* (Mo.) *Sun*, Aug. 22, 1918.

46. "Roy Thornburgh Severely Wounded," *Greenville* (Mo.) *Sun*, Aug. 15, 1918.

47. "Cross Roads Program," *Greenville* (Mo.) *Sun*, Aug. 15, 1918.

48. "Honor Roll War Savings Stamps," *Greenville* (Mo.) *Sun*, Aug. 15, 1918.

49. See "Local and Personal" and "With Our Boys in the Service," *Greenville* (Mo.) *Sun*, Aug. 22, 1918.

50. "Program Wayne County Teachers Convention," *Greenville* (Mo.) *Sun*, Aug. 22, 1918.

51. "Flag Raising in Every School District," *Greenville* (Mo.) *Sun*, July 4, 1918.

52. "'Old Glory' Floats on School Campus," *Greenville* (Mo.) *Sun*, Sept. 5, 1918.

53. See Michael S. Neiberg, *Dance of the Furies: Europe and the Outbreak of World War I* (Cambridge: Belknap Press of Harvard University Press, 2011), 7.

54. See "Mrs. Frank Wilkinson" and "Local and Personal," *Greenville* (Mo.) *Sun*, Aug. 15, 1918.

55. See "Williamsville Boy Killed in Action," *Greenville* (Mo.) *Sun*, Sept. 12, 1918; Harve Akes draft registration card, June 5, 1917, Wayne County, Mo.; *Draft Registration Cards, 1917–1918* (Family History Library Microfilm [FHL] roll 1683936); Records of the Selective Service System (World War I), 1917–1939, Record Group 163 (RG 163); National Archives and Records Administration-Southeast Region, Morrow, Ga. (NARA-Southeast); Harve Akes death record, American Battle Monuments Commission, *World War I, World War II, and Korean War Casualty Listings* (Provo: Ancestry.com Operations, Inc., 2005), *Ancestry.com* (Dec. 2, 2015).

56. "Arthur Lee Clayton Killed in Action," *Greenville* (Mo.) *Sun*, Sept. 26, 1918; Arthur Lee Clayton death record, *U.S., Find a Grave Index, 1600s–Current* (Provo: Ancestry.com Operations, Inc., 2012), *Ancestry.com* (Dec. 2, 2015).

57. Arthur Lee Clayton draft registration card, June 5, 1917, Wayne County, Mo.; *Draft Registration Cards, 1917–1918* (FHL roll 1683936); RG 163; NARA-Southeast.

58. "With Our Boys in the Service," *Greenville* (Mo.) *Sun*, Sept. 12, 1918.

59. William Oda Dees draft registration card, June 5, 1918, Wayne County, Mo.; *Draft Registration Cards, 1917–1918* (FHL roll 1683936); RG 163; NARA-Southeast; "Thirty-Seven Men Left Here Tuesday," *Greenville* (Mo.) *Sun*, Aug. 29, 1918.

60. "With Our Boys in the Service," *Greenville* (Mo.) *Sun*, Sept. 12, 1918.

61. John M. Barry, *The Great Influenza: The Epic Story of the Deadliest Plague in History* (New York: Viking, 2004), 169–74.

62. See *History of the 124th Machine Gun Battalion*, 15; Clayton Slack interview, WHS.

63. Huidekoper, *History of the 33rd Division*, 55–57; Clayton Slack interview, WHS.

64. See Jonathan H. Ebel, *Faith in the Fight: Religion and the American Soldier in the Great War* (Princeton: Princeton University Press, 2010) and *G.I. Messiahs: Soldiering, War, and American Civil Religion* (New Haven: Yale University Press, 2015).

65. Ebel, *Faith in the Fight*; Edward A. Gutiérrez, *Doughboys on the Great War: How American Soldiers Viewed their Military Experience* (Lawrence: University Press of Kansas, 2014), 40, 152–53; David Laskin, *The Long Way Home: An American Journey from Ellis Island to the Great War* (New York: Harper Perennial, 2011), 196; Nancy Gentile Ford, *Americans All! Foreign-born Soldiers in World War I* (College Station: Texas A&M University Press, 2001), 117–23; Cooke, *All-Americans at War*, 67–68.

66. Cooke, *All-Americans at War*, 58–61.

67. George Waring Huston to Nellye Huston, Sept. 6, 8, and 9 (two ltrs.), 1918, folder 3, box 1080, Huston Papers, UASC.

68. Streeter, *Love Letters of Bill to Mable*, 281.

69. George Waring Huston to Nellye and Robert Huston, Sept. 1, 1918, folder 3, box 1080, Huston Papers, UASC. For the Forty-Second in the Aisne-Marne see Coffman, *War to End All Wars*, 254.

70. Frazer, *Send the Alabamians*, 146; James H. Hallas, ed., *Doughboy War: The American Expeditionary Force in WWI* (Mechanicsburg, Penn.: Stackpole Books, 2009), 197; Cooke, *All-Americans at War*, 61.

71. George Waring Huston to Nellye Huston, Sept. 4, 1918, folder 3, box 1080, Huston Papers, UASC.

72. Transcribed diary, Sept. 2–11, 1918, p. 17, Takes Papers, Veterans Survey Collections, USAHEC.

73. George Waring Huston to Robert Huston, Sept. 14, 1918, folder 3, box 1080, Huston Papers, UASC.

74. John Keegan, *The First World War* (New York: Alfred A. Knopf, 1999), 411; Coffman, *War to End All Wars,* 271–77; Edward G. Lengel, *To Conquer Hell: The Meuse-Argonne, 1918* (New York: Henry Holt, 2008), 49–53.

75. Cooke, *All-Americans at War,* 67.

76. Allan M. Brandt, *No Magic Bullet: A Social History of Venereal Disease in the United States Since 1880* (New York: Oxford University Press, 1985), 101.

77. See Cooke, *All-Americans at War,* 67.

78. See Susan Zeiger, *Entangling Alliances: Foreign War Brides and American Soldiers in the Twentieth Century* (New York: New York University Press, 2010), 11–37. Jennifer Keene argues for the accommodation strategy in *Doughboys, the Great War, and the Remaking of America* (Baltimore: Johns Hopkins University Press, 2001).

79. See Borch, "Anatomy of a Court-Martial," 1–6; Williams, *Torchbearers of Democracy,* 171.

80. See Williams, *Torchbearers of Democracy,* 172; Mary Louise Roberts, *What Soldiers Do: Sex and the American GI in World War II France* (Chicago: University of Chicago Press, 2013), 195.

81. Quotations and this material from Williams, *Torchbearers of Democracy,* 159–60.

82. See Barbeau and Henri, *Unknown Soldiers,* 142; Williams, *Torchbearers of Democracy,* 167–69.

83. For Buckner's hanging see Budreau, *Bodies of War,* 59; Borch, "Anatomy of a Court-Martial," 1–6; Williams, *Torchbearers of Democracy,* 171–72.

84. Huidekoper, *History of the 33rd Division,* 56.

85. See Whitman, *Story of the 325th,* 22; Lengel, *To Conquer Hell,* 52; Coffman, *War to End All Wars,* 278–79.

86. See Frazer, *Send the Alabamians,* 150–55; Lengel, *To Conquer Hell,* 52; Coffman, *War to End All Wars,* 281; "Amazing Graveyard on St. Mihiel Hill," *New York Times,* Sept. 18, 1918.

87. See Buxton, Jr., *Official History of 82nd Division,* 24–25; Richard Wheeler, ed., *Sergeant York and the Great War: His Own Life Story and War Diary* (San Antonio: Vision Forum, 2011), 136–37.

88. See Lengel, *To Conquer Hell,* 52–53; Coffman, *War to End All Wars,* 283.

89. "Glorious Page Was Added to American History . . . ," *Atlanta Constitution,* Sept. 22, 1918.

90. See "St. Miehiel [*sic*] Falls, Americans Take 12,000 Germans," *Selma* (Ala.) *Journal,* Sept. 13, 1918; "Yanks Continue Drive on Metz," *Watertown* (Wisc.) *News,* Sept. 16, 1918.

91. "Greeted in St. Mihiel," *Washington Post,* Sept. 15, 1918.

92. See "St. Mihiel Women Kiss Baker's Hand," *New York Times,* Sept. 15, 1918; "20,000 Taken at St. Mihiel," *San Francisco Chronicle,* Sept. 15, 1918;

"Pershing's Army Makes Further Gain on the Moselle," *St. Louis Post-Dispatch*, Sept. 16, 1918; "Greeted in St. Mihiel," *Washington Post*, Sept. 15, 1918; "Glorious Page Was Added to American History . . . ," *Atlanta Constitution*, Sept. 22, 1918.

93. "20,000 Taken at St. Mihiel," *San Francisco Chronicle*, Sept. 15, 1918.

94. See Frazer, *Send the Alabamians*, 156.

95. George Waring Huston to Nellye Huston, Sept. 16, 1918, folder 3, box 1080, Huston Papers, UASC.

96. Transcribed diary, Sept. 13, 1918, p. 18, Takes Papers, Veterans Survey Collections, USAHEC.

97. See Coffman, *War to End All Wars*, 324; Whitman, *Story of the 325th*, 22; Cooke, *All-Americans at War*, 77.

98. George Waring Huston to Nellye Huston, Sept. 17, 1918, folder 3, box 1080, Huston Papers, UASC

99. Transcribed diary, Sept. 17, 18, and 23, 1918, pp. 18–19, Takes Papers, Veterans Survey Collections, USAHEC.

100. Transcribed diary, Sept. 24, 1918, p. 19, Takes Papers, Veterans Survey Collections, USAHEC.

101. George Waring Huston to Nellye Huston, Sept. 24, 1918, folder 3, box 1080, Huston Papers, UASC.

102. "New Draft, 18 to 45," *Washington Post*, Aug. 4, 1918.

103. *Congressional Record*, Senate, 65th Congress, 2nd sess., Aug. 24, 1918, 9465, 9470.

104. "Draft Extension from 18 to 45 Years Passed by Senate," *Atlanta Constitution*, Aug. 28, 1918.

105. *Congressional Record*, Senate, 65th Congress, 2nd sess., Aug. 24, 1918, 9465, 9466, 9471.

106. John Whiteclay Chambers II, *To Raise an Army: The Draft Comes to Modern America* (New York: The Free Press, 1987), 155, 196–98.

107. "18 to 45 Men, in the New Draft, to Register September 12," *St. Louis Post-Dispatch*, Aug. 31, 1918.

108. "For Festal Draft Day," *Baltimore Sun*, Sept. 10, 1918; "All Men 18 to 46 Must Register for Draft Tomorrow," *St. Louis Post-Dispatch*, Sept. 11, 1918.

109. "Expect Draft Here Will Reach 800,000," *New York Times*, Sept. 14, 1918; "Nation's Greatest Registration Today," *Washington Post*, Sept. 12, 1918; "Atlanta Pastors Urge Registration," *Atlanta Constitution*, Sept. 9, 1918; "18–45 Draft Bill Passes Senate," *Watertown* (Wisc.) *News*, Aug. 28, 1918; "Manpower Bill Is Completed," *Selma* (Ala.) *Journal*, Aug. 29, 1918; "19–20 and 32–36 Class to Be Called First," *Greenville* (Mo.) *Sun*, Sept. 19, 1918.

110. "25,526 Atlantans Enroll for Duty Registration Day," *Atlanta Constitution*, Sept. 13, 1918.

111. "Urges Women to Encourage Men in Duty to Register," Committee on Public Information, *Official Bulletin*, Sept. 4, 1918, vol. 2, no. 403, p. 4.

112. "All Men 18 to 46 Must Register for Draft Tomorrow," *St. Louis Post-Dispatch*, Sept. 11, 1918.

113. Chambers, *To Raise an Army*, 198.

114. "Whole Country Goes Over Top in 18–45 Draft," *Chicago Daily Tribune*, Sept. 13, 1918; "Huge Army Now Enrolled to Support United States, *Watertown* (Wisc.) *News*, Sept. 13, 1918; "Registration May Exceed 14,000,000," *Selma* (Ala.) *Journal*, Sept. 13, 1918; "Total Registration in County 1411," *Greenville* (Mo.) *Sun*, Sept. 19, 1918.

115. Harry Bill Huston draft registration card, Sept. 12, 1918, Maury County, Tenn.; *Draft Registration Cards, 1917–1918* (FHL roll 1877494); John Leander Bilbrey draft registration card, Sept. 12, 1918, Wayne County, Mo.; *Draft Registration Cards, 1917–1918* (FHL roll 1683936); RG 163; NARA-Southeast.

116. Huidekoper, *History of the 33rd Division*, 56-7, 65; *History of the 124th Machine Gun Battalion*, 15.

117. See Lengel, *To Conquer Hell*, 91.

118. "Large Crowds Attend Waterloo Patriotic Day," *Watertown* (Wisc.) *News*, Aug. 12, 1918.

119. Marie Doran, *The Girls Over Here: A Patriotic Play Act in One Act* (New York: Samuel French, 1917), 20, 29.

120. "Put it There, Son!" *Watertown* (Wisc.) *News*, Aug. 19, 1918; "Soldiers of the Soil," *Watertown* (Wisc.) *News*, Aug. 21, 1918; "Working men of America . . . ," *Watertown* (Wisc.) *News*, Aug. 26, 1918.

121. "Patriotic Sunday Draws Big Crowd at Lake Mills," *Watertown* (Wisc.) *News*, Aug. 28, 1918.

122. "Army of Labor Like the Army Over There," *Watertown* (Wisc.) *News*, Sept. 2, 1918.

123. "Women and Children Must Be Made Safe," *Watertown* (Wisc.) *News*, Sept. 6, 1918. Emphasis added.

124. "Mothers for Foe Defeat," *Watertown* (Wisc.) *News*, Sept. 20, 1918.

125. "Help the World to Clean House," *Watertown* (Wisc.) *News*, Sept. 11, 1918.

126. "Patriotic Sunday Draws Big Crowd at Lake Mills," *Watertown* (Wisc.) *News*, Aug. 28, 1918.

127. See "In War Time," *Watertown* (Wisc.) *News*, Aug. 2, 1918.

128. "Fear of the Draft Causes R. Harder to Take His Life," *Watertown* (Wisc.) *News*, July 19, 1918.

129. See Coffman, *War to End All Wars*, 291–303.

130. See Coffman, *War to End All Wars*, 299–301; Lengel, *To Conquer Hell*, 57.

131. Coffman, *War to End All Wars*, 303–6.

Chapter 6: Yankee Doodle Do or Die

1. *History of the 124th Machine Gun Battalion, 66th Brigade, 33rd Division, A. E. F.* (publisher unknown, 1919), 16–19.

2. Edward G. Lengel, *To Conquer Hell: The Meuse-Argonne, 1918* (New York: Henry Holt, 2008), 90–92; Frederic Louis Huidekoper, *The History of the 33rd Division, A. E. F.*, Vol. 1 (Springfield, Ill.: Illinois State Historical Library, 1921), 56–83, 334n100; Clayton K. Slack interview (sound recording), Oct. 12, 1964, UC box 22, Wisconsin Historical Society, Madison, Wisc. (WHS).

3. Transcribed diary, p. 1B, Henry G. Weinberg Papers, 33rd Division, 131st Infantry Regiment, Veterans Survey Collections, U.S. Army Heritage and Education Center, Military History Institute, Carlisle, Penn. (USAHEC).

4. Transcribed diary, Sept. 26, 1918, p. 5, Selmar Waldemar Papers, 33rd Division, 131st Infantry Regiment, Veterans Survey Collections, USAHEC.

5. Transcribed diary, Sept. 26, 1918, p. 19, Fred H. Takes Papers (Takes Papers), 82nd Division, 325th Infantry Regiment, Veterans Survey Collections, USAHEC.

6. See Lengel, *To Conquer Hell*, 172, 213; Walter M. Whitman, *The Story of the 325th* (Bordeaux: Saugnac and Drouillard, 1919), 22–23; James J. Cooke, *The All-Americans at War: The 82nd Division in the Great War, 1917–1918* (Westport, Conn.: Praeger: 1999), 86; "Report on the Operations of the 82nd Division in the Argonne-Meuse Offensive," p. 2; box unknown; Records of the 82nd Division; Combat Divisions, 1917–1919; Records of the American Expeditionary Forces (World War I), Record Group 120 (RG 120); National Archives and Records Administration, College Park, Md. (NACP).

7. George Waring Huston to Nellye Huston, Sept. 29, 1918, folder 3, box 1080, Huston Family Papers (Huston Papers), W. S. Hoole Special Collections Library, University of Alabama, Tuscaloosa, Ala. (UASC).

8. Transcribed diary, Sept. 29, 1918, p. 20, Takes Papers, Veterans Survey Collections, USAHEC.

9. "That Liberty Shall Not Perish from the Earth," *Birmingham Age Herald*, Sept. 29, 1918, folder 3, box 1080, Huston Papers, UASC.

10. Arthur E. Barbeau and Florette Henri, *The Unknown Soldiers: Black American Troops in World War I* (Philadelphia: Temple University Press, 1974), 118–21; Laurence Stallings, *The Doughboys: The Story of the AEF, 1917–1918* (New York: Harper and Row, 1963), 319; Chad L. Williams, *Torchbearers of Democracy: African American Soldiers in the World War I Era* (Chapel Hill: University of North Carolina Press, 2010), 136.

11. Barbeau and Henri, *Unknown Soldiers*, 122–28; Williams, *Torchbearers of Democracy*, 136.

12. Barbeau and Henri, *Unknown Soldiers*, 131–36; Williams, *Torchbearers of Democracy*, 137–38.

13. Barbeau and Henri, *Unknown Soldiers*, 128–31; Williams, *Torchbearers of Democracy*, 137.

14. See, for example, "Why Negroes Failed in Argonne Offensive," *Atlanta Constitution*, Nov. 8, 1919.

15. Barbeau and Henri, *Unknown Soldiers*, 137–63; Williams, *Torchbearers of Democracy*, 138–43; Edward M. Coffman, *The War to End All Wars: The American Military Experience in World War I* (Lexington: University Press of Kentucky, 1998 ed.), 314–20.

16. Barbeau and Henri, *Unknown Soldiers*, 121.

17. Coffman, *War to End All Wars*, 320.

18. See Mark Ethan Grotelueschen, *The AEF Way of War: The American Army and Combat in World War I* (New York: Cambridge University Press, 2007), 320–22; Richard Slotkin, *Lost Battalions: The Great War and the Crisis of American Nationality* (New York: Henry Holt, 2005), 287–89; Cooke, *All-Americans at War*, 88.

19. For Whittlesey see Slotkin, *Lost Battalions*, 79–82.

20. George Waring Huston to Nellye Huston, Oct. 3 (two ltrs.), 1918, folder 3, box 1080, Huston Papers, UASC. For Takes see Cooke, *All-Americans at War*, 88.

21. American Battle Monuments Commission, *2d Division: Summary of Operations in the World War* (Washington: U.S. Government Printing Office, 1944), 50–60; Thomas Boyd, *Through the Wheat: A Novel of the World War I Marines* (Lincoln: University of Nebraska Press, 2000), xii; Coffman, *War to End All Wars*, 284; Martin Gus Gulberg, *A War Diary* (Chicago: The Drake Press, 1927), 43; Steven Trout, *On the Battlefield of Memory: The First World War and American Remembrance, 1919–1941* (Tuscaloosa: University of Alabama Press, 2010), 150.

22. Boyd, *Through the Wheat*, 265.

23. John W. Scott, *Natalie Scott: A Magnificent Life* (Gretna, La.: Pelican Publishing Co., 2008), 191–204.

24. Natalie Scott to Martha Scott, Sept. 1, 1918, folder 9, box 2, Correspondence, Natalie Scott Papers (Scott Papers), Manuscripts Collection 123, Louisiana Research Collection, Tulane University, New Orleans, La. (LaRC).

25. For women's gun clubs see Kimberly Jensen, *Mobilizing Minerva: American Women in the First World War* (Urbana: University of Illinois Press, 2008), 36–59.

26. See Jonathan H. Ebel, *Faith in the Fight: Religion and the American Soldier in the Great War* (Princeton: Princeton University Press, 2010), 129–37.

27. See Susan Zeiger, *In Uncle Sam's Service: Women Workers with the American Expeditionary Force, 1917–1919* (Ithaca: Cornell University Press, 1999); Jensen, *Mobilizing Minerva*.

28. Natalie Scott to Martha Scott, Sept. 8, 1918, folder 9, box 2, Scott Papers, LaRC.

29. For Stimson see Jensen, *Mobilizing Minerva*, 136–38.

30. Natalie Scott to Martha Scott, Sept. 8, 1918, folder 9, box 2, Scott Papers, LaRC.

31. Natalie Scott to Martha Scott, Sept. 10, 1918, folder 9, box 2, Scott Papers, LaRC.

32. Natalie Scott to Martha Scott, Sept. 19, 1918, folder 9, box 2, Scott Papers, LaRC.

33. Natalie Scott to Martha Scott, Sept. 25, 1918, folder 9, box 2, Scott Papers, LaRC.

34. Natalie Scott to Martha Scott, Oct. 23, 1918, folder 10, box 2, Scott Papers, LaRC.

35. See Scott, *Natalie Scott*, 205.

36. Lengel, *To Conquer Hell*, 190–93.

37. John M. Barry, *The Great Influenza: The Epic Story of the Deadliest Plague in History* (New York: Viking, 2004), 175–76.

38. Coffman, *War to End All Wars*, 321.

39. Slotkin, *Lost Battalions*, 283–85, 293; Coffman, *War to End All Wars*, 313–14; Williams, *Torchbearers of Democracy*, 139.

40. "The 325th Infantry in its Meuse-Argonne Operations—October 10–31, 1918," undated, p. 1; box 16; Records of the 82nd Division; RG 120; NACP.

41. Lengel, *To Conquer Hell*, 188.

42. Whitman, *Story of the 325th*, 23; Transcribed diary, Oct. 5, 1918, p. 20, Takes Papers, Veterans Survey Collection, USAHEC.

43. See Coffman, *War to End All Wars*, 321–23; Cooke, *All-Americans at War*, 88.

44. See Lengel, *To Conquer Hell*, 218, 265–73.

45. Jonathan H. Ebel, *G.I. Messiahs: Soldiering, War, and American Civil Religion* (New Haven: Yale University Press, 2015), 49–58; Slotkin, *Lost Battalions*, 466–80.

46. See Whitman, *Story of the 325th*, 23–24; Transcribed diary, Oct. 8, 1918, pp. 20–21, Takes Papers, Veterans Survey Collections, USAHEC.

47. See Lengel, *To Conquer Hell*, 278–79.

48. G. Edward Buxton, Jr., *Official History of 82nd Division, American Expeditionary Forces, 1917–1919* (Indianapolis: Bobbs-Merrill Co. Publishers, 1920), 58–62; Coffman, *War to End All Wars*, 324; Lengel, *To Conquer Hell*, 279–82; Richard Wheeler, ed., *Sergeant York and the Great War: His Own Life Story and War Diary* (San Antonio: Vision Forum, 2011), 167.

49. Transcribed diary, Oct. 9, 1918, p. 21, Takes Papers, Veterans Survey Collections, USAHEC.

50. See Lengel, *To Conquer Hell*, 294–95; Buxton, Jr., *Official History of 82nd Division*, 66–67.

51. See Whitman, *Story of the 325th*, 27.

52. Lengel, *To Conquer Hell*, 295–96.

53. Transcribed diary, Oct. 10, 1918, pp. 21–2, Takes Papers, Veterans Survey Collections, USAHEC.

54. "The 325th Infantry in its Meuse-Argonne Operations—October 10–31, 1918," undated, p. 1; box 16; Records of the 82nd Division; RG 120; NACP.

55. "Gives His Life for Cause of Freedom," newspaper unknown, Nov. 15, 1918, Walter F. Owens Papers, 82nd Division, 325th Infantry Regiment, Veterans Survey Collections, USAHEC.

56. See Whitman, *Story of the 325th*, 26–32; Cooke, *All-Americans at War*, 92–93.

57. See Lengel, *To Conquer Hell*, 303–5; Coffman, *War to End All Wars*, 325.

58. Society of the First Division, *History of the First Division During the World War, 1917–1919* (Philadelphia: John C. Winston Co., 1922), 208–9.

59. "Dead on the Field of Honor," *Greenville* (Mo.) *Sun*, Nov. 28, 1918.

60. "Letters from Selma Boys 'Over There'," *Selma* (Ala.) *Journal*, Oct. 1, 1918.

61. David L. Snead, ed., *An American Soldier in World War I* (Lincoln: University of Nebraska Press, 2006), 123.

62. Nimrod T. Frazer, *Send the Alabamians: World War I Fighters in the Rainbow Division* (Tuscaloosa: University of Alabama Press, 2014), 156–61.

63. "By Fourth Liberty Bonds: 'Don't Let the SON Go Down'," *Greenville* (Mo.) *Sun*, Oct. 3, 1918.

64. "They Got There in Time," *Watertown* (Wisc.) *News*, Sept. 27, 1918. See also "Forward!" *Watertown* (Wisc.) *News*, Oct. 2, 1918.

65. "Finish the Job Now," *Greenville* (Mo.) *Sun*, Oct. 17, 1918.

66. "Sporting Writer Gives Two Tragic Bond Arguments" and "Buy Another Bond Even If You Must Mortgage Future," *Greenville* (Mo.) *Sun*, Oct. 17, 1918.

67. See "While Heads Are Bared," *Watertown* (Wisc.) *News*, Oct. 4, 1918. The line served as the epigraph of Dinsmore Ely, *Dinsmore Ely: One Who Served* (Chicago: A. C. McClurg & Co., 1919).

68. "Yanks," *Selma* (Ala.) *Journal*, Oct. 4, 1918.

69. "Don't Be a 'Slacker,'" *Watertown* (Wisc.) *News*, Oct. 4, 1918.

70. "Pouring Forth Our Earthly Treasures . . . ," *Watertown* (Wisc.) *News*, Sept. 30, 1918.

71. "A Bit of Home within the Camp," *Watertown* (Wisc.) *News*, Oct. 16, 1918; *Greenville* (Mo.) *Sun*, Oct. 17, 1918.

72. See Barry, *Great Influenza*, 169–76.

73. "Influenza Stops New Draft Call," *Watertown* (Wisc.) *News*, Sept. 27, 1918; "Camp Head Ends Life" and "Ferd. Schoechert a Watertown Boy Succumbs in Camp," *Watertown* (Wisc.) *News*, Oct. 9, 1918.

74. Ben Fluegel to Mother, Nov. 3, 1918, Letters folder (call no. SC 1931), Ben (Bernhard) Fluegel Papers (Fluegel Papers), WHS.

75. See "Influenza Taking Hold in Missouri," *Greenville* (Mo.) *Sun*, Oct. 17, 1918; "Influenza Is Gaining Way in Selma Now," *Selma* (Ala.) *Journal*, Oct. 8, 1918.

76. "Francis W. Barnes Severely Wounded While in Action" and "News of the Boys," *Watertown* (Wisc.) *News*, Sept. 27, 1918.

77. "Back the Boys with Bonds," *Watertown* (Wisc.) *News*, Oct. 14, 1918.

78. "U.S. Men Wade Waist Deep to Take Grandpre," *Watertown* (Wisc.) *News*, Oct. 18, 1918.

79. See "Ralph Ewing Writes from the Front," *Greenville* (Mo.) *Sun*, Oct. 24, 1918; "From the Boys in the Service," *Greenville* (Mo.) *Sun*, Nov. 7, 1918.

80. "Asa Cradic Killed in Action in France," *Greenville* (Mo.) *Sun*, Oct. 31, 1918; C. Asa Cradic draft registration card, June 5, 1917, Wayne County, Mo.; *Draft Registration Cards, 1917–1918* (Family History Library Microfilm roll 1683936); Records of the Selective Service System (World War I), 1917–1939, Record Group 163, National Archives and Records Administration-Southeast Region, Morrow, Ga.

81. "The Origin, Design and Proper Display of Service Flag," Committee on Public Information, *Official Bulletin*, May 25, 1918, vol. 2, no. 319, pp. 12–14. Emphasis added.

82. See "John F. Moriarty Corporal in France Succumbs to Wounds," *Watertown* (Wisc.) *News*, Oct. 30, 1918; "Asa Cradic Killed in Action in France," *Greenville* (Mo.) *Sun*, Oct. 31, 1918.

83. Huidekoper, *History of the 33rd Division*, 84.

84. See Coffman, *War to End All Wars*, 326; Clayton Slack interview, WHS.

85. Lengel, *To Conquer Hell*, 275–82.

86. See *History of the 124th Machine Gun Battalion*, 27–28, 49.

87. See Coffman, *War to End All Wars*, 326–27.

88. See Lengel, *To Conquer Hell*, 309–11; Transcribed diary, Oct. 11, 1918, pp. 22–23, Takes Papers, Veterans Survey Collections, USAHEC; "The 325th Infantry in its Meuse-Argonne Operations—October 10–31, 1918," undated, p. 1; box 16; Records of the 82nd Division; RG 120; NACP.

89. See Whitman, *Story of the 325th*, 27; Maj. Oliver Q. Melton, "'K' Company in the Argonne-Meuse Drive," p. 1; box 16; Records of the 82nd Division; RG 120; NACP.

90. See *The Gold Chevron: A History of the Fifty-Third U.S. Infantry*, pp. 13–15; box 12; Records of the 6th Division, 53rd Inf. Regt.; RG 120; NACP.

91. See Eliga Dees to Mae Dees, Oct. 5 and 8, 1918, Eliga and Mae Dees Letters (Dees Letters), Collection R1453, State Historical Society of Missouri, Columbia, Mo. (SHSM).

92. Edward Streeter, *Love Letters of Bill to Mable: Comprising Dere Mable, "That's Me All Over, Mable," and "Same Old Bill, eh Mable!"* (New York: Frederick A. Stokes Co., 1918, 1919), 228.

93. Streeter, *Love Letters of Bill to Mable*, 234.

94. See Eliga Dees to Mae Dees, Oct. 5 and 8, 1918, Dees Letters, SHSM.

95. Eliga Dees to Mae Dees, Oct. 22, 1918, Dees Letters, SHSM.

96. See Cooke, *All-Americans at War*, 102–3; Buxton, Jr., *Official History of 82nd Division*, 129; Transcribed diary, Oct. 11, 1918, p. 23, Takes Papers, Veterans Survey Collections, USAHEC; "The 325th Infantry in its Meuse-Argonne Operations—October 10–31, 1918," undated, pp. 4–5; box 16; Records of the 82nd Division; RG 120; NACP.

97. See Frazer, *Send the Alabamians*, 180–81.
98. See Lengel, *To Conquer Hell*, 341–42; Whitman, *Story of the 325th*, 44–49; Maj. Oliver Q. Melton, "'K' Company in the Argonne-Meuse Drive," p. 2; box 16; "The 325th Infantry in its Meuse-Argonne Operations—October 10–31, 1918," undated, p. 6; box 16; Records of the 82nd Division; RG 120; NACP.
99. Whitman, *Story of the 325th*, 40, 47; U.S. Army Field Messages; box 16; "The 325th Infantry in its Meuse-Argonne Operations—October 10–31, 1918," undated, p. 6; box 16; Records of the 82nd Division; RG 120; NACP. For friendly fire see Slotkin, *Lost Battalions*, 471; Byron Farwell, *Over There: The United States and the Great War, 1917–1918* (New York: W. W. Norton, 1999), 243, 246, 307, 312.
100. Buxton, Jr., *Official History of 82nd Division*, 134.
101. Reminiscences, p. 6, Knud J. Olsen Papers; Eighty-Second Division, 325th Infantry Regiment, Veterans Survey Collections, USAHEC.
102. "The 325th Infantry in its Meuse-Argonne Operations—October 10–31, 1918," undated, p. 7; box 16; Records of the 82nd Division; RG 120; NACP.
103. Maj. Oliver Q. Melton, "'K' Company in the Argonne-Meuse Drive," p. 3; box 16; Records of the 82nd Division; RG 120; NACP.
104. Maj. Oliver Q. Melton, "'K' Company in the Argonne-Meuse Drive," p. 2; box 16; Records of the 82nd Division; RG 120; NACP.
105. "The 325th Infantry in its Meuse-Argonne Operations—October 10–31, 1918," undated, p. 11; box 16; Records of the 82nd Division; RG 120; NACP.
106. Cooke, *All-Americans at War*, 106–9.
107. Lengel, *To Conquer Hell*, 373.
108. Transcribed diary, Oct. 18, 1918, p. 24, Takes Papers, Veterans Survey Collections, USAHEC.
109. Buxton, Jr., *Official History of 82nd Division*, 213.
110. See Lengel, *To Conquer Hell*, 345.
111. Lengel, *To Conquer Hell*, 359–61.
112. Ben Fluegel to Mother, Nov. 3, 1918, Fluegel Papers, WHS.
113. *History of the 124th Machine Gun Battalion*, 55.
114. *History of the 124th Machine Gun Battalion*, 29–34.
115. Diary from July 5, 1918 to June 4, 1919, p. 1, Sol J. Arouesty Papers; Wayne Turner to Mother, Dec. 13, 1918, Wayne O. Turner Papers (Turner Papers); 6th Division, 53rd Infantry Regiment, Veterans Survey Collections, USAHEC; *Gold Chevron*, pp. 15–17; box 12; Records of the 6th Division; RG 120; NACP.
116. Lengel, *To Conquer Hell*, 381–403.
117. See Frazer, *Send the Alabamians*, 193–94.
118. See "German Military Forces are Under Civilian Rule," *Watertown* (Wisc.) *News*, Oct. 28, 1918; "Suspect Hun Trickery" and "Austria Asks for Peace

As Soon As Possible," *Watertown* (Wisc.) *News*, Oct. 30, 1918; "Ottoman Empire Quits," *Watertown* (Wisc.) *News*, Nov. 1, 1918; "Emperor of Austria Has Fled Vienna," *Selma* (Ala.) *Journal*, Nov. 1, 1918; "Teutons are in Retreat East of Meuse River," *Watertown* (Wisc.) *News*, Nov. 4, 1918; "America Must Feed Neutrals After the War," *Greenville* (Mo.) *Sun*, Nov. 7, 1918.

119. "Peace Talk," *Selma* (Ala.) *Journal*, Oct. 28, 1918; "Selma Parents Receive Notice of Son's Death," *Selma* (Ala.) *Journal*, Sept. 3, 1918.

120. "From the Boys in the Service," *Greenville* (Mo.) *Sun*, Nov. 7, 1918.

121. Wayne Turner to Mother, Dec. 13, 1918, Turner Papers, Veterans Survey Collections, USAHEC.

122. See *Gold Chevron*, p. 18; box 12; Records of the 6th Division; RG 120; NACP.

123. Maj. Gen. John F. O'Ryan, *The Story of the 27th Division*, Vol. 1 (New York: Wynkoop Hallenbeck Crawford Co., 1921), 386–98. Casualty statistics from Vol. 2, p. 1106.

124. Barbeau and Henri, *Unknown Soldiers*, 157–63.

125. "Lt. G. W. Huston Reported Killed at Battle Front," *Selma* (Ala.) *Journal*, Nov. 6, 1918.

126. Whitman, *Story of the 325th*, 58.

127. Cooke, *All-Americans at War*, 109.

128. Thomas Alexander Boyd to Mother, Oct. 27, 1918, folder 1, box 1, Thomas Boyd Papers (Boyd Papers), Ohio Historical Society, Columbus, Ohio (OHS).

129. See Scott, *Natalie Scott*, 204–10.

130. Natalie Scott to Martha Scott, Oct. 1918 [likely Oct. 26], folder 10, box 2, Scott Papers, LaRC.

131. Natalie Scott to Martha Scott, Oct. 1918 [likely Oct. 26], folder 10, box 2, Scott Papers, LaRC.

132. Natalie Scott to Martha Scott, Nov. 4, 1918, folder 11, box 2, Scott Papers, LaRC.

133. *History of the 124th Machine Gun Battalion*, 35.

134. See "Plan of Defense—Troyon Sector: Terrain," in Frederic Louis Huidekoper, *The History of the 33rd Division, A. E. F.*, Vol. III (Springfield, Ill.: Illinois State Historical Library, 1921), 379–80.

135. Office of the Adjutant General, *Histories of Two Hundred and Fifty-One Divisions of the German Army which Participated in the War (1914–1918)* (Chaumont, France: American Expeditionary Forces, 1919), 577–78, 660–61. For the 439th see "Plan of Defense—Troyon Sector" in Huidekoper, *History of the 33rd Division*, Vol. 3, 373–83; General Staff, Intelligence Section, *The German and American Combined Daily Order of Battle, 25 September, 1918—11 November 1918* (Chaumont, France: American Expeditionary Forces, 1919), p. 22; Collection of the American Expeditionary Forces, General Staff, G-2, Special

Collections, Combined Arms Research Library, Fort Leavenworth, Kans. William J. Bacon, ed., *History of the Fifty-Fifth Field Artillery Brigade* (Memphis: William J. Bacon, 1920), 173, references the 439th but misidentifies it as Bavarian.

136. See Benjamin Ziemann, *War Experiences in Rural Germany, 1914–1923* (Oxford: Berg, 2007), 102.

137. See *History of the 124th Machine Gun Battalion*, 35–37; Robert Cowley, "The Road to Butgnéville—November 11, 1918," in Byron Hollinshead, ed., *I Wish I'd Been There: Twenty Historians Bring to Life Dramatic Events that Changed America* (New York: Anchor Books, 2006), 223–41; "Report of Active Operations," Nov. 17, 1918, p. 11; box 19; Records of the 33rd Division, 124th Machine Gun Battalion; RG 120; NACP.

138. See Joseph E. Persico, *Eleventh Month, Eleventh Day, Eleventh Hour: Armistice Day, 1918: World War I and Its Violent Climax* (New York: Random House, 2005), 344.

139. "Report of Active Operations," Nov. 17, 1918, p. 11; box 19; Records of the 33rd Division, 124th Machine Gun Battalion; RG 120; NACP.

140. See Cowley, "The Road to Butgnéville," 233–34.

141. See Bacon, ed., *History of the Fifty-Fifth Field Artillery Brigade*, 171–72; Persico, *Eleventh Month*, 345.

142. See "Liggett Says Truce Put Troops in Danger," *New York Times*, Jan. 21, 1920.

143. Quoted in Persico, *Eleventh Month*, 347.

144. Ben Fluegel to Mother, Jan. 26, 1919, Fluegel Papers, WHS.

Chapter 7: It's Over Over There

1. Edward M. Coffman, *The War to End All Wars: The American Military Experience in World War I* (Lexington: University Press of Kentucky, 1998 ed.), 299.

2. *History of the 124th Machine Gun Battalion, 66th Brigade, 33rd Division, A. E. F.* (publisher unknown, 1919), 43–44.

3. *Watertown* (Wisc.) *Weltbürger*, Feb. 19, 1921; Interview with James R. Huebner, Aug. 4, 2012, Fish Creek, Wisc.

4. See John W. Scott, *Natalie Scott: A Magnificent Life* (Gretna, La.: Pelican Publishing Co., 2008), 210–29.

5. Report on the American Red Cross Evacuation Hospital 36, folder 9, box 6, Red Cross Report, Natalie Scott Papers (Scott Papers), Manuscripts Collection 123, Louisiana Research Collection, Tulane University, New Orleans, La. (LaRC).

6. Natalie Scott to Martha Scott, Dec. 10, 1918, folder 12, box 2, Scott Papers, LaRC.

7. Natalie Scott to Martha Scott, Dec. 10, 1918, folder 12, box 2, Scott Papers, LaRC.

8. "Text of President Wilson's Address to Congress. . . ," *Washington Post*, Dec. 3, 1918.

9. See "Peace Summary," *Los Angeles Times*, Nov. 12, 1918; "Unity in Peace as in War Urged," *Christian Science Monitor*, Nov. 21, 1918; "Entire Nation Gives Thanks," *Louisville Courier-Journal*, Nov. 29, 1918; "U.S. Thanks God of Nations for Victory Peace," *Chicago Daily Tribune*, Nov. 29, 1918.

10. "The United War Work Campaign," *New York Times*, Nov. 11, 1918; "Peace Summary," *Los Angeles Times*, Nov. 12, 1918; "Hartford Prays in Thanksgiving Over End of War," *Hartford Courant*, Nov. 15, 1918; "Unity in Peace as in War Urged," *Christian Science Monitor*, Nov. 21, 1918; "Peace Christmas Brings Joy to City," *New York Times*, Dec. 26, 1918; "Obtain $8,191,262 in War Work Drive," *New York Times*, Nov. 12, 1918.

11. "Rejoicing Throngs on Roads to Mons," *New York Times*, Nov. 14, 1918.

12. "The United War Work Campaign," *New York Times*, Nov. 11, 1918.

13. "Pastor Speaks on Patriotism," *Nashville Tennessean*, Nov. 25, 1918.

14. "No Heroics When Heroes Go," *Louisville Courier-Journal*, Nov. 17, 1918.

15. "For the Men Who Fought for Us," *New York Times*, Nov. 12, 1918; "The United War Work Campaign," *New York Times*, Nov. 11, 1918.

16. See Byron Farwell, *Over There: The United States and the Great War, 1917–1918* (New York: W. W. Norton, 1999), 147.

17. See John M. Kinder, *Paying with Their Bodies: American War and the Problem of the Disabled Veteran* (Chicago: University of Chicago Press, 2015), 76–79.

18. See, for example, "7,740 More War Veterans Return from Europe," *Hartford Courant*, Dec. 12, 1918; "129 Wounded Veterans Here," *Louisville Courier-Journal*, Dec. 11, 1918; "7,740 Maimed Yanks Land at New York," *Louisville Courier-Journal*, Dec. 12, 1918; "Huns Blame Marines," *Washington Post*, Dec. 13, 1918; "Heroes of War Home," *Los Angeles Times*, Dec. 12, 1918.

19. "7,740 Maimed Yanks Land at New York," *Louisville Courier-Journal*, Dec. 12, 1918.

20. "President Pays Honor to U.S. War Veterans," *San Francisco Chronicle*, Dec. 23, 1918.

21. "The Returned Disabled Soldier," *Outlook*, Dec. 11, 1918. See also "Our Crippled Soldiers," *Chicago Daily Tribune*, Dec. 18, 1918.

22. Beth Linker, *War's Waste: Rehabilitation in World War I America* (Chicago: University of Chicago Press, 2011), 4.

23. "People Facing Grim Tragedy of Almost 190,000 Wounded," *San Francisco Chronicle*, Dec. 15, 1918; "Face War Tragedies," *Washington Post*, Dec. 15, 1918.

24. "President Pays Honor to U.S. War Veterans," *San Francisco Chronicle*, Dec. 23, 1918.

25. "The Returning Crippled Soldier," *Washington Post*, Dec. 16, 1918. See also "When the Boys Come Home," *Hartford Courant*, Dec. 22, 1918.

26. "Lieut. G. W. Huston," *Selma* (Ala.) *Journal*, Nov. 18, 1918.

27. "Official Announcement of Death of Lieut. G. W. Huston Is Made," *Selma* (Ala.) *Journal*, Nov. 19, 1918.

28. G. B. Duncan to Nellye Huston, Nov. 23, 1918, folder 4, box 1080, Huston Family Papers (Huston Papers), W. S. Hoole Special Collections Library, University of Alabama, Tuscaloosa, Ala. (UASC).

29. Walter M. Whitman to Nellye Huston, Dec. 26, 1918, folder 4, box 1080, Huston Papers, UASC.

30. W. W. Harper to Nellye and Walter Huston, Nov. 23, 1918, folder 4, box 1080, Huston Papers, UASC.

31. J. W. L., "In Memory of Lt. G. Waring Huston," undated, folder 22, box 1080, Huston Papers, UASC.

32. Robert Cater draft reg. card, June 5, 1917, Dallas County, Ala.; *Draft Registration Cards, 1917–1918* (Family History Library Microfilm roll 1509378); Records of the Selective Service System (World War I), 1917–1939, Record Group 163; National Archives and Records Administration-Southeast Region, Morrow, Ga.

33. R. B. Cater to Walter Huston, Dec. 5, 1918, folder 4, box 1080, Huston Papers, UASC.

34. G. Claiborne Blanton to Nellye Huston, Dec. 1, 1918, folder 4, box 1080, Huston Papers, UASC.

35. Pressley Cleveland to Nellye Huston, Dec. 26, 1918, folder 4, box 1080, Huston Papers, UASC.

36. My thanks to Dr. Bruce Fleegler and Georgia Sylke, RN, for assistance with this material.

37. Arthur Huebner removal file, author's collection.

38. *History of the 124th Machine Gun Battalion*, 44–46.

39. See Jennifer D. Keene, *Doughboys, the Great War, and the Remaking of America* (Baltimore: Johns Hopkins University Press, 2001), 119–20.

40. *Watertown* (Wisc.) *Weltbürger*, Dec. 14, 1918.

41. "The Roll of Honor," *Watertown* (Wisc.) *News*, Dec. 13, 1918; "Casualty List," *Watertown* (Wisc.) *News*, Dec. 18, 1918.

42. See "Report of Death May Be Untrue," *Watertown* (Wisc.) *News*, Dec. 16, 1918; "Pvt. Dan M'Carthy Dies in France," *Watertown* (Wisc.) *Daily Times*, date unknown.

43. See Frederic Louis Huidekoper, *The History of the 33rd Division, A. E. F.*, Vol. 3 (Springfield, Ill.: Illinois State Historical Library, 1921), 541; *History of the 124th Machine Gun Battalion*, 55, 59; W. M. Haulsee, F. G. Howe, and A. C. Doyle, comps., *Soldiers of the Great War*, Vol. 3 (Washington, D.C.: Soldiers Record Publishing Association, 1920), 459.

44. See *The Gold Chevron: A History of the Fifty-Third U.S. Infantry*, pp. 18–21; box 12; Records of the 6th Division, 53rd Inf. Regt.; Combat Divisions, 1917–1919; Records of the American Expeditionary Forces (World War I), Record Group 120 (RG 120); NACP.

45. Wayne Turner to Brother, Jan. 5, 1919, Wayne O. Turner Papers (Turner Papers), 6th Division, 53rd Infantry Regiment, Veterans Survey Collections, U.S. Army Heritage and Education Center, Military History Institute, Carlisle, Penn. (USAHEC).

46. See "Dead on the Field of Honor" and "Williamsville School Destroyed by Fire," *Greenville* (Mo.) *Sun*, Nov. 28, 1918.

47. Eliga Dees to Mae Dees, Jan. 24, 1919, Eliga and Mae Dees Letters (Dees Letters), Collection R1453, State Historical Society of Missouri, Columbia, Mo. (SHSM).

48. Eliga Dees to Mae Dees, Feb. 7, 1919, Dees Letters, SHSM.

49. Eliga Dees to Mae Dees, Mar. 23, 1919, Dees Letters, SHSM.

50. Eliga Dees to Mae Dees, Dec. 30, 1918, Dees Letters, SHSM.

51. Eliga Dees to Mae Dees, Feb. 7, 1919, Dees Letters, SHSM.

52. Eliga Dees to Mae Dees, Jan. 3, 1919, Dees Letters, SHSM. For relaxed censorship after the armistice see Keene, *Doughboys*, 133.

53. Eliga Dees to Mae Dees, Dec. 23, 1918 and Jan. 24, 1919, Dees Letters, SHSM.

54. Ben Fluegel to Mother, Jan. 26, 1918, Letters folder (call no. SC 1931), Ben (Bernhard) Fluegel Papers (Fluegel Papers), Wisconsin Historical Society, Madison, Wisc. (WHS).

55. For the battalion in 1919 see *History of the 124th Machine Gun Battalion*, 46.

56. See G. Edward Buxton, Jr., *Official History of 82nd Division, American Expeditionary Forces, 1917–1919* (Indianapolis: Bobbs-Merrill Co. Publishers, 1920), 214–22.

57. See Scott, *Natalie Scott*, 216–19; Natalie Scott to Martha Scott, Dec. 26, 1918, folder 12, box 2, Scott Papers, LaRC.

58. See Scott, *Natalie Scott*, 219.

59. Natalie Scott to Martha Scott, July 16, 1919, folder 1, box 3, Scott Papers, LaRC.

60. Eliga Dees to Mae Dees, Feb. 7 and Mar. 2, 1919, Dees Letters, SHSM; Wayne Turner to Mother, Feb. 2, 1919, Turner Papers, Veterans Survey Collections, USAHEC.

61. Eliga Dees to Mae Dees, Feb. 9, 1919, Dees Letters, SHSM.

62. Eliga Dees to Mae Dees, Mar. 6, 1919, Dees Letters, SHSM.

63. Mother to Eliga Dees, Apr. 27, 1919; Mae Dees to Eliga Dees, Apr. 21, 1919, Dees Letters, SHSM.

64. Eliga Dees to Mae Dees, Feb. 15, 1919, Dees Letters, SHSM.

65. Eliga Dees to Mae Dees, Feb. 23, 1919, Dees Letters, SHSM.

66. Eliga Dees to Mae Dees, Mar. 2, 1919; Mae Dees to Eliga Dees, May 11, 1919; Dees Letters, SHSM.

67. Eliga Dees to Mae Dees, Mar. 2, 1919, Dees Letters, SHSM.

68. Eliga Dees to Mae Dees, Feb. 17, 1919, Dees Letters, SHSM.

69. Eliga Dees to Mae Dees, Mar. 2, 1919, Dees Letters, SHSM.

70. Eliga Dees to Mae Dees, Mar. 2, 1919, Dees Letters, SHSM.

71. Eliga Dees to Mae Dees, Feb. 23, 1919, Dees Letters, SHSM.

72. Eliga Dees to Mae Dees, Mar. 13, 1919, Dees Letters, SHSM.

73. Eliga Dees to Mae Dees, Feb. 17 and Mar. 2, 1919, Dees Letters, SHSM.

74. Mae Dees to Eliga Dees, May 15, 1919, Dees Letters, SHSM.

75. Eliga Dees to Mae Dees, Feb. 28 and Mar. 2, 1919, Dees Letters, SHSM.

76. Eliga Dees to Mae Dees, Mar. 21, 1919, Dees Letters, SHSM.

77. Eliga Dees to Mae Dees, Feb. 28, 1919, Dees Letters, SHSM.

78. Eliga Dees to Mae Dees, Apr. 13, 1919, Dees Letters, SHSM.

79. See John M. Barry, *The Great Influenza: The Epic Story of the Deadliest Plague in History* (New York: Viking, 2004), 383–87, 397.

80. Mae Dees to Eliga Dees, Apr. 13, 1919, Dees Letters, SHSM.

81. Mae Dees to Eliga Dees, May 19, 1919, Dees Letters, SHSM.

82. Eliga Dees to Mae Dees, Apr. 14 and 20, 1919; Mae Dees to Eliga Dees, Apr. 21, 24, and 25 and May 11, 1919; Dees Letters, SHSM.

83. See David M. Kennedy, *Over Here: The First World War and American Society* (New York: Oxford University Press, 2004 ed.), 185; Michael McGerr, *A Fierce Discontent: The Rise and the Fall of the Progressive Movement in America* (New York: Oxford University Press, 2003), 294.

84. See Robert H. Zieger, *America's Great War: World War I and the American Experience* (Lanham, Md.: Rowman and Littlefield, 2000), 149–51; Kimberly Jensen, *Mobilizing Minerva: American Women in the First World War* (Urbana: University of Illinois Press, 2008), 166–7.

85. See "Yanks Not Hilarious over Dry Amendment," *Los Angeles Times*, Jan. 17, 1919; "Brands Reports as False," *Baltimore Sun*, Jan. 20, 1919.

86. "Hartford Prays in Thanksgiving over End of War," *Hartford Courant*, Nov. 15, 1918.

87. See "Suffrage Success Held to Be Assured," *New York Times*, Dec. 9, 1918; "Women at Peace Table," *New York Times*, Nov. 19, 1918.

88. See Jensen, *Mobilizing Minerva*, 167.

89. "Text of President Wilson's Address to Congress . . . ," *Washington Post*, Dec. 3, 1918.

90. "Women's Service Paid Tribute in Washington," *Nashville Tennessean*, Dec. 15, 1918.

91. See Lisa M. Budreau, *Bodies of War: World War I and the Politics of Commemoration in America, 1919–1933* (New York: New York University Press, 2010), 34–81.

92. Arthur Huebner burial file, author's collection.

93. Interview with James R. Huebner, Aug. 4, 2012, Fish Creek, Wisc.

94. See Budreau, *Bodies of War*, 24.
95. Mae Dees to Eliga Dees, May [date unknown], 1919, Dees Letters, SHSM.
96. Mae Dees to Eliga Dees, Apr. 13 and 24, 1919, Dees Letters, SHSM.
97. Eliga Dees to Mae Dees, Mar. 21, 1919, Dees Letters, SHSM.
98. Wayne Turner to Mother, Jan. 29, 1919, Turner Papers, Veterans Survey Collections, USAHEC.
99. Mae Dees to Eliga Dees, Apr. 25, 1919, Dees Letters, SHSM.
100. "Jilted, Sues as Soldier Brings War Bride Home," *Chicago Daily Tribune*, July 10, 1919.
101. "Jilted, Sues as Soldier Brings War Bride Home," *Chicago Daily Tribune*, July 10, 1919.
102. Susan Zeiger, *Entangling Alliances: Foreign War Brides and American Soldiers in the Twentieth Century* (New York: New York University Press, 2010), 39–70.
103. Eliga Dees to Mae Dees, Feb. 28, 1919, Dees Letters, SHSM; Wayne Turner to Brother, Jan. 5, 1919, Turner Papers, Veterans Survey Collections, USAHEC.
104. Eliga Dees to Mae Dees, Apr. 13, 1919, Dees Letters, SHSM; Wayne Turner to Mother, Jan. 18, 1919, Turner Papers, Veterans Survey Collections, USAHEC.
105. See Eliga Dees to Mae Dees, May 5, 12, 13, and 22, 1919, Dees Letters, SHSM.
106. Wayne Turner to Mother, May 9, 1919, Turner Papers, Veterans Survey Collections, USAHEC.
107. See Keene, *Doughboys*, 120–26.
108. Wayne Turner to Mother, May 9, 1919, Turner Papers, Veterans Survey Collections, USAHEC.
109. See Zeiger, *Entangling Alliances*, 48–49.
110. See Mae Dees to Eliga Dees, May 4, 1919; Eliga Dees to Mae Dees, May 12 and 17, 1919; Dees Letters, SHSM.
111. *Gold Chevron*, pp. 21–24; box 12; Records of the 6th Division; RG 120; NACP.
112. Eliga Dees to Mae Dees, May 12, 1919, Dees Letters, SHSM.
113. Mae Dees to Eliga Dees, May 4 and 19, 1919, Dees Letters, SHSM.
114. Eliga Dees to Mae Dees, May 17, 1919, Dees Letters, SHSM.
115. Eliga Dees to Mae Dees, June 13, 1919, Dees Letters, SHSM.
116. Eliga Dees to Mae Dees, June 19, 1919, Dees Letters, SHSM.
117. Eliga Dees to Mae Dees, June 15, 1919, Dees Letters, SHSM.
118. Kennedy, *Over Here*, 357–59.
119. See Kinder, *Paying with Their Bodies*, 87.
120. Eliga Dees to Mae Dees, June 19, 20, and 28, 1919; Mae Dees to Eliga Dees, June 22 and 25, 1919; Dees Letters, SHSM.
121. Mae Dees to Eliga Dees, June 22 and July 7, 1919; Dees Letters, SHSM.
122. Mae Dees to Eliga Dees, July 8, 1919, Dees Letters, SHSM.

123. Eliga Dees to Mae Dees, June 28, 1919; Mae Dees to Eliga Dees, July 7, 1919, Dees Letters, SHSM.

124. Eliga Dees to Mae Dees, July 16, 1919, Dees Letters, SHSM.

125. See *https://www.abmc.gov/node/322744#.WOZoCI5Ok8Z* (Apr. 6, 2017); Fred L. Borch III, "Anatomy of a Court-Martial: The Trial and Execution of Private William Buckner," *The Army Lawyer* (Oct. 2011), 6; Lisa M. Budreau, *Bodies of War: World War I and the Politics of Commemoration in America, 1919–1933* (New York: New York University Press, 2010), 59.

126. Chad L. Williams, *Torchbearers of Democracy: African American Soldiers in the World War I Era* (Chapel Hill: University of North Carolina Press, 2010), 127–28.

127. For black troops after the armistice see Arthur E. Barbeau and Florette Henri, *The Unknown Soldiers: Black American Troops in World War I* (Philadelphia: Temple University Press, 1974), 164–89. For Service of Supply in the queue see Keene, *Doughboys*, 132.

128. See Richard Slotkin, *Lost Battalions: The Great War and the Crisis of American Nationality* (New York: Henry Holt, 2005), 480–81.

129. For this paragraph and quotations see Barbeau and Henri, *Unknown Soldiers*, 177, 182, 185.

130. See Budreau, *Bodies of War*, 214.

131. Natalie Scott to Martha Scott, Oct. 18, 1919, folder 1, box 3, Scott Papers, LaRC.

132. For Natalie's homecoming see Scott, *Natalie Scott*, 228–29.

133. Eliga Dees to Mae Dees, Oct. 25 and 26, 1919; Mae Dees to Eliga Dees, Oct. 25, 1919; Dees Letters, SHSM.

134. Mae Dees to Eliga Dees, Nov. 26, 1919, Dees Letters, SHSM.

135. Mae Dees to Eliga Dees, Dec. 7, 1919, Dees Letters, SHSM.

136. See Eliga and Mae Dees; p. 43A, lines 47 and 48, Enumeration District 171, Camp Grant, Winnebago County, Ill. Census of Population; *Fourteenth Census of the United States, 1920* (National Archives Microfilm Publication [NAMP] T625, roll 416); Records of the Bureau of the Census, Record Group 29 (RG 29); National Archives Building, Washington, D.C. (NAB).

137. See Eliga Dees Service Record; Missouri Digital Heritage; Soldiers' Records: War of 1812—World War I, *sos.mo.gov/archives/soldiers* (Sept. 12, 2016).

138. See Helen Mae Dees; p. 3B, line 53, Enumeration District 112–8, Lost Creek Township, Wayne County, Mo. Census of Population; *Fifteenth Census of the United States, 1930* (NAMP T626, roll 1251); RG 29; NAB. Helen Mae's birthdate comes from her grave marker in Greenville Cemetery.

139. See Kinder, *Paying with Their Bodies*, 78; Linker, *War's Waste*, 8–9; Stephen R. Ortiz, *Beyond the Bonus March and GI Bill: How Veteran Politics Shaped the New Deal Era* (New York: New York University Press, 2010), 15.

140. See Kinder, *Paying with Their Bodies*, 101–14.

141. See Ortiz, *Beyond the Bonus March and GI Bill*, 25–27.

142. *Watertown* (Wisc.) *Weltbürger*, Feb. 19, 1921.

143. See "7,800 Hero Dead Arrive," *Watertown* (Wisc.) *Daily Times*, May 18, 1921; *Watertown* (Wisc.) *Weltbürger*, May 21, 1921. Other papers had the number as 5,112 or 5,212. See, for example, "5,212 Dead Soldiers Back from France," *New York Times*, May 19, 1921; "Honor 5,112 American Dead," *Washington Post*, May 23, 1921.

144. See Budreau, *Bodies at War*, 77–8; "Only 2 Unclaimed Soldier Dead Here," *New York Times*, April 16, 1921.

145. For Kohls and Knaak see Jefferson County Directory, 1921–1922, p. 215, Watertown Public Library, Local History Collection, Watertown, Wisc.; Arthur Huebner removal file, author's collection.

146. Funeral record, St. Mark's Lutheran Church, Watertown, Wisc.

147. *Watertown* (Wisc.) *Weltbürger*, June 11, 1921.

148. See Roger Daniels, *Guarding the Golden Door: American Immigration Policy and Immigrants since 1882* (New York: Hill and Wang, 2004), 49–58; Nancy Cott, *Public Vows: A History of Marriage and the Nation* (Cambridge: Harvard University Press, 2000), 132–55; Robert L. Fleegler, *Ellis Island Nation: Immigration Policy and American Identity in the Twentieth Century* (Philadelphia: University of Pennsylvania Press, 2013), 12.

149. Quoted in Zeiger, *Entangling Alliances*, 51.

150. Nancy Cott notes the same irony: The exclusion of polygamists suggested "disloyalty to monogamy [was] equivalent to overthrowing the government." See Cott, *Public Vows*, 139.

151. See *http://freepages.genealogy.rootsweb.ancestry.com/~wcmc/dees_chapel/dees_william_clifford_death.jpg* (Aug. 25, 2016).

152. See *http://www.archives.alabama.gov/goldstar/images/card/Huston_GeorgeW. pdf* (Sept. 22, 2016).

153. For Waring's funeral see "He Had One Life and He Gave That When His Country Called," *Selma* (Ala.) *Times-Journal*, Sept. 4, 1921.

154. See Steven Trout, *On the Battlefield of Memory: The First World War and American Remembrance, 1919–1941* (Tuscaloosa: University of Alabama Press, 2010), 37.

155. "'Unknown' Made War to End War, Wells Asserts," *Chicago Daily Tribune*, Nov. 12, 1921.

156. Jonathan H. Ebel, *G.I. Messiahs: Soldiering, War, and American Civil Religion* (New Haven: Yale University Press, 2015), 55.

157. Carrie Goodwin to Nellye Huston, Apr. 7, 1920, folder 14, box 1080, Huston Papers, UASC. Emphasis added.

158. "R. H. L. Recalls Good Old Days of Journalism," *Chicago Daily Tribune*, Mar. 28, 1924.

Epilogue

1. See Chad L. Williams, *Torchbearers of Democracy: African American Soldiers in the World War I Era* (Chapel Hill: University of North Carolina Press, 2010), 349; Christian G. Appy, *American Reckoning: The Vietnam War and Our National Identity* (New York: Viking, 2015), 137–40; Beth Bailey, *America's Army: Making the All-Volunteer Force* (Cambridge: Belknap Press of Harvard University Press, 2009), 258–59; Arthur E. Barbeau and Florette Henri, *The Unknown Soldiers: Black American Troops in World War I* (Philadelphia: Temple University Press, 1974), 178–89; Jennifer Mittelstadt, *The Rise of the Military Welfare State* (Cambridge: Harvard University Press, 2015), 118.

2. See Lynn Dumenil, *The Second Line of Defense: American Women and World War I* (Chapel Hill: University of North Carolina Press, 2017); Kara Dixon Vuic, *Officer, Nurse, Woman: The Army Nurse Corps in the Vietnam War* (Baltimore: Johns Hopkins University Press, 2010); Heather Marie Stur, *Beyond Combat: Women and Gender in the Vietnam War Era* (New York: Cambridge University Press, 2011); Yvonne Tasker, *Soldiers' Stories: Military Women in Cinema and Television since World War II* (Durham: Duke University Press, 2011); Margot Canaday, *The Straight State: Sexuality and Citizenship in Twentieth-Century America* (Princeton: Princeton University Press, 2009); Susan Zeiger, *In Uncle Sam's Service: Women Workers with the American Expeditionary Force, 1917–1919* (Ithaca: Cornell University Press, 1999), 163, 168–74; Kimberly Jensen, *Mobilizing Minerva: American Women in the First World War* (Urbana: University of Illinois Press, 2008), 140–41, 174–75; Nancy K. Bristow, *Making Men Moral: Social Engineering during the Great War* (New York: New York University Press, 1996), 179–214; Jennifer D. Keene, *World War I: The American Soldier Experience* (Lincoln: University of Nebraska Press, 2001), 120; Bailey, *America's Army*, 130–71. For similar assertions on the war's impact on postwar European gender roles see Susan R. Grayzel, *Women's Identities at War: Gender, Motherhood, and Politics in Britain and France during the First World War* (Chapel Hill: University of North Carolina Press, 1999); Mary Louise Roberts, *Civilization without Sexes: Reconstructing Gender in Postwar France, 1917–1927* (Chicago: University of Chicago Press, 1994).

3. See Nancy Gentile Ford, *Americans All! Foreign-born Soldiers in World War I* (College Station: Texas A&M University Press, 2001), 144–45; Christopher M. Sterba, *Good Americans: Italian and Jewish Immigrants during the First World War* (New York: Oxford University Press, 2003).

4. See Tom Engelhardt, *The End of Victory Culture: Cold War America and the Disillusioning of a Generation* (Amherst: University of Massachusetts Press, 1995).

5. See Robert D. Kaplan, *Imperial Grunts: On the Ground with the American Military, from Mongolia to the Philippines to Iraq and Beyond* (New York: Vintage Books, 2005), 4.

6. Stephen R. Ortiz, *Beyond the Bonus March and GI Bill: How Veteran Politics Shaped the New Deal Era* (New York: New York University Press, 2010), 1–28.

7. Jennifer D. Keene, *Doughboys, the Great War, and the Remaking of America* (Baltimore: Johns Hopkins University Press, 2001), 198–203.

8. See Keene, *Doughboys*, 205–14; Ronald Schaffer, *America in the Great War: The Rise of the War Welfare State* (New York: Oxford University Press, 1991).

9. See Mark Boulton, *Failing Our Veterans: The G.I. Bill and the Vietnam Generation* (New York: New York University Press, 2014); Ortiz, *Beyond the Bonus March and GI Bill*, 201; Keene, *Doughboys*, 213.

10. Mittelstadt, *Rise of the Military Welfare State*, 220–28.

11. See Michael S. Sherry, *In the Shadow of War: The United States since the 1930s* (New Haven: Yale University Press, 1995), 9; Jackson Lears, *Rebirth of a Nation: The Making of Modern America, 1877–1920* (New York: HarperCollins, 2009), 11.

12. For the intertwining of family and political history in the late twentieth century see Michael Stewart Foley, *Front Porch Politics: The Forgotten Heyday of American Activism in the 1970s and 1980s* (New York: Hill and Wang, 2013); Robert O. Self, *All in the Family: The Realignment of American Democracy since the 1960s* (New York: Hill and Wang, 2012); Jefferson Cowie, *Stayin' Alive: The 1970s and the Last Days of the Working Class* (New York: The New Press, 2010).

13. See *obamawhitehouse.archives.gov/the-press-office/2013/04/27/remarks-president-white-house-correspondents-association-dinner* (March 14, 2017).

14. See Susan A. Brewer, *Why America Fights: Patriotism and War Propaganda from the Philippines to Iraq* (New York: Oxford University Press, 2009), 90; Chris Rasmussen, " 'This Thing Has Ceased to Be a Joke': The Veterans of Future Wars and the Meanings of Political Satire in the 1930s," *Journal of American History* 103 (June 2016): 84–106.

15. Quoted in Tom Digby, *Love and War: How Militarism Shapes Sexuality and Romance* (New York: Columbia University Press, 2014), 156–57.

16. Steven Trout, *On the Battlefield of Memory: The First World War and American Remembrance, 1919–1941* (Tuscaloosa: University of Alabama Press, 2010), 150.

17. See John Milton Cooper, Jr., "The World War and American Memory," *Diplomatic History* 38 (Sept. 2014): 732.

18. See Mary L. Dudziak, "How War Lost Its Politics," *Dissent* (Summer 2016).

19. Thomas Boyd, *Through the Wheat: A Novel of the World War I Marines* (Lincoln: University of Nebraska Press, 2000), 266.

20. See Trout, *On the Battlefield of Memory*, 6–9.

21. My first book, like many others, provoked debate over the character of war imagery. For that example see Andrew J. Huebner, *The Warrior Image: Soldiers in American Culture from the Second World War to the Vietnam Era* (Chapel Hill: University of North Carolina Press, 2008); Michael J. Allen, "The Limits and Fears of Flesh and Blood," *Reviews in American History* 38 (Sept. 2010): 539–47; Andrew J. Bacevich, "Review of *The Warrior Image*," *Journal of Cold War Studies* 11 (Winter 2009): 150–51; Bacevich, *The New American Militarism: How Americans Are Seduced by War* (New York: Oxford University Press, 2005). For WWII's shifting meanings see John Bodnar, *The "Good War" in American Memory* (Baltimore: Johns Hopkins University Press, 2010).

22. Robert Walter Huston death record, *Alabama, Deaths and Burials Index, 1881–1974* (Provo: Ancestry.com Operations, Inc., 2011), *Ancestry.com* (August 16, 2012).

23. See Cleveland family; p. 15B, lines 80–82, Enumeration District 34, Selma, Dallas County, Ala. Census of Population; *Fifteenth Census of the United States, 1930* (National Archives Microfilm Publication [NAMP] T626, roll 14); Records of the Bureau of the Census, Record Group 29 (RG 29); National Archives Building, Washington, D.C. (NAB). Waring H. Cleveland death record, *U.S., Find a Grave Index, 1600s—Current* (Provo: Ancestry.com Operations, Inc., 2012), *Ancestry.com* (Apr. 5, 2017).

24. See Nellye Smith Huston death record, *Alabama, Deaths and Burials Index, 1881–1974* (Provo: Ancestry.com Operations, Inc., 2011), *Ancestry.com* (July 26, 2013); Selma, Ala., telephone directory, Edwin Condie Godbold Local History Collection, Selma-Dallas County Public Library, Selma, Ala.

25. George Waring Huston Lapsley service record, *Muster Rolls of U.S. Navy Ships, Stations, and Other Naval Activities, 1939–1949*; ARC ID: 594996; Records of the Bureau of Naval Personnel, 1798–2007, Record Group 24; National Archives and Records Administration, College Park, Md.

26. Selma City Directory, 1957, Vol.3, p. 346, *U.S., City Directories, 1822–1995* (Provo: Ancestry.com Operations, Inc., 2011), *Ancestry.com* (Apr. 5, 2017); John W. Lapsley death record, *U.S., Social Security Death Index, 1935–2014* (Provo: Ancestry.com Operations, Inc., 2011), *Ancestry.com* (Apr. 5, 2017). In 2013, I went to see the place on Church Street, but it was gone. Although still appearing on Google Earth, a "suspicious" fire had claimed the empty house three years earlier. See "Historic Home Destroyed," *Selma Times-Journal*, Oct. 2, 2010.

27. See Dees family; p. 3B, lines 51–55, Enumeration District 0008, Lost Creek Township, Wayne County, Mo. Census of Population; *Fifteenth Census of the United States, 1930* (NAMP T626, roll 1251); RG 29; NAB; Dees family; p. 2A, lines 21–24, Enumeration District 112–15, Cowan

Township, Wayne County, Mo. Census of Population; *Sixteenth Census of the United States, 1940* (NAMP T627, roll 2163); RG 29; NAB.

28. Eliga Dees and Mae Dees death records, *U.S., Social Security Death Index, 1935–2014* (Provo: Ancestry.com Operations, Inc., 2011), *Ancestry.com* (Apr. 5, 2017).

29. John W. Scott, *Natalie Scott: A Magnificent Life* (Gretna, La.: Pelican Publishing Co., 2008), 16, 459–60.

30. See Richard Slotkin, *Lost Battalions: The Great War and the Crisis of American Nationality* (New York: Henry Holt, 2005), 480–88, 519–20.

31. "Last-Hour '18 Hero Will Get the D. S. C.," *New York Times*, Nov. 12, 1939.

32. For quotation and Whittlesey see Richard Slotkin, *Lost Battalions: The Great War and the Crisis of American Nationality* (New York: Henry Holt, 2005), 466–80.

33. See Jonathan H. Ebel, *G.I. Messiahs: Soldiering, War, and American Civil Religion* (New Haven: Yale University Press, 2015), 61; "Lost Battalion Chief Commits Suicide at Sea," *Baltimore Sun*, Nov. 29, 1921; "Col. Whittlesey, of the 'Lost Battalion,' Vanishes from Ship," *New York Times*, Nov. 29, 1918.

BIBLIOGRAPHY

Archival Collections

Alabama Department of Archives and History (archives.alabama.gov), Montgomery, Ala.

Alabama Civil War Service Database
World War I Gold Star Database

Ancestry.com Operations (ancestry.com), Provo, Utah.

Alabama, Deaths and Burials Index, 1881–1974
Alabama, Marriage Index, 1800–1969
Missouri, Marriage Records, 1805–2002
U.S., Sons of the American Revolution Membership Applications, 1889–1970
U.S., City Directories, 1822–1995
U.S., Civil War Soldiers, 1861–1865
U.S., Confederate Soldiers Compiled Service Records, 1861–1865
U.S., Find a Grave Index, 1600s–Current
U.S., Social Security Death Index, 1935–2014
World War I, World War II, and Korean War Casualty Listings

Combined Arms Research Library, Fort Leavenworth, Kans.

Collection of the American Expeditionary Forces, General Staff, G-2.

Library of Congress, Washington, D.C.

World War I Sheet Music Collection

National Archives and Records Administration, Southeast Region, Morrow, Ga.

Records of the Selective Service System (World War I), 1917–1939, Record
Group 163

National Archives and Records Administration, College Park, Md.

Records of the Bureau of Naval Personnel, 1798–2007, Record Group 24
Records of the Committee on Public Information, Record Group 63
Records of the Office of the Quartermaster General, 1774–1985, Record
Group 92
Records of the Signal Corps (World War I), Record Group 111
Records of the American Expeditionary Forces (World War I), Record Group 120
    Records of the 6th Division, 53rd Infantry Regiment
    Records of the 33rd Division, 124th Machine Gun Battalion
    Records of the 82nd Division, 325th Infantry Regiment
Records of the War Department General and Special Staffs, 1860–1952,
Record Group 165

National Archives and Records Administration, Washington, D.C.

Records of the Bureau of the Census, Record Group 29
Records of the Provost Marshal General's Bureau (Civil War), Record Group 110

Ohio Historical Society, Columbus, Ohio.

Thomas Boyd Papers

St. Mark's Lutheran Church, Watertown, Wisc.

Funeral Records

Selma-Dallas County Public Library, Selma, Ala.

Edwin Condie Godbold Local History Collection

State Historical Society of Missouri, Columbia, Mo.

Eliga and Mae Dees Letters, Collection R1453
Russell and Bernadine How Collection
Soldiers' Records: War of 1812–World War I (sos.mo.gov)

Tulane University, Louisiana Research Collection, New Orleans, La.

Natalie Scott Papers

United States Army Heritage and Education Center, Military History Institute, Carlisle, Penn.

Veterans Survey Collection (World War I Veterans Survey Inventories)
    George H. Anderson Papers
    Sol J. Arouesty Papers
    William L. Ashton Papers
    James E. Collins Papers
    William L. Helberg Papers
    Knud J. Olsen Papers
    Walter F. Owens Papers
    Fred H. Takes Papers
    Wayne O. Turner Papers
    Selmar Waldemar Papers
    Henry G. Weinberg Papers

University of Alabama, W. S. Hoole Special Collections Library, Tuscaloosa, Ala.

Alabama Collection
Huston Family Papers
Wade Hall Collection of Southern History and Culture: Sheet Music

Watertown Public Library, Watertown, Wisc.

Local History Collection

Wisconsin Historical Society, Madison, Wisc.

Ben Fluegel Collection
Clayton Slack Oral History

Wisconsin Veterans Museum Research Center, Madison, Wisc.

Clayton K. Slack Collection
Charles R. Reuber Collection

Periodicals

Atlanta Constitution
Baltimore Sun
Birmingham Age Herald

Boston Globe
Chicago Daily Tribune
Chicago Defender
Christian Science Monitor
Cleveland Gazette
Crimson White (Tuscaloosa, Ala.)
Daily Independent (Harrisonburg, Va.)
Eau Claire (Wisc.) Leader
Emmetsburg Palo Alto (Iowa) Tribune
Greenville (Mo.) Sun
Hartford Courant
Jefferson County (Wisc.) Union
Kansas City Advocate
Los Angeles Times
Louisville Courier-Journal
Montgomery (Ala.) Advertiser
Nashville Tennessean
New York Herald
New York Times
Piedmont (Mo.) Banner
Racine (Wisc.) Journal-News
Reveill-E (Wisc.)
San Francisco Chronicle
Savannah Tribune
Selma (Ala.) Mirror
Selma (Ala.) Times
Selma (Ala.) Times-Journal
St. Louis Post-Dispatch
Trench and Camp
Washington Bee
Washington Post
Watertown (Wisc.) Daily Times
Watertown (Wisc.) Gazette
Watertown (Wisc.) News
Watertown (Wisc.) Weltbürger
Wayne County (Mo.) Journal

Published Primary Sources

American Battle Monuments Commission. *2d Division: Summary of Operations in the World War*. Washington: U.S. Government Printing Office, 1944.

Bacon, William J., ed. *History of the Fifty-Fifth Field Artillery Brigade*. Memphis: William J. Bacon, 1920.

Boyd, Thomas. *Through the Wheat: A Novel of the World War I Marines*. Lincoln: University of Nebraska Press, 2000.

Brewer, Willis. *Alabama, Her History, Resources, War Record, and Public Men: From 1540 to 1872.* Montgomery, Ala.: Barrett & Brown, 1872.

Bureau of the Census. *Statistics of the Population of the United States at the Tenth Census (June 1, 1880).* Washington: U.S. Government Printing Office, 1881.

Bureau of the Census. *Thirteenth Census of the United States, 1910, Vol. 2: Population, Alabama-Montana.* Washington: U.S. Government Printing Office, 1913.

Bureau of the Census. *Twelfth Census of the United States, 1900, Vol. 1: Census Reports: Population, Part I.* Washington: U.S. Census Office, 1901.

Bureau of the Census. *Thirteenth Census of the United States, 1910, Vol. 3: Population, Nebraska-Wyoming.* Washington: U.S. Government Printing Office, 1913.

Buxton, Jr., G. Edward. *Official History of 82nd Division, American Expeditionary Forces, 1917–1919.* Indianapolis: Bobbs-Merrill Co. Publishers, 1920.

Committee on Public Information. *German War Practices, Part I: Treatment of Civilians*, Jan. 1918. Washington, D.C.: Committee on Public Information.

Committee on Public Information, *Official Bulletin.* Washington, D.C.: Committee on Public Information.

Committee on Public Information, *War Information Series, Why America Fights Germany*, Mar. 1918, no. 15. Washington, D.C.: Committee on Public Information.

Congressional Record containing the Proceedings and Debates of the First Session of the Sixty-Fifth Congress and Special Session of the Senate of the United States of America, Vol. 55 Washington: Government Printing Office, 1917.

Congressional Record containing the Proceedings and Debates of the Second Session of the Sixty-Fifth Congress of the United States of America, Vol. 56 Washington: Government Printing Office, 1917.

Crane, Stephen. *The Red Badge of Courage.* New York: Modern Library, 2000.

Creel, George. *How We Advertised America.* New York: Harper and Brothers, 1920.

Dallas County, Alabama Genealogical Records, Vol. 3: Inscriptions—Live Oak Cemetary [sic]*, Selma, Alabama Prior to June, 1968.* Selma, Ala.: The Sturdivant Museum Association, 1969.

Doran, Marie. *The Girls Over Here: A Patriotic Play Act in One Act.* New York: Samuel French, 1917.

Douglas, Paul H. "The War Risk Insurance Act." *Journal of Political Economy* 26 (May 1918): 461–83.

Ely, Dinsmore. *Dinsmore Ely: One Who Served.* Chicago: A. C. McClurg & Co., 1919.

Fuller, Ruth Wolfe. *Silver Lining: The Experiences of a War Bride.* Boston: Houghton Mifflin Co., 1918.

Grant, Madison. *The Passing of the Great Race or The Racial Basis of European History.* New York: Charles Scribner's Sons, 1916.

Gulberg, Martin Gus. *A War Diary.* Chicago: The Drake Press, 1927.

Haulsee, W. M., F. G. Howe, and A. C. Doyle, comps., *Soldiers of the Great War*, Vol. 3. Washington: Soldiers Record Publishing Association, 1920.

History of the 124th Machine Gun Battalion, 66th Brigade, 33rd Division, A. E. F. Publisher unknown, 1919.

Hoole, William Stanley. *Historical Sketch of the Fifth Alabama Infantry Regiment, C. S. A.* University, Ala.: Confederate Publishing Co., 1985.

Huidekoper, Frederic Louis. *The History of the 33rd Division, A. E. F.* Vols. 1–3. Springfield, Ill.: Illinois State Historical Library, 1921.

Illinois in the World War: An Illustrated History of the Thirty-Third Division. Chicago: States Publications Society, 1920.

Kelley, Ethel M. *Over Here: The Story of a War Bride.* Indianapolis: Bobbs-Merrill Co., 1918.

Macaulay, Thomas Babington. *Lays of Ancient Rome.* London: George Routledge and Sons, 1888.

March, William. *Company K.* Tuscaloosa: University of Alabama Press, 1989 ed.

McLaughlin, Marie Whaley, and Carolyn Ward Vintson, comps., *Dallas County Alabama Marriage Records, 1818–1918.* Selma, Ala.: Prestige Research and Publishing, 1992.

O'Ryan, Maj. Gen. John F. *The Story of the 27th Division.* New York: Wynkoop Hallenbeck Crawford Co., 1921.

Office of the Adjutant General. *Histories of Two Hundred and Fifty-One Divisions of the German Army which Participated in the War (1914–1918).* Chaumont, France: American Expeditionary Forces, 1919.

Plat Book of Wayne County, Missouri. Rockford, Ill.: W. W. Hixson & Co., 1930.

Riis, Jacob A. *How the Other Half Lives.* New York: Dover Publications, 1971 ed.

Roosevelt, Theodore. "American Preparedness." *The European War, Vol. 4, July—September, 1915, Current History.* New York: The New York Times Company, 1915.

Snead, David L., ed. *An American Soldier in World War I.* Lincoln: University of Nebraska Press, 2006.

Society of the First Division. *History of the First Division During the World War, 1917–1919.* Philadelphia: John C. Winston Co., 1922.

State of Alabama Department of Archives and History. *Alabama Official and Statistical Register, 1915.* Montgomery: Brown Printing Company, 1915.

Streeter, Edward. *Love Letters of Bill to Mable: Comprising Dere Mable, 'That's Me All Over, Mable,' and 'Same Old Bill, eh Mable!'* New York: Frederick A. Stokes Co., 1918, 1919.

Summers, Florence Elizabeth. *Dere Bill: Mable's Love Letters to Her Rookie.* New York: Frederick A. Stokes Co., 1918, 1919.

Verhaeren, Emile. "The Uncivilizable Nation." *The European War, Vol. 4, July—September, 1915, Current History.* New York: The New York Times Company, 1915.

Wheeler, Richard, ed. *Sergeant York and the Great War: His Own Life Story and War Diary.* San Antonio: Vision Forum, 2011.

Whitman, Walter M. *The Story of the 325th.* Bordeaux: Saugnac and Drouillard, 1919.

Books and Articles

Adams, Michael C. C. *The Great Adventure: Male Desire and the Coming of World War I*. Bloomington: Indiana University Press, 1990.

Appy, Christian G. *American Reckoning: The Vietnam War and Our National Identity*. New York: Viking, 2015.

Bacevich, Andrew J. *The New American Militarism: How Americans Are Seduced by War*. New York: Oxford University Press, 2005.

Bailey, Beth L. *From Front Porch to Back Seat: Courtship in Twentieth-Century America*. Baltimore: Johns Hopkins University Press, 1988.

Bailey, Beth L. *America's Army: Making the All-Volunteer Force*. Cambridge: Belknap Press of Harvard University Press, 2009.

Barbeau Arthur E., and Florette Henri. *The Unknown Soldiers: Black American Troops in World War I*. Philadelphia: Temple University Press, 1974.

Barry, John M. *The Great Influenza: The Epic Story of the Deadliest Plague in History*. New York: Viking, 2004.

Beckett, Ian F. W. *The Great War*. London: Pearson Longman, 2007 ed.

Bederman, Gail. *Manliness and Civilization: A Cultural History of Gender and Race in the United States, 1880–1917*. Chicago: University of Chicago Press, 1995.

Blight, David W. *Race and Reunion: The Civil War in American Memory*. Cambridge: Belknap Press of Harvard University Press, 2001.

Bodnar, John. *Remaking America: Public Memory, Commemoration, and Patriotism in the Twentieth Century*. Princeton: Princeton University Press, 1992.

Bodnar, John. *The "Good War" in American Memory*. Baltimore: Johns Hopkins University Press, 2010.

Borch III, Fred L. "Anatomy of a Court-Martial: The Trial and Execution of Private William Buckner." *The Army Lawyer* (Oct. 2011): 1–6.

Boulton, Mark. *Failing Our Veterans: The G.I. Bill and the Vietnam Generation*. New York: New York University Press, 2014.

Brandt, Allan M. *No Magic Bullet: A Social History of Venereal Disease in the United States Since 1880*. New York: Oxford University Press, 1985.

Brewer, Susan A. *Why America Fights: Patriotism and War Propaganda from the Philippines to Iraq*. New York: Oxford University Press, 2009.

Bristow, Nancy K. *Making Men Moral: Social Engineering during the Great War*. New York: New York University Press, 1996.

Budreau, Lisa M. *Bodies of War: World War I and the Politics of Commemoration in America, 1919–1933*. New York: New York University Press, 2010.

Canaday, Margot. *The Straight State: Sexuality and Citizenship in Twentieth-Century America*. Princeton: Princeton University Press, 2009.

Capozzola, Christopher. *Uncle Sam Wants You: World War I and the Making of the Modern American Citizen*. New York: Oxford University Press, 2008.

Chambers II, John Whiteclay. *To Raise an Army: The Draft Comes to Modern America*. New York: The Free Press, 1987.

Clement, Elizabeth Alice. *Love for Sale: Courting, Treating, and Prostitution in New York City, 1900–1945*. Chapel Hill: University of North Carolina Press, 2006.

Coffman, Edward M. *The War to End All Wars: The American Military Experience in World War I*. Lexington: University Press of Kentucky, 1998.

Coffman, Edward M. *The Regulars: The American Army, 1898–1941*. Cambridge: Belknap Press of Harvard University Press, 2004.

Cooke, James J. *The All-Americans at War: The 82nd Division in the Great War, 1917–1918*. Westport, Conn.: Praeger: 1999.

Cooper, John Milton, Jr. "The World War and American Memory." *Diplomatic History* 38 (Sept. 2014): 727–36.

Cott, Nancy. *Public Vows: A History of Marriage and the Nation*. Cambridge: Harvard University Press, 2000.

Cowie, Jefferson. *Stayin' Alive: The 1970s and the Last Days of the Working Class*. New York: The New Press, 2010.

Cowley, Robert. "The Road to Butgnéville—November 11, 1918." In *I Wish I'd Been There: Twenty Historians Bring to Life Dramatic Events that Changed America*, edited by Byron Hollinshead. New York: Anchor Books, 2006.

Cramer, Rose Fulton. *Wayne County, Missouri*. Cape Girardeau, Mo.: Ramfre Press, 1972.

Daniels, Roger. *Guarding the Golden Door: American Immigration Policy and Immigrants since 1882*. New York: Hill and Wang, 2004.

Demm, Eberhard. "Censorship." In *1914–1918 Online: International Encyclopedia of the First World War*, edited by Ute Daniel et al. Berlin: Freie Universität Berlin, 2014.

Digby, Tom. *Love and War: How Militarism Shapes Sexuality and Romance*. New York: Columbia University Press, 2014.

Dudziak, Mary L. *War-Time: An Idea, Its History, Its Consequences*. New York: Oxford University Press, 2012.

Dumenil, Lynn. *The Second Line of Defense: American Women and World War I*. Chapel Hill: University of North Carolina Press, 2017.

Ebel, Jonathan H. *Faith in the Fight: Religion and the American Soldier in the Great War*. Princeton: Princeton University Press, 2010.

Ebel, Jonathan H. *G.I. Messiahs: Soldiering, War, and American Civil Religion*. New Haven: Yale University Press, 2015.

Eksteins, Modris. *Rites of Spring: The Great War and the Birth of the Modern Age*. Boston: Houghton Mifflin, 1989.

Ellis, John, and Cox, Michael. *The World War I Databook*. London: Aurum Press, 2001.

Engelhardt, Tom. *The End of Victory Culture: Cold War America and the Disillusioning of a Generation*. Amherst: University of Massachusetts Press, 1995.

Farwell, Byron. *Over There: The United States and the Great War, 1917–1918*. New York: W. W. Norton, 1999.

Faust, Drew Gilpin. *This Republic of Suffering: Death and the American Civil War*. New York: Knopf, 2008.

Fitts, Alston, III. *Selma: Queen City of the Black Belt*. Selma, Ala.: Clairmont Press, 1989.

Fleegler, Robert L. *Ellis Island Nation: Immigration Policy and American Identity in the Twentieth Century*. Philadelphia: University of Pennsylvania Press, 2013.

Foley, Michael Stewart. *Front Porch Politics: The Forgotten Heyday of American Activism in the 1970s and 1980s*. New York: Hill and Wang, 2013.

Ford, Nancy Gentile. *Americans All! Foreign-born Soldiers in World War I*. College Station: Texas A&M University Press, 2001.

Foster, Gaines M. *Ghosts of the Confederacy: Defeat, the Lost Cause, and the Emergence of the New South*. New York: Oxford University Press, 1987.

Frazer, Nimrod T. *Send the Alabamians: World War I Fighters in the Rainbow Division*. Tuscaloosa: University of Alabama Press, 2014.

Gallagher, Gary W. *The Confederate War*. Cambridge: Harvard University Press, 1997.

Gallagher, Gary W. *The Union War*. Cambridge: Harvard University Press, 2011.

Gibbs, Christopher C. *The Great Silent Majority: Missouri's Resistance to World War I*. Columbia: University of Missouri Press, 1988.

Gier, Christina. "Gender, Politics, and the Fighting Soldier's Song in America during World War I." *Music and Politics* 2 (Winter 2008): 1–20.

Gilbert, Martin. *The First World War: A Complete History*. New York: Henry Holt, 1994.

Gilbert, Martin. *The Routledge Atlas of the First World War*. 3rd ed. London: Routledge, 2008.

Gilmore, Glenda Elizabeth. *Gender and Jim Crow: Women and the Politics of White Supremacy in North Carolina, 1896–1920*. Chapel Hill: University of North Carolina Press, 1996.

Gordon, Linda. *Pitied But Not Entitled: Single Mothers and the History of Welfare, 1890–1935*. New York: The Free Press, 1994.

Grayzel, Susan R. *Women's Identities in War: Gender, Motherhood, and Politics in Britain and France during the First World War*. Chapel Hill: University of North Carolina Press, 1999.

Grayzel, Susan R. *Women and the First World War*. London: Longman, 2002.

Grayzel, Susan R., and Tammy M. Proctor, eds. *Gender and the Great War*. New York: Oxford University Press, 2017.

Gregory, Adrian. *The Last Great War: British Society and the First World War*. Cambridge: Cambridge University Press, 2008.

Grotelueschen, Mark Ethan. *The AEF Way of War: The American Army and Combat in World War I*. New York: Cambridge University Press, 2007.

Gutiérrez, Edward A. *Doughboys on the Great War: How American Soldiers Viewed Their Military Experience*. Lawrence: University Press of Kansas, 2014.

Hallas, James H., ed. *Doughboy War: The American Expeditionary Force in WWI*. Mechanicsburg, Penn.: Stackpole Books, 2009.

Hallas, James H. "War Letters: Communication between Front and Home Front." In *1914–1918 Online: International Encyclopedia of the First World War*, edited by Ute Daniel et al. Berlin: Freie Universität Berlin, 2014.

Harris, Ruth. " 'Child of the Barbarian': Rape, Race and Nationalism in France during the First World War." *Past and Present* 141 (November 1993): 170–206.

Haynes, Robert V. "The Houston Mutiny and Riot of 1917." *Southwestern Historical Quarterly* 76 (Apr. 1973): 418–39.

Higham, John. *Strangers in the Land: Patterns of American Nativism, 1860–1925.* New York: Atheneum, 1970.

Higonnet, Margaret Randolph, Jane Jenson, Sonya Michel, and Margaret Collins Weitz, eds. *Behind the Lines: Gender and the Two World Wars.* New Haven: Yale University Press, 1987.

Hoganson, Kristin L. *Fighting for American Manhood: How Gender Politics Provoked the Spanish-American and Philippine-American Wars.* New Haven: Yale University Press, 1998.

Horne, John, and Alan Kramer. *German Atrocities, 1914: A History of Denial.* New Haven: Yale University Press, 2001.

Huebner, Andrew J. *The Warrior Image: Soldiers in American Culture from the Second World War to the Vietnam Era.* Chapel Hill: University of North Carolina Press, 2008.

Huebner, Andrew J. "Gee! I Wish I Were a Man: Gender and the Great War." In *The Routledge History of Gender, War, and the U.S. Military*, edited by Kara Dixon Vuic. New York: Routledge, 2018.

Hunter, Kathryn M. "Australian and New Zealand Fathers and Sons during the Great War: Expanding the Histories of Families at War." *First World War Studies* 4 (Oct. 2013): 185–200.

Irwin, Julia F. *Making the World Safe: The American Red Cross and a Nation's Humanitarian Awakening.* New York: Oxford University Press, 2013.

Iwan, Wilhelm. *Die Altlutherische Auswanderung um die Mitte des 19. Jahrhunderts (The Old Lutheran Emigration at the Middle of the 19th Century)*, Vol. 2. Ludwigsburg: Eichhorn Publishing, 1943.

Jackson, Walter M. *The Story of Selma.* Birmingham, Ala.: Birmingham Printing Co., 1954.

Jacobson, Matthew Frye. *Whiteness of a Different Color: European Immigrants and the Alchemy of Race.* Cambridge: Harvard University Press, 1998.

Jacobson, Matthew Frye. *Barbarian Virtues: The United States Encounters Foreign Peoples at Home and Abroad, 1876–1917.* New York: Hill and Wang, 2000.

James, Pearl, ed. *Picture This: World War I Posters and Visual Culture.* Lincoln: University of Nebraska Press, 2009.

Janney, Caroline E. *Remembering the Civil War: Reunion and the Limits of Reconciliation.* Chapel Hill: University of North Carolina Press, 2013.

Jensen, Kimberly. *Mobilizing Minerva: American Women in the First World War.* Urbana: University of Illinois Press, 2008.

Joiner, Thekla Ellen. *Sin in the City: Chicago and Revivalism, 1880–1920.* Columbia, Mo.: University of Missouri Press, 2007.

Kaplan, Robert D. *Imperial Grunts: On the Ground with the American Military, from Mongolia to the Philippines to Iraq and Beyond.* New York: Vintage Books, 2005.

Kazin, Michael. *War Against War: The American Fight for Peace, 1914–1918*. New York: Simon and Schuster, 2017.

Keegan, John. *The First World War*. New York: Alfred A. Knopf, 1999.

Keene, Jennifer D. *Doughboys, the Great War, and the Remaking of America*. Baltimore: Johns Hopkins University Press, 2001.

Keene, Jennifer D. *World War I: The American Soldier Experience*. Lincoln, Neb.: University of Nebraska Press, 2011.

Keith, Jeanette. *Rich Man's War, Poor Man's Fight: Race, Class, and Power in the Rural South during the First World War*. Chapel Hill: University of North Carolina Press, 2004.

Kennedy, David M. *Over Here: The First World War and American Society*. 25th anniversary ed. New York: Oxford University Press, 2004.

Kennedy, Kathleen. *Disloyal Mothers and Scurrilous Citizens: Women and Subversion during World War I*. Bloomington: Indiana University Press, 1999.

Kennedy, Ross A. *The Will to Believe: Woodrow Wilson, World War I, and America's Strategy for Peace and Security*. Kent: Kent State University Press, 2009.

Kerber, Linda K. *Women of the Republic: Intellect and Ideology in Revolutionary America*. Chapel Hill: University of North Carolina, 1980.

Kiessling, Elmer C. *Watertown Remembered*. Watertown, Wisc.: Watertown Historical Society, 1976. Kindle electronic edition.

Kinder, John M. *Paying with Their Bodies: American War and the Problem of the Disabled Veteran*. Chicago: University of Chicago Press, 2015.

Kingsbury, Celia Malone. *For Home and Country: World War I Propaganda on the Home Front*. Lincoln: University of Nebraska Press, 2010.

Kuhlman, Erika. *Of Little Comfort: War Widows, Fallen Soldiers, and the Remaking of the Nation after the Great War*. New York: New York University Press, 2012.

Laskin, David. *The Long Way Home: An American Journey from Ellis Island to the Great War*. New York: HarperCollins, 2010.

Lears, Jackson. *Rebirth of a Nation: The Making of Modern America, 1877–1920*. New York: HarperCollins, 2009.

Lengel, Edward G. *To Conquer Hell: The Meuse-Argonne, 1918*. New York: Henry Holt, 2008.

Lentz-Smith, Adriane. *Freedom Struggles: African Americans and World War I*. Cambridge: Harvard University Press, 2009.

Leuchtenberg, William E. *The Perils of Prosperity, 1914–1932*. 2nd ed. Chicago: University of Chicago Press, 1993.

Linker, Beth. *War's Waste: Rehabilitation in World War I America*. Chicago: University of Chicago Press, 2011.

Luebke, Frederick C. *Bonds of Loyalty: German Americans and World War I*. De Kalb: Northern Illinois University Press, 1974.

MacLean, Nancy. *Behind the Mask of Chivalry: The Making of the Second Ku Klux Klan*. New York: Oxford University Press, 1994.

Manning, Chandra. *What This Cruel War Was Over: Soldiers, Slavery, and the Civil War*. New York: Knopf, 2007.

Matt, Susan J. *Homesickness: An American History*. New York: Oxford University Press, 2011.

Mayers, David. *Dissenting Voices in America's Rise to Power*. New York: Cambridge University Press, 2007.

McCartney, Helen B. *Citizen Soldiers: The Liverpool Territorials in the First World War*. Cambridge: Cambridge University Press, 2005.

McGerr, Michael. *A Fierce Discontent: The Rise and the Fall of the Progressive Movement in America*. New York: Oxford University Press, 2003.

McGuire, Danielle L. *At the Dark End of the Street: Black Women, Rape, and Resistance: A New History of the Civil Rights Movement from Rosa Parks to the Rise of Black Power*. New York: Vintage Books, 2010.

McPherson, James. *Battle Cry of Freedom: The Civil War Era*. New York: Oxford University Press, 1988.

Meigs, Mark. *Optimism at Armageddon: Voices of American Participants in the First World War*. New York: New York University Press, 1997.

Mittelstadt, Jennifer. *The Rise of the Military Welfare State*. Cambridge: Harvard University Press, 2015.

Mock, James R., and Cedric Larson. *Words That Won the War: The Story of the Committee on Public Information, 1917–1919*. Princeton: Princeton University Press, 1939.

Morton, Desmond. *Fight or Pay: Soldiers' Families in the Great War*. Vancouver: University of British Columbia Press, 2004.

Moyd, Michelle. "Centring a Sideshow: Local Experiences of the First World War in Africa." *First World War Studies* 7 (July 2016): 111–30.

Murphy, Paul L. *World War I and the Origin of Civil Liberties in the United States*. New York: W. W. Norton, 1979.

Neiberg, Michael S. *Dance of the Furies: Europe and the Outbreak of World War I*. Cambridge: Belknap Press of Harvard University Press, 2011.

Neiberg, Michael S. *The Path to War: How the First World War Created Modern America*. New York: Oxford University Press, 2016.

O'Leary, Cecilia Elizabeth. *To Die For: The Paradox of American Patriotism*. Princeton: Princeton University Press, 1999.

Ortiz, Stephen R. *Beyond the Bonus March and GI Bill: How Veteran Politics Shaped the New Deal Era*. New York: New York University Press, 2010.

Persico, Joseph E. *Eleventh Month, Eleventh Day, Eleventh Hour: Armistice Day, 1918: World War I and Its Violent Climax*. New York: Random House, 2005.

Plant, Rebecca Jo. *Mom: The Transformation of Motherhood in Modern America*. Chicago: University of Chicago Press, 2010.

Pula, James S. *The Sigel Regiment: A History of the Twenty-Sixth Wisconsin Volunteer Infantry, 1862–1865*. Campbell, Calif.: Savas Publishing Co., 1998.

Quinn, Erika. "Love and Loss, Marriage and Mourning: World War One in German Home Front Novels." *First World War Studies* 5 (July 2014): 233–50.

Rable, George C. *God's Almost Chosen People: A Religious History of the American Civil War*. Chapel Hill: University of North Carolina Press, 2010.

Rasmussen, Chris. " 'This Thing Has Ceased to Be a Joke': The Veterans of Future Wars and the Meanings of Political Satire in the 1930s." *Journal of American History* 103 (June 2016): 84–106.

Roberts, Mary Louise. *Civilization without Sexes: Reconstructing Gender in Postwar France, 1917–1927*. Chicago: University of Chicago Press, 1994.

Roberts, Mary Louise. *What Soldiers Do: Sex and the American GI in World War II France*. Chicago: University of Chicago Press, 2013.

Roper, Michael. *The Secret Battle: Emotional Survival in the Great War*. Manchester: Manchester University Press, 2009.

Rosenberg, William G. "Reading Soldiers' Moods: Russian Military Censorship and the Configuration of Feeling in World War I." *American Historical Review* 119 (June 2014): 714–40.

Rubin, Richard. *The Last of the Doughboys: The Forgotten Generation and Their Forgotten World War*. Boston: Houghton Mifflin Harcourt, 2013.

Schaffer, Ronald. *America in the Great War: The Rise of the War Welfare State*. New York: Oxford University Press, 1991.

Scott, John W. *Natalie Scott: A Magnificent Life*. Gretna, La.: Pelican Publishing Co., 2008.

Self, Robert O. *All in the Family: The Realignment of American Democracy since the 1960s*. New York: Hill and Wang, 2012.

Sheehan-Dean, Aaron. *Why Confederates Fought: Family and Nation in Civil War Virginia*. Chapel Hill: University of North Carolina Press, 2007.

Shenk, Gerald E. *"Work or Fight!" Race, Gender, and the Draft in World War One*. New York: Palgrave Macmillan, 2005.

Sherry, Michael S. *In the Shadow of War: The United States since the 1930s*. New Haven: Yale University Press, 1995.

Skocpol, Theda. *Protecting Soldiers and Mothers: The Political Origins of Social Policy in the United States*. Cambridge: Belknap Press of Harvard University Press, 1992.

Slotkin, Richard. *Regeneration through Violence: The Mythology of the American Frontier, 1600–1860*. Middletown, Conn.: Wesleyan University Press, 1973.

Slotkin, Richard. *The Fatal Environment: The Myth of the Frontier in the Age of Industrialization, 1800–1890*. Norman: University of Oklahoma Press, 1985.

Slotkin, Richard. *Lost Battalions: The Great War and the Crisis of American Nationality*. New York: Henry Holt, 2005.

Stallings, Laurence. *The Doughboys: The Story of the AEF, 1917–1918*. New York: Harper and Row, 1963.

Sterba, Christopher M. *Good Americans: Italian and Jewish Immigrants during the First World War*. New York: Oxford University Press, 2003.

Stevenson, David. *Cataclysm: The First World War as Political Tragedy*. New York: Basic Books, 2004.

Stone, Geoffrey R. *Perilous Times: Free Speech in Wartime from the Sedition Act of 1798 to the War on Terrorism*. New York: W. W. Norton, 2004.

Strachan, Hew. *The First World War*. New York: Penguin Books, 2003.

Stur, Heather Marie. *Beyond Combat: Women and Gender in the Vietnam War Era.* New York: Cambridge University Press, 2011.

Tasker, Yvonne. *Soldiers' Stories: Military Women in Cinema and Television since World War II.* Durham: Duke University Press, 2011.

Thomas, William H. *Unsafe for Democracy: World War I and the U.S. Justice Department's Covert Campaign to Suppress Dissent.* Madison: University of Wisconsin Press, 2008.

Trout, Steven. *On the Battlefield of Memory: The First World War and American Remembrance, 1919–1941.* Tuscaloosa: University of Alabama Press, 2010.

Vuic, Kara Dixon. *Officer, Nurse, Woman: The Army Nurse Corps in the Vietnam War.* Baltimore: Johns Hopkins University Press, 2010.

Wallman, Charles J. *The German-Speaking 48ers: Builders of Watertown, Wisconsin.* Madison: Max Kade Institute, 1992.

Westbrook, Robert B. *Why We Fought: Forging American Obligations in World War II.* Washington, D.C.: Smithsonian Books, 2010.

Whalan, Mark. *The Great War and the Culture of the New Negro.* Gainesville: University Press of Florida, 2008.

Williams, Chad L. *Torchbearers of Democracy: African American Soldiers in the World War I Era.* Chapel Hill: University of North Carolina Press, 2010.

Williamson, Joel. *A Rage for Order: Black/White Relations in the American South Since Emancipation.* New York: Oxford University Press, 1986.

Winter, Jay. Review of Steven Trout, *On the Battlefield of Memory* and John Bodnar, *The "Good War" in American Memory. American Historical Review* 116 (June 2011): 755–58.

Zeiger, Susan. "She Didn't Raise Her Boy to Be a Slacker: Motherhood, Conscription, and the Culture of the First World War." *Feminist Studies* 22 (Spring 1996): 7–39.

Zeiger, Susan. *In Uncle Sam's Service: Women Workers with the American Expeditionary Force, 1917–1919.* Ithaca: Cornell University Press, 1999.

Zeiger, Susan. *Entangling Alliances: Foreign War Brides and American Soldiers in the Twentieth Century.* New York: New York University Press, 2010.

Zieger, Robert H. *America's Great War: World War I and the American Experience.* Lanham, Md.: Rowman and Littlefield, 2000.

Ziemann, Benjamin. *War Experiences in Rural Germany, 1914–1923.* Oxford: Berg, 2007.

Zuckerman, Larry. *The Rape of Belgium: The Untold Story of World War I.* New York: New York University Press, 2004.

INDEX

Page numbers in italics refer to illustrations.